GUHIN, Michael A. John Foster Dulles; a statesman and his times. Columbia, 1972. 404p il bibl 72-5873. 12.95. ISBN 0-231-03664-7

CHOICE   APR. '73

History, Geography & Travel

North America

A revision of a doctoral dissertation that has both the advantages and disadvantages of such a work. It sets out to explain Dulles' thought and foreign policy in terms of his background — religious, political, and social — though not always successfully. Well-documented but somewhat overwritten, the book has much more information on Dulles as a product of his environment than on Dulles as a statesman, although it does reveal some interesting aspects of his term as Secretary of State. It emphasizes that Dulles understood that a nation's power brings responsibilities, although it does not clearly explain how these should be defined. Index; bibliography. More useful to the advanced reader. Should be read in conjunction with Louis Gerson's *John Foster Dulles* (CHOICE, May 1968).

JOHN FOSTER DULLES
A Statesman and His Times

Lisa Larsen, Life

JOHN FOSTER DULLES
A STATESMAN AND HIS TIMES

Michael A. Guhin

Columbia University Press
NEW YORK AND LONDON 1972

Permission to quote is gratefully acknowledged:

War, Peace and Change, by John Foster Dulles. Reprinted by permission of Harper & Row.

"The Christian Citizen in a Changing World," by John Foster Dulles, in *The Church and International Disorder.* Reprinted by permission of SCM Press Limited.

War or Peace, by John Foster Dulles. Copyright © 1950, 1957 by John Foster Dulles. Reprinted by permission of The Macmillan Company.

Full Circle, by Sir Anthony Eden (Earl of Avon). Reprinted by permission of Cassell & Company and Houghton Mifflin Company.

The White House Years: Mandate for Change 1953–1956 and *The White House Years: Waging Peace 1956–61,* by Dwight D. Eisenhower. Copyright © 1963 and 1965 by Dwight D. Eisenhower. Reprinted by permission of Doubleday & Company and William Heinemann Limited.

Present at the Creation: My Years at the State Department, by Dean Acheson. Copyright © 1969 by Dean Acheson. Reprinted by permission of W. W. Norton & Company and Hamish Hamilton Limited.

Permission to quote from articles and speeches by John Foster Dulles is gratefully acknowledged the Committee for the *John Foster Dulles Papers* (Princeton University Library), *Foreign Affairs,* and *Life.*

LIBRARY OF CONGRESS CATALOGING IN PUBLICATION DATA

Guhin, Michael A.   1940–
    John Foster Dulles: A Statesman and His Times.

    Bibliography: p. 375–95
    I. Dulles, John Foster, 1888–1959.
E835.D85G8   973.921'092'4 [B]   72.5873
ISBN 0-231-03664-7

To my Mother and Father,
Sister and Brother,
Always there, always Love

PREFACE

A Statesman and His Times is addressed not only to those interested in the life, policies, and politics of John Foster Dulles, but also to those concerned with American foreign policy generally and some of the dilemmas of statesmanship. The work contains one clear bias, which has contributed much to its tone and which was expressed by Stefan Zweig thusly: "Mir persönlich macht es mehr Freude, Menschen zu verstehen, als sie zu richten." (It gives me more pleasure to understand men than to judge them.)

The work grew out of my dissertation, "The Political Philosophy of John Foster Dulles: An Examination of Its Foundations and Its Influence upon His Conduct of American Foreign Policy," approved by the University of London for the award of the Ph.D. degree. For this and the earlier product I am deeply grateful to Dr. F. S. Northedge, my tutor at the London School of Economics and Political Science, for his trenchant and constructive criticisms, his helpful guidance and instruction in broadening my understanding of international politics, and his enduring patience with my twists and turns in seeking to understand John Foster Dulles.

There have been some friends and acquaintances who have helped me along, perhaps in most cases unknowingly, in their own particular ways. A thought here, a comment there, a prod now and again, and a friend's reassurance at a trying moment—all contributed to the content and completion of this work.

I would also like to thank Mr. Alexander P. Clark and each member of his staff at Princeton University Library for all their help with the *Dulles Papers* over the past six years; and Barbara for her untiring assistance in preparing the manuscript during the long hours of the last throes.

For their keen insights and kind help, I am especially grateful to Mr. John W. Hanes, Jr., and Mrs. Eleanor Lansing Dulles. Bob Osgood's and Alexander George's comments and constructive criticisms and Bob Tilley's guidance and enormous patience are likewise much appreciated.

Finally, there is the very special place for Sarah B., who put up with this endeavor during long and beautiful months and who pitched in with support and help whenever needed. Without her, the evolution of this work would have been far less meaningful and satisfactory to me.

The drafting and research for this book were completed prior to my having the honor of serving as a member on the staff of the Assistant to the President for National Security Affairs. Any views expressed herein are wholly personal and in no way represent the official views of the United States government.

MICHAEL A. GUHIN

Washington, D.C.

CONTENTS

ILLUSTRATIONS

(FOLLOWING PAGE 60)

John Foster Dulles

With Allen Dulles

With Margaret, Allen, Eleanor Lansing, and Nataline Dulles

With fellow Princetonians, Allen W. Dulles and Walter S. Davison

With Janet Avery Dulles

Dulles Family

Dulles and the American Commission to the Paris Peace Conference

Ambassador Jessup, Secretary Acheson, Ambassador Harriman, and Ambassador Dulles at Paris

Dulles and Japanese Prime Minister Yoshida

John Foster and Janet Dulles with Frances and Thomas E. Dewey

Richard Nixon, General Eisenhower, and Dulles in 1952

(FOLLOWING PAGE 220)

British Foreign Secretary Eden and Dulles

Dulles and German Chancellor Konrad Adenauer

Soviet Foreign Minister Molotov, British Foreign Secretary Macmillan, Secretary Dulles, and Austrian Foreign Minister Figl

Secretary Dulles, Soviet Premier Bulganin, and Communist Party First Secretary Nikita Khrushchev at the Summit

Soviet Foreign Minister Shepilov, British Foreign Secretary Lloyd, Secretary Dulles, and Ambassador Lodge at the United Nations

With Generalissimo Chiang Kai-shek

With Indian Prime Minister Nehru

General Eisenhower, Sir Winston Churchill, and Dulles

Dulles sailing

JOHN FOSTER DULLES
A Statesman and His Times

IN SEARCH OF DULLES

During his last days of suffering, in 1959, John Foster Dulles (1888–1959) reportedly requested a recording of several hymns and, night after night, found solace in the words of "The Spacious Firmament on High," "Work for the Night is Coming," and "Through the Night of Doubt and Sorrow," among others. The seeming implication of such a final scene tended to confirm the view that the Secretary of State was, after all, an extremely religious man, reared within and indelibly marked by the puritanical strain of American tradition. Almost every work on the subject of Dulles draws some attention to the idea that an understanding of the man and his policy preferences involves considerations of his religious home environment, strong religious convictions, a sense of Christian mission, and a subsequent universalization of and missionary zeal for American ideals.

John Foster Dulles, the elder son of a Presbyterian minister, has been frequently categorized as a type of cold war ideologue in his approach to international affairs or, at minimum, a statesman with a distorting pair of moral spectacles. Thorough investigation of his background, development, positions, and actions, however, disproves the notion that his pattern of interpreting policy issues and his policy preferences were derived from or distorted by either moralistic premises or strictly defined ideological considerations. The philosophical foundations of his views on human nature, on the inevitability of conflict and disharmony, on government, and on

politics essentially coincide with what one of the foremost spokes-
men of the "realist school" has defined as the "principles of
realism." [1] Were one inclined to attach labels, Dulles' approach
would fall somewhere in the category of "realistic liberalism" or
"Christian realism" [2]—as long as the "Christian" half is taken in a
liberal, naturalistic theological sense.

Nevertheless, with few exceptions,[3] an inaccurate image of Dulles
continues to be commonly accepted in both academic communities
and general publics at home and abroad. Those critical of Dulles'
actions not infrequently exaggerate the importance of supposed but
ill-defined religious influences and motivation. On the other hand,
such critics have been ineffectively countered by equally naive and
superficial apologetics. As is often the case in the politician's realm,
Dulles appears to have elicited either admiration or animosity, with
the former sometimes bordering on veneration and the latter on
moral contempt. Neither the "pro-Dulles" nor the "anti-Dulles"
camp has perceived its subject as a thoroughly pragmatic craftsman
whose approach to international politics was unimpaired by ideological or moral precepts. Moreover, both camps tend to assign insufficient attention to the political context and the force of circumstances within which Dulles weighed the diverse considerations and
pressures of his times.

Even after making allowances for varying authors' assumptions
and viewpoints, political sympathies and prejudices, there persists a
wide divergence of views and interpretations which is not so readily
explainable. Dulles has been described as an "idealist," a classic example of the "legalistic-moralistic" approach to international politics, a "realistic conservative," and a "sober realist." [4] He has been
called a "dedicated pessimist in his general theory of international
politics" and one of "the pioneers of faith." [5] Some thought he had
an "almost schizophrenic attitude"; others viewed him as "a man of
one piece." [6] Much of this disagreement apparently springs from essentially three interrelated sources.

*First, there has been a conspicuous dearth of research into and
discussion about his background, early experiences, and the development of his thoughts.* Dulles is generally remembered in the light
of a single span in his career, the purely political period of problem-

atical balancing acts between international requirements and public acceptance, between American diplomacy and American politics. During most of his career in international affairs, however, he functioned as a technical adviser or competent negotiator. His experiences and activities at the Versailles conferences in 1919, combined with his activity and positions regarding the settlement of the political-diplomatic-financial problems plaguing the years between the two world wars, established the basis of his approach to and theory of international politics.

These early experiences resulted in an understanding of international affairs which was, for all practical purposes, nonlegalistic, nonmoralistic, and nonideological. Although Dulles was not a realist's realist, his approach was constructed on the pragmatic standards of statesmanship and contained strong doses of antilegalism, antimoralism, and anti-ideology. A consistent theme in his writings from the early 1920s was the avoidance of simple solutions, of holier-than-thou self images, and of diabolical enemy images. A noteworthy example appeared in an early essay analyzing the attitudes and policies of the French government after Versailles:

Moral distinctions, though pleasing to those who draw them, are hard to sustain in fact, and I know of no historic reasons to justify our approaching these problems of international relations with the complacent assumption that we are party to a clashing of the forces of good and evil, and that solution is to be found in the moral regeneration of those who hold views contrary to our own.[7]

Chapters I, II, and III deal with Dulles' background and early experiences, ranging from the particular puritanical strains, religious themes, formative influences, and basic impressions in his upbringing, through his roles and reactions during the Versailles peace conferences in 1919 and throughout the interwar years, to his emergence as a political figure. While laying the groundwork for further in depth analysis, these chapters do not pretend at definitive biography.

A second basic source of misunderstanding regarding Dulles has been the lack of the necessary differentiation between the politician and the statesman, between political rhetoric and the actual content of policies, or between "style" and "stuff". According to Dulles, the philosophical inclinations of those who govern should be determined by a study of both utterances and actions, for the nature of policy cannot "be ascertained merely from what its officials say." [8] Yet, in his own case, the politician's indispensable references to moral principles and the common good, plus his tributes to the semi-official ideology, have been taken too much at face value. His earlier writings, for example, contained neither moralistic nor ideological references or overtones. Such overtones, with concomitant alterations in his style of presenting issues and policies, became a part of the pattern only upon his emergence as a national political figure. They were, for the most part, natural products of his perceived requirements for political viability, both personally and for policy preferences, and of his role as a decision-maker in the domestic and international environments at mid-century.

In fairness to those who have misinterpreted Dulles, it should be noted that he was partially responsible for the misunderstanding and the images by which he is often remembered. Although practical, international and political considerations were normally the determining factors in his decision-making as Secretary of State, he was by no means disinclined to employ moralistic rhetoric and ideological overtones in the process of rallying support for decisions once made. Depending upon the particular issue and the circumstances surrounding its presentation, his moralisms, ideological appeals, and hyperbole could spring from one or a combination of factors including, for example, his belief in the power of idealism in social dynamics, perhaps particularly in breaking through barriers of American isolationism; his perception of effective and necessary tools for operating in the American political system; his view of useful propaganda techniques with respect to the cold war competition on the ideological level; or simply the conscious or unconscious political habit of identifying particular interests with wider schemes of interests and values.

The fact is that the language of domestic politics "looks to a common denominator that can more often be found in moral generalities or in broad principles" and "prefers militant slogans to qualified truths." [9] Moreover, except in special and crisis circumstances, American foreign policy oftentimes had "to labor under a handicap" of having "to shout loudly to be heard even a little." [10] To be sure, many statements designed for domestic consumption might be better left unsaid or surely otherwise stated as far as international relations are concerned. In Europe, the American politician may sometimes appear as Mozart's Tamino, accompanied by three gentle spirits to protect and guide him to "truth":

> Their counsel they will lend at need,
> Only to them shall you give heed.

But this appearance results in large part from the fact that Europeans and others, not to mention Americans themselves, are apparently better acquainted with America's "semiofficial ideology" than with its "practical justice." [11] The what, how, and why of actual deeds are far less familiar subjects than the rhetoric and slogans which colored the 1950s. In addition, the process of differentiating between "style" and "stuff" in politics is often further complicated by a common dilemma of statesmen:

The normal tension between a government restrained by prudence and an ideologically impelled people remains, compelling every government to decide how it will reconcile foreign policy considerations with popular pressures at home.

One of the standard means by which governments meet this dilemma is by a more or less cultivated inconsistency between word and deed.[12]

In the task of differentiating between the statesman and the politician, Chapters IV and V represent a search for the spectacles through which Dulles viewed the world, the substratum of philosophical tendencies and attitudes, of ideas on politics and international affairs with which he approached specific problems. The validity of the popular notion that he had an incurably "legalistic-moralistic" approach is tested in the process.[13]

Since the cold war was the predominant background for the evolution of foreign policy in the post-World War II world, no attempt to understand Dulles' approach to various policy problems would be complete without a grasp of his interpretations of communism, "the unholy union of Marx's communism and Russia's imperialism," [14] and the cold war. These subjects, along with the argument that he acquired an ideological outlook sometime after

1945, are examined in Chapters VI and VII. If, as has been suggested, Dulles "believed in the ideals of the West with the same intensity as Khrushchev believed in Communism," [15] there yet remain important questions regarding the degrees to which leaders are themselves "believers" in, "victims" of, and "manipulators" of both the ideologies they represent and the movements which bring them to power.

Chapter VIII traces Dulles' emergence as a political figure, his political adjustments at mid-century, the forces at work in these adjustments, and his role and the issues in the presidential campaign of 1952. Thus one enters the realm of the politician, keeping in mind part of Laertes advice to Ophelia:

> He may not, as unvalued persons do,
> Carve for himself . . .

A third and equally important source of misunderstanding surrounding Dulles has been the abstraction of the man from the foreign policy processes and the overall political context of his era. It is commonly assumed that, as Secretary of State, Dulles had a relatively unlimited field for operation. The extreme of such an assumption is reflected in the contention that he could have pursued whichever course he chose without fear of serious domestic opposition.[16] Even when some basic limitations on his options and maneuverability as Secretary are taken into account, the actual impact of various political and even technical considerations on particular decisions has all too frequently been underestimated.

Conversely, the room for individual maneuverability or the ability to implement personal preferences have been grossly overestimated. Dulles' frequent use of television appearances and radio broadcasts served to inculcate the impression that the Secretary was in absolute command of all foreign policy matters. Eisenhower unquestionably granted his Secretary of State a generous latitude in the formulation and the presentation of policy. But the concept of a "free hand" in the making of American foreign policy contradicts the very essence of the policy-making process. Basic foreign policies cannot be understood as a Secretary's so-called pet projects. Chapters IX, X, and XI reopen some of the major issues of Dulles' secretaryship—"agonizing reappraisal," "massive retaliation," "brink-manship," the 1954 Geneva Conference on Indochina, the Suez crisis, and the subject of "neutralism"—with the aim of placing the Secretary and his decisions in more proper political perspective by concentrating on the conditions outside and inside the government which directly or indirectly affect the making of foreign policy.

The international conditions of the particular cold war and essentially bipolar environment of the 1950s constituted a first order of considerations in the defining of policy options and the weighing of their political, military, psychological, and economic advantages and disadvantages. But international considerations inter-react with a range of other political factors and, in a very real sense, foreign policy decisions cannot be judged merely in terms of inherent soundness or unsoundness with respect to the international situation. Other political factors included such items as Dulles' protecting the relationship of trust with the President from which the Secretary's generous latitude flowed. This would mean not only constantly taking into account Eisenhower's views and predicaments but also not interfering or issuing serious challenges in areas where the General or other advisers held the upper hand. The struggle for power within the Republican party and the search for party unity constituted another important element in the political pattern of the first years of Dulles' secretaryship. Both he and particularly the President as party leader were necessarily concerned with the pressures within the party, and the White House could not without serious political risk ignore the presence and power of the party's right flank.

But, apart from international considerations, the most important and fundamental factor in the definition and exercise of policy options relates to the general state of affairs and the normal balancing act between Congress and the Executive. Dulles took great pains, as did the President, to cultivate a better relationship with Congress. In three years after taking office, the Secretary had met with committees or subcommittees over one hundred times. It has been contended that he paid the price of stagnation in foreign policy for domestic or congressional success.[17] The necessary price for and desired extent of cooperation may be debated, but the indispensability of congressional cooperation remains beyond question.

The prevailing mood of the American people, the political temperament, climate, and environment represent the broad political context of American foreign policy. Near one end of the political spectrum of the early 1950s, although a few Republicans formed the leadership of the so-called McCarthy movement, various forms of "McCarthyism" and "right-wingism" were powerful forces spreading through both political parties and were manifested in the congressional and public moods. At the middle of the political spectrum and of crucial importance to understanding foreign policy, the historical and political "truth" for the United States in the 1950s was not the same as it is today. The period from the late 1940s until at least the mid-1960s was characterized by a "grand consensus" on certain basic policies such as firm opposition to any type or appearance of Soviet or communist expansionism. Although there were some real debates over strategies and implementing tactics, the premises on which basic policies rested "were not centrally at issue." [18] Dulles, as Secretaries before and after him, was perforce a partial incarnation of the period within which he operated.

While international and domestic conditions generally combine to set broad limits on the number of practicable policy alternatives at any given time, international conditions themselves remain the prime concern of the statesman and create a force of circumstances effectually defining the major problems with which he must deal. During the first few years of Dulles' secretaryship, for example, it appeared to some that he had become preoccupied with the military and containment aspects of American foreign policy in spite of his trenchant criticisms of such a trend shortly before assuming office. But the fact was that in the trail of the "loss of China" episode and the miscalculation leading to and the experiences of the Korean War, not to mention the war in Indochina, how to establish more effective or forceful containment and how to deal with the novelty of applying this concept in the gray areas of Asia, as compared to the sharper shades of Europe, emerged as major foreign policy problems of the early 1950s. Another major problem was how to place American foreign policy and strategy of deterrence on an efficient dollar basis which would retain the support of the

American people and be supportable by the national economy over the long haul. The pressures for saving money would expectedly be somewhat stronger if the Republicans came into power, but both of these problems would have been similarly defined for any administration in 1953. Although Eisenhower and Dulles' responses in attempting to answer such questions sometimes seemed exaggerated and abstract to a few of their contemporaries and to others later, an understanding of the responses requires not only an understanding of the "grand consensus" on the broad lines of American foreign policy and the force of international circumstances but also an appreciation of how the problems appeared then and the available tools for dealing with them.

The conclusions of the following chapters raise a broad question relating to trends and habits in political analysis. While there is nothing profound nor unique in recognizing the inescapably political nature of the foreign policy process, a proclivity to abstract policy-makers and policies from their purely political surroundings has contributed to what has been described as the "popular fallacy of equating the foreign policies of a statesman with his philosophic or political sympathies, and of deducing the former from the latter." [19] Since this manner of analysis has become fashionable in assessments of Dulles and decisions during the Eisenhower years, there is more than a modicum of irony in the fact that Dulles knew and counseled against such superficial, popular approaches:

The attitude of great nation is not determined by the personalities of in dividual statesmen or politicians. . . . It is basic economic and political conditions which determine the broad lines of national policy. It is these we must study and with which we must deal.[20]

He advised Americans to "avoid the error of assuming that the foreign policy which runs athwart our own is due to the personal views and idiosyncrasies of some foreign politician who may have temporarily secured an ascendancy over his fellows." [21]

The elements of personality—preferences, prejudices, ego-involvement, style, and especially operational code[22]—are not unimportant to the study of the day-to-day operations and the processes of decision-making; and, at times, a particular personality may even affect or modify the long-range course. But, foreign policy analysis requires first that the individual involved be accurately evaluated, and, second, that his role be considered in terms of the climate, considerations, and pressures of the day which define the political game. As described by one noted philosopher, the challenge of all biography is to enter "into the magic circle of that phenomenon to witness the momentous objective event which that life was" and to view the participant as "only one ingredient." [23]

Two points should, however, be clearly established at the outset. The following discourse is concerned far less with the soundness or unsoundness of particular decisions than with the reasons behind them; and a defense of Dulles against unwarranted and irrelevant criticism in no way immunizes him against all forms of adverse criticism. The conclusion that common assumptions regarding his theory and approach do not coincide with fact, and further that he was fundamentally realistic and pragmatic, does not mean that Dulles possessed an infallible view of world problems or that he never slipped in the balancing act between international and domestic requirements. Furthermore, recognition of the several and sometimes severe limitations upon the Secretary's field for operations does not mean that all his actions, particularly the day-to-day operations, were effectually predetermined by the situation. There surely exists room for criticism in terms of policy tactics, his style of politics and diplomacy, and sometimes the lack of finesse in the implementation of American foreign policy. One need only review the balancing act between European allies and the emerging nations.

Nonetheless, the conclusion that Dulles was fundamentally a pragmatic statesman may serve as a healthy reminder that the source of error in policy is rarely to be found strictly with the individual no matter how powerful he may be within the system. An understanding of statesmen and their policies "requires an appreciation of conditions and forces at work outside the Cabinet room which are often by no means what the responsible authorities would wish," and "the proper understanding of foreign policy demands compassion." [24] Whatever else can be said about John Foster Dulles, he was unmistakably a man responsive to his times, a reflection of the major signposts which characterized America and the world during his turn at the helm of American foreign policy.

CHAPTER ONE

‿‿‿

BACKGROUND INFLUENCES
AND EXPERIENCES

THE EARLY YEARS AND LATER REFLECTIONS

Arriving on February 25, 1888, John Foster Dulles was the firstborn child of the Reverend Allen Macy Dulles, pastor of the Trumbull Avenue Church in Detroit, Michigan, and Edith Foster Dulles, daughter of the prominent American statesman, John Watson Foster. Shortly thereafter, the family moved to Watertown, New York, where Dr. Dulles served as pastor of the First Presbyterian Church. Learning and intellectual inquiry were emphasized in this household, and although Foster Dulles graduated from the local high school, most of his precollege education was acquired through a small private school. In spite of the close contact with community activities, which resulted from his father's profession, it is apparent that, in a very real sense, young Dulles never experienced the "rough and tumble of humanity":

To the outsiders the Dulles's were a formidable and unusual family, just a bit larger than life, full of spirit and character.[1]

All in all, he experienced a perfectly normal and probably exceptionally happy childhood. In later years, as is the wont of political personalities, Dulles frequently referred to his childhood background which genuinely reflected several aspects of the ideals and traditions associated with the "American way of life." These early circumstances, combined with his excellent intellectual equipment and the studious years in philosophy and psychology at Princeton, were conducive to the development of a philosophical detachment and a pervasive strain of moderate liberalism tempered by realism and conservative tendencies.

Broadly speaking, the two most important early influences in Dulles' life were his father, Reverend Allen Macy Dulles, and the family patriarch, John Watson Foster. There was, in fact, a confluence of the teachings and ways of these two forceful figures operating in Dulles' upbringing. There was neither an inherent incompatibility nor any real antagonisms between the Presbyterianism and principles of the pastor's home and the practical affairs and worldliness of the statesman. Allen Macy Dulles and John Watson Foster represented different, but by no means disparate, expressions of a similar American strain. Moderate teachings of a Presbyterian Christianity blended with the ideas of a frontier liberalism to form the pragmatic foundation of Dulles' conceptual framework.

Although interpretations of Dulles' Presbyterian background have ranged from the fundamentalistic-moralistic type to, in terms of the times, the very liberal, neither impression accurately describes the nature of his religious inheritance. To be sure, as the elder son of a Presbyterian minister, he experienced a rigorous training in religion and the religious backbone of the family left a strong impression. Moreover, the puritan fiber generally has been inextricably woven into the fabric of American society and "the influence of puritanism, in the broad Calvinistic sense . . . contributed uniquely and profoundly to the making of the American mind when the American mind was in the making." [2] But such naked facts fail to illumine the subject. An almost infinite number of possible combinations were made possible in the mixing of eighteenth-century democratic liberalism and seventeenth-century puritanism, regardless of their common emphases on individualism and on man as a social being with certain rights and moral relations. Dulles' "rigorous training" needs to be defined and clarified in terms, not of hours and services, but of the religious themes and emphases in the pastor's household and church.

While the consistency of particular themes and the kind of everyday talk in the Watertown church and the Dulles home are not exactly known, several passages in Reverend Dulles' major theological work, *The True Church*,[3] suggest that he was basically a church moderate with at least three important inclinations toward a liberal theological viewpoint. These inclinations appeared in his general view of the Church, his emphasis on social utility, and his attitude toward intellectual inquiry and science.

The True Church was written as a defense of the evangelic concept against the forces of ecclesiasticism and denominationalism. Reverend Dulles' criticism of the latter was not confined to the Catholic notion of divine authority: "It is not to be denied that this delusion of divine authority has at times taken possession of some protestant communions . . . . Each and all have erred most grievously both in practice and in precept." [4] The treatise was concerned less with particular forms and formulae than with the widespread idolatry within the Church—namely, the worship of the organization itself and the concomitant petrification of the different approaches through rules and dogma. The work concluded that the "problem of problems for The Church is, first—itself." [5]

Reverend Dulles accentuated the idea of social duty by reiterating that the three Christian duties—love of God, love of man, and edification of the spirit—were inseparable.[6] Accordingly, social utility constituted the standard by which individuals and religious organizations were to be measured. Regarding such judgment, however, man's inherent finitude precluded finality and absolutes.[7] The concepts of human finitude and social utility not only were part and parcel of Dr. Dulles' teachings but also apparently made lasting impressions on his firstborn. John Foster Dulles' own writings later were permeated by the ideas of necessary imperfection and relativity; his philosophical framework and views on religion were structured around utilitarian foundations.

Reverend Allen Macy Dulles clearly dissociated himself from the die-hard clergy, the stubborn fundamentalists, in his attitude toward intellectual inquiry and science, both of which he strongly encouraged,[8] and in his view that acceptance of the "virgin birth" was not necessary to Christian belief. But the expression and existence of a number of liberal tendencies and sentiments did not, in the complete sense, a "liberal theologian" make. Although such tendencies were no doubt significant relative to Dulles' upbringing and religious training, the reverend actually had his strongest ties to the middle ground between the fundamentalist and liberal, or "modernist," camps. It was on the basis of this middle position that, in 1924, he encouraged and aided his elder son in taking up the cause of the "modernists" in their battle against the fundamentalist movement in the church.

The fundamentalist movement in the Presbyterian church attempted to establish "five points" as both fundamental to true belief and essential to the right to preach the gospel in the church. These "five points" included the literal inerrancy of the Scriptures, the virgin birth, bodily or physical resurrection, substitutionary atonement, and miracles. The fundamentalists succeeded in having the 1923 Presbyterian General Assembly instruct the New York Presbytery to investigate the matter of Doctors Harry Emerson Fosdick and Henry P. Van Dusen and their orthodoxy. After the New York Presbytery found no reason to challenge the ordinations of Fosdick and Van Dusen, the Philadelphia Presbytery, according to Allen Macy Dulles, "especially was dissatisfied and has gone on a heresy hunt." [9] The fundamentalists' goals, in the 1924 General Assembly, were to have it instruct the New York Presbytery to terminate Fosdick's relationship with the church, primarily because of his questioning of the virgin birth, and further to establish that the church's constitution gave the General Assembly powers to enforce adherence to its deliverances such as the "five points" by the Presbyteries.

In a letter to his son Foster, Reverend Dulles outlined the issues most likely to be presented at the assembly, mentioned the senselessness of dividing the church, and briefly and hastily ventilated his own views as to why the "five points" were not essential to Christian belief:

Let those who want testify to Fundamentals, and let the truth prevail; but why use force and excommunication and anathema in this day and generation? Cannot Fundamentalists win through the truth, without persecution and prosecution? . . . Paul's "gospel" never made these "five points" fundamental. . . . What *kind* of a body Jesus had, Paul never made fundamental. The exact *method* of the generation of Jesus Paul never mentions. *What constitutes* a miracle is never defined in the New Testament. The *exact significance* of the death of Jesus has never been determined by the church universal. . . . Any and every scholar knows that no theory of Atonement has had anything approaching unanimity in the church. Inerrancy of the Scriptures is, of course, an absurdity.[10]

But Reverend Dulles' "defense" of the "modernists" was motivated less by any particular agreement with their theological positions or disagreement with the fundamentalists' "five points" than by his adherence to the principle that the "modernists" had a right to hold and to preach their beliefs. While strongly disagreeing with the bases and divisive methods of the fundamentalists' "heresy hunt," he was not necessarily pleased with the "modernists." He was personally "little interested" in the dispute and felt like saying "(a) plague on both your houses." [11] Of interest, however, he advised his son that one of the main objectives should be to secure time and "time is on the side of the Liberals." [12]

During April and May, Foster Dulles prepared for participation in the 1924 General Assembly, primarily by studying the legal and constitutional questions involved, to "assist . . . in breaking lances with [William Jennings] Bryan on behalf of the Modernists." [13] The approach of the "modernists" to the assembly, with which Dulles agreed, was "to avoid discussion of doctrine" and "to raise an issue of constitutional procedure." [14] At the assembly itself, he was in "the thick of the fight" as a member of the Liberal Steering Committee of three and experienced a "most interesting and exciting" week.[15] With the "modernists" being defended on legal and constitutional grounds, the "fight" was in large measure a successful exercise in church law and politics as set forth in Dulles' own recounting of the episode:

We succeeded in wresting control . . . away from the Fundamentalists (Bills and Overtures Committee) and I was almost daily in controversy with Bryan. . . . The Fundamentalists had a very well and closely organized machine and had the votes on us throughout the proceeding. The only way we were able to secure a victory was through getting the Judicial Commission to assume jurisdiction in the case of Fosdick and of the Philadelphia Overture, which I do not think they really had, and then when it came to a question of accepting or reviewing the decision of the Judicial Commission, the Fundamentalists were, for the first time, unable to hold their votes in line.[16]

The New York Presbytery was not instructed to terminate Fosdick's relationship with the church and, of greater importance to Dulles, the decision in the case of the Philadelphia Overture held that "the attempt to enforce adherence to such deliverances of the Assembly as the 'five points' . . . is unconstitutional." [17] After congratulating his son in the handling of the cases, Reverend Dulles agreed that "it was certainly *not* a case for the Judicial Commission" and, perhaps wearying of the divisive dispute or possibly concerned regarding Foster's firm alignment with the liberal camp, added that the "modernists have no adequate standing ground" since the "Fundamentalists are *logically* correct in their attitude to the Confession and the Bible." [18] The battle between the camps continued and, for his part, Foster Dulles kept in contact with the controversy throughout the following year and prepared two more legal briefs in defense of the New York Presbytery's actions regarding four other ministers. His argument for the "modernists" again concentrated on the constitutional power of the Presbyteries over the licensure of candidates for the ministry. He concluded that "if any particular Presbytery cannot be trusted, then the remedy is to exscind that Presbytery. . . . Such a procedure is infinitely to be preferred over one which, for the purpose of controlling one Presbytery, would bind the whole church with legalism and formalism. . . ." [19]

Although Dulles was indeed "churchy" and an active Presbyterian elder, religion or religious doctrine as such appeared to play a relatively minor role in his life from the time of entering the university (1904) and even after the Oxford Conference on "Church, Community and State" (1937). Even if he had graduated from the Watertown church with a somewhat restricted religious viewpoint, his writings during these years contained no evidence of parochialism and virtually no references to Christianity, religion, or moral laws. The influence of the grandfather, the experiences of university life, travel abroad, the many years as a skilled practitioner in law, diplomacy, and politics all had a broadening effect. In 1918 he was questioning whether or not he really had any religion.[20] Although he avoided doctrinal issues while defending the "modernists" against the fundamentalists' heresy trials, his active association with the liberal cause suggests a far more sympathetic alignment than the more middle-of-the-road position of his father. Even after the very refreshing experience at the 1937 Oxford Conference, he described himself as a Christian layman with "somewhat diluted beliefs." [21] His own utilitarian view of religion, which is discussed in Chapter VI, was a logical development considering his religious training and background. This early religious environment did not encourage any parochialism or "true believer" tendencies which would, practically speaking, affect the evolution of his political thinking and approach to international politics.

Of greater import in Dulles' background was the vast common ground shared by Allen Macy Dulles and John Watson Foster, where the influence of the father and that of the grandfather generally complemented and reinforced each other. By 1888, the various religions in the United States had already either adapted or been molded to the American setting. In this sense, Reverend Dulles represented not only American Presbyterianism but also "protestant Americanism." As a layman of Christian upbringing, John Watson Foster was representative of a similar strain. Both men adhered to a moderate, individualistic, political liberalism which favored gradual evolution and change in the preservation, promotion, and expansion of political liberty, and generally opposed conservatism's tendency toward the preservation of the *status quo* and established privilege as well as radical liberalism's tendency toward abrupt change and revolution. While favoring evolutionary change, however, moderate political liberalism could not escape the proposition that revolution was the logical retaliation against repression. Also, within this context of political liberalism, both the Presbyterian pastor and the august grandfather, whom Bryce once called "the most distinguished diplomat of our time," [22] were genuinely internationally minded.

The key to both men's political liberalism was its moderateness. Reverend Dulles' theological approach revolved around the concern for unity, stability, tolerance, and freedom of the individual. These same values probably carried over into and formed the foundations of his political thinking. Although there exists only very scant evidence relating to his political preferences, there are no indications that he possessed any strong sense of imaginative reform or "political creativeness." John Watson Foster, a thoroughgoing Republican of the liberal, internationalist variety, expressed his understanding of diplomatic affairs in the conclusion, reached in 1873, resolving the matter of his hesitation to enter the diplomatic service because of lack of experience:

The practice of diplomacy was not, after all, so very different from that of any other profession and . . . success could come only through strict devotion to duty and through understanding of the matters at hand.[23]

While his ability as a statesman remained beyond question, he did come into some criticism for plodding and lacking imagination.

As representatives of nineteenth-century American liberalism's concern for expanding political liberty, Secretary Foster and Reverend Dulles were strong adherents of the democratic idea. Campaigning for Abraham Lincoln in two elections, when antislavery was not a popular issue along the Kentucky border, the former "was so keen in the cause that he was often called an abolitionist, an opprobrious epithet in those times."[24] Although not nearly so inclined toward political activism, the latter appears to have accepted the implications of his statement that the color of a man's skin is not essential.[25] In terms of domestic political issues, John Foster Dulles' inherited belief in political liberalism and commitment to the democratic idea found their sharpest expression in some strong statements after World War II against segregation, discrimination, and racism in the United States.

Secretary Foster was obviously internationally minded. He became a dedicated diplomat and a member of the internationalist school before the arrival of his grandson whom he encouraged along a similar path. Reverend Dulles, a firm believer in learning and languages, in traveling and living abroad, also encouraged interests in international affairs. He always had a streak of cosmopolitanism, having furthered his studies in both France and Germany. Foster Dulles, not to mention the other children of the family, inherited a serious interest in international relations well before he departed for Princeton in 1904. If, like his grandfather, he lacked a certain spark of imagination, his life and career, from the university to 1959, reflected similar possession of a devotion to duty and to understanding the matters at hand.

The common strains of moderate political liberalism and internationalism, represented in his father and grandfather, were very consequential early influences in Dulles' background. His entire political philosophy was based on the premise of the inevitability of change either by peaceful or violent means and a clear concomitant preference for evolutionary progress as contrasted to the *status quo* and to radical change. According to this political complexion, the task of authority is to "create a condition of flexibility which will give qualified and balanced satisfaction to both the dynamic and static elements" which, because "underlying conditions are constantly in flux," can only be attained by ever-temporary adaptations and changes.[26] This broad principle was applied to internal and international relations, with the task of leadership in both areas defined by Dulles as being "constantly on the watch for symptoms which foreshadow the necessity for change":

If detected at an early state, adjustment can be offered which will serve to prevent a damming up of dynamic forces to a degree such that violent and drastic change becomes inescapable. . . . The ideal form of change . . . avoids that spectacular and grandiose massing of dynamic and static elements which in itself excludes intelligence from any guiding role.[27]

The successful operation of this balancing principle was more often easier said than done, however, since those in positions of authority "naturally proceed from the viewpoint that the conditions which have brought them into the position . . . are not conditions which should be changed."[28]

The combination of Dulles' moderate political liberalism and internationalism prevented any identification with the noninternationally minded, more conservative segment of American society. He never did belong to the die-hard group of the Grand Old Party and, at times, his internationalist complexion caused him either to shift party alliances or to disagree openly with the more conservative element. Although John W. Davis, Democratic candidate for the presidency in 1924, was a friend of Dulles, familiarity was not the only, if even the main, reason why the latter supported Davis in 1920 and 1924. In short, Ambassador Davis was internationally minded and Dulles was strongly advocating, among other things, United States membership in the League of Nations and no "return to normalcy." When Davis failed to receive the Democratic nomination in 1920, Dulles was "considerably disappointed" with both candidates and awaited developments to decide whether to be a Republican or Democrat.[29] In a more personal note after the election of Warren G. Harding, he found that "nothing so far has gone to change the impression originally created that Harding has not much of a mind of his own." [30]

In 1924 Dulles wholeheartedly supported Davis and supplied him with a list of issues on which he thought the Republicans were particularly vulnerable to criticism. Dulles supported the Harding-Hughes plan for adherence to the Permanent Court of International Justice, while claiming that President Coolidge, in spite of announced support, was actually indifferent to the proposal. He favored returning the over $300 million worth of private alien property held by the United States since seizure under the Trading with the Enemy Act, during the war, on the grounds of moral considerations and good business practice and, incidentally, since control of such sums by political appointees "cannot but breed favoritism and dishonesty" no matter which party happens to be in power. Dulles proposed doing away with the absurd fiction that the Kerensky group in the United States were representatives of the Russian government and then determining whether and, if so, on what terms to renew diplomatic relations. Stating that recognition of the Soviets as the government of Russia, which they unquestionably were, would neither require resumption of diplomatic relations nor "imply amity or friendship," he was aware that the distinctions in the issue may be "too subtle to be of any use." Turning to the Western hemisphere, he thought that "some effective contrast could be made between our feeble and rather timid policy toward the really vital international problems and our bullying and imperialistic policy toward the smaller nations to the South." [31]

On the question of his overall reaction to the international posture of the Coolidge Administration, Dulles' private memorandum for Ambassador Davis left no room for doubt: "The attitude of the Republican Administration toward the great problem of reparation strikingly illustrates the futility and folly of a policy of attempted isolation." Referring to the Dawes Plan of 1924, he maintained that it bordered "upon the ludicrous that the Republican party should now, after the event, so eagerly seek to take credit onto itself for a course of action which it neither initiated nor officially aided." [32] Dulles' approach to the campaign of 1924 also reflected the inherited brand of moderate political liberalism: "It is out of extreme conservatism of the Coolidge type that extreme radicalism emerges." Therefore, "it must be demonstrated that the welfare of the country in the long run requires a liberal government and that persistence of an ultra-conservative government . . . quickly bears fruit in a radical party of increasing menace and power." [33] The same liberal foundations would later account for his antiextremism and anti-isolationism after World War II, as well as for the difficulties and many disagreements with both the right wing of the Republican party and the generally antiliberal mood of the country at mid-century.

DEVELOPING SEEDS OF PRAGMATISM

Foster Dulles entered Princeton University in 1904 at the young age of sixteen. Obviously quick and possessing an excellent power of concentration, he excelled in his studies and exhibited that rare ability to work hard and play hard. He was a serious student who "kept greatly to himself" so that few of the "classmates knew him well." [34] His keeping to himself was probably also a product of the fact that most of his classmates were older.

Having received an invitation from his grandfather in 1907, Dulles experienced an adventure in firsthand diplomacy at the second Hague Peace Conference. Grandfather Foster attended the conference as the special counsel to the Chinese delegation, and young John Foster as the delegation's official secretary. The representatives at the second Hague Peace Conference reaffirmed belief in arbitration, revised and improved upon the methods of arbitration, and passed upon more extensive rules to humanize warfare. But the absence of an agreement to control arms production left a mark of failure in the minds of many participants.

The experience provided two basic impressions for young Dulles: first, evidence of hope and possibilities for increased cooperation between nations and, second, the fact that realities and not hope constitute the context of foreign relations. His grandfather's *Diplomatic Memoirs* illustrated this combination: "It is visionary to expect that wars among nations will cease, but let us hope that there is the dawn of a new day." Describing the conference as "in some respects, the most important event in the history of the human race," he also recorded that a general spirit of skepticism and cynicism prevailed in Europe.[35] Aside from Dulles' dealings with other governments as part of his law practice, his next experiences in diplomacy would result from the explosion of World War I seven years later.

Dulles returned from the conference to complete his senior year at Princeton. Majoring in philosophy, which entailed several courses in psychology, he wrote a revealing and lengthy piece entitled "Pragmatism." Analyzing the works of William James, John Dewey, and F.C.S. Schiller, the essay dealt primarily with ontological and epistemological objections to the philosophical foundations of pragmatism. His main objection was that pragmatism, in its more narrow sense, failed "to be a better or more adequate explanation than many now existing philosophies," particularly as a theory of reality, a theory of thought, or a theory of truth.[36] Dulles also believed that pragmatism went too far when it tried "to supplant all reason by feeling and desire" and when it appealed "to reason to deny its own validity." Although "it may well be that feeling and will verify the decisions of reason," he concluded that "reason must be left the ultimate judge of truth."[37]

The exposition reveals that the author mostly failed to grasp the core and meaning of the pragmatists' thoughts and, consequently, underrated their impact and importance. On the other hand, he considered pragmatism "valuable" insofar as it was "a protest against rationalism which ignores feeling" and viewed its thrusts as serving a salutary purpose: "It has infused life and spirit in certain

fields of thought, and by its attacks on rationalism it will undoubtedly lead to a readjustment and improvement of that doctrine." [38]
If, at this stage, Dulles perceived his actual affinity with pragmatic
thinkers, the association did not come out in this essay. But neither
did these early intellectual objections alter this developing affinity,
particularly with the thoughts and sentiments of William James.

Another essay, "The Theory of Judgment," won Dulles the Chancellor Green Mental Science Fellowship for one year of study at the
Sorbonne. He graduated with honors, Phi Beta Kappa and vale-
dictorian of his class, and the family departed for Paris in 1908.
Dulles took some interest in the international law courses at the
Sorbonne, but found more interest in Henri Bergson's lectures in
philosophy. Perhaps Bergson's concept of "creative evolution"—
especially the idea that the intellect is merely one factor in biological
adaptation serving a pragmatic function in the struggle for life—
played a role in the strengthening of the young Princetonian's naturalistic leanings. (These leanings and his philosophy generally
were interestingly reflected in his keen interests, developed in his
youth and lasting throughout his career, in nature and the outdoors
and in sailing.)

In 1909, beginning his law studies at George Washington Law
School, Dulles moved in with his grandparents in Washington. For
two years, he burned the proverbial candle at both ends. Completing the three year course in two years and keeping a busy social
schedule, he reportedly attained the highest academic marks
granted by the school. While excelling in his legal studies, he also
became well acquainted with Washington circles and had, through
his grandfather, open entree into all levels of Washington's society.
His list of friends included Andrew Carnegie and young Robert
Taft. He also spent much time with his uncle, Robert Lansing, who
later offered him the first real opportunities in diplomacy.

Dulles began his career as a fifty-dollar-a-month law clerk with
one of New York's more respected law firms, Sullivan and Cromwell. His success in law came rapidly. He was soon traveling to Central America as counsel for the firm and, in 1926, became senior active partner, a position which often took thirty years to achieve. His
association and practice with Sullivan and Cromwell continued

until the demands of public service, at mid-century, required giving up the practice of law.

Dulles was successful early in life and tasted no real defeat. Helped by his grandfather and later by his uncle, he never failed and usually surpassed the trust placed in him. Although not symbolic of the typical Horatio Alger rags-to-riches or famine-to-fame figure, he was "essentially a self-made man." [39] As his political philosophy adjusted to changing circumstances over the years and became increasingly liberalized through his involvement in international affairs, its basic foundations would remain intact as would his separation from "the rough and tumble of humanity."

BEGINNINGS IN DIPLOMACY

When United States entry into World War I became imminent in 1917, President Wilson and Secretary of State Lansing made preparations to prompt Panama and Cuba into following the United States lead in the declaration of war on Germany. After sounding out officers of the State Department, Lansing selected his twenty-nine-year-old nephew, John Foster Dulles, to act as special emissary on an unofficial mission. On the first day of April, the latter departed for Panama. As Lansing recorded in his *War Memoirs,* his nephew was entirely successful in the mission. The day after the United States entered the war, both Panama and Cuba proclaimed a state of war with the German Empire.[40]

After consulting with the Panamanian government, Dulles proceeded to Costa Rica where, in January, General Tinoco had gained control by revolution. The United States had withheld recognition of the Tinoco government. Dulles' assignment was to consult with the leaders, survey the situation, and recommend a course of action. In a confidential memorandum to the Secretary of State, dated May 21, 1917, he strongly advocated recognition of the revolutionary regime. The recommendation was adopted by the State Department but was not approved by President Wilson.[41] This relatively minor and obscure incident illustrates three important aspects of Dulles' development.

First, it is the earliest indication of his basic approach, which was expressed more systematically some twenty-two years later in *War, Peace and Change,* toward the subject of recognition. In 1917, he concluded that "non-recognition, in the case of a government exercising undisputed control, is . . . a measure rarely to be availed of. . . . The United States cannot . . . lay down as a general principle, applicable even to the Caribbean states alone, the non-recognition of *every* government which comes into power through a revolution." This was particularly so because "actual revolution is often the only effective method of preventing an indefinite perpetuation of power." [42]

Second, the incident brought out one of the many unbridgeable differences between Wilson and Dulles. Although he never criticized Wilson personally, Dulles unequivocally disapproved of the policy of nonrecognition and nonintercourse which he later described as squeezing Costa Rica dry and destroying "a decade of progress." [43] In 1917, he had described such a policy as "negative and destructive in its operation" unless it were "in aid of a specific constructive program." [44]

Third, Dulles concluded from the incident that good motives and theoretical principles of morality were guarantees of neither morally virtuous nor politically successful policies: "The policy which we did adopt, although it could not be said to involve the slightest infraction of the highest theoretical standards of international law, in fact constituted an interference of a most burdensome nature." Given the circumstances and the stance of Wilson, a military expedition would have perhaps accomplished a change of government more expeditiously and, in this sense, been preferable to economic strangulation affecting all the Costa Ricans. [45]

CHAPTER TWO

COMING OF STATESMANSHIP

Dulles' poor eyesight, a product of quinine doses during an earlier bout with malaria in Panama, precluded his enrolling in active military service during World War I. He was commissioned at the rank of captain and became a legal assistant to the chairman of the War Trade Board, Vance McCormick. McCormick, also chairman of the Democratic National Committee, acquired a lasting admiration for his assistant's abilities, and the two men corresponded for years following their work together during the war and at Versailles. In the War Trade Board position, Dulles frequently worked with the chairman of the War Industries Board, Bernard Baruch. Although the details of his activity in this capacity are relatively unimportant, his performance led to a promotion to major, recognition as "the" economics and legal expert, and a request to accompany the American delegation to the Paris Peace Conference of 1919.

THE PARIS PEACE CONFERENCE

As did other technicians accompanying peace commissioners to Versailles, Dulles soon came to realize that what the War Trade Board knew was not of great interest to them.[1] Invited to attend the conference as legal adviser to the American delegates concerned with the financial aspects of the settlement, he served on various commit-

tees and commissions. He later became a member of the American
delegation's steering committee and was generally responsible for
the economic sections of the treaties with Austria, Hungary, and
Bulgaria. His most significant work at the conference, however, was
done in the capacity of a United States representative on the Reparations Committee, where he found himself helping to construct
and presenting the arguments of the United States against the
claims of Great Britain and France. In this task, he worked closely
with the senior members of the delegation to the Reparations
Committee—Bernard Baruch, Vance McCormick, Thomas Lamont,
and Norman Davis. Officially serving only as counsel to this group,
Dulles soon became, in fact, its principal draftsman and spokesman.[2]

As reflected in his draft memoranda and statements, the counsel
to the United States delegation to the Reparations Committee was
in sharp disagreement with the British and French proposals to
exact very large reparations from Germany on the principle of holding it responsible for war costs or all loss and damage resulting
from the war. War costs, in this sense, included reparation not just
for damage done the civilian population and property but also for
the costs and damage imposed upon the allied governments. These
latter costs could actually range from reparations for war pensions
and separation allowances to those for the costs involved in war
production and nonmilitary and military capital destruction resulting from the war. War cost demands could easily lead to the ridiculous and, according to Bernard Baruch, one of the allies went so far
as to "make claim for loss and damage resulting from the fact that
the Armistice was concluded so unexpectedly that the termination
of hostilities involved it in financial losses."[3] Moreover, the actual
calculation of war costs was, for all practical purposes, impossible
and inevitably led to astronomical figures.

But the French and the British, largely because of their serious
financial difficulties after the war and because of strong domestic
political pressures and public sentiments against Germany, pressed
for high reparations based on the war costs principle. This occurred
in spite of the fact that "(m)ost experts agreed that Germany's capacity to pay . . . was less than the cost of the war to the Allies and

less than the most conservative estimates of that damage." [4] Dulles interpreted the demands for war costs as unmanageable, imprudent, and, in light of the pre-Armistice and Armistice approach to the Germans, unjust. His skills as a master of the technicalities of negotiation and compromise were exemplified in his arguments and reactions during the reparations episode at Versailles.

President Wilson had proclaimed that the treaty with Germany should be "just." The general arguments of the British and French delegations, after a lengthy course of reasoning and quotations, boiled down to the contention that for Germany to pay the costs of the war would be in accordance with theoretical principles of justice. Their arguments also relied upon a particular, completely open-ended, interpretation of Article 19 of the Armistice Agreement which read: "With the reservation that any future claims and demands of the Allies and the United States of America remain unaffected, the following financial conditions are required: reparation for damages done." Referring to the open-endedness of this statement, John Maynard Keynes later pointed out that it was "merely the usual phrase of the draftsman, who, about to rehearse a list of certain claims, wishes to guard himself from the implication that such list is exhaustive." [5] To identify war cost demands as consistent with Wilson's "just peace" took a long stretch of the imagination as, beyond reparation for civilian damages, the President opposed any punitive demands upon Germany. On February 23, 1919, he stated the fundamental American objection to the argument of France and the United Kingdom:

I feel that we are bound in honor to decline to agree to the inclusion of war costs in the reparation demanded. The time to think of this was before the conditions of peace were communicated to the enemy. . . . We should dissent and dissent publicly if necessary not on the ground of the intrinsic injustice of it but on the ground that it is clearly inconsistent with what we deliberately led the enemy to expect and cannot now honorably alter simply because we have the power. [6]

Dulles skillfully countered the arguments for inclusion of war costs. Although continuing to reiterate the idea that Germany should be made to pay to the uttermost, "uttermost" for him meant neither the inclusion of war costs nor the holding back of Germany's economic development. He perceived great danger both in seeking high damages and in failing to arrive at a reasonable fixed sum. By destroying economic incentive thusly, the willingness and ability of Germany to pay could only be adversely affected. In short, Dulles wanted Germany as a stabilizing, productive, and consuming factor in the world economy.[7] His approach to the issue of reparations essentially coincided with the ideas presented by Keynes, whose position history has vindicated. Keynes declared that the British and the French arguments for reparations inclusive of war costs "were . . . overwhelmed by the speeches made on behalf of the American delegates by Mr. John Foster Dulles." [8]

As far as the legal aspects of the matter were concerned, Dulles accepted neither the casuistry nor the intricacies of the British arguments. His case was based upon the fact that the pre-Armistice Agreement with Germany, the Allied note of November 5, 1918, had specifically stated "that compensation will be made by Germany for all damages done to the civilian population of the Allies and their property by the aggression of Germany." [9] This condition limited the Allies' rights to claims only for such civilian damages:

Our bargain has been struck for better or for worse; it remains only to give it a fair construction and practical application.[10]

Germany's corresponding obligation was thereby defined as "contractual liability," more than a strictly legal liability and less than liability under equity. Proceeding from this argument, Dulles insisted that there existed, under the principles of international law, no bases whereby Germany could become a debtor for the general costs of the war. He covered the flanks with other legalistic arguments:

We are also compelled to recognize that in so far as we base our claims, not upon contractual law but on the law of torts, we are restricted to damage arising from *illegal* acts. It is not enough that an act be immoral, that it be cruel, that it be unjust, unless at the same time it be illegal. It is the quality of illegality alone which in law gives rise to a right of reparation.[11]

As the contending political forces and possible "trade-offs" effectually shut the door on reaching a reparations settlement along the lines recommended by the American delegation and other experts, Dulles began preparing fallback positions. In a memorandum of June 3, 1919, he had asserted that a fixed sum for reparations should be established: "It seems far more probable that to continue to perpetuate uncertainty as to the amount of Germany's payments will merely postpone an awakening until a time when the situation may be even more critical." [12] However, when the proposal for a fixed sum failed, along with the suggestion to establish at least minimum and maximum amounts, he came up with a plan whereby the decision as to the amount of reparations would be left to a Permanent Reparation Commission. According to Colonel House, this idea was rapidly seized upon by both Lloyd George and Georges Clemenceau.[13]

The search for workable compromises had, several months earlier, led to Dulles' original part in the process which finally resulted in Article 231, the so-called war guilt clause. Even after Belgium's Van den Heuvel agreed to safeguards for the small powers and objected to the inclusion of war costs, the gap between the major powers persisted. On February 21, Dulles drafted an unofficial text reflecting the position of the American delegation. According to this draft plan, Germany would be held responsible for war costs only in theory and only by certain governments: "Certain of the governments at war with Germany, believing that it is just and within the contemplation of the principles agreed to . . . that the German Government shall . . . make reparation for the entire cost of the war . . . the Government of Germany recognizes its liability in the premises." But, the draft then stipulated: "It is agreed, however, that the ability of the German Government . . . to make reparation is limited . . . and accordingly the governments at war with Germany renounce the right to insist upon reparation other than is expressly specified for herein." [14]

The draft was distributed and, of course, revised several times. Although the basic concepts were those which ultimately became embodied in Articles 231 and 232 of the treaty, the final product differed significantly from Dulles' original text. The changes in successive revisions, especially those resulting from Lloyd George's position that the statement be a direct affirmation of an allied right, substantially altered the tone of the final text of Article 231: "The Allied and Associated Governments affirm and Germany accepts the responsibility of Germany and her allies for causing all the loss and damage to which the Allied and Associated Governments and their nationals have been subjected as a consequence of the war imposed upon them by the aggression of Germany and her allies." The final text of Article 232 recognized the impossibility of Germany's making reparation for "such loss and damage" and limited actual liability to reparation for damage done to civilian population and property and for damages as defined in an annex to the treaty.

Dulles' original draft was clearly and simply an economic thesis of liability vis-à-vis certain allied governments and Germany. Even though the final article emerged as a similar economic thesis,[15] its different thrust and tone were no doubt far more abrasive from the German standpoint, which later interpreted the charge of "causal responsibility" as "moral responsibility" and Article 231 as the "infamous war guilt" clause. The emotional and psychological significance of this article was apparently not evident to Dulles or the American delegation at the Paris Peace Conference. At any rate, in the bargaining with Britain and France, it emerged as the delegation's least undesirable workable option.

Dulles had initially hoped for a clean and reasonable reparation settlement generally along the lines of Keynes' approach. When such a settlement was not attained, he yet hoped that reason, guided by consideration of real economic factors and expert advice, would be given a better hearing in the decision-making process of a Permanent Reparation Commission. He, therefore, found himself in disagreement with the inauspicious prospects presented in Keynes' *The Economic Consequences of the Peace:*

If every ambiguity in the Treaty is to be resolved in a sense oppressive to Germany; if it be assumed that the Reparation Commission is to exercise its functions in a spirit obviously destructive of the interests of the Allies and of the economic reestablishment of Europe; then Mr. Keynes's condemnation of the Treaty is explicable. . . . If the broad constructive purpose of the Treaty is borne in mind, and its provisions (already elastic) are liberally construed and applied; and if a Reparation Commission is created which will, as intended, exercise its powers with wisdom and in accordance with the true interests of the nations which it represents; then the Treaty can be regarded as a statesmanlike accomplishment.[16]

As it turned out, Keynes' reply to Dulles more accurately assessed the situation and outlook:

I fancy we agree pretty much at heart about what happened in Paris, and only differ as to the tactics and procedures of the immediate future. For my own part I feel very strongly that matters have now gone too far for anything but an outward and visible change to be adequate to the situation.[17]

Such a change was not forthcoming. Reflecting on the "historical genesis of German reparation" in 1938, Dulles concluded that the "scope of what man can usefully attempt is constantly restricted by his lack of knowledge, and by moods which render unavailing that little knowledge which he does possess." [18]

When Dulles returned from the Paris Peace Conference, he had gained in international respect and was recognized as one of America's experts on reparations and international finance.[19] Had the United States Senate authorized official American membership on the Reparation Commission, he was a likely and logical candidate for the job. (If, as has been reported, he declined the offer to serve as the unofficial American representative, it was probably due to his perceived need to return to the practice of law.) The experiences at Versailles left many important impressions in terms of his career, the development of his thinking, and his political operational code. The episode included instructions not only in the field of international politics but, most poignantly, in the relationships between foreign policy and domestic politics. All of these lessons would be uniquely combined, three decades later, in Dulles' handling of the Japanese Peace Treaty negotiations.

DULLES AND PRESIDENT WILSON

Probably the most significant lessons of this period derived from the political failure of President Wilson and the related refusal of the United States to become a member of the League of Nations. Although Dulles accepted many of the ideals and some of the programs promulgated by Wilson, and in spite of the fact that he often quoted and had high praise for Wilson as a great statesman (albeit one with many recognized faults not the least of which being political) and both men were sons of Presbyterian ministers, the two men were of decisively different temperaments and political operational principles. Their differences went well beyond substantial disagreement on policy issues, such as whether or not to recognize the Tinoco regime in Costa Rica.

During the Paris Peace Conference, another more minor disagreement arose regarding the President's decision to accept the British plan to hold the Germans responsible for pensions. Dulles carefully presented the arguments, shared by other members of the delegation, against accepting the British proposal: First, it could be manipulated to cover war costs; second, even if it were not extended to cover war costs, the pension scheme alone violated the pre-Armistice Agreement with Germany; and third, it simply went against the rules of logic. His own account of the incident, at the time, was rather restrained: "The President stated that he did not feel bound by considerations of logic and that . . . it was a proper subject of reparation under the agreed terms of peace." [20] Actually, on later report, the President is reputed to have retorted: "I don't give a damn for logic. I'm going to include pensions." [21]

While Dulles wholly supported Wilson's basic program for international cooperation and an organized League of Nations, there was scarce room for respect regarding the latter's approach either to the conduct of the negotiations or to the handling of politics back home. According to Secretary Lansing, no one seemed to know just how the President proposed to conduct the negotiations. The Secretary later considered it fair to assume that Wilson neither had nor wished drawn up a negotiating program.[22] Although Wilson and Lansing never really got along well, there existed a good case for the latter's description of the former's inflexibility:

Mr. Wilson's mind once made up seemed to become inflexible. It appeared to grow impervious to arguments and even to facts. . . . He might break, but he could not bend. This rigidity of mind accounts in large measure for the deplorable, and, as it seems to me, needless conflict between the President and the Senate over the Treaty of Versailles.[23]

It was, indeed in large part, Wilson's imprudent inflexibility, or refusal to modify or clarify one word in the document he brought home for the Senate's advice and consent to ratification, which prevented the United States from entering into the League of Nations.

When referring to the Versailles Treaty episode during his own campaign for international organization in the early 1940s, Dulles was inclined to consider President Wilson and his ideas as ahead of their times. Even this form of apologetic praise, however, contained the lesson that an inability or refusal to make certain compromises to political realities usually spells a prescription for failure. Dulles fully recognized that Wilson both failed in his program and tended to operate with too little regard for political factors and demands.[24] The lessons in Wilson's failure and its repercussions for American policy were driven deep into Dulles' own political or operational code. In broad terms, these impressions were that policy-makers must recognize and accept the implications of political realities, that one's political power base and lines to other necessary bases must not be allowed to deteriorate, and that the essence of political and diplomatic success is often a willingness to compromise. In everyday terms, the most significant lesson Dulles learned from the fight over the Versailles Treaty was the need to have the support of and, as necessary to this end, to placate the United States Senate.

REPARATIONS AND ALLIED DEBTS

Dulles returned to his New York law practice, devoting most of his time to legal work concerned with various Latin American and European governments. He continued to take an active interest in the postwar problems of German reparations and allied indebtedness to the United States. In fact, from 1920 to 1923, nearly all of his writings related to these two inseparable issues.

With respect to reparations, he persistently advocated establishing a fixed amount of the indemnity. From Dresden in 1920, he reported to the Assistant Secretary of the Treasury that the deadening influence in Germany was the manner in which the reparations clauses of the treaty were being applied, combined with the uncertainty as to the nature and extent of obligations. Referring to the "vexatious misapplication of the economic clauses," he wrote that the time had "come for the Reparation Commission to accord that definiteness of obligation and that economic freedom which we always hoped and expected would result from an intelligent exercise of the discretionary clauses of the Treaty." [25] He also recommended that the United States work toward the establishment of such conditions as economic equality for Germany throughout the world and economic unity with East Prussia. These were only two of several conditions which would have to be met before Germany would be able to pay a very substantial sum.[26]

A crux of the matter, however, was that the establishment of normal economic relations in Europe and the rehabilitation of Germany depended largely upon actions of the United States. Thus, while advocating a fixed amount regarding Germany's obligation, Dulles also insisted that United States responsiblity in the matter required the moderation of its demands as creditor of Great Britain and France. Writing to the French Minister of Liberated Regions, Louis Loucheur, in 1921, he found some room for hope: "I feel that there is a growing recognition in this country that the United States cannot consistently urge upon France that she be moderate toward her debtor, while the United States, as creditor of France . . . displays no qualities of moderation." [27] In so many words, Dulles deplored the attitude of the United States toward its debtors. At home, seriously concerned lest venom and not balm be added to the "gaping wound . . . draining the vitality of modern civilization," he counseled against emotional and self-righteous approaches to the issues of allied debts and reparations.[28]

Several months later, Dulles recommended that the United States contribute to a general settlement in Europe by canceling as much of the allied debts as reason and experience showed to be uncollectable at any rate, which meant the greater portion of the debts. According to this plan, the United States should use the prospects of debt cancellation and of more American cooperation generally as leverage in an attempt to reach an understanding which would free France, Germany, and Great Britain from any excessive burdens. Although tying substantial debt cancellation to a general settlement, including particularly fixing a reasonable amount of reparations and some political guarantees, he found no justification for the suspicion that Great Britain and France merely sought an escape from payment. Dulles concluded that if some such course were not adopted by the United States, it would bear major responsibility for continuing chaos:

What will be our response? The easy way is to let matters drift, to postpone decisive and irrevocable action. Will we thus assume the responsibility of dragging the world through more years of political and economic unrest in order to satisfy ourselves by personal experimentation that the Allied debts are, in the main, uncollectable? Or shall we avail ourselves of the present temper of Europe to effect a general settlement of the most disturbing of post-war problems? [29]

Recognizing that there was a good argument for outright cancellation of the debts, he preferred using them for some political leverage:

From an economic standpoint, I believe that it would enhance the general good if these debts were cancelled. . . . However . . . so far as action on the part of our own Government is concerned, any adjustment of the War debts should be made a part of some general settlement which will insure more sane and settled conditions in Europe and thus bring about benefit to us actually much greater than we would receive were we to attempt to collect the actual money.[30]

But the most important and pivotal move, as he saw it, was for the United States to sit down with the allies in a spirit of "cooperation and sympathy" for the real problems of Europe.[31] This the United States did not do.

During the first two weeks of July 1923, approximately six months after the French occupation of the Ruhr, Dulles made several trips between Hamburg, Brussels, Paris, and Berlin in an unofficial attempt to work some sort of settlement of the Ruhr conflict. After consultations with German Chancellor Cuno, Belgian Premier Theunis, French Minister of Justice Barthou, and Louis Loucheur, Dulles met with Cuno, Minister of Foreign Affairs von Rosenberg, and Under Secretary von Maltzan from July 12 to 15. He presented a plan which declared, without stipulating for the evacuation of the Ruhr, that Germany would resume delivery of reparation in kind, take steps promptly to stabilize its currency and balance its budget, and give some kind of guaranty regarding further reparation payments.[32] This attempt to settle the Ruhr conflict met with failure:

I had something worked out which I thought might have been successful, but at the last minute, Mr. von Rosenberg . . . threw the plan down after Mr. Cuno had accepted it.[33]

While Dulles was hardly alone in his positions, the United States under President Coolidge rather unsympathetically continued to dun its debtors and to apply financial and political pressures for payment. In 1922 the prevailing viewpoint in Washington was that the key to the problem was to untangle the reparations knot in order to receive debts due. After all, so the reasoning went, if Germany were able to make payments to Great Britain and France, then France could pay both the United States and Great Britain, and Great Britain could pay the United States. (This financial merry-go-round completed the circle when it turned out that Germany's ability to meet its obligations depended upon private loans from the United States.) [34] Following the suggestions of Secretary of State Hughes, the Reparation Commission decided in November of 1923 to appoint the Dawes Committee. The product of this committee, the Dawes Plan of 1924, attempted to untangle the reparations knot by providing loans for Germany and by moderating its payments for a few years.

Dulles fully supported the measures, but believed that they fell far short of what the situation required primarily because of the political limitations imposed on the members of the committee.[35] To Dulles' way of thinking, the main weaknesses of the plan stemmed from the committee's lack of authority to set a fixed amount of Germany's obligations and a date when payments would cease. This meant that the plan did not include the necessary incentives for Germany to want to free itself of debt and foreign controls by meeting its obligations. If the plan were to prove unworkable, he concluded it would be because of these defects which flowed "inevitably from the limitations which were initially imposed upon the committee's powers." [36]

On the favorable hand, the Dawes Plan introduced a system of checks and balances to facilitate equitable adjustments in the future. It also appeared to place the reparations issue more on an economic and business basis. These factors accounted for Dulles' hopes that the flaws of the plan could be corrected in the near future and that future adjustments would not be so dependent upon or restricted by political factors. Most important, in spite of the plan's imperfections, something had to be done:

If the Dawes Committee plan is not utilized it can confidently be predicted that the financial disintegration of Europe cannot be arrested and that political unrest will steadily increase.[37]

Throughout the 1920s and 1930s, Dulles continued to combine law, international finance, and diplomacy. In 1927, he was retained by the Federal Reserve, the Bank of England, and the Bank of France to act as counsel in the project to stabilize the Polish zloty. In spite of the damaging effects of the Great Depression, this stabilization plan was considered a success. Four years later, Dulles was summoned by President Hoover to consult with Ogden Mills, Under Secretary of the Treasury, on the worsening allied debt and reparation problem. Dulles recommended that the United States discount future annuities but refrain from canceling all debts for a few years. He proposed the continuance of some token payments on the grounds that France, for various political and financial reasons, would not agree to a complete cancellation. His primary conclusion, however, was that something positive had to be set in motion. When Ogden Mills stated a preference for a two years' suspension of all payments, Dulles replied emphatically: "I realize that the most important thing is promptly to develop *some* plan and that any plan, which is both practicable and can reasonably be expected to have a proper psychological effect, is better than delay incident to difference of opinion as to what would be the most ideal plan." [38]

Dulles represented the United States at the 1933 Berlin Conference on Germany's foreign debts. Believing that the situation was critical, but not necessarily irreparable, he set out to persuade the president of the Reichsbank, Hjalmar Schacht, that Germany should attempt to meet its obligations where possible. Returning from Berlin, Dulles and Mr. Cromwell agreed that the firm of Sullivan and Cromwell should move out of Germany. The process began in 1934, when the German clients were asked to withdraw their accounts.

THE CONCEPT OF PEACEFUL CHANGE

Dulles had been occupied with the idea of peaceful change ever since Versailles. In the 1920s and 1930s, he began to define his ideas on the subject more systematically. His first essay on the subject of war was written in 1924 as a result of his appointment by the New York Presbytery to the Presbyterian General Assembly's Committee on War. In this essay, he clearly differentiated between his intellectual, theoretical conclusions and his practical approach and conclusions. Interestingly, he included a proposal for speculative, unilateral disarmament as an example for other nations and indicated that his overall program, although worthy of the followers of Christ, did not necessarily proceed from a peculiarly Christian premise.[39] The key to his approach toward the subject of solving the problem of war was that "there will always be differences of opinion and conflicts of interest; and always ways will be found of settling them. War is the most primitive, the nearest at hand, and it will surely be resorted to unless some effective substitute be provided." [40]

In a subsequent essay analyzing the economic origins of conflict and based for the most part on the World War I experience, Dulles considered conservatism's tendencies toward a rigid preservation of the *status quo* as the primary impediment to peaceful change:

Most peace plans have consisted of machinery designed to hold the world in a static condition. . . . That this is possible, is the illusion upon which the peace efforts in the past have failed. . . . You must proceed from the premise that change is inevitable. The problem is not to retard or prevent such change, it is rather to facilitate it, to remove the resistance to change which creates the friction which ignites war.[41]

His various efforts and writings throughout this period finally culminated in *War, Peace and Change*,[42] an extensive expression of his general thoughts on man, society, and international relations.

The work was written not long after his participation in the 1937 Oxford Conference on "Church, Community and State." Shortly before the Oxford Conference, however, Dulles had attended the Tenth International Studies Conference in Paris, sponsored by the International Institute of Intellectual Cooperation. He also had served, in preparation for this conference, as chairman of a committee studying the procedural methods of peaceful change. *War, Peace and Change* contains no indications that the Oxford Conference experience substantially altered his outlook and, in most respects, the work "appears to be more the product of his experiences at Paris than of his experiences at Oxford." [43]

In *War, Peace and Change,* Dulles undertook no less a task than to understand how "to attack and solve the . . . international phase of the primitive problem of eliminating force as the solvent of conflicting desires." [44] War had "long been tolerated" in the age of professional armies, limited operations, and "relatively immune" civilian populations. But, through the experiences of World War I, it was generally recognized that war "was no longer tolerable" in an age of industrialization, modern science, national mobilization, mechanized armies, and, by no means last, very vulnerable populations. Nevertheless, the "war system" still prevailed and one could not "expect to eradicate" such a fundamental system without both understanding "its origins and causes" and applying "the lessons taught by centuries of experimentation with the elimination of violence." The crux of the problem, as he viewed it, was how to effectuate peaceful change or how to reorganize "society, within the limits permitted by human nature, so as to substitute for force some other procedures." [45]

After rather carefully analyzing prerequisites of totalitarian war, broad ethical and political requisites to a system of peaceful change, limitations upon their realization, and means of overcoming the limitations and of avoiding false and inadequate solutions, Dulles found that it was largely the "ideology of nationalism" which "has developed characteristics which threaten our destruction." To counter these characteristics, measures should be taken to check the tendencies "to identify one's personified state with deity" and "the other-national personality with evil," to "dilute the concept of one's own state as sole benefactor," to alter substantially the concept of "national sovereignty," and to secure "elasticity" in the treaty structure and in the political and economic relations between states.[46] He considered such measures valuable, necessary, and possible within existing mores. But they were essentially stopgap in nature unless accompanied by persistent efforts to change some basic weaknesses in human nature and society:

It should not be permanently accepted that human action should be dictated by emotion to the virtual exclusion of reason. . . .

We should not accept as permanent a situation wherein only a few are motivated by a broad sense of duty to fellow-men, and wherein those who have a corporate responsibility . . . are deemed immune from the application of broad ethical concepts of the general welfare.

We should not acquiesce in human nature being such that mass effort and sacrifice are largely dependent upon the ideology of conflict.

We should not accept the increasing tendency of the group authority to destroy individual freedom and initiative. . . . We should not accept the present form of world organization as embodying the ultimate possibilities of the conception of a commonwealth.[47]

Broadly speaking, *War, Peace and Change* was essentially designed as a tract against *status quo* thinking and myopic nationalism or, in a positive vein, a call for enlightened self-interest and internationalism.

The endeavor to analyze the fundamental factors which gave rise to war in general, at a time when a particular war was imminent, resulted in his conclusions regarding "shared responsibility" for the current state of affairs. While *War, Peace and Change* was not a justification of the expansionist tendencies and policies of Germany, Italy, and Japan, it did argue that these despotisms and their revolt against the international system could be fully understood only in terms of the political and economic policies pursued by the allied nations:

Throughout these twenty years England, France and the United States . . . have earnestly and sincerely preached peace. It is tragic that good intentions have borne such fruit.

The cause is simple and fundamental. There has been grave misconception of the nature of peace. Peace has been identified with the *status quo*, stability with rigidity. Exponents of force are the inevitable product of a society within which change can occur only through force.[48]

His concentration on the problem in general also resulted mostly in silence on the particularly charged issues of 1939, although this did not "imply any lack of recognition of the importance of dealing with them." [49] (The dearth of references to the Czechoslovakian crisis also derived from the fact that, for all practical purposes, the work was completed prior to the invasion of Czechoslovakia.) Such factors, especially his emphasis on shared responsibility and the absence of any broadside condemnation of parties in the brewing conflict, led to accusations, in 1944 and thereafter, of pro-Nazism. While this charge was completely unfounded, Dulles himself realized that he was treading on tender ground in *War, Peace and Change:*

The reasoning of this study may be repellent to some, as suggesting a defense of those powers which are in rebellion against the present scheme of things. . . . [But] *to seek to understand the cause is not to defend the evil.* Such understanding is, indeed, essential if our efforts are to be intelligently directed. It was through lack of understanding that the power and influence of the democracies have operated to produce results diametrically opposite to those which were intended.[50] (Emphasis added.)

The concept of "peaceful change" became an ever more persistent theme in Dulles' writings. Given "change" as "the ultimate fact to which we must accommodate ourselves," there "must be either a *peaceful* way of change or a *violent* way of change." [51] The ideas and problems of war, peace, and evolutionary change became the primary occupation for the remainder of his life.

NEO-WILSONIANISM AND THE COMING OF WAR

As the twenty-year armistice collapsed and hostilities recommenced in Europe, Dulles was firmly advocating that the United States avoid participation as a defender of the *status quo.* This quasi-Wilsonian stance was combined with trenchant criticisms of the post-Versailles actions and inactions of the *status quo* powers, and particularly the United States. While profoundly regretting both Germany's decision to occupy Bohemia and the policies of Germany and Japan generally, he nevertheless maintained, in March of 1939,

that "no other evolution could be expected of dynamic and re-
pressed peoples." [52] The seeds of this comment and of his position
prior to World War II were sown at Versailles and continued to
grow during the interwar years.

When Secretary of State Lansing first read the draft Treaty of
Versailles in its entirety, he commented that "the impression made
by it is one of disappointment, of regret, of depression." On the day
following the delivery of these conditions to Germany, the Secretary
wrote: "Resentment and bitterness, if not desperation, are bound to
be the consequences of such provisions." [53] His nephew, however,
did not take such a bleak view of the situation so early. But before
long, or by 1920, Dulles became impatient with the policies of the
dominant powers. Apart from what he considered the unreasonable
approaches of the allies to reparations and of the United States to
allied debts,[54] he had been very disappointed by the United States
rejection of membership in the League of Nations and by the prevailing attitude toward Europe in 1920: "I do not expect to stay
longer in Paris than is necessary, as I will be rather ashamed to
meet again my former colleagues after the way in which the Peace
Treaty and the European situation in general have been treated by
the Senate and American public opinion." [55]

From an economic standpoint, in 1922, he found that the victors
had fallen "prey to illusions," dealing in terms of billions and placing their homes in paper schemes and paper budgets.[56] The following year, he claimed that the nations had become shortsighted ever
since the armistice, each perceiving its own troubles looming large
with little or no concern for the real troubles of each other. Until
the legitimate needs of others were considered, the situation would
continue to be one of "confusion, interference and ill-will." [57] Nine
years later, looking back on New York's emergence as the financial
center of the world in the 1920s, it was clear that "the use which we
made of that opportunity is looked back upon as one of the less
creditable incidents of a now discredited period." [58] Attempting to
avoid a repeat postwar performance by the United States at mid-
century, Dulles described the American people after World War I
as a people "turned soft, sentimental and undisciplined. . . . We
adopted an attitude of illusory aloofness. . . . We sought to enclose

our economy and be an oasis of prosperity in a world of misery." [59]

Reflecting on the post-World War I situation, shortly before American entry into World War II, Dulles still maintained that the problems caused by the allied "breach of faith" with Germany, the harsh language of the treaty, and the severe manner in which it had been imposed upon the German leaders "need not have been more than a passing phase." But the agencies which "might have corrected initial defects" did not.[60] He had in 1921, for example, believed that there was a good chance that some sort of customs union or organization of the Central European states would come about after some time "for national feeling to subside." [61] Twenty years later, he concluded that "it was the height of folly to acquiesce in the demand of such groups that they should be accorded the full rights of sovereignty." [62] But the principal problem, as he viewed it in 1937, was that for all concerned the Versailles Treaty "emerged as a rededication of the nations to the old principles of sovereignty," to "extreme nationalism" and "national isolation." [63]

The depth and sincerity of Dulles' sharp criticisms during the pre-World War II period can be measured by his basic beliefs on the economic origins of conflict. In his 1925 essay on the subject, he maintained that "the real danger of war" resulted "from motives which we all possess and respect":

To covet the wealth of others we are prone to condemn. But to seek to retain our own is a homely virtue which we honor. Yet here, I think we find the underlying economic cause of war. For we then have a group of individuals who have attained great wealth and power, who influence, or are in a position to influence, governmental action, and who have become conservative and seek to resist any change which threatens the position which they have acquired.[64]

Believing that the main economic cause of conflict was not greed for gain, but rather the effort to perpetuate the *status quo* by those in power, he granted that "in most cases those who are responsible do not themselves desire a war," particularly since such a "desire is generally parallel to their interests" in maintaining existing conditions.[65]

This 1925 analysis was admittedly based for the most part on Dulles' views of the policies of the Austro-Hungarian Empire and

Czarist Russia prior to World War I and supported by references to the United States war with Mexico (1848) and the American Revolution. But he applied a similar thesis to the policies of the United States, Great Britain, and France during the interwar years. The tragedy to him, in the mid-1930s, was that a wealthy and powerful United States had become merely one of the conservative defenders of the *status quo* in international politics. Since it was "the powerful, self-satisfied nations which" exercised "the initiative in international affairs," it was "not surprising" that there had been no major program which sought "peace through the framework of change." [66] A "natural cycle" which he had described in 1925 was completing itself again ten years later:

Those whose lives fall in pleasant places, contemplate with equanimity an indefinite continuation of their present state. "Peace" means to them that they should be left undisturbed. It is those who seek change that are the disturbers of the peace. "Aggression" becomes the capital international crime and "security" the watchword. . . . Knowing that change is inevitable, they seek to postpone it by attaching the label of "peace" to the existing status. [67]

As the designs of Hitler's Germany were unraveling in March of 1939, Dulles was concerned that the policies of the United States were dedicated to recapturing through grants and armaments "a preponderance of power" for the *status quo* powers "which will permit them to resume the same blind policies." So long as this remained the case, he was opposed to throwing the resources of the United States into world politics: "I dislike isolation, but I prefer it to identification with a senseless repetition of the cyclical struggle between the dynamic and static forces of the world." Rather his "intense desire" was "that there be a changed mentality which perceives that peace is an elastic" state of affairs, for "then indeed we could act." [68] As the United States edged toward supporting Great Britain and France, Dulles perceived no such changed mentality in official quarters:

The tragedy is that we seem to have learned nothing. I hear the same talk about "sanctity of treaties," "law and order," "resisting aggression" and "enforcing morality." Such phrases have always been the stock in trade of those who have vested interests which they wish to preserve against those in revolt against a rigid system.

Unhappily, our own would-be "liberal" government is today the principal exponent of this *status quo* philosophy. . . . It is we who . . . are to create a new world bloc committed to the doctrine of the divine right of things as they are.[69]

Without condoning the actions of Germany, he was convinced that nothing was to be gained by assuming a "holier-than-thou" attitude. Recognizing that denunciation was difficult to avoid, he advised that it should be used sparingly both because it created in those who denounce a sense of moral superiority and because it could play into the hands of such leaders as Hitler, who could utilize foreign denunciations as a means of strengthening the German national will to sacrifice for the "cause." [70]

The period from 1919 to 1945 contained some of Dulles' "finest days" and, in several respects, 1935 to 1942 constituted one of his "finest hours." He rejected all "devil theories" and moralistic explanations for the current conflict. He was against the infection of war passions during his neo-Wilsonian stand not to enter the war in defense of the *status quo ante bellum* and also advocated calmness, sanity, and postwar planning throughout the conflict. Although these positions obviously buttressed his preference for noninvolvement, he had unquestionably developed over the years a "definite distaste" [71] for nonrational, anti-intellectual appeals. He continued to emphasize the idea of shared guilt as a heavy responsibility on the shoulders of the dominant powers. No nation was guiltless in the generation of "widespread unrest, great violence and immense disaster," and a "great burden" rested on the United States for having "fallen far short of that which was required." [72] Accepting the genuineness of the American preference for peace, Dulles nevertheless seriously questioned the sources of this preference:

Our blindness was not an affliction from without, but a result of our smug complacency and narrow selfishness. And to profess a love for peace is no great virtue in those who control so disproportionate a share of the world's wealth that to retain it is their principal concern.[73]

He viewed the United States in March of 1941 as still desperately attempting to hold "the richest and most productive area of the world . . . as our exclusive preserve." This end violated "both morality and political expediency" and, in seeking it, the United States "will ultimately succumb—and should succumb" to those subjected "to the irresponsible use of our power." [74]

In another significant respect, however, this very same period represents one of Dulles' "worst hours." Having warned of possible severe repercussions unless corrective actions were taken, dating from his arguments before the Reparation Committee at the Paris Peace Conference, his attitude evolved from one of a qualified modicum of admiration for the German revival in the early 1930s to one bordering on *tout comprendre est tout pardonner* later. The fact was that, by the late 1930s and largely because of his detached viewpoint, he seriously misjudged the real dangers of Hitler's Germany and manifested less sensitivity than many of his contemporaries to what he labeled the "evil manifestations" of Nazism and Fascism. His position was not an ostrich-like neutrality. Stressing the need for political objectives and a new mentality to guide America's actions, in 1939, he recognized that it would be tragic were the United States immobilized and entertained "no idea that peace should now be sought merely by throwing sops to the dynamic powers." [75] Nevertheless, he had seriously underestimated the violence, scope, and repercussions of the impending war and, consequently, failed to sense the urgency of arming and aiding Great Britain and France.

THE WAR YEARS

Not inclined to place personal blame on the leaders of the United States, Great Britain, and France, Dulles aimed most of his attacks at the accepted "dictates of the sovereignty system." [76] (He similarly refused to place blame on the German, Italian, and Japanese peoples. He was not, however, at all disposed to excuse the German, Italian, and Japanese leadership as implied by the shift in his statements from not placing blame on the *Allied leadership* to also not placing blame on the *Axis peoples*.) The fault was defined as that "of the system" wherein conflict or war was bound to recur unless one understood the "political axiom" that "there are always . . . those who are eager to lead the masses in ways of violence. They can be rendered innocuous only by preventing the many from feeling that they are subject to power which is exercised without regard for their welfare and which condemns them to inequalities and indignities." [77]

In pursuit of altering the system, from 1939 through 1945, most of Dulles' energies were devoted to campaigning for an international organization and to building a public opinion which both favored such cooperation and accepted the concept of a flexible, changing state of affairs in international politics. In 1940, he became a member of the Commission to Study the Organization of the Peace and was invited by the Federal Council of the Churches of Christ in America to become chairman of the committee of direction for the Commission to Study the Bases of a Just and Durable Peace.

Throughout this campaign, he continually promulgated the need for a federative type of international organization, flexible and powerful enough to allow and adjust to change. When President Roosevelt and Prime Minister Churchill set forth an eight-point declaration on common aims for a peace program, in August of 1941, Dulles viewed the so-called Atlantic Charter as a step forward, but a "tentative and incomplete statement" which was either doubtless or hopefully regarded as such by its authors. To Dulles the declaration seemed "to reflect primarily the conceptions of the old sovereignty system" and to "follow too closely the pattern of Versailles, without, however, any of the liberalizing international institutions." Thus, "in the absence of mechanisms creating rights on a basis of equality, there would probably result an Anglo-Saxon military and economic hegemony whose self-interest would be bound to the maintenance of the *status quo*." [78]

If the United States fell victim to the reasoning that peace meant to reproduce and stabilize the prewar world, it "will be defending the indefensible . . . attempting the impossible" and, in effect, lose the struggle to which it was committed. Considering "the old order . . . gravely defective," [79] he conducted an incessant campaign—aiding various study groups and speaking in many parts of the country—for international organization and a public opinion favoring American participation in it. He was part of the growing movement for international cooperation which existed before Roosevelt assigned Cordell Hull to the task.

Some of Dulles' utterances during this period were clearly on the utopian side in comparison to his more pragmatic earlier views. The task for the United States, for example, required "that we use our power, not to perpetuate itself, but to create, support and eventually give way to international institutions drawing their vitality from the whole family of nations." [80] However, as discussed in Chapter IV, his approach to the formation of a viable organization was by no measure idealistic or utopian. He was under no illusions regarding the possibility of eradicating "blocs," balances of power, and conflicting interests, or of establishing a world government. One of his major themes, from the early 1940s until his death in 1959, was that "waging peace" was a "long, hard task." By 1945, he reportedly "indicated great misgivings as to whether the hopes of the nation for an international peace organization . . . might not be raised to too great heights" since, even with an organization, the problems of peaceful change would continue to perplex the postwar world. [81]

During the war, Dulles also journeyed to England presumably to confer with churchmen, although, in actuality, most of his time was spent with officials of the British Foreign Office and Colonial Office. The episode included several interesting meetings and reactions recorded by Dulles. He was, for example, not impressed by Clement Attlee and Ernest Bevin, but was favorably impressed by Sir William Jowett, Sir George Cater, Lord Astor, Tom Jones, and Barbara Ward. He also found his ideas "very closely allied" with those of Professor E. H. Carr, who "is a great believer in the necessity of federation in Europe and . . . feels that the era of small, independent states is past." Impressed by Sir Stafford Cripps' "fine mind and liberal attitude" during their first meeting, the second encounter resulted in a different reaction: "He seemed to be more narrow in his thinking. . . . Perhaps I was sensitive because one of the things he said was that we will have to destroy Wall Street. I tried to get him to explain. . . . But he did not add anything to that." [82]

The most important meetings and discussions took place with the British Foreign Secretary, Anthony Eden, and the Colonial Secretary, Lord Cranbourne. Dulles stressed the necessity for postwar planning and his view that British-American cooperation and coordination on European policy were absolutely essential after the war. Otherwise, "the whole situation might easily get out of hand with turmoil and confusion in Europe for many years." There was also in these meetings "a lot of talk about English colonial policy." Eden and Cranbourne raised the idea of sending lecturers to the United States to show that England's colonial policy was "not all imperialism." Dulles implicitly recognized that it was not all imperialism but considered it of little value to argue "an old idea" since "the American attitude was deeply rooted." If it were "believed, rightly or wrongly, that collaboration is collaboration in imperialism and exploitation, then the opposition in the United States will be formidable." Consequently, if Britain "wished for American postwar collaboration in the development of the great colonial areas of the world," he "felt it would be necessary for the British to pocket their pride and accept the idea of a new approach to the problem." [83]

While not favoring the British idea to send some lecturers to the United States, Dulles interestingly took occasion to act in such a capacity upon his return. With regard to the "white man's burden," he wrote in *Life:* "Today we laugh at that phrase, but under its influence hundreds of thousands of Britain's best youth went forth to do what they believed to be in the general welfare. Britain gained, but in the process more was done to improve the lot of mankind than ever before in any comparable period of time." [84] He had departed England with a very favorable impression, maintaining that "the preservation of free political institutions and of tolerance in the face of grave danger is proof that British peculiarly exemplifies the spirit and practice of human liberty." But he was still somewhat concerned that there appeared "a public psychology" which favored the old *status quo* and did "not adequately appreciate the fundamental changes which the war is working." [85]

CHAPTER THREE

POLITICS, CONTROVERSY, AND DIPLOMACY

The year 1937 in Dulles' life is perhaps most significant for the fact that it marks the beginning of the Dewey-Dulles relationship. Thomas Dewey was then a young public servant in the process of prosecuting the racket operations in New York. The two men frequently met, and, before long, Dulles offered Dewey a senior partnership in Sullivan and Cromwell. Soon after declining this invitation, Dewey, with some help from Dulles, conducted a successful campaign for district attorney. At the time of Dewey's first campaign for the presidency in 1944, Dulles was a well-known member of this eastern Republican circle, Dewey's expert on foreign affairs, and the probable nominee for Secretary of State in the event of a Republican victory at the polls.

Not only did Dulles begin to appear as a *political* figure in his own right; but, more important, he emerged and was identified as a member of the mellow, liberal, internationally minded school of Republicans. In 1944, the powerful and isolationist old-line party members neither embraced nor welcomed Dewey's advocacy of international cooperation. (As a balance to the young New Yorker, the Republicans selected the isolationist-minded Governor Bricker of Ohio as their vice-presidential candidate.) Regardless of political associations or contacts, Dulles' international complexion naturally demanded allegiance to the moderate camp of the Republican

party. Several of his later trials would be affected by the problems
of the necessary balancing acts, not only between the two major parties but also within the Grand Old Party itself.

EMERGENCE AS POLITICAL FIGURE

Certainly before 1944, and in many respects until 1949, Dulles' efforts had been neither identified as party tasks and accomplishments
nor necessarily constructed along any party lines. His initiation into
diplomacy stemmed from President Wilson and Robert Lansing.
He actively supported the Democratic candidate, Ambassador John
W. Davis, in 1924. Although he received assignments from Secretary
of State Hughes in the 1920s and somewhat later from President
Hoover, many of his close associates were Democrats, and he
thought very little of President Harding and far less of President
Coolidge. After World War II, he fraternized and collaborated with
various members of the Truman Administration, especially with
Secretaries Byrnes, Marshall, and Acheson. All in all, Dulles was essentially a noncontroversial, nonpolitical figure until the Dewey
campaign of 1944. Even as late as 1949, he was not really considered
a "party man" and, in some Republican circles, was viewed as a
crypto-Democrat.

While the lines of opposition became more clearly drawn during
the contest of 1944, this mild affair hardly resembled an American
presidential tussle. Dulles performed, as he did again in 1948, more
like a career Foreign Service Officer than a political combatant.
The relative mildness of the 1944 election and the amount of apparent agreement between the opposing parties were products largely
of the fact that the United States was still at war. The more positive
consideration was that the presidential candidates of both parties favored the formation of an international organization. On August
25, Hull and Dulles agreed and it was announced that "the subject
of future peace would be kept out of politics." Although the latter
added that this "agreement did not preclude full public nonpartisan discussion of the means of attaining lasting peace," [1] it was decided in effect that the United Nations *per se* and many of its as-

pects should not become campaign issues. For all practical purposes, Dewey concentrated his fire on the domestic policies and shortcomings of the Democrats. President Roosevelt, for his part, reportedly violated the Hull-Dulles agreement only once late in the campaign.[2]

During the campaign, Dulles frequently consulted with Secretary of State Hull about the project for international organization. The former's suggestion to describe the endeavor as "bipartisanship" was vetoed by Roosevelt and the Democrats. The President preferred the term "nonpartisanship" because, according to Secretary Hull, "the word 'bipartisanship' might concede the Republicans an equal status in a project that was now presumed to be politically profitable."[3] Nevertheless, the Democrats were careful to avoid repeating Woodrow Wilson's fatal mistake with the League of Nations project—namely, virtually excluding and defying the opposition. There was close cooperation between the two parties as the United Nations Charter negotiations proceeded. After Senator Vandenberg and others placed some pressure on the Truman Administration in 1945, Dulles became one of the principal advisers to the United States delegation at the United Nations Conference in San Francisco.

By this time, in spite of his generally bipartisan approach, Dulles was beginning to pay one of the prices of emergence as an active political figure. The year 1944 marked the first in a brief series of not very effective, but nevertheless serious and calumnious, charges against him. The charge of pro-Nazi sentiments first appeared in 1944 and reappeared several times throughout the 1940s, becoming most frequent from 1947 to 1949.

Of course, Dulles inherited a host of natural "enemies" upon entering the realm of political competition. But the attempts to identify him as pro-Hitler, pro-Nazi, and sympathetic to the German-American Bund inordinately exceeded the limits of normal, reasonable criticism. This attack was carried mainly by a few left-wing publications of questionable accuracy and objectivity. It had commenced, however, with a speech by Senator Joseph F. Guffey on the floor of the United States Senate.[4] Senator Guffey's pointed questions and remarks were mild compared to the more immoderate diatribes in 1947 by Senator Claude Pepper and Representative Adolph J. Sabath.[5] Similar charges appeared in several New York newspapers, in the form of a political advertisement sponsored by the New York Democratic State Committee, during the 1949 senatorial contest between Herbert Lehman and Dulles.[6]

All of these denunciations relied upon tenuous or faulty guilt by association reasoning and less than half-truths. The charges appear to have derived from similar, perceptible origins such as an abhorrence or phobia of anything resembling big business or Wall Street, a corresponding odium or fear of Germany, a sympathetic attitude toward the Soviet Union, and an unrestricted desire to vilify a political opponent. Ignoring the charges publicly, Dulles privately distributed a detailed confutation of the accusations.[7]

COOPERATION WITH DEMOCRATS

At a Cabinet luncheon on January 29, 1946, Secretary Byrnes commented that Senator Vandenberg's and Dulles' activities now "could be viewed as being conducted on a political and partisan basis." [8] This observation, apparently based on some of Dulles' comments after the 1945 Council of Foreign Ministers meeting in London, which he attended as a representative of the opposition and counselor to Secretary Byrnes, was perhaps slightly premature. In many respects, Dulles continued to perform as a nonpartisan and noncombatant until 1949.

He was invited by President Truman to become one of the American delegates to the United Nations General Assembly in 1946 and continued to serve in this capacity until 1948. During the 1948 presidential contest, the Truman Administration set up a special wire communications system between Dewey in America and Dulles in Paris. Robert D. Murphy, who was in contact with Dulles at the time, later reported that the likely Secretary of State exhibited no recognizable partisan attitude—"he might as well have been a career Foreign Service Officer." [9] In 1950, he again served as a member of the United States delegation to the General Assembly, where he helped handle the American campaign for a "Uniting for Peace" resolution and, incidentally, sided with Secretary Acheson on a specific issue which arose with the Republican chairman of the United States delegation, Henry Cabot Lodge, who was advocating a tougher line against Soviet membership on the proposed Peace Observation Committee.[10]

There existed, of course, disagreements between Dulles, Secretary Byrnes, Secretary Marshall, and Secretary Acheson. But these differences of degree never appeared great enough to reveal any outstanding dissimilarities between their respective approaches toward foreign relations, international organization, and European policy. Whether Dulles entirely or reservedly agreed with some or all of the foreign policies developed during the 1945–1949 phase of the Truman Administration was of less consequence to his political standing, particularly within the Republican party, than the fact that he continued to collaborate with the Democrats.

Approximately nine months before Secretary Acheson handed the Japanese Peace Treaty project over to Dulles, the latter experienced firsthand a brief adventure in Senate politics. When Robert F. Wagner, Sr., resigned from the Senate because of illness in 1949, New York's Governor Dewey appointed John Foster Dulles to fill the vacancy. On July 8, 1949, he was sworn into the Senate and resigned from the firm of Sullivan and Cromwell. His legal career was technically at its end.

Dulles' relative nonpartisanship, which had been fading throughout the 1940s, was still exemplified in the Senate but not unnaturally disappeared in the Senate campaign four months later. During the very brief tenure as Senator from New York, he broke the tradition of silence among newcomers. Challenging Senator Taft and others, he vigorously advocated ratification of the North Atlantic Treaty Organization:

Far from being a step backward, NATO is a step forward. It is apparent now, as it already had begun to be apparent at San Francisco, that security could not be achieved at a single step through a single world organization. It is going to be necessary to advance progressively through a series of organizations for collective self-defense. . . . The Treaty can, and I believe will, lift from the UN a burden and anxiety which it was never designed to carry.[11]

Fifteen months before these comments in the Senate, Dulles had met with Secretary Marshall, Under Secretary Robert A. Lovett, and Senator Vandenberg in order to discuss the idea of some sort of regional pact. At this meeting he expressed the view that a unilateral statement of American intentions, along with practical military cooperation similar to that with Canada, "might be better than a formalized agreement." Adhering to the idea of a more united Europe, he was concerned lest any extensive commitments would tend to encourage the governments of Western Europe to insulate, rather than integrate, their particular economic and social experiments.[12] Despite these initial questions, in 1948, on the value and effect of a relatively long-term formal agreement, he wholeheartedly supported the proposed treaty in the 1949 Senate debates and no instance in his later career suggested any lack of firmness in his commitment to Atlantic defense and Atlantic cooperation.

While Dulles was defending NATO on the floor of the Senate, President Truman campaigned for Dulles' opponent, Herbert Lehman, in the New York senatorial contest. Dulles had originally accepted the appointment with the understanding that he had no intentions of running for election at the end of the remaining term. But the persuasions of Senator Vandenberg, Governor Dewey, and other Republican leaders prevailed.[13] Only a few months after the appointment, he was campaigning as the Republican candidate against a powerful Democrat and a former governor of New York.

This heated senatorial campaign generally revolved around absurd issues. Dulles rarely ventured into the subject of foreign policy and restrained his criticism whenever the subject arose. He continued to support the broad outlines and the basic programs of United States foreign policy developed since the war. He concentrated his fire on domestic policies where he denounced the trend toward "welfarism." Also, though careful to point out that Lehman personally had no communist sympathies, Dulles attacked the former governor indirectly by maintaining that communist groups would vote for him. In his turn, Lehman attacked Dulles for being reactionary, bigoted, and anti-Semitic. Not only was it a poor show for both candidates, but, as is often the case in such campaigns, the party organizations accentuated the absurdities.[14] Upon losing the election, as was generally expected, Dulles found himself temporarily "unemployed."

WAR OR PEACE

Dulles soon thereafter published his second book, *War or Peace,* in which he popularized several of the ideas contained in his first work. However, the second book, written in a matter of weeks, was much more of a political tract than *War, Peace and Change.* In *War or Peace* Dulles was obviously less concerned with fundamental sources and theories and more concerned with particular policies, effects, and needs. The work was a rather quick attempt to place his ideas of peace into the context of the cold war, to describe the Russian communist threat in terms of its impact upon and meaning for America and relative stability. Dulles presented the challenge in the following manner:

The scene is constantly shifting. There is no simple formula for peace, and no single act that will assure peace. Any who preach that are dangerously deluded. Only the combined result of many efforts at different levels, and at many places, will assure peace.[15]

Again, the goal was relative stability or order—or nonviolent competition—and the author thoroughly denounced three common American misconceptions: (1) peace as isolation; (2) peace as American dominance; and (3) peace as the perpetuation of the *status quo.*[16]

JAPANESE PEACE SETTLEMENT

Following Senator Vandenberg's insistence upon bipartisanship in foreign policy matters, Dulles became a consultant to the State Department in March of 1950. Secretary Acheson soon assigned to him the Japanese Peace Treaty project, which had been floundering in the department for over three years. Although there occurred some unfortunate misunderstandings, especially between Dulles and two

British Foreign Secretaries, Herbert Morrison and Anthony Eden, the negotiation of the Japanese Treaty was a notable achievement. Excepting the areas of misunderstanding for the time being, with the support of Acheson Dulles adroitly handled such conflicting interests as the demands for high reparations and trade restrictions versus the support for very few restrictions and a more productive Japan. In this instance especially, and given the still young communist take-over in China, he was not about to near repeating some of the fateful clauses of the Versailles settlement. His approach to potential Russian obstructions—namely, leaving a wide open but carefully guarded door—proved effective.

Internally, Dulles successfully managed the issues between the Department of State and the Pentagon. For example, after the commencement of hostilities in Korea, there "were many in the Pentagon" supporting the position that no further steps be taken toward a peace settlement until the Korean conflict was brought to a close. This position was based on the argument that the United States military position under occupation was superior to what it would be under any conceivable agreement.[17] Very shortly after the outbreak of the Korean conflict, however, Dulles had urged that the process of making peace with Japan should not be delayed because of the war. He maintained that the Korean crisis presented more reason to hasten a settlement with Japan, and he accelerated the timetable for negotiations.[18] Another issue outstanding between the State Department and the Pentagon related to the status of Okinawa under a settlement. The Pentagon was not necessarily pleased with Acheson's and Dulles' compromise position which took form in the concept of Japanese "residual sovereignty" over the island.

The affairs of these treaty negotiations in many respects mirrored his lessons from the Versailles experience and presaged many of the difficulties Dulles encountered later as Secretary of State. Besides the basic foreign policy considerations, three recurring, related problems had to be considered throughout the negotiations: (1) the conflicts of interest between the United States and Great Britain; (2) the indispensability and difficulties of Senate cooperation and approval; and (3) the growing seeds of trouble within the right wing. Similar problems continued to pose dilemmas during his secretaryship, most noticeably from 1953 to 1955. His handling of the Japanese Peace Treaty negotiations particularly illustrated his keen concern regarding Senate cooperation and its advice and consent to ratification.

The conflicts of interest between the United States and Great Britain revolved around the two interrelated subjects of *de jure* recognition of the People's Republic of China and British economic and commercial interests. The British were concerned with recognition not completely or necessarily for reasons of *realpolitik,* but as well for reasons of trade and commerce in the East. These latter interests played a predominant role in the determination of Britain's position. As far as the United States was concerned, for the reasons detailed in Chapter V, the recognition issue was virtually unapproachable. In brief, war in Korea and the unanimous Senate opposition to recognition of Communist China, which had broad support in American public sentiment and which was not unaided by the attitude and actions of Communist China, effectually precluded any negotiations with and recognition of Peking.

The disagreement between the two governments became apparent at the beginning. Transmitting the United States draft treaty to interested governments sometime in February or March of 1951, the United States requested replies by May 1. Great Britain replied quickly with an extensive document, including a copy of its draft treaty. The British proposals included, among other things, several economic obligations without reciprocity, limitations upon shipbuilding, the confiscation of gold and precious metal reserves, and the seizure of assets in neutral countries. While a few inconsequential details were accepted by the United States— items which Dulles would still have preferred to leave out of the treaty because they gave "an aura of compulsion" to matters which he considered the Japanese would likely affect voluntarily anyway—the British eventually dropped most of their particular demands.[19]

But the major issue of China remained outstanding. Early in March, the British Foreign Office had presented Dulles a brief *aide-memoire,* which stated the propositions that Communist China should be brought into the negotiations and that Formosa should be restored to the People's Republic of China by the peace treaty.[20]

President Truman and Secretary Acheson had already made it abundantly clear, in December of 1950, that such moves would be impossible.[21] On April 10, 1951, Dulles privately related that there existed many difficulties surrounding the negotiations, not only within the American power structure but "also because of the present attitude of the British Foreign Office under Morrison."[22]

Great Britain was chiefly concerned with directing Japan's trade toward the Chinese mainland, which would mean less Japanese competition for the British in other parts of Asia such as Malaya, Singapore, Hong Kong, and India. London, less anxious than Washington about the prospect or possibilities of communist expansion in the Far East, set out to link Tokyo and Peking closely together. On the other hand, the United States wanted to keep Japan relatively independent of the mainland, at least for the time being. Washington recognized, however, that some trade would have to develop between the two Far Eastern neighbors, and that it would tend to increase over the years.

The naïvete of the proposals from the Foreign Office, under Herbert Morrison, is shown in two ways: first, by the notion that the United States Senate would even consider ratifying a treaty which included either recognition of the People's Republic of China or abandonment of Formosa, or a treaty which left the door clearly open for such eventualities; and second, by the reluctance in London to admit that Japan realized her eggs were in the American basket. Anthony Eden, who succeeded Morrison, expressed similar views: "Japan's attitude towards the two Chinese Governments should be entirely her own concern."[23]

But Japan's attitude toward the two Chinas question could not, in view of American and British pressures, be "entirely her own concern." Japanese interests would still reside primarily in following the lead of the United States, although Prime Minister Yoshida would admittedly have desired more latitude regarding future trade relations with the mainland: "Red or White, China remains our next-door neighbor. . . . Economic laws will, I believe, prevail in the long run over any ideological differences."[24] Yet, he was justifiably less concerned with problems of future trade relations than with the problem of securing the independence of Japan. In the final

John Foster Dulles

With Allen Dulles (1893)

With Margaret, Allen, Eleanor Lansing, and Nataline Dulles (1900)

With fellow Princetonians,
Allen W. Dulles and Walter
S. Davison (1910)

With Janet Avery Dulles,
shortly after their marriage
(June 1912)

Dulles Family (1916): Left to right, seated, Dr. and Mrs. Dulles, Mr. and Mrs. Foster (Dulles' grandparents), Mr. and Mrs. Avery; standing, Nataline, Allen, Eleanor Lansing, John Foster, and Janet Avery Dulles; front, John Watson Dulles, Margaret Dulles Edwards, Robert Lansing Edwards, and Lillias Dulles

Dulles and the American Commission to the Paris Peace Conference (1919) Left to right, seated, Colonel Edward M. House, Secretary of State Robert Lansing, President Wilson, Ambassador Henry White, and General Tasker H. Bliss; Dulles behind President Wilson and Secretary General Joseph C. Grew

Ambassador Jessup, Secretary Acheson, Ambassador Harriman, and Ambassador Dulles at American Embassy, Paris, for Council of Foreign Ministers Meeting (June 1949)

LEFT: Dulles and Japanese Prime Minister Yoshida (June 1951)

RIGHT: John Foster and Janet Dulles with Frances and Thomas E. Dewey

Richard Nixon, General Eisenhower, and Dulles, during the 1952 campaign

event, this independence required ratification of a peace treaty by the United States Senate. Acceptance of the British proposals would have no doubt spelled the doom of any peace treaty possibilities as far as the United States and Japan were concerned.

Unable to reach agreement on the question of which China, Dulles accepted a compromise whereby neither the Nationalist regime nor the Communist regime would be mentioned in the text of the treaty.[25] Several senators remained dissatisfied with this arrangement, which they interpreted as leaving the door open for the eventual recognition of the People's Republic of China by Japan. Senator H. Alexander Smith, one of the senators accompanying Dulles to the treaty conference in San Francisco, decided to meet Prime Minister Yoshida before the formal opening of the conference on September 4, 1951. According to Smith's memorandum, Yoshida "said that Japan might postpone . . . making a peace treaty with either group." Without definitely committing himself, Yoshida implied that Japan was interested in negotiating with Chiang Kaishek, and under no conditions with the communists.[26] Smith, a supporter of the treaty, but also a "foremost Formosan," concluded that perhaps ratification should be delayed "until we see what Japan is likely to do with China." [27]

Smith commended the treaty upon his return from the conference, but others on the Hill were still concerned about the "indecision" over the question of the recognition of China. Fifty-six senators joined in a letter to the President desiring "to make it clear" that they "would consider the recognition of Communist China by Japan or the negotiating of a bilateral treaty with the Communist Chinese regime to be adverse to the best interests of the people . . . of Japan and the United States." [28] The White House and State Department could not very easily ignore the warning.

The difficulties brewing in the Senate confronted both the Democratic Administration and Dulles with the following dilemma: how to secure the Senate's advice and consent to ratification of the treaty without severe reservations or delays, and without bluntly repudiating the "hands-off" agreement concluded with Britain.[29] Early in December, Dulles, accompanied by the two very important Senators Smith and Sparkman, departed for Japan. On December 11, Smith

made the following notation in his *Diary:* "The situation is bad.
. . . The British are standing pat on their policy of recognition of
Communist China and we fear that they are putting the heat on the
Japanese . . . to make trade agreements with Communist China but
no peace treaties with the Nationalists." [30] Both Smith and Spark-
man, concerned about what would be Japan's policy toward China,
were members of the Senate Foreign Relations Committee and its
Far Eastern subcommittee.

During this visit Dulles prepared the letter which was to be
signed by Prime Minister Yoshida and which upset Great Britain
when released on January 16. The letter was a clarification of Japanese intentions designed to allay the concerns of those United States
senators who were inclined to support either restrictive reservations
or delays in ratification of the multilateral treaty unless the China
issue were clarified to their liking. After mentioning that Japan
hoped ultimately "to have a full measure of political peace and
commercial intercourse with China," the letter maintained that, for
the time being, diplomatic movement would be in the direction of
the Nationalist regime. The two key points of the "Yoshida letter"
were as follows: First, the Japanese government intended promptly
to explore the subject of a bilateral treaty with the Nationalist government on Taiwan; and second, the Japanese government had no
intention to conclude a bilateral treaty with the Communist regime
in Peking. [31]

Although Eden later claimed that he was only generally aware of
the contents of this letter, anything more than a general awareness
was probably unnecessary and any lack of awareness of its details
was no doubt a matter of natural selective attention or inadequate
communication between the two sides and within the British system. During Dulles' visit to Japan the note was revealed to the British Ambassador in Tokyo, Sir Esler Dening. There was never any
design on the part of the United States to keep either its contents or
its nature a secret from the British. [32]

On January 5, 1952, Prime Minister Churchill and Eden arrived
in Washington for a series of British-American discussions ranging
from differences over the Atlantic Command in NATO to Far Eastern questions and the Middle East. Five days later, Eden and the

British Ambassador in Washington, Sir Oliver Franks, met with Acheson and Dulles. Acheson again talked "about the need for a public statement by the Japanese on the China policy." Although the actual letter may not have been discussed, it had "been shown to Ambassador Franks." [33] After Dulles explained the domestic difficulties surrounding the Senate's advice and consent to ratification of the Japanese Treaty, Eden replied that he understood, "but that the view of His Majesty's Government had not changed." [34]

Nevertheless, according to Smith's later account of a meeting with Dulles, Eden did agree that the United States should be allowed to take the lead in developing the relation of Japan to China. He also reluctantly agreed to the formula proposed by Dulles whereby Japan would negotiate a treaty with Formosa, but would not explicitly recognize the Nationalists as the legal government of the Chinese mainland.[35] The formula did not preclude arrangements for trade with Communist China, but it did mean that Japan would not recognize Peking. By Acheson's account, there certainly appeared agreement on both sides that neither "wished to risk failure of American ratification of the peace treaty because of Senate misapprehension of Yoshida's intentions," and neither "wished Mr. Eden to face opposition criticism in a suspicious House of Commons for rescinding an agreement obtained by his predecessor. Leaving the matter to the Japanese [that is, the announcement] seemed a skillful solution." [36]

Eden departed for London on January 15. The following day, as he arrived there, the Yoshida letter was released in Washington and Tokyo. The British reacted immediately to this "undisguised attempt to implicate" Great Britain in the American formula. It was the timing which surprised and upset the Churchill government.[37] But was it really an attempt to implicate the British? The Senate hearings on the treaty were to begin on January 21, which meant that Acheson and Dulles had five days in which to release the letter. Would a few days have made any difference in the British reaction? Unfortunately, on January 10, when the nature of a public announcement had been discussed with Eden, the specifics of timing of release may not have been raised.

At any rate, in writing to Canada's Secretary of State for External

Affairs a few days later, Acheson mentioned the affair of the Yoshida letter: "To some degree I think we were at fault in not being
more explicit about the whole matter and not informing him
[Eden] specifically about the publication, but I think in some degree also there was some fumbling and error on the British side." [38]
[It is fair to assume that Ambassador Franks had been apprised of
the specifics of publication.] The unfortunate incident was by no
means a product of bad faith on the part of Dulles or any party.
Eden later wrote that Acheson's assurances "terminated an unnecessary misunderstanding." [39] But Acheson's replies did not alter the
Foreign Secretary's opinions of Dulles. In 1952 Eden asked General
Eisenhower not to appoint Dulles in the event of a Republican election victory.[40]

Aside from the conflicting judgments as to timing, was the letter
necessary? At this point, the observer peers through a glass darkly as
the question remains unanswerable. There was always the possibility, as Dulles suggested, that without this concession to Senate Republicans and many Democrats the Japanese Peace Treaty could
have been virtually defeated or indefinitely delayed by reservations
such as those proposed by Senator William Jenner.[41] From the Truman Administration's and Dulles' point of view, was it not prudent
to play it safe on all sides in the light of the very strong opposition
to recognition of the People's Republic of China, and in light of the
unusually great degree of distrust developing between the two
branches of the government?

From the Senate's point of view, the powerful Republican from
California, William F. Knowland, highlighted on the Senate floor
his strong desire that there be no delay in Japan's establishing
treaty relations with the Nationalists—it would be a "great service
if it could be done before Senate ratification of the Japanese treaty."
Supporting the treaty with Japan, he noted that objections raised to
it were mostly based on "doubts as to the advisability of ratifying it
on the possibilities of what Japan may do in dealing with Communist China." [42] The Yoshida letter appeared a useful and skillful solution. Regarding Japan's intentions and relations with China, Senator Connally of Texas reported to the Senate that "on that score I
think we have the best assurances we can get." [43]

The steady efforts of Dulles and the administration to cultivate congressional support came to fruition on March 20, 1952, when the Senate gave its advice and consent to ratification by a vote of sixty-six to ten. Dulles resigned from the State Department and began to concentrate on the 1952 elections.

CHAPTER FOUR

THOUGHTS ON INTERNATIONAL POLITICS, PART I

BASIC FOUNDATIONS AND THE ABSENCE OF ABSOLUTES

Experiences at the Paris Peace Conference and involvement in the international predicaments between the two world wars constitute the backdrop to the development of Dulles' thoughts on international politics. Although training in law may have accounted for some minor aspects of his political style, his involvement in and reflections on these diplomatic-political-financial matters were the most significant factors in the formation of his general theory and approach. This background made him highly critical of all "devil" theories and simplistic solutions. Rather he directed his attention toward the economic, political, psychological, and sociological origins of conflict. These experiences also highlighted the relationships between domestic conditions and international postures which would much later, for example, find expression in the form of the "domestic change" thesis vis-à-vis the Soviet Union and include a "conduct and example" lesson for the United States. On several subjects pertaining to international affairs, his theory and operations throughout his career continued to reflect the background of the Versailles Treaty and its aftermath.

Emerging from the international and domestic crises of the 1920s and 1930s, Dulles' approach was dominated by a salutary dosage of political-economic determinism. Although economic and political determinants would change and could be intelligently modified with time, at any given moment their influence and course constituted an indispensable reference for action. In 1925 he concluded that "politics and economics cannot be divorced" for they "are interdependent and can only progress *pari passu*." [1]

Since general political stability and overall economic well-being were inescapably intertwined, Dulles concentrated on the importance of international and domestic economic matters to foreign affairs. He found that when domestic and foreign needs conflicted— as they often did—enlightened self-interest would sometimes dictate that the foreign needs be given priority. This became vitally true if a decision in favor of domestic requirements would increase the areas of discontent and economic disease.[2] United States policies, throughout the interwar years, had in this respect been all too often selfish and shortsighted:

The United States has in the past been a principal violator of good international practice. We have treated our foreign trade as though it were of no legitimate concern to anyone but ourselves.[3]

He found also that the Constitution was defective: "Under it tariff making has been treated as domestic-revenue legislation to be dealt with by Congress." Dulles believed that trade, monetary controls, and immigration should become the responsibility "of that branch of government which is also responsible for foreign relations and the maintenance of peace." [4]

This early political-economic orientation contained other salutary tendencies. It meant, for example, that international and allied cooperation could not be sustained on purely military bases. The continual emphasis, in the 1950s, upon political and military security against communism was considered a necessary tool in garnering congressional consent and public approval for such items as otherwise unpopular aid programs. The emphasis, however, neither meant that the Secretary himself operated under such simplifications nor reflected the subtleties of his more sophisticated political-economic approach to international problems. He simultaneously maintained that the economic programs and overall cooperation with allies were as vital, if not more vital in the long-run, than the military aspects; and he frequently called for an intensification of mutual security programs in both areas.[5] But the actions of Congress at mid-century hardly tended to disprove his belief that the United States had not adjusted to meeting the demands of international responsibility on the political and economic fronts. Speaking on the subject of international trade and cooperation in 1953, he warned that conflict between the Western nations and the disintegration of the beginning steps toward a more unified approach were inevitable if the United States were "blind to the fact that the Communist thesis includes some valid elements. We could by our own mistakes make the Soviet predictions come true." [6]

Concentration on the interdependence between economic factors and political stability led Dulles to the proposition that the "problem of international peace is but an extension of the problem of internal peace." [7] Without equating the domestic and international systems and their political processes in all specifics, the proposition did reflect a first principle of "political realism": namely, the operation of objective laws in all political-economic spheres. To Dulles, favorable economic conditions were requisite not only for maximum self-fulfillment but also for minimizing the amount of discontent which thereby reduced the effectiveness of any appeals from radical or revolutionary elements in society. But the establishment of reasonably balanced, mixed-enterprise economic systems by no means represented a panacea for international discord. Dulles asserted in 1949 that the profound conflicts of international relations should not be approached and could not be solved simply by extending relatively free economies. The economic factor, while very important, constituted only one ingredient in the mixture. The "economic answer" of simply extending free economies represented a gross oversimplification of the multifaceted network of international politics.[8] Absolute models—whether economic, political, or moral—were a part neither of the real world nor of Dulles' understanding of it.

Most important, the experiences at Versailles and thereafter tended to confirm several basic assumptions regarding the nature of man, human interaction, and politics which were ingrained in Dulles' background and which formed the first foundations for his political theory, his thoughts on international politics, and his political operational code. According to this understanding, while admitting that there were surely exceptions to the rule, man is generally a self-seeking, self-interested being: "Man is by nature selfish." [9] Self-interest was considered "the dominating human motive power" or "the driving force . . . that most frequently achieves practical results." [10] In the process of defining self-interest, Dulles deprecated emotion as an unreliable source of human motivation which led to extremes and created "blindness and inadequate perception." [11] Nonetheless, he believed that man operated essentially on emotion and habit in defining and seeking his own self-interest: "We like to feel that reasoning and logical argument are the most persuasive means of inducing human action. Actually this is far from being the case. . . . In the main we act unthinkingly, under the impulse of emotion and physical desires or in accordance with tradition or the custom of the social group of which we happen to form a part." This held true even for "the most intelligent" of men.[12]

In broad terms Dulles viewed society as consisting of two basic forces. "Static" forces were defined as those self-satisfied people who, because of contentedness with their financial condition, power or position, desired no change in the *status quo*. "Dynamic" forces referred to those who wished change in the form of a better, if not necessarily larger, "piece of the pie." Recognizing that these terms were arbitrary, Dulles preferred them to "haves" and "have-nots" because of the latter terms' possible misleading connotations. A "have" could, for example, seek to change the *status quo* and a "have-not" could be dissatisfied but still not actively pursue a change in social conditions.[13] Society or the "association of human beings . . . places in juxtaposition the static and dynamic and enhances the possibility of struggle between them." [14]

This view of man and human relations added up to a state of inevitable disharmony and discord: "Whenever human beings are thrown together, there will be conflicts of interest." [15] Such conflicts were signs neither of moral perversity nor irrationality. Even "Christ's command to love one's enemies implicitly recognizes . . . the persistence of human disagreement." [16] The idea of eradicating conflicts of interest was both an impossible and a poor goal: "Men will never solve the problem of how to end problems. . . . Indeed human nature is such that we would not long be happy if we did not have problems to tackle. . . ." [17] In instances of serious disagreement, however, the opponents would surely resort to force "unless some effective substitute be provided." [18] Because the "force system" was unsatisfactory for many, "there grew up a demand for a social mechanism which would permit human beings to derive the advantages of association without incurring the acute disadvantages incident to force being the only method of resolving the conflicts." [19]

The primary challenge to Dulles was one of "eliminating force as the solvent of conflicting desires." [20] This meant not only the establishment of accepted political mechanisms for change but also a general recognition that self-interest could "be served only if it be enlightened self-interest." [21] Peaceful change demanded constant striving for more "rule of reason" in the affairs of men. Intelligence was a unique quality which while "it cannot stop the forces which make change inevitable, it can *to some extent* modulate and direct these forces so as to affect the character of change." [22] But in the end, if all conditions for peaceful change were met, only a compromise of the ideal was ever attainable: "The existence of imperfections does not prove that the system is wrong. . . . Human nature at best is imperfect, and any system which is based on human nature is bound to have defects." [23]

Dulles' line of reasoning relative to international politics followed the same course as his general theory. Taking the egotism of political man for granted, one cannot normally expect men or nations to deviate from perceived self-interest: "All nations are inherently selfish and we are no different from any other. . . . It is easy to fall into the illusion that our policy is dictated by altruistic motives. This view will not . . . stand the test of impartial scrutiny." Disharmony and conflict are part of the given international situation for it is "inevitable that nations interfere with each other and influence each other." In a never static world, transformation and transmutation are ineluctable: "There must be either a *peaceful* way of change or a *violent* way of change." The challenge is to arrive at ever-temporary settlements, to adjust the constantly shifting balance between static and dynamic elements, to "discover the restraining envelope which creates the pressure," and to "provide outlets such that the dynamic forces become peacefully diffused." Failure to provide adequate outlets resulted in conditions where "ruthless men, who otherwise would be impotent minorities, are afforded the opportunity to become formidable and violence grows in frequency, intensity and scope." [24]

The central concept to Dulles' understanding was the inevitability of change. Active movements directed against the *status quo*, although capable of being interrupted and dammed up temporarily, were ultimately irresistible. Repression served only "to postpone, but not prevent, change and to exaggerate its violence when it occurs." [25] As a rule, therefore, resort to arms represented either a last ditch effort on the part of those fearing any alterations in the division and structure of power, or a natural reaction to unenlightened rigid programs devised by self-satisfied controlling groups, or some blending of the two. The key to the problem of peaceful change was viewed as enlightened self-interest, or a willingness to adapt and change on the part of the controlling interests or powerful nations. This was far more easily stated than realized because of the natural tendency to secure and perpetuate one's power base rather than to risk or open it to competition. With Machiavellian insight, Dulles found it "a curious fact that people seem more fearful of losing their property than their lives." [26]

The balance of power clearly emerged as Dulles' active principle in governmental and international relations. Contrary to the assumption that he sought absolutes, his approach precluded any "absolutization" of the finite and recognized the essence of international politics as an endless process of adjustment-disequilibrium-adjustment. In *War, Peace and Change* he advised: "*In international affairs—as indeed elsewhere—we should seek to abolish any sense of finality. 'Never' and 'Forever' are words which should be eliminated from the vocabulary of statesmen.*" [27] (Emphasis added.) The capsheaf of his international theory was not some panacean solution, but a two-sided affair: first, the nurturing and growth of a functional substratum of international community interests; and second, political procedures or diplomatic processes of settlement which would both decrease the occurrence and mitigate the scope and intensity of violence.

THE ETHICAL SOLUTION

The roles of two interrelated principles of solution relative to the problem of avoiding explosions of human energy—the "ethical" and the "authoritarian-political" solutions—were detailed by Dulles in *War, Peace and Change*. The "authoritarian solution" dealt with political channels and mechanisms which, while protecting the foundations and tending toward stability, allowed for peaceful change. The "ethical solution" dealt with the subject of altering the psychological impediments to increased international cooperation by creating awareness and acceptance of the facts of interrelatedness and interdependence. In a similar vein, and in the same year as *War, Peace and Change*, E. H. Carr expanded upon the theme that peaceful change is a problem both of international politics and of international morality.[28]

An unmistakable impression from the days of Versailles was Dulles' realization that the international behavior of a government was limited and, at times, determined not only by the balance of power at home but also by the conceptions and attitudes of the governed. Answering the charges by Keynes against President Wilson in 1920, although really in agreement with the former's arguments at and after Versailles, Dulles responded by referring to Keynes' own conclusion in the chapter entitled "Remedies": "A great change is neccessary in public opinion before the proposals of this chapter can enter the region of practical politics." [29] Discarding both "great man" and "devil" theories, on the grounds that such theories presupposed a nonexistent degree of free will in the stream of political-economic-historical forces, Dulles described the sources of the French posture thusly in the early 1920s:

The attitude of a great nation is not determined by the personalities of individual statesmen or politicians. The explanation of the position of France is not to be found in the mental processes of a Clemenceau or a Poincare. Such individuals are merely brought into emergence by great fundamental forces of which they will be the mouthpiece. . . . It is basic economic and political conditions which determine the broad lines of national policy. It is these we must study and with which we must deal.[30]

Dulles also concluded that, while limitations within the balance of power structure itself were unavoidable political phenomena, restrictions imposed by the public temperament and conceptions generally, and as expressed in official or congressional attitudes, could be abated. The "ethical solution" aimed at individuals and public opinion. It represented a slow process of enlightenment through education, emphasizing interrelatedness and interdependence. This process would, by design, eventually erode the foundations of isolationism and extreme nationalism and generate the growth of a functional substratum of international community interests. The strategy of the "solution" involved three steps: (1) avoiding the other-nation-devil mentality or diabolical enemy images; (2) diluting the concepts of one's own state as quasi deity and sole benefactor; and (3) redefining the meaning of sovereignty.

Avoiding Diabolical Enemy Images

From the early 1920s the avoidance of the other-nation-devil mentality became a consistent theme in Dulles' writings. In the 1930s, his campaign against self-righteousness and "holier-than-thou" attitudes derived partly from a preference not to become identified with "a senseless repetition of the cyclical struggle between the dynamic and static forces." His "antimoralistic" position was, nonetheless, not a mere affectation of this preference and the day. He had a persistent antipathy for explanations which relied upon "devils" or supposed differences in morality.

Dulles, accordingly, placed responsibility for the collapse of the Versailles Treaty not on any single nation or national leader, but on a series of ill-conceived actions and untimely inactions on the part of the United States, Great Britain, Germany, and France. Avoiding any tendency in the direction of diabolical enemy images, Dulles' criticism fell hardest on what he considered the irresponsible aloofness of the United States, although, true to his understanding, this criticism was not directed against individual personalities. The general target of his criticisms was widespread

American misconceptions and attitudes in approaching the subject of international relations. Thus, in 1941, he stated that the Versailles Treaty and its aftermath "should be studied, not for the purpose of shifting responsibility to the past, not for the purpose of excusing the present, but in order that we may identify the forces which caused that failure and combat them today, for they are still with us." [31]

A most noteworthy expression of his distaste for diabolical enemy images appeared in an early essay analyzing the French government's attitudes after Versailles:

In approaching this international difference, I trust we can avoid two errors which commonly intrude themselves in such discussion. The first is the assumption that any difference between ourselves and a foreign nation is due to the inherent righteousness of our cause and the inherent perverseness of our neighbors. Moral distinctions, though pleasing to those who draw them, are hard to sustain in fact, and I know of no historic reasons to justify our approaching these problems of international relations with the complacent assumption that we are party to a clashing of the forces of good and evil, and that solution is to be found in the moral regeneration of those who hold views contrary to our own.[32]

A similar approach characterized his view of Germany's foreign policy prior to World War II. Viewing the Nazi movement in terms of political, economic, psychological, and sociological origins in June of 1939, he asserted that the source of Germany's foreign policy was "not to be found in a different standard of morals." [33] After the war, as discussed in Chapter VII, he did not conceive of the Soviet Union or communism as inherently "evil" forces of His Satanic Majesty.

While Dulles had advocated American cooperation in international affairs upon returning from Versailles, the country withdrew into "normalcy" and many sought "scapegoats" for international conflicts of interest. The scapegoat position was unacceptable to Dulles:

Let us also avoid the error of assuming that the foreign policy which runs athwart our own is due to the personal views and idiosyncrasies of some foreign politician who may have temporarily secured an ascendancy over his fellows.[34]

But the mood of the United States was not one of shared responsibility and international cooperation. The interwar phase in America was characterized by isolationist congresses, reports of the Nye Committee, and, on a much more refined level, Charles Beard's *The Devil Theory of War*.[35] In his opposition to such interpretations, Dulles displayed a keen awareness of the psychological roots of the "devil theory of causation" approach:

The popular view is that, by some unlucky coincidence, four great nations of the world . . . happened . . . to fall under the domination of a few evil men.

The "devil" theory of causation has always been popular. Thus we used to explain floods and other violent outbreaks of nature. We still thereby seek to explain the explosions of human energy. This is simple; it saves us from mental exertion and relieves us of all causal responsibility.[36] (Emphasis added.)

In *War, Peace and Change,* he categorically denounced the "devil" theory as superficial and childish. Although responsive to primitive human desires, it was no longer necessary "as evidenced by its being discarded in the religious field." [37]

Diluting One's Own National Obsessions

The converse of avoiding diabolical enemy images was refraining from the deification of one's own group. According to Dulles, moral denunciation was usually not only unwarranted but equally dangerous in that it created in those who denounced "a sense of moral superiority." [38] Both other-nation-villain and own-nation-hero were related conceptual traps which worked against reason and peaceful settlement of disputes. Progress in breaking the common habit of forming diabolical enemy images "will . . . operate to dilute the feeling of the individual that his group authority is an indispensable protector and shield against the ever-present threat of violence from without." [39]

An early example of Dulles' own avoidance of these traps was his disapproval in the 1920s of programs which called forth or relied upon denunciation of others or glorification of self. Critical of some foreign governments' trade practices, he sympathized with the proposal to establish a body similar to the British Board of Trade.

However, it would be regrettable "if it were necessary . . . to arouse our public opinion with charges of treachery and trickery on the part of foreign governments." Consequently, he supported the idea of closer contact and coordination between the United States government and America business *only* if it could be "brought about without creating the public impression that we are 100 per cent perfect and other nations 100 per cent wrong. Such a public attitude would get us nowhere—except, perhaps into war." [40] His reaction to the American First Committee contained the same aversion to hyperbolic nationalism. While opposing United States entry into the war as a defender of the *status quo,* he also decried "the exaggeration of nationalism." [41]

When speaking of diluting the concept of one's own state as sole benefactor, Dulles was not merely attacking extreme nationalism and promulgating the liberal concept of interdependence. There was also a deep concern for the escape from freedom through total identification with a collectivity. While communism, fascism, and nazism constituted prime examples of total identification, he maintained that all societies contained some tendencies in this direction. Therefore, care had to be taken to avoid nurturing conditions conducive to "true believers," and "the concept of what is worthy of devotion and sacrifice" had to be broadened to overcome "this deification of the nation which . . . developed so dangerously" in the 1930s. [42]

The broadening of the concept of that which is worthy was a primary task, although not exclusively, for the churches and religious leadership. It was in this sense, in the 1930s, that Dulles launched a series of charges specifically against the churches when speaking before religious groups or gatherings and against national leadership generally in other speeches. All had contributed to the ascendancy of the false gods of nationalism. [43] The idea of corporate bodies becoming ends in themselves—whether church, state, race, or class—remained a classical form of idolatry, incompatible with democratic theory, Protestant belief, and Dulles' approach.

The dilution of the concept of the nation as "sole-benefactor" presented some different problems because, at least theoretically, its origins were not the same: "The nation-benefactor concept is primarily consequent upon considerations of material expediency. The nation-deity concept is responsive primarily to the yearning . . . for identification with some spiritually superior entity." [44] Dulles perceived room for moderating the former concept by such moves as lessening the "barrier aspect of boundaries," making individuals less "boundary conscious," and providing reasonable opportunity abroad for individuals without their having to "pay the price of blind allegiance to their sovereign." [45] This would include greater movement of people, goods, and capital, but he was under no "illusions as to the possibility of fundamentally altering world economy with a view to equalizing opportunity." Nevertheless, he thought there could "be a broader and longer range vision of . . . the best interest of the domestic economy," an "avoidance of minor obstructions which produce" disproportionate irritations and, above all, "a change of technique and of manners" in the handling of international and domestic economic affairs so as to enhance the possibilities of cooperative understanding and to avoid unnecessary retaliation. [46]

Redefining National Sovereignty

As a third and related step in the "ethical solution," Dulles sharply attacked what he considered to be an outdated and unhealthy concept of national sovereignty. The "ethical solution" was designed to help eradicate the "great affections" for the division of peoples and nations "by artificial lines into compartments." He noted that the "system of dividing the surface of the earth among some sixty nations and allowing each to do as it pleases has become as obsolete as the unregulated public utility." [47] In 1941 he extended his case to the point of asserting that, if the United States were to attempt to preserve the practice of self-centered sovereignty, the nation would and should succumb in the long-run. [48]

The goal of the "ethical solution" was based upon the idea that "if boundaries cannot be made changeable as to their location, they can at least be altered in character." [49] As far as everyday means of altering the exclusive nature of boundaries were concerned, Dulles placed personal exchanges and contacts, the dissemination of ideas, and less obstructions in communications above trade and commerce. But, only through the combined intercourse of people, ideas, and goods would it be possible to gain a "better understanding and a reconciliation of different viewpoints." [50] The liberal conviction of interdependence was manifested in all three steps in the "ethical solution." The same conviction would later lead both to his disapproval of the secretive nature of the Soviet Union and his promotion of cultural and scientific exchanges.

In the nineteenth century, Dulles once recalled, a committee to study the causes and results of war was appointed by the Christian Massachusetts Peace Society. This committee discovered, among other causes, what they referred to as an "infatuation" and "delusion" by which individuals identified themselves with the nation to which they happened to belong. If moral light were to increase in the future, the members predicted that this sentimental attachment would "be regarded by posterity as . . . most childish and absurd." Several generations later, in 1939, Dulles directed the "ethical solution" against the same type of "infatuation" and "delusion" which, contrary to the committee's prediction, had become "the most powerful and dangerous force in the world." [51]

THE AUTHORITARIAN SOLUTION

In 1924, with reference to the Dawes Plan, Dulles reminded his audience that all efficacious schemes take into account the limitations imposed by the political environment. Nonetheless, he was inclined to express the expert's distaste for political conditions which precluded the handling of a problem on the basis of its intrinsic qualities and which sometimes prevented reasonable settlement altogether. He maintained that the Dawes Plan served a valuable purpose, among others, in that some machinery had been established which could help ensure equitable adjustments in the future. He hoped that the necessary adjustments could "come into play almost automatically" and "not be dependent upon political factors." [52] Regardless of this note of optimism, the experiences of the Permanent Reparation Commission provided adequate evidence that no adjustments actually come into play "almost automatically."

The "authoritarian solution" was not viewed as a simple matter of setting up authorities and commissions; it was rather a gradual, political evolution toward increased international cooperation. To Dulles, the direction and success of this political evolution could not be separated from the direction and success of the "ethical solution."

The "authoritarian solution" dealt with the establishment of political devices and mechanisms which would facilitate peaceful change in the international system through contact and cooperation. The "solution" necessarily included both diplomatic processes and political mechanisms.[53] But, in *War, Peace and Change*, Dulles' concentration was almost entirely upon the latter. His emphasis upon international organization and a revitalization of the peaceful change concept as embodied in the League of Nations Covenant imparts the impression that he had only scant regard for the role of traditional diplomatic methods as one aspect of the "authoritarian solution." [54] The work only very indirectly recognized the vital role to be played by traditional diplomacy in its discussion of such topics as establishing flexible treaty structures to allow for continuous disequilibrium-adjustment-disequilibrium. But the absence of detail on this account resulted mostly from the fact that *War, Peace and Change* was not a study of day-to-day adjustments, principles of operation in negotiations, and diplomatic methods. Also, compared to his discussion of the "ethical solution" and its application to different periods, the approach to the "political solution" in *War, Peace and Change* was thoroughly embedded in the particular problems and issues of the 1930s. Consequently, his actions and other writings offer more insight into his broad understanding of, regard for, and interest in the normal diplomatic channels:

So long as the world is organized along national lines, it is . . . impracticable to attain peace through the establishment of an international tribunal empowered to dictate momentous changes. . . . Important changes can usually be best effected through the direct interplay of opposing tendencies.[55]

Actually, Dulles' approach to the "political solution" was best exemplified in his campaign for international organization and his views on international law. During World War II his campaign against isolationist tendencies and for international organization with American participation was characterized by a call to "idealism," in the sense of future possibilities, and a demand for "realism," in recognition of necessary gradualness and imperfections. To avoid repetition of the American refusal to ratify the Versailles Treaty and participate in the League of Nations, Dulles reasoned that with a resolute public opinion favoring participation in international organization, there would be less likelihood of squabbles in the Senate and intergroup conflicts reaching a peak where the baby would be thrown out with the bath water.

Although specific proposals on organization were offered, he was less concerned with immediate powers basic jurisdiction than with the decisive step of developing an initial means of collaboration which would serve as the foundation for increasing cooperation.[56] His campaign for international organization included the counsel that: (1) the organization could not, would not, and should not be an American formula; (2) some foundations had to be actualized before the Allies drifted apart; (3) police force and weighted voting schemes were quagmires and differences of opinion or debates on them should not impede establishment of a basic framework for cooperation; and (4) emphasis should be placed on the functional agencies whose quiet results could bring about concrete products and increased cooperation. The predominant motif was the idea that the development of a functional world organization would be "a long, hard task." [57]

Another important recurring theme was that any international organization should be constructed on a universal base: "If we are not to *fail utterly,* we must remember that world order cannot be just an *American* formula. . . . Our thinking must be kept *flexible.* For world order must be organized so that *all* can cooperate." [58] Dulles disagreed with the notion of the so-called democratic countries organizing alone or controlling the organization: "I think . . . there is needed some form of world organization which will be representative of, and feel a sense of responsibility toward, all of these peoples [non-democratic countries such as Russia, China, and some Latin American states] as well as the vanquished." [59]

Dulles' approach to this subject tends to corroborate the conclusion that the founders of the United Nations Charter "exhibited a keen awareness of the problem of power and of the difficulties of dealing with it." [60] He both disbelieved in and warned against any utopian schemes or aspirations:

Let there be no misunderstanding. Nothing that the San Francisco Conference can do will of itself assure lasting peace. Indeed, the Conference will wholly fail unless its limitations are understood and respected.[61]

Concerned lest disillusionment and disenchantment would result from any utopian aspirations running into reality, he counseled that official statements should not instill hopes so high that they would obscure the very real difficulties ahead. In 1945, according to the *Forrestal Diaries,* he "indicated great misgivings as to whether the hopes of the nation for an international peace organization . . . might not be raised to too great heights. He said that these questions . . . have been perplexing the minds of statesmen for centuries and that it was unwise . . . to assume they would be settled now over night." [62]

Throughout this period, Dulles opposed the advocates of "world government" primarily on the grounds that the energies spent in such a direction distracted attention from present realities. Early in this campaign for international organization, he set forth four reasons why "world government" schemes were impractical and unachievable. First, interdependence and interrelation existed on a world scale in some areas of concern, but fell short of being universal in other areas. Second, there was still no pervasive awareness of the extent to which nations and peoples were, in fact, interdependent. People were largely uneducated as to interdependence, which they could not, figuratively speaking, see with their own eyes. Third, there was lacking a set of common mores, a necessary condition to rules being understood and deemed reasonable, on any world scale. Fourth, the extensive complications and vast scope of such an operation would preclude a practical performance of world-wide trustee responsibility of general import.[63] In 1951 he became even more critical of this diversion of human energy: "The World Federalists are, in the main, somewhat unrealistic idealists. . . . The error they fall into is to assume that the present prosecution of their ideal will help solve the very difficult and dangerous problems of the present." [64]

Keeping with his earlier views toward the "ethical" and "political" solutions, however, Dulles was concerned during his campaign for international organization that "national governments must be seen to be what they are—pieces of political mechanism which involve no sanctity and which must be constantly remolded and adapted to meet the needs of a world which is living, and therefore a changing organism." [65] The great difficulty, as he saw it, was not in finding a particular political formula, but rather in assuring "that popular understanding and acceptance without which no formula, however ingenious, will work." [66] Behind Dulles' pragmatic approach to the subject and his reservations regarding specific proposals, there was a deep and lasting commitment to the establishment and continuing viability of an international organization.

The remainder of his career also reflected a belief that a favorable "popular understanding" had, for the most part, been achieved. When President Eisenhower and Dulles met with British Prime Minister Macmillan and Foreign Secretary Lloyd in 1957, not long after the United States had supported United Nations opposition to the British, French, and Israeli actions against Egypt in the Suez crisis, the President and Dulles reaffirmed their general policy in support of the United Nations. The latter further remarked that "the American people were a moralistic and perhaps sentimental people, but they had a real faith and belief in the United Nations and United States policy remained faithful to it." When the President indicated that there was very strong sentiment against Peking's admission to the United Nations, his Secretary of State added that "while congressional sentiment was very strong, recent polls had indicated that public opinion as a whole favored staying in . . . even if Communist China were admitted." [67]

LAW AND ANTILEGALISM

A similar nonidealistic strain pervaded Dulles' approach to international law and treaties. Before examining these views, however, a few general definitions should be noted. "Legalism" or the "legalistic approach" to international affairs involves the transplantation from the legal sphere of principles, rules, and procedures, which have proved effective in some national systems, to the international political sphere. The basic weaknesses inherent in the approach have been described by George Kennan. First, the idea of many individual states being subordinated to an international juridical regime implies a degree of contentedness that does not exist. Second, international relationships cannot be contained in a static legal framework or "legal strait jacket." Third, the "legalist" ignores or is ignorant of the complexities of sanctions against violations.[68] In a real sense, "legalism" represents an escape from the arduous tasks of diplomacy.

In a 1925 address Dulles asserted that the judicial process "was well devised to meet the psychological attitude of hostile or unfriendly nations." Since the speech was advocating United States participation in the Permanent Court of International Justice and acceptance of compulsory jurisdiction, he could hardly have stated otherwise. But he also emphasized that law should never be viewed as a solution in itself and would always reflect existing ambiguities.[69] Orderly legal processes depended upon laws being mostly self-enforcing, which meant mirroring "what most of the community thinks is right, or at least acceptable." Consequently, international law could only be constructed upon a "general consensus of world opinion." [70] In none of his writings did he assert that consensus had attained a level whereby law could function as an effective mold for all international relationships, although it could and did serve a useful function in regulating some aspects of international intercourse. In spite of his many tributes to the concept and goal of international order under law, similar explicit or implicit qualifications normally accompanied such tributes.

From the premise that law depended on public acceptance or acquiescence, Dulles logically concluded that it must develop along with the community to keep astride of changing conditions. Therefore, any establishment of a functional system of international law required "that such laws should be changeable to meet changing circumstances, for basic moral principles may require certain conduct at one time and different conduct at another time." [71] The necessity of a flexible, adjustable, and nonstatic system of laws also elicited his counsel that the international law of the distant future should not deal exclusively with states, but with states and individuals. Otherwise, it was "almost sure to be an effort to preserve the *status quo*." [72] Law, as a negative or static force, would inevitably encourage rupture and revolution—exactly what Dulles sought to prevent. A "strait-jacket" approach was foreign to his entire theory which held that any framework, legal or political, had always to be flexible.

Again in contrast to the "legalistic" syndrome, Dulles was fully aware of the complexities involved in the application of sanctions against offenses and violations. In a 1932 analysis of the nature of economic sanctions, his approach was characterized by selectivity and flexibility. Viewing economic sanctions as a series of intricate compromises between self-interest and "justice," he concluded that the precise form of sanctions to be effectuated was one "of the most difficult and complex problems" in the field of international relations. [73]

Dulles' understanding of international relations was not merely "nonlegalistic" but also contained an "antilegalistic" strain. In the early 1940s when Philip Jessup proposed the idea of "freedom under law" as a primary guideline for foreign policy, Dulles reacted thusly: "I think we are following a vain illusion if we assume that the slogan 'freedom under law' has sufficient substance to be the 'living principle of U. S. foreign policy.' " In reply to the suggestion that the United States generally represented an exception to the widespread inclination to twist international law to suit national interests, he responded: "But that is not accurate. I can cite many treaties we have violated." [74] On another occasion, in 1942, he was similarly disinclined to cite the United States as an exception to the normal rules of power politics: "It is difficult for me to think of any situation where substantive gains were renounced when we had the power to achieve them, but feared that the use of power would be improper." [75] In reality, nations could be relied upon to accept as "law" those customs, practices, and treaties which were in accordance with the authorities' conceptions of national interest. As early as 1929, Dulles indicated that concepts such as "the rule of law" may serve as an inspiration, but "in the meantime there are practical situations which must be dealt with." [76]

This antilegalistic strain extended to his views on pacts and treaties. When asked in 1950 if he favored a Pacific Pact, he replied in part: "Sometimes . . . a mutual pact may be necessary. . . . But if there is not a long association among nations, it is better that they not place their relationships on a legalistic basis." [77] In a similar vein, after visiting the Middle East in 1953, he came to the conclusion that there existed no basis for an overall defensive arrangement in the area. Though he soon thereafter supported the "nothern tier plan," he was not at all enthusiastic about any broader or general arrangements in the Middle East:

> We must . . . avoid becoming fascinated with concepts that have no reality. We should rather, through measures such as the above (Point IV and economic assistance), seek to improve the general situation without demand for specific *quid pro quo* on our part. Where we do require certain guarantees on the part of local States, these should be simple, direct and devoid of legalisms.[78]

Furthermore, Dulles often stressed that treaties generally should be viewed not as ends in themselves but as means for action, as reflections of common interests with their ambiguities, qualifications, and changing conditions. All treaties, therefore, should be subject to reconsideration or renegotiation at least once in every generation and preferably even more frequently. Notably, only seven years after the accomplishment of the diplomatic settlement, he recommended that the Japanese Peace Treaty be reconsidered in light of the altered situation in the Far East.

A sense of ever-changing conditions and a preference for a more united Europe led to his expression of some reservations, in 1948, about a very long-term, formalized agreement with Western Europe. During a meeting with Secretary of State Marshall, Under Secretary Lovett, and Senator Vandenberg, Dulles agreed that there was need for some form of United States guarantee, but questioned the advisability of a long-term regional arrangement. Chiefly concerned lest any semipermanent arrangement would be interpreted and applied as a guarantee of the *status quo,* he was inclined to think that a unilateral statement of United States intentions, combined with practical military cooperation similar to that which existed with Canada, might be preferable to a broad formalized agreement. (Later as Secretary, such diverse positions as "agonizing reappraisal" and the proposal to broaden the NATO agenda reflected the inherent tension between the United States commitment and guarantee to Europe and the United States preference for increased European unity.)

Dulles' reservations in 1948 derived from a concern that long-term, formalized commitments could tend to inculcate a sense of permanency and easily prove counterproductive to the interest in increased European cooperation:

I emphasized again my fear that any firm commitment, either military or economic, would be used by the governments of western Europe as an excuse to continue their own particular social and economic experiments, which required insulation from others, and that there would be advantage in keeping our policy in our own hands as I did not see very well how it would be possible to draft a convention which would promise a growth and development rather than guaranty an existing status.[79]

In spite of these reservations, the indispensability of some form of commitment to western Europe was not questioned by Dulles. Once the actual form began to take shape, the plan received his unequivocal support. But major parts of his 1949 supportive speech before the Senate Foreign Relations Committee on the North Atlantic Treaty Organization still mirrored his original concerns. He noted that, combined with the European Recovery Program, the pact could serve to stimulate the impulse toward European unity or at least toward greater European cooperation, especially in the economic realm. Also, he warned that the pact should not result in a system of group consultations which would in effect destroy the value of the United Nations Organization as the "town meeting of the world."

The first order of emphasis, however, was that the pact was necessary to eliminate doubt that the Atlantic community would act quickly and unitedly for common defense. For their part, Americans had to recognize that the security and economic welfare of western Europe were of vital interest to the United States, and that the overall effectiveness and vitality of the arrangement would largely depend upon a genuine sense of identification and common interests. But Dulles stressed that the agreement should not lead to the conclusion that the necessary military commitment and arrangements provided either the total or the main answer to the Soviet challenge and the cold war issues. Military security, though indispensable, would prove insufficient substance for a vital Atlantic alliance. He therefore concluded that the "Pact should not be operated primarily as a military instrument." Nor should the proposed organization be interpreted as a standard guarantee of the *status quo*. Rigid defense of the *status quo*, "merely because communism attacks it," would be imprudent and impractical. The Atlantic organization's viability demanded dynamic and creative approaches: "It is not a mere framework for goods and guns, but a framework for constructive programs that will catch men's imagination and enlist their support." [80]

Dulles' positive approach to the North Atlantic Treaty Organization remained constant over the years. As Secretary of State, he attempted to expand the areas of political cooperation and consultation within NATO. In 1957 the Secretary defined the long-term aim of NATO as the development of "the Atlantic Community" with its "roots . . . far deeper than those necessary for the common defense." [81] A year later, he was sympathetic with General de Gaulle's suggestion that political consultation be expanded to include issues and actions outside the NATO region. Both Dulles and President Eisenhower agreed with the aim. In the words of the former: "The idea that you can deal only with problems just within the NATO area is illusory. How to broaden this relationship is the difficult problem." [82] But de Gaulle's proposed methods—a directorate composed of France, Great Britain, and the United States within the organization—did not sit well with either the President or his Secretary of State. As a temporary measure until there developed agreement on means, a special committee, composed of Under Secretary Robert Murphy and the British and French ambassadors, was set up in Washington to discuss broad ranges of issues. From

1948 to 1959 Dulles' approach consistently reflected his belief that military security should not be viewed as the "be-all" and "end-all" either of NATO or of foreign policy generally.

The impressions of the Versailles to Munich period are apparent in Dulles' general approach to treaties and pacts: "The treaties on which men depend for immediate self-preservation should . . . set up forces which make them self-enforcing." [83] The process of negotiation was never "just a matter of finding words," for "the total dictionary of noble words has already been exhausted by treaties which today are merely crumpled bits of paper littering the cruel path which humanity has had to tread." [84] The demand for self-enforcing terms did not, however, necessarily reflect a tendency to approach outstanding issues on the basis of a legal brief as exemplified by the following statement, shortly after the Yalta Conference in 1945, in an address on the "Peaceful Settlement of International Disputes" and in the context of a discussion of the limitations of international law:

> Most of the expansion of the American nation has been through war or the threat of war. Was that illegal and should the United States have been forever confined to its original strip of territory along the Atlantic seaboard? . . . To turn to current politics, how about the rebirth of Russia and the dynamism of the U.S.S.R.? *There are no legal principles which enable us to re-determine the boundaries of Poland.*[85] (Emphasis added.)

Although Dulles was by nature a cautious negotiator in the international arena, his expressed concern about the need for achieving self-enforcing terms and avoiding attractive, airy generalities really did not emerge until the cold war climate at mid-century. During this period, as noted in Chapter VII, his views toward treaties and pacts were heavily influenced by the state of world politics and by his concern that the American people would just as soon substitute symbol for substance in order once again to give way to an impulse toward nonparticipation and nonpreparation.

Judging by Kennan's delineation of "legalistic traits," no portion of Dulles' earlier or later approach suggests a propensity toward "legalism" in international affairs. His conception of the role of international law was basically positivistic and realistic. He did not possess the so-called lawyer's trust in written agreements. The experiences of the Versailles Treaty and its aftermath produced a keen awareness of the fact that agreements, whether with allies or with nonallies, were ineffective unless they reflected a substantial concurrence of interests and will. In short, the name of Dulles' game was not international law but international politics.

CHAPTER FIVE

THOUGHTS ON INTERNATIONAL POLITICS, PART II

RECOGNITION: AN ANTIMORALISTIC APPROACH

In April of 1917, after successfully completing an unofficial mission to prompt Panama and Cuba to follow the lead of the United States in declaring war on the German Empire, Dulles proceeded to Costa Rica, where the regime of General Tinoco had gained control by revolution in January. The United States had withheld recognition. Dulles was assigned to survey the situation and recommend a course of action. In a memorandum for Secretary of State Robert Lansing, he strongly advocated United States recognition of the Tinoco government.

Moreover, with regard to a policy of nonrecognition in general, Dulles wrote:

Non-recognition, in the case of a government exercising undisputed control, is . . . a measure rarely to be availed of. Non-recognition, unless in aid of a specific constructive program, is negative and destructive in its operation. . . . The United States cannot . . . lay down as a general principle, applicable even to the Caribbean states alone, the non-recognition of *every* government which comes into power through a revolution.[1]

Granting that nonrecognition "may be a useful aid in carrying out a specific program," he had "heard no one suggest any such concrete program for Costa Rica." [2] Stating that each case had to be decided on the basis of its own peculiar facts, he found that the condemnation of revolutionary action frequently amounted to the unwarranted transplantation of values to other systems. Since "actual revolution is often the only effective method of preventing an indefinite perpetuation of power," one "cannot deny *in toto* the right of revolution." [3]

Thus, nonrecognition without a supplementary constructive plan of action was considered at best a feeble instrument of national policy. Dulles did not belong to that school of international lawyers which maintains that, in the absence of other machinery, nonrecognition "must be regarded as a supplementary weapon of considerable legal and moral potency." [4] But this was not to say that the power of political suggestion should be completely ignored when in the process of granting recognition. Although not "a weapon of considerable legal and moral potency," in 1917 Dulles thought that the United States might use the prospect of recognition to influence the Costa Rican leaders to hold Senate elections. Compliance with such suggestions, however, was not to be judged a precondition for recognition. [5]

His recommendation that the United States recognize the Tinoco regime, as noted in Chapter 1, was adopted by the State Department but not approved by President Wilson. Wilson's determination not to recognize revolutionary regimes in Latin America had its moralistic overtones. Dulles, both in his recommendation of 1917 and later, clearly dissociated himself from this policy approach. The Costa Rican experience led him to the conclusion that good motives and sound theoretical principles were guarantees of neither morally virtuous nor politically successful policies. [6] His 1917 memorandum was the earliest example of his distaste for the injection of unwarranted moral judgments and inapplicable legal standards into international affairs.

Regarding the revolutionary regime in Moscow, Dulles suggested in 1924 that it was absurd to sustain the fiction that the Kerensky group in the United States represented the government of Russia. Although not proposing immediate and complete diplomatic relations with the Soviet government, he commended that the fiction be destroyed so that the United States could decide on terms for dealing with the Soviets and whether to renew diplomatic relations. [7] A few days after President Roosevelt's inauguration in 1933, and approximately six months before Roosevelt reportedly called for a complete review of the nonrecognition policy vis-à-vis Moscow, Dulles not only remained opposed to the perpetuation of the legal fiction that the Soviet government did not exist but also privately supported recognition of the Soviet Union without conditions or reservations.[8] (Later in the fall, President Roosevelt met with Maxim Litvinov and, in January of 1934, Ambassador Troyanovsky presented his credentials.)

Besides the issue of recognizing regimes which come into power by force within a country, there was a more difficult question regarding boundary changes affected by force. Henry L. Stimson, Secretary of State from 1929 to 1933 under President Hoover, discarded the Wilson practice of nonrecognition as it had been applied in the Western Hemisphere. On the other hand, the Stimson Doctrine of 1932, relating to alterations brought about by force across boundaries (Japan in Manchuria), to some extent derived from the belief that the withholding of *de jure* recognition could serve as a consequential tool of foreign policy. The doctrine was not simply a derivative of any "legalistic-moralistic" tendencies on Stimson's part, for numerous considerations and complications, plus the dearth of viable alternatives at the moment, combined in its formulation. Nevertheless, as Stimson later declared, the declaration of a legal principle undeniably failed as an instrument of United States policy.[9]

To Dulles again, as well as to the Japanese, the instrument appeared as an impuissant reply to the situation. He did not know, in 1935, whether the changes in the Far East were actually warranted by the facts, but he found it at least conceivable that Japan in Manchuria represented "a logical and inevitable tendency." From this position he criticized the American approach to nonrecognition: "Nor is the cause of peace advanced by closing one's eyes to actual changes merely because they result from the only mechanism for change which is available." [10] Dulles neither maintained that all fruits of aggression should be automatically recognized, nor entertained accepting Japanese tutelage over China.[11] But he did conclude, as before, that a policy of nonrecognition without the backing of supplementary actions was ineffective, and that recognition offered a better chance of possible influence over the direction of future relationships.

Dulles put all his thoughts together on the problem of nonrecognition in *War, Peace and Change* in 1939, and forcefully and extensively censured the American inclination toward "moralism" on the subject:

Non-recognition by one state of a *de facto* situation created by another . . . involves certain political inconveniences to both. . . . Consular and diplomatic relations are interrupted or continued only through ingenious and complicated subterfuge.

For a nation to base its relations with the outside world on the assumption that change brought about by force is in fact non-existent, is a policy of absurdity. . . . For any nation to close its eyes to such changes . . . means the election of such nation to live in a world as unrelated to reality as that of "Alice in Wonderland."

It appeals to our moral sense to have our government refrain from "recognizing" changes effected through the aggression of others.

Such an approach, however, involves . . . carrying over into the international field judgments which derive from social units in which the authoritarian solution is operative. We can condemn the use of violence in a society which provides for peaceful evolution and change. . . . But we cannot . . . indiscriminately carry forward moral judgments of aggression into a society within which neither the political nor ethical solutions are operative.

International practice over the centuries has made it clear that "recognition" merely constitutes taking cognizance of certain admitted facts. No moral judgment is involved.[12]

Ten years later, as the anticommunist movements gained momentum in the United States, he perceived no reason to recall diplomatic representatives from the Soviet satellite countries. The presence of the missions "did not involve any moral approval" of the regimes and could "perhaps help to promote the interests" of the United States.[13] Up to this point, Dulles' approach to the subject of recognition was clear and consistent.

However, also in 1949, he hesitated to recognize the communist regime in China. He offered two legitimate reasons for hesitation. First, preferring a noncommunist government on the mainland—a preference founded upon considerations of national interest—he hoped that the Chinese communists would encounter insurmountable obstacles in their attempt to gain and retain control. Second, in light of the many decades of chaos in China, he supported this hope with the requirement (and a normal requirement in the American habit) that every government should be tested over a period of time in order to establish the fact of control.

But shortly before the outbreak of war in Korea, at the same time that he was proposing a delay in recognition, Dulles twice stated that, if the Peking regime proved its ability to govern without serious domestic difficulties, the People's Republic of China should be admitted to the UN. Along with this argument, however, he expressed discontentment with the Truman Administration's "total neglect of an effective cold war offensive for this area." [14]

There were no substantial contradictions, in terms of overall national interest, between proposing to admit the People's Republic of China to the UN and simultaneously withholding official United States recognition. (As will be noted below, two distinct advantages inhered in this course.) As it turned out, however, the United States found itself unable to support either admission or recognition because of a combination of factors including: (1) the developments within China and the policies of the People's Republic; (2) the opposition of the American public and Congress; and (3) the inheritances from past administrations. (With reference to UN admission, for example, the issue was made even more difficult, if not actually unmanageable under the circumstances prevailing in the 1950s, by the inheritance of "China's" permanent seat on the Security Council.) [15] Nevertheless, an interesting twist is reflected in Dulles' position-taking. The qualified proposal to admit Peking to the UN was completely in line with his earlier pragmatic approach to such problems; but the proposal to delay official recognition did not necessarily indicate a tendency in the opposite direction or toward "moralism."

During his campaign for postwar cooperation in the early 1940s, as noted in Chapter IV, Dulles supported a universal international organization regardless of a government's political coloring. Before the outbreak of the Korean War, he consistently argued for, and accepted, the logical implications of a universal base for the United Nations. In *War or Peace* (1950), he declared that the organization "will best serve the cause of peace if its Assembly is representative of what the world actually is, and not merely representative of the parts which we like." A government in control "should be represented in any organization" purporting to mirror world reality. If the Chinese communist regime proved its ability to retain control, "then it . . . should be admitted to the United Nations." [16]

This belief led him to recommend amending the UN Charter to provide clearly for universality. Article 4 (1) "makes a vote for the admission of a new member in effect a vote of confidence in the moral quality of the nation. . . . *As between nations, diplomatic recognition involves no element of moral approval. It should be the same with admission to the United Nations.*" [17] (Emphasis added.) On another occasion, in 1950, he phrased the issue thusly:

Communist governments today dominate more than 30 per cent of the populations of the world. We may not like that fact; indeed, we do not like it at all. But if we want to have a *world* organization, then it should be representative of the world as it is.[18]

After the opening of hostilities by North Korea, a gradual shift in emphasis began to emerge in some of his utterances. He still maintained that the UN should be constructed upon a universal base, but "universality should not turn the United Nations into an impotent organization." [19] Since the Soviet Union had often exercised its veto power in the Security Council, there was naturally some concern that the granting of a permanent seat to the People's Republic of China would increasingly hinder the operations of that body. This was a potent issue during the time of crisis and conflict in Korea since the Soviet Union's absence from the Security Council had in effect enabled it to take action.

At this stage Dulles' various comments indicated that, while he yet hoped the Chinese communist experiment would encounter insuperable obstacles and fail, he was careful to allow room for any future adjustments which would be necessitated in the event of communist success. The suggestions of UN membership for Peking had two advantages. First, had circumstances allowed for follow through along this course, a form of contact with the revolutionary regime would have been established. Second, this might have been accomplished hopefully without the administration risking political crisis or suicide by further infuriating the American Congress and public.

Dulles' position, as well as Acheson's and the Truman Administration's policy, on the issues of UN admission and recognition of the People's Republic of China can be understood only in terms of the political conditions, international and domestic, at the time. There were many sides to the issues, and the answer to the question —why the proposal to delay recognition?—did not lie chiefly within the American sphere: "The Communists themselves . . . by their action in the Angus Ward and similar cases, had effectually shelved the question of U. S. diplomatic recognition for the foreseeable future." [20] Even after the ill-treatment of United States officials by communist authorities—Angus Ward in Mukden and other incidents in Dairen, Nanking, and Shanghai—the Truman Administration and the State Department entertained no illusions about the possibility of a reversal of events and were careful not to adopt an inflexible and irreversible position. On January 5, 1950, the President announced that the United States still had no intentions of becoming embroiled in China's civil war. Implied in this position was United States acceptance of the view that Formosa should be considered an integral part of China. Truman stated further that, although economic aid would continue under legislative authority, the United States would provide neither military aid nor advice to the Nationalist forces which had retreated to Formosa in December. The day following the speech, a communist order to seize the former military barracks in Peking, which housed the consular offices of the United States, resulted in the withdrawal of all American personnel from Communist China.

Dulles agreed with Truman's and Acheson's policy toward Formosa in two fundamental respects: The United States "should refrain from action that would involve us in fighting in the Chinese Civil War or imply that we have predatory designs on Formosa." [21] However, as evidenced by his draft press releases, draft responses to inquiries, and correspondence just after the President's statement on January 5, Dulles did not favor having the fate of the six or seven million Formosans decided on the basis that Formosa was an integral part of China. Noting that the Formosans had "a distinctive economic, social and cultural life," had "no political ties with China" for about two generations, and were in number "greater than . . . at least twenty nations members of the United Nations," he thought the United States should explore "taking Formosa to the United Nations Assembly on the theory that Formosa was a non-self-governing territory, and that the best solution might be an interim period at least of trusteeship under Article 77, providing for trusteeship of 'territories which may be detached from enemy states as a result of the Second World War'." It seemed to him "little short of scandalous" for the United States to adopt a policy course and theory which appeared to mean that the Formosans would "be subjected to the cruel fate of being the final battleground between the Red regime and the Nationalist Army." [22] By suggesting that the matter be taken to the United Nations as a non-self-governing territory issue, the basic idea was "to neutralize Formosa." [23] However, Dulles found his analysis largely academic because, as he wrote Senator Vandenberg the day following Truman's announcement, "of the finality of the President's and Acheson's statements and the fact that probably at this late date the United Nations would resent having the problem dumped in its lap." [24]

Regarding the issue of whether or not to recognize the People's Republic of China, Dulles agreed with Acheson's statement that it was "premature." Believing that the communist regime would find it very difficult to establish its rule in China, the former maintained that the United States should not aid the process by granting recognition early. To Dulles and to the Truman Administration, the decision to hold off appeared reasonable in itself given China's internal problems, given Washington's welcome for difficulties that contributed to hindering communist control, and given the preference for a ruling faction more in keeping with American interests. But the matter was already slipping out of the hands of the Executive. To favor immediate recognition publicly would have been the equivalent of playing political Russian roulette with, at best, a single empty chamber. A Gallup poll, on June 2, 1950, found 40 per cent of those interviewed opposed to recognition, 44 per cent undecided or without opinion, and only 16 per cent in favor of recognition. More poignant was the fact that, on January 19, 1950, the House of Representatives voted against the White House request for $60 million of new economic aid to Korea, as pro-Formosans and a Southern Democrat-Republican coalition tied their demand for more aid for the Nationalist Chinese to the administration's request for aid to Korea.

In a very real sense, the blending of the actions of the People's Republic of China and the United States Congress effectually slammed the door which the Truman Administration and Dulles were willing to keep ajar. Neither the administration nor Dulles hastened to adopt any hard and fast lines for policy in the area. The United States neither bolted the door on the subject of recognition nor demanded that the admission issue be considered an "important question" which would require a two-thirds majority in the General Assembly. During a span of approximately eight months, the official United States position was essentially and pragmatically ambivalent. The circumstances changed and lines became hardened when hostilities began in Korea.

If, at this stage, there had been the slightest hope for adjustments, such anticipations vanished as a political possibility with the Chinese attitude toward and participation in the Korean War. The fact that recognition was nowhere within the realm of the possible was reiterated several times by Truman and Acheson during their meetings, in December of 1950, with British Prime Minister Attlee.[25] A few weeks later, James Reston wrote that Acheson's policy on China had reversed itself within a year. According to this report, Peking's participation in the Korean War "started a chain of events in American national and international politics that is now extremely hard to control." [26] Acheson's letter of September 26, 1951, reflected the hardening of the political scene and the American attitude. During the hearings concerned with the nomination of Philip Jessup as a United States delegate to the United Nations, the nominee was accused of having favored the immediate recognition of the People's Republic of China. Senator H. Alexander Smith, a member of the Senate Foreign Relations Committee, stated that his experiences in 1949 had left the impression that the United States was moving toward recognition. Countering Senate suspicions and charges, Acheson wrote that the Truman Administration had consistently opposed and continued to oppose, for itself and for friendly governments, the following: (1) recognizing the Peking regime; (2) seating representatives from Peking at the UN or any other international agency; (3) turning over Formosa to the Chinese communists. The letter also stated opposition to linking an armistice in Korea to the last two points. The Secretary maintained that he had informed British Foreign Secretary Ernest Bevin, in late 1949, that the United States was not considering recognition. Dean Rusk, Assistant Secretary of State for Far Eastern Affairs, went a step further with the assertion that no important official of the State Department had recommended recognition.[27]

From the outbreak of the Korean War, if not from October 1, 1949, until Dulles' first hints toward possible rapprochement and recognition in 1958, the door remained firmly closed on the recognition question. *Strictly in terms of the balance between international and national interests, it cannot be assumed that extending recognition would have been either possible or prudent.* Since the unification and control process in China depended largely upon the existence of a concrete enemy—"Uncle Sam" and "United States imperialism"—what reason was there to suppose that the communist regime would desire adjustments or entertain early recognition? Did not the maneuvers of Peking's leaders clearly indicate the low priority attached to any prospect of recognition by or rapprochement with the United States? Considering the vast differences between the situations of China and Yugoslavia, was there any validity in the British idea of "Titoism"? Even if a comparison were plausible, would a type of "Titoism" in China be less in conflict with United States interests? In the early stages, was it not a better bargain to have the Chinese communists identified as the tools of Soviet masters? Would not this identification tend both to hinder the effectiveness of Peking's propaganda to overseas Chinese and to lessen possible Chinese influence in the Far East, especially Japan, and Southeast Asia? With respect to the issue of UN membership, did not both the Nationalists and Communists reject any form of "two China" solution?

Given the combination of international and domestic factors in the early 1950s, the above questions became practically academic. The Truman Administration had been made painfully aware of the absence of alternatives within the domestic political environment; and, as will be noted, similar political realities severely restricted the freedom of action or maneuverability of succeeding administrations in this region. December of 1950 was not yet the heyday of "McCarthyism" and the China Lobby was only beginning to gather steam. Public and congressional opinion, which did not begin to mellow on the issue until more than a decade later, became more resolute and entrenched in its opposition. The following months produced a unanimously passed (91–0) Senate resolution demanding that the People's Republic of China not be admitted to the United Nations. Unanimity became the standard thereafter for expression of congressional opposition to any change in the China policy of the United States.* A Gallup poll release, on July 25, 1954, found that 78 per cent of the respondents opposed admitting the Peking regime to the UN.

The background explains the questions relating to Dulles' positions both before and during his secretaryship. Why did he find it necessary gradually to shift emphasis? Why did his advocacy of UN admission for the People's Republic of China fade until, finally, it was supplanted by firm opposition? Why did he not propose recognition after a reasonable period of time had elapsed? Why did Formosa become a political and psychological bastion for "free China" rather than an island for the Formosans? [28] Why were there no substantial changes throughout the 1950s? The answers to such questions reside in several considerations, including Peking's intense anti-Americanism and its prognostications for the future of Asia, and the effects of these developments upon American thinking

---

* "Language objecting to the recognition and/or seating of Communist China in the UN was incorporated each year, from 1953 through 1964, in State Department or foreign aid appropriations acts or both. Separate resolutions to the same effect were adopted by one or both chambers in 1954, 1956, and 1961. Support for the *status quo* was recorded by roll call on eight occasions: by the House, July 15, 1954, 381–0; July 18, 1956, 391–0; August 17, 1959, 368–2; and August 31, 1961, 395–0; and by the Senate, June 3, 1953, 76–0; July 29, 1954, 91–0; July 23, 1956, 86–0; and July 28, 1961, 76–0." *Congress and the Nation 1945–1964* (Washington: Congressional Quarterly Service, 1965), p. 104.

and public opinion; the impact of the Korean War and Chinese participation upon official thinking and public attitudes in the United States; American support for and commitment to the Nationalist regime; and the restraints imposed by domestic reactions and congressional attitudes or power groups on governmental processes and maneuverability. Throughout these changes in the early 1950s, however, Dulles perceived the main objective of United States policy toward Peking not as the dissolution of communism in China but as breaking "the present ties between China and Moscow." Under the circumstances of 1952, he concluded that this could best be done by keeping on pressures.[29]

The Truman Administration's decision to "let the dust settle in China," regardless of its rationality relative to the international situation, had its measure of tragic repercussions. If the administration had genuinely decided to accept either victor in China's internal struggle, it failed to cultivate congressional acquiescence and prepare the American public for this eventuality. The failure of United States policy in China was described in 1952 as "one of the most resounding defeats our foreign policy" had "ever sustained." [30] The magnitude of the congressional and domestic reaction to that policy meant that, for several years to come, the two groups most directly concerned with foreign policy would have extremely scant room for any maneuver, and could only incur unnecessary political difficulties by raising the issue of possible recognition or admission to the UN. Political survival normally takes priority over political education. The matter no longer rested within the realm of the State Department or the Executive.

Realistically speaking, therefore, Dulles had little alternative but to shift his emphasis, to oppose admission of Peking to the United Nations and remain silent on the subject of recognition. From 1950 to 1951 on, his remarks were couched in a continuous stream of "if's" and "but's," the inevitable products of a delicate balance between domestic demands, the exactions of leadership, and international requirements. As far as his position as Secretary of State is concerned, there will remain some legitimate questions regarding certain tactics and policy maneuvers, such as the ring of security pacts or arrangements in Asia, and whether or not there could have been a consequential shade more flexibility in those few instances where it appeared possible. But the basic policies of nonrecognition and nonadmission were irrefragably determined before he set foot in office, and no practicable alternative to these broad policy lines emerged during his term. There was little, if any, change on the domestic scene; and, throughout the 1950s, Peking's attitude reflected a basically nonconciliatory approach and the communists continued to threaten the take-over of Formosa—a commitment and symbol which no American administration could risk losing without also risking its own and its party's career, not to mention the possibility of another dangerous flux in American public and congressional opinion.

It may be debatable whether a time for education and preparation had existed during the Roosevelt Administration and the early years of the Truman Administration. But, by the time Dulles took office, a cram course quite logically appeared beyond reach. Happenings and events, as one student of presidential politics points out, determine the educational projects and subjects of the president and his advisers.[31] After a definite, even if slight, relaxation in the cold war climate and on the domestic fronts, the Kennedy Administration found it imprudent either to suggest positively or to pursue actively a path toward eventual recognition and Peking's admission to the UN. The change in United States tactics at the UN in 1961 was a shift in tactics only, not in policy, designed to strengthen the American hand against Peking's admission.*

Only during the past few years did it become apparent that the opposition to any proposals concerning rapprochement with, eventual recognition of or UN membership for the People's Republic of China no longer existed with the same hypersensitive rigidity. In 1968, both Richard Nixon and Hubert Humphrey found it politically advantageous to advocate rapprochement with Peking.[32] Similar utterances would have bordered on political suicide during the 1950s and would have been considered highly controversial as late

---

* The Kennedy Administration agreed to debate the China issue but maintained that it was an "important question" requiring a two-thirds majority. The General Assembly accepted this interpretation by a vote of 61–34 with 7 abstentions on December 15, 1961.

as 1964. In 1965 Senator Fulbright concluded: "I do not think that the United States can or should recognize Communist China or acquiesce in her admission to the United Nations under present circumstances." [33]

If part of the American practice has been "using recognition to express moral or political approval of new regimes," [34] it was not inherent in Dulles' practice. In 1950 he left the future open for possible adjustments in United States relations with China until those became politically impossible. In 1958 he appeared to be searching for an eventual way toward increased intercourse and conciliation. On January 16 he asserted: "Any time it will serve the interests of the United States to recognize the Communist Chinese regime, we will do it." [35] Twice in June, and again in December, he maintained that, although official recognition would not serve the interests of the United States at the time, the Eisenhower Administration did and would continue to deal with the Chinese People's Republic whenever it appeared expedient. [36] Earlier in March he had been concerned with the renegotiation of the Japanese Peace Treaty in a manner which would recognize the need for an extension of trade between Japan and mainland China. [37] In October he counseled the Nationalist regime to abandon the "civil war complex," and to begin thinking in terms of an armistice along the present lines of division. [38] China's turn inward later in 1958, the Chinese invasion of Tibet in March of 1959, the frontier disputes with India, and Peking's inflexible and not infrequently hostile attitude toward the United States were among the factors which precluded further action in the direction of possible conciliation as hinted by Dulles.

Yet, clearly, the United States had to take account of the fact that the People's Republic of China did exist and could not be ignored: "And where we can deal with it on a *de facto* basis with relation to a particular matter, if we fail to do that through a policy of non-recognition, that would be equally stupid." [39] Dulles' support for establishing the Geneva and Warsaw talks corroborates the conclusion that he realized the importance of having contact with Peking. Respecting the types of contact, however, the maneuverability of the Secretary was restricted, as exemplified in his approach to the 1954 Geneva Conference on Indochina. Political concerns were evident in the wording of his announcement, upon returning from the Four Power Foreign Ministers Conference at Berlin in February, that the United States would not refuse to meet indirectly with the Chinese People's Republic. He found it necessary to justify, to an American public with vivid memories of Yalta, the decision to go to the conference table.[40]

The unraveling of the issues between the People's Republic of China and the United States cannot be viewed as a one-way American street. Advocates of recognition often placed the cart before the horse, as though the issue constituted the cause, rather than a reflection, of instability in the area and Sino-American variance. For the rest, there remained the overriding domestic difficulties which effectively eliminated any real room for possible flexibility on anything touching broad policy. The United States policy of nonrecognition of the People's Republic has been categorized as "a classic example of the 'moralistic approach' to international politics."[41] But such was not the case at least with regard to a good deal of official thinking. The reasons for nonrecognition, nonadmission, and for certain actions in 1954, lay deep in the international circumstances at the time and in both the national interest as perceived by American leadership and the relationship between domestic political situations and international postures.

THE PROBLEMS OF POWER

With its coming of age and power during the first half of the twentieth century, the shifts and starts of the United States support Reinhold Niebuhr's observation on an American "schizophrenia" on the subject of power.[42] Thus, what was first viewed as a European trade rivalry of little concern to the United States became, within a very few years, a mission "to make the world safe for democracy." Returning to till its own garden, after World War I, the United States failed to comprehend "that the disavowal of the responsibility of power can involve an individual or nation in . . . grievous guilt."[43] This disavowal of the responsibility of power by the United States was a principal target of Dulles' criticism from his advocacy of participation in the League of Nations to his assertions of shared guilt and contributory negligence before and during World War II. The period was characterized, to his way of thinking, as nothing more nor less than national irresponsibility.

Generally speaking, no signs of "schizophrenia" on the subject of power appeared in Dulles' thinking. First, he was not inclined to ignore the indispensability of power: "Policies are of little use unless behind them lies the power, moral or material, potential or actual, to make them good." [44] Second, he did not entertain the myth that power could transcend interest. Accordingly, in the 1920s, the United States was no exception to the dictum that "all nations are inherently selfish" and, in broad terms, "we want the rest of the world to grow richer so that we may get some of its wealth." Many years later, in 1954, the American aspiration for peaceful change reflected neither moral superiority nor altruism, but rather the fact that the "interests of the United States are best protected by a world at peace." [45]

The tension between his positions, on such subjects as power and the responsibility of power, and the context within which he operated from the late 1930s to approximately mid-century reflected lessons drawn from both America's mistakes and some of his own. This tension resulted in several descriptions of what he considered to be the weaknesses and misconceptions in the "American approach" toward the exercise of power in world politics. Although nonparticipation or noninterference in particular events under certain circumstances remained rational alternatives in Dulles' scheme, he thought the most dangerous American weakness was a general tendency toward nonparticipation and isolationism. In 1941, the forces for a repeat of the post-World War I performance—whether products of idealistic, nostalgic, isolationist, nationalistic, or other propensities—were, to Dulles, still very active in the American fabric. [46] This pronounced American weakness had by no means been entirely corrected to his liking by 1945, when he found a public psychology accepting the idea of collaboration but actually fearing it as a reality:

The fact is that this nation has not yet adjusted itself to the working conditions of collaboration. Too many Americans prefer to see our government stand aloof, and utter lofty pronouncements which pander to their sense of moral superiority.[47]

Viewing one of the sources of the American disavowal of the responsibility of power as a propensity to place "war" and "peace" into two entirely disconnected compartments, Dulles frequently censured this disposition to disconnect political and military considerations. A primary objection to embarking upon a course and mood of war, in 1939, was his concern that the United States had given inadequate attention to political objectives and political interests and to how best to achieve these aims. In a deliberate quasi-Wilsonian stance, he preferred nonparticipation to setting out merely in defense of the *status quo ante bellum* and then, throughout the war years, his statements concentrated on political objectives, such as the formation of a viable international organization, which should attend any victory. Shortly after the outbreak of war in Korea in 1950, he pictured the tendency to dichotomize "war and peace" thusly:

The United States has one very bad habit. In times of fighting we usually forget all about political objectives. . . . We Americans usually look on war as a kind of prize fight. The objective is to knock out your opponent. If you do knock him out, the job is done. Then it is in order to go home, break training, and enjoy yourself. . . .

If we have even a childish capacity to learn by experience, World War II should have taught us the folly of that attitude.[48]

Yet, to Dulles, the post-World War II attitudes of the United States generally seemed to represent substantial shifts, rather than a healthy balance, between extremes. At this stage, his attention began to focus on the problem of a responsible defense posture, a subject which rarely appeared in his earlier writings except by implication. The developments in this subject, however, surely reflected one of his most constant concerns—American disavowal of the responsibility of power. Immediately following the war, the nation set upon a course of rapid demobilization. From 1945 through 1946, the armed forces dropped from approximately 12 million men to around 2 million men. The official goal, for July of 1947, was slightly over 1.6 million. From the Truman Administration's point of view, the move was not predicated upon unrealistic expectations of real tranquillity or of broad cooperation with the Soviet Union. Nor was the move simply a giving in to public and congressional pressures, although these factors carried much weight in the process of defining policy options. The demobilization course no doubt derived from a combination of conclusions, perhaps the most decisive being the idea that the Soviet Union was not about ready to plunge into another war.

Regardless of the reasoning, what some considered a very rapid demobilization policy reflected in part the familiar habit of separating military and political considerations. While agreeing that the Soviet Union was neither prepared nor wanting to enter upon a course of major conflict, Dulles maintained that power was necessary for deterrence, for symbolic meaning, for diplomatic leverage, and bargaining purposes. In 1945 he warned that the United States was demobilizing far too rapidly in terms of both numbers and quality. Less than a year later, he supported the immediate enactment of legislation which would, through a draft if necessary, enable the country to maintain a "position of strength." [49]

On the other side of the American coin, there emerged a type of "Fortress America mentality" which placed confidence in "military solutions" to the cold war. The "solution" tended in the direction of "all or nothing" or "absolute security" behind a line of atomic weapons. To Dulles, a "position of strength" was requisite for positive, effective foreign policy measures and aims. But as the coin turned, he thoroughly deprecated the notion that military power alone could serve as either the primary substance or the "be-all" and "end-all" of the United States posture. From 1948 to 1953, he expressed alarm regarding the spreading tendency to think in military terms and the increasing influence of the military establishments. He declared in 1948 that "in the United States great emphasis is being placed upon achieving military supremacy and military counsels are more influential than has normally been the case in that republic." [50] The objective tone of this statement changed as he became increasingly concerned with the role of the military and military considerations in the decision-making processes. Although a note that America was "fast becoming a military dictatorship" was discarded in 1952, he warned that concentration upon the military side of the cold war would not only prove counterproductive to the interests and foreign policy aims of the United States, but also adversely affect the nation's economy and the national character itself.[51]

A part of Dulles' concern, particularly in 1948 and 1949, stemmed from his view that the organizational structure for the conduct of American foreign policy was too divided and gave the military too much influence. Writing to Congressman Christian A. Herter, shortly after Dewey's defeat at the polls in 1948, Dulles did "not envy anyone the job" of Secretary of State not only because of the international problems confronting the United States but also because the Secretary had "an appearance of responsibility much greater than his authority." For example, the War Department essentially conducted foreign affairs relative to Germany and Japan, and the authority for strategic matters resided in the National Security Council. This "division of authority and the question of what to do about it" had been worrying Dulles.[52] In the broader respect, however, his concern about military influence and military thinking derived from the proposition that the nation's economy could not bear crisis years and crisis military expenditures. What was needed, therefore, was a "long haul" approach to sustain the support of the American people without a large drain on the nation's resources and without having the nation's economic health dependent on military spending.

But, in its broadest sense, Dulles' concern was that the increasing emphasis upon military aspects and the currency given "military solutions" resulted largely from isolationist propensities, from a superficial outlook on international politics, and, generally, from the failure of the United States to meet the severe test of prosperity. In so many words, Americans had become too materialistic in their approach and too static in their thinking. At mid-century the search for security through stress on military and economic forces presented a situation which Dulles considered incongruous at best:

It is ironic . . . that we who so proudly profess regard for the spiritual should rely so utterly on material defenses while the avowed materialists have been waging a winning war with social ideals, stirring humanity everywhere.[53]

While developments in the United States attitude toward power, in the environment after World War II and during the cold war, caused Dulles much concern, the problems were not new. He had long recognized dilemmas in the acquisition and maintenance of military power. Discussing the problems of armaments in *War, Peace and Change* (1939), he had perceived great difficulty in maintaining a reasonable defense posture without undermining the moral, psychological, and economic fibers of the people. There was indeed some "force in the contention that war becomes less likely as its destructive consequences become more assured." But, on balance, he considered vast armament a very dangerous trend since "the creation of vast armament in itself calls for a condition midway between war and peace. Mass emotion on a substantial scale is prerequisite. . . . A sense of peril from abroad must be cultivated." Such conditions already put one "a long way on the path toward war" where it was "dangerous to rely upon reasoning as to consequence to restrain against the small additional transition necessary to the actual attainment of war." It was also "dangerous . . . to rely upon the ability of group authorities to prevent wars which they would avoid as lacking adequate possibilities of success." [54]

Although this analysis was firmly rooted in the prewar environment of 1939, its generalizations would have obvious applicability in the postwar situations when he was concerned with the problems of sustaining a reasonable defense posture and of restraining the tendency toward military solutions and military thinking in both official quarters and the public psychology. In a major speech on "Not War, Not Peace" in 1948, Dulles defined the major struggle between East and West as one "to be fought with food and fuel and with creative ideas and lofty ideals." The statement was natural enough given the fact that the address was designed in part as a defense of the Marshall Plan for aid to Europe. However, he continued that while "military factors are not to be ignored . . . let the military be an instrument of national policy, not itself the maker of that policy." A further note of caution was added in his conclusion describing the task as a very difficult one of "waging peace" and manifesting that "free societies can generate forces for construction":

Much depends on other people. . . . Much also depends on us. We must plan and act on a grand scale. We must do mighty deeds such as are usually inspired only by war itself. We must do that without generating a war-like spirit or striking a military posture which will, itself, make war more likely.[55]

Having taken a very dim view of those who considered vast armament an answer to the problem of peace in 1939, Dulles nevertheless considered armament a natural consequence in a system which did not provide for peaceful change. One could not "expect armament to be placed permanently on a non-competitive basis unless we first demote force from its role of supreme arbiter of change." [56] The limitation of armaments would, in this light, generally be a reflection rather than a cause of easing tensions. But he did not "underestimate the importance of reversing present armament trends. Only thus can we avoid economic wastage and emotional aberrations which rival war itself in impairing our material and spiritual welfare." [57] After the war he was obviously more concerned with countering any return to disarmed isolation. Nevertheless, his other basic concerns remained as strong as before. His postwar statements outlining the need for military power as a deterrent also counseled that the deterrent had to be achieved without "economic wastage" and "emotional aberrations."

THE MORAL EQUIVALENT OF WAR

In approaching the subjects of power, force, revolution, and war, Dulles' position was essentially naturalistic. In the absence of adequate outlets or channels for the nonviolent diffusion of dynamic energies and of a willingness to accept and compete in changing conditions, there would be resort to violent measures or explosions of human energy. These explosions—war and revolution—were basically understood by Dulles in terms of political, economic, and socio-psychological circumstances. Whenever peaceful channels for compromise and adjustment were inadequate or nonexistent, the to-be-expected products were widespread discontentment and ultimately violence, either in the form of a revolt against a rigid system or in the form of the established power attempting to protect its position by means of repression internally or of adventures externally. The "cycle of rise and fall and the effort to resist the fall are inevitable and it can never be eliminated. The only encouraging aspect . . . is that while the cycle is inevitable, war is not a necessary part . . . but rather a by-product. There is no inherent reason why this by-product cannot be eliminated." [58] Its elimination, however, involved nothing less than peacefully channeling the recurrent "rise and fall."

In 1924 Dulles had reached the theoretical conclusion that the act of war in itself could not automatically be defined as either "evil" or "unchristian." Having arrived at this theoretical conclusion, however, he admitted that, in reality, the conduct of war would overpower any initial righteous motives or good intentions and, almost inevi ably, involved suffering disproportionate to any obtainable good. By connecting war with its concomitant "fruits," he asserted that war "if persisted in . . . may well involve the human race in self-destruction." [59] The self-destructive aspect of war became more self-evident after the spectre of nuclear holocaust appeared on the horizon: "Another world war would engulf all humanity in utter misery and make almost impossible the achievement of the good ends for which, no doubt, the combatants would profess to be fighting." [60] The tasks of the statesmen—to work for increased avenues of cooperation while carefully balancing conflicting interests and, thereby, avoiding major explosions—remained basically unchanged with the advent of the nuclear age. To Dulles one could not escape the fact that war represented the "ultimate failure of statesmanship." [61]

If civilization and war, as a way of international change, could no longer go on together, neither could conflicts of interest be eradicated. Consequently, his theory of international relations was concerned not with the idealistic aim of eliminating power struggles, but with keeping those struggles within certain bounds. Peace and security in the popular senses were not even necessary by-products of the scheme. The "end" was a constantly fluctuating balance, a delicate equilibrium which allowed for and encouraged change while simultaneously protecting the roots upon which the future would be constructed: "The achievement of a state of 'insecurity' which is adequate and not excessive is the really difficult task of authority." [62] Some years before, William James had defined this "zone of insecurity" as the area "in which all the dramatic interest lies," the "zone of formative processes, the dynamic belt of quivering uncertainty, the line where past and future meet." [63] The concept of "absolute security" as a primary end of foreign policy was, to Dulles, both wrong and impractical. Such a state of security was a chimera which "we should not waste our time and energy pursuing." [64]

He described the conditions of "peace" in various terms: (1) "a rugged art, not very different from the art of winning victory in war"; (2) "essentially a way of life," whereby political mechanisms functioned "not to impose peace but to establish channels of contact and collaboration" without which peaceful change was virtually impossible; (3) not United States isolation or United States domination, but "a condition of community, of diversity, and of change"; and (4) "the avoidance of the use of force and . . . the creation of conditions of justice." [65] "Peace" neither depended upon nor implied a prior ironing out of differences. The goal of his scheme was "peaceful coexistence." The description of the international political game as "neither peace nor war," for which phrase Dulles credited Trotsky, summarized the former's understanding and approach to international politics.

It is not known precisely what effect William James' works had on Dulles at Princeton, but the latter was very familiar with and influenced by the thoughts of the august Harvard professor. The reference to James underlines two aspects of Dulles' approach and theory. First, his view of the nature of peace coincided with James' "moral equivalent of war." Second, the popularized version of "waging peace" reflected James' conclusion that "the war against war is going to be no holiday excursion or camping party." [66] In fact, the views of both men incidentally coincided at several points. For example, James considered "martial virtues" as "absolute and permanent goods." Dulles referred to the sacrificial spirit and comradeship as two "of the finest human qualities." [67] The tragedy to both men was that these qualities appeared to come to the fore, in any considerable quantity, only for great and dramatic causes against equally great and dramatic threats. Dulles summarized the problem in the following words:

Men have never looked on peace as something that needs to be waged. . . . War has had a near monopoly of moral fervor and the determination and courage and sacrifice it produces. It is that discrepancy in favor of war which must be changed. . . . Peace, no less than war, requires idealism and self-sacrifice and a righteous and dynamic faith.[68]

The challenge of the "moral equivalent of war" was to devise means and appeals whereby these qualities would be actively directed against the common enemies of mankind—conditions of intolerance, repression, injustice, and economic want—rather than serving to cement historically accidental groupings against one another. The challenge involved a difficult problem of motivation. Could sufficient human energies be directed toward the betterment and balance of conditions and causes before they reached the breaking point? Neither Dulles nor James considered the challenge simple. When the former asserted that "waging peace" required sacrifices and risks, he was fully aware that sacrifices and risks were not the stock and trade of the established, contented, and self-satisfied peoples and nations.

James viewed the solution as "but a question of time, of skillful propagandism, and of opinion-making men seizing historic opportunities." [69] In *War, Peace and Change,* Dulles viewed the task as nothing short of fundamental, stressing that "we should not acquiesce in human nature being such that mass effort and sacrifice are largely dependent upon the ideology of conflict." [70] Ten years later, in *War or Peace,* he defined the idea of "waging peace" thusly: "While we are at peace, let us mobilize the potentialities, particularly the moral and spiritual potentialities, which we usually reserve for war. That is perhaps asking a good deal." [71]

The approach of the practitioner, compared to that of the theorist, ended on a less optimistic note. Shortly before assuming office, Dulles expressed awareness of the inherent difficulties: "I am not blind to the difficulty and risk of waging peace with positive policies. . . . It calls for patience on the part of the people and their leaders, for only long-range policies will work." [72] Patience and long-range approaches were constant educational themes in his writings from the early 1940s to 1959. But patience did not become a predominant public quality in reacting to foreign policy matters. His experience in office left little room for naive optimism. In 1957, discouraged by the propensity to "wage war" or "wage nothing" and by the reluctance to contribute to the creative processes of "waging peace," Dulles concluded: "It is a hard task and . . . a task which the peoples of the world must devote themselves to far more vigorously than they do now if we are going to succeed." [73] A "moral equivalent of war" was the focusing point for Dulles' theory and motivation.

SUMMARY BASIS FOR FOREIGN POLICY

The preceding investigation has concentrated on Dulles' experiences, actions, and the development of his thoughts on certain subjects prior to his becoming Secretary of State. The seeds sown in his early experiences left indelible marks throughout the remainder of his career. Late in his secretaryship, many of these seeds were summarized in a note setting forth the basic ingredients for the recipe of sound policy:

Sound policy cannot be derived from a priori concepts, whether moralistic, materialistic or legalistic. It must always have a wholesome infusion of the pragmatic. Our national interest requires that we relate our policies to the actual conditions of the world about us. *This means that we must understand both the realities we confront, and the limitations on our power.*[74] (Emphasis added)

Three years before taking over at Foggy Bottom, he picturesquely and sharply criticized the habit of acting and talking "as though God had appointed us to be the Committee of Admissions to the Free World and as though the qualifications for membership were to be found by our looking into a mirror." [75] Yet, as a political figure later in his career and in his role as one of the authorities, Dulles frequently utilized ideological and moral camouflage in the presentation of decisions. This type of icing has been and no doubt will remain an indispensable political implement: "Moves in practical politics must be articulated in such a way as to pay tribute to moral principles." [76] It is important to note that Dulles was well aware of the tendency to cover the political cake with ideological or moral icing. On several occasions before his secretaryship, he expressed displeasure over the fact that explanations couched in ideological terminology were given priority over interpretations in terms of interest, and he understood the camouflage process very well.[77] In 1939 he surely classified himself as one "not duped by the nation-hero, nation-villain personifications." [78] But the question later arose whether, upon his emergence as part of America's official authority, he was "seduced to some degree by the persuasiveness of his own free world ideology." [79]

CHAPTER SIX

RELIGION AND AMERICA

THE OXFORD CONFERENCE AND RELIGIOUS FORCES

The Oxford Conference on "Church, Community and State," in July of 1937, was convened not to extol the churches and Christianity, but to analyze the shortcomings of the Christian churches in modern society and, more specifically, to appraise the role of Christians in relation to the continuing problem of world peace. There was no design to outline a simple solution or panacea, and the tone of the conference had a distinct ring of the "modernist" school in Christian thought at the time:

No Christian Church has the right to preach to an age which we call secular without a contrite recognition of the shortcomings of historic Christianity, which are one cause of the disavowal by the modern age of its Christian faith.[1]

The conference as a whole and the measure of agreement at Oxford surpassed the expectations of most of the representatives. It no doubt created a feeling among the participants that forces were in motion which would revive and revitalize Christianity in terms of its relevancy to the times and the world's troubles.

Attending the conference as a representative appointed by the Universal Christian Council, Dulles experienced a limited and intellectual type of "conversion" in the sense that he departed with the impression that religion could serve as a significant social force in the process of breaking down the trappings of nationalism and the barriers of the "sovereignty system." It represented, therefore, a most effective tool in moving toward increased international cooperation. Recalling Browning's lines, shortly before the conference, he had wondered if Christianity would survive such formidable rivals as communism and fascism: "Has Christianity become a painted thing, good only to serve some silent gallery; to be forgotten when there intrudes some vital force of breath and blood?" [2] As evidenced by various statements and activities after the gathering at Oxford, his interest and belief in religion as a possible dynamic social agent had been stimulated. This was essentially a utilitarian view of religion—namely, that it should be valued in terms of social utility or social "fruits"—which continued to harmonize with Dulles' naturalistic outlook.

Following on this stimulated belief, his campaign for international cooperation and organization with American participation was geared primarily through the Federal Council of Churches and other church organizations. He became a member of the Commission to Study the Organization of the Peace under the Federal Council, and served as chairman of the committee of direction for the Commission to Study the Bases of a Just and Durable Peace. In this capacity he defined the task of the churches as preparing "the hearts and minds of Christian people for fair and objective dealing with all international situations." Fair dealing presupposed "a will to cooperate; a willingness to accept, in certain areas, a surrender or pooling of the exclusive perquisites of national sovereignty and a sharing of economic advantages; a learning of the techniques whereby men come to accord through processes other than those of military and economic warfare." [3] The religious movement throughout the country and elsewhere could "and should create the underlying conditions indispensable to the attainment of a better international order" by educating the public to be "willing that their political leaders should exercise the powers of sovereignty for ends loftier than the achievement of some immediate sectional advantage." [4] "To create the moral foundation for world order" was, to Dulles, the foremost "task of the churches." [5]

Within the context of this broad duty, he defined several specific and special, although by no means unique, responsibilities of the churches. They should, for example, serve to restore "God as the object of human veneration," which would preclude extreme nationalism or the deification of any state, class, or religion; to insist "that any human organization is a mere mechanism which enjoys no sanctity or immutability, and which cannot rightfully absorb men's spiritual allegiance"; to recreate "in man a sense of duty to fellow man"; to proclaim "eternal verities in terms such that their practical significance is made plain"; and to avoid "sponsoring specifics that necessarily must be compromises compounded out of worldly knowledge." [6] Dulles figured above all that "anybody who is truly a Christian person cannot very well be ultra-nationalistic," [7] and this was surely a prime key to effecting the "ethical solution" set forth in *War, Peace and Change.*

Church structures, like other organizations, contained an inherent tendency toward becoming static ends in themselves and this, according to Dulles, was precisely what made many churches socially irrelevant, anemic, lifeless, and in effect useless in the interwar years. The worship and righteous perpetuation of the structure— whether it be religious, political, class, or otherwise—was, as the Reverend Allen Macy Dulles had taught, a fundamental form of idolatry. The lesson was not lost on his elder son. Dulles considered the Christian religion a dynamic creed by definition:

Christianity is, above all, a dynamic and revolutionary creed. Wherever Christianity is vital, there will be tension between Christians and the political structure of the time. . . . No Christian could be true to his faith if he sought an organization dedicated to perpetuate the given scheme of things.[8]

But to function as a positive social force, he hammered on the idea that the churches had to take account of "realities." While emphasizing the power of idealism and faith in his public "secular" utterances, Dulles' habit before religious gatherings was to caution against idealism or a utopian approach to the hard world of politics:

Practical political action is not often a subject for authoritative moral judgments of universal scope. Those who act in the political field must deal with the possible, not with the ideal; they must try to get the relatively good, the lesser evil; they cannot, without frustration, reject whatever is not wholly good; they cannot be satisfied with proclaimed ends, but must deal with actual means.[9]

He found that the complaint that Christian leadership was "too prone to rely upon high motivation without regard to practical limitations" was "often valid." [10] To avoid the utopian trap, and to perform effectively as an agent in the "ethical solution," Christians should learn to "conform their daily conduct to their judgment of relative good and relative evil," to understand that Christianity was never a "substitute for factual knowledge, practical experience and tested wisdom," and always to "take account of what men are, not what the Church thinks they ought to be." [11]

Later, in the cold war context, Dulles neither altered nor reinterpreted the churches' functions in order that they might coincide more with the particular interests of the United States or the West. He believed, however, that the churches now faced the challenge of shaking the American people out of their suicidal, materialistic mood. This mood contributed to the acceptance of the "Soviet thesis of the inevitability of violent conflict" and such a thesis "Christians must reject." Also, Christians "must not imitate Soviet leadership by placing reliance on violent means." On the more positive side, "Christians must see to it that their nations demonstrate that peaceful methods can realize the goals which we all espouse." [12]

As a dynamic and progressive social force, religion could revitalize the connection between principle and practice and, in this sense, the churches were undeniably viewed as national assets and important forces in the American fabric. But, as a channel for the operation of the "ethical solution" in international relations, the churches could not be considered strictly national assets or adjuncts to American power. To undermine successfully the foundations of the traditional sovereignty system and narrow nationalism, there had to be both distance and tension between religion and the governing authorities. In *War, Peace and Change,* Dulles deprecated the "assumption by secular rulers of divine authority" primarily because religion thereby ceased "to be an effective medium for the internationalizing of the ethical solution." Conversely, he was highly critical of churches which allowed themselves to become servants or tools of the state and state authorities or which identified "righteousness with . . . national cause." [13]

During the period from the 1937 Oxford Conference through his active participation in church organizations in the 1940s, Dulles' naturalistic and utilitarian view of religion remained intact without tending toward a parochial Christian viewpoint. The emphasis on religion as a part of the "ethical solution" was neither exclusively Christian nor an attempt to "Christianize" the world. If his program for peaceful change, as outlined in 1924 at the Presbyterian General Assembly, did not proceed from a peculiarly Christian premise, he considered it all the better.[14] Twenty years later he reminded Christian audiences that they do not "alone possess the qualities of mind and soul upon which solution depends." [15] Although "Christians believe that the moral law has been most perfectly revealed by Jesus Christ," it had to be recognized that "the moral, *or natural,* law is revealed through other religions, and can be comprehended by all men, so that it is a force far more universal than any particular religion." [16] (Emphasis added.) At mid-century, the "ethical solution" still operated by applying the principles "of the natural and moral law which have wider acceptance than Christianity." [17] If anything, his association with church circles probably exerted a broadening or liberalizing effect on Dulles' already established outlook.

On the other hand, his participation in religious circles unquestionably tended to accentuate the typically Christian aspects of his naturalistic approach. Moreover, his discovery of the churches as a potentially powerful force for change and international cooperation was constantly reinforced by the Christian movement in the country during the 1940s and 1950s. Church membership steadily and sometimes startlingly increased and, by 1947, church leaders had surpassed government officials and businessmen in the polls concerning who could do the most good for the United States.[18] Throughout all his activities, however, there appeared no increased interest in church doctrine or creed as such. Also, he rarely, if ever, peddled religion in private and was apparently disinclined even to mention such subjects.[19] Most importantly, there emerged no changes in substance from his earlier normative and operational ethics. In sum, it was clearly "his Utilitarian ethic which brought about his acceptance of Christianity and not vice versa." [20]

MORAL LAW AND MORAL POWER

This fact was further evidenced by the apparent meaning behind the religious references and terminology—moral law, righteous faith, and spiritual or moral power—which became an integral part of Dulles' speeches and writings during this period, which reappeared in various forms throughout the remainder of his career, and which had been conspicuously absent in all his earlier writings and speeches. Prior to the introduction of the concept of moral law, he was inclined to define the "natural law" as "biological, economic, and political" laws which produced "disagreeable results" whenever man acted contrary to their operation.[21] These natural laws tended to justify selfish and established interests unless tempered by reason, which meant that real self interest could "be served only if it be enlightened self-interest." [22] Enlightenment, as defined in Dulles' earlier works, demanded a value system and an operational ethic with the general welfare or "the greatest good for the greatest number" at its apex.

During the interwar years, however, he found little to suggest that enlightened self-interest generally prevailed over strictly self-centered motivation and actions in the lives of either individuals or, particularly, nations. To counter the centripetal, selfish forces in men and nations, Dulles began to identify and emphasize "moral law" as the "natural law" in the early 1940s. This moral law undergirded the world "no less than physical law," and was "relevant to the corporate life of men and the ordering of human society." If mankind was "to escape chaos and recurrent war, social and political institutions must be brought into conformity with this moral order." [23] Conversely, the ills which afflicted society were "fundamentally due to non-conformity with a moral order, the laws of which are as imperative and as inexorable as are those that order our physical world." [24]

Contrary to some idealistic overtones in statements such as above, and while maintaining that moral law could "serve mightily to direct the conduct of nations into ways consonant with peace," Dulles postulated no absolute standards of right and wrong. Moral law was "variously expressed and understood" and its implications did "not seem to all to be the same." [25] Although a degree of general agreement about " 'right' and 'wrong' in their broad outlines" was possible, the moral law was "never immediately and universally effective." [26] It did "not automatically or of itself bring order and well being into human affairs"; nor did it "do away with the need for thorough knowledge, technical skill and a resolute will." [27] Such qualifications, coupled with the idea that common moral standards could *evolve* out of the intercourse in the General Assembly and between nations generally,[28] suggest that Dulles was basically positivistic in his conceptions of international morality.

While proclaiming the universality of a "moral law" which could be ignored only at the risk of failure, Dulles presented no dogma concerning the content of this law except that it demanded a genuine concern for others by recognizing "the obligation of man to fellowman, and the obligation to make sacrifices for the social welfare." [29] It was actions and beliefs contrary to these principles which were bound to fail, whether it was the United States preserving a practice of self-centered sovereignty and pursuing selfish economic policies, or the Axis powers' perverse concept of racial and national superiority and its "evil fruit," or communism's denial of moral principle and its profession that "the end justifies any means." Broadly speaking, the discipline of the moral law served as a lubricant which made a relatively stable and free society of nations and individuals possible. In virtually all his writings, there surfaced no clear distinction between Dulles' concept of moral law and his earlier concept of enlightened self-interest. The demand for conformity to the former was equivalent to his previous pleas for the latter or for more reason, self-restraint, and cooperation in human and international affairs.

Within the domestic context, the concept of moral law was utilized by Dulles to support the idea of international responsibility and cooperation, to accentuate the moral, psychological, and politi-

cal aspects of the Soviet challenge, and to counter tendencies toward
militaristic and materialistic approaches to the cold war. Within the
international context, however, the concepts of moral law and
moral power rather naturally assumed roles as instruments in the
cold war competition and were utilized by Dulles as such. Classify-
ing himself as a "believer in the power of moral principle," he proclaimed that "more effective use of moral power" was needed.[30] For
his part, he openly admitted taking such a course:

What has given Soviet Communism its tremendous influence over men
everywhere in the world? It is the moral slogans which they have adopted
and expressed. . . . They are nothing but the same slogans—the same beliefs . . . for which America has stood. . . . The leaders of the Soviet
Communist Party have been smart enough to see that the way to get influence in the world is to sponsor great moral principles.[31]

There was, needless to say, "some hypocrisy" on all sides. But the
fact that it seemed "necessary to present a moral facade" was, to
Dulles, "proof that the moral law is a recognized power." [32] He was,
according to one student of the period, a "complex man who understood very well that the espousal of moral principles could be a useful weapon—even an essential weapon—in a struggle which took
place on a number of levels, including the moral one, simultaneously." [33]

Although Dulles surely hoped to strengthen America's political
and propaganda position by invoking moral and spiritual forces,
moral law and moral power were not, in the final analysis, crusading instruments wielded in the cold war confrontation between East
and West. First, the mere espousal of moral principles was not sufficient since actions contrary to the general welfare could not for long
be protected or hidden by any amount of moralistic camouflage.
Second, "moral law" and "moral power" simply did not represent a
crusading spirit, but commanded patience, endurance, and hope.
Dulles' belief in the ultimate victory of moral law was not dissimilar
to William James' faith in the final triumph of those "invisible mo-
lecular moral forces that work from individual to individual," the
"eternal forces of truth which always work in the individual and
immediately unsuccessful way." [34] According to Dulles, "moral
power arises from the most humble to the most mighty. It works

inexorably, even though slowly. It will not suit the impatient. But it can achieve solid results." [35] His postwar writings on the nature of the communist challenge emphasized the need for a steady approach in an historical competition.

THE UNITED STATES AND MORAL POWER

Dulles' "righteous faith" was similarly little more than the term he applied to acceptance of the dictates of enlightened self-interest. He believed that no nation is great or strong "unless its people are imbued with a faith." To survive the course over the long haul, this had to "be a *righteous* faith . . . compatible with the welfare and the dignity of others." [36] Following the rule that power had to be tempered by a broad concern for others, in 1949, he could imagine "nothing . . . more dangerous and destructive than to have the present great material power of the United States rattling around in the world detached from the guiding direction of a righteous faith." [37] Yet, in some important respects, this was precisely how he viewed the situation. His emphasis and, as it were, "preaching" on moral law, moral power, moral determination, and righteous faith clearly related to his views regarding the shortage of these resources in the United States and the importance of these resources to the political, economic, psychological, and spiritual aspects of the cold war competition.

One of the primary challenges for the United States, as defined by Dulles in 1943, was how to regain its "soul" or righteous faith which it had lost in the process of evolving from a wealthy to a materialistic society, a society promoting material prosperity as the "all-sufficient end" and, thereby, being "drawn away from long-range creative effort." [38] It was conceivable that the "work of creation" for America had come to an end, but he thought not and it "need not be so." [39] Two years later, however, he asserted that the Americans presented "the spectacle of a people who" had "lost confidence in themselves." [40] Several months before the outbreak of war in Korea in 1950, he still found the national mood basically "defensive and materialistic," seeking security "through military and economic power." This mood, if persisted in, would spell failure for the American experiment. Moreover, making security "an end in itself" or "a principal goal" was "the surest way to lose security." [41]

Militaristic and materialistic tendencies were suicidal according to two of Dulles' articles of faith: The dynamic prevails over the static, and nonmaterial forces (for example, moral and intellectual) were more powerful historical forces than those that were merely material (for example, military). He sincerely believed that the American heritage was by no means inexhaustible and that its institutions and social fabric could not possibly survive unless constantly replenished by the democratic faith which had given them birth. As set forth in *War, Peace and Change* and highlighted in the postwar environment, he perceived no inherent righteousness or moral power in the American position and cause which would of its own accord prevail.

Having combatted isolationism and the return to tilling America's hedged gardens after World War I, Dulles was not sanguine about the prospects for a similar reaction after the second conflict. Those who live comfortably, in 1950, did "not want the ugly aspects of life to intrude upon the pleasant tenor of their ways" and therefore "practice isolation and non-recognition." [42] It was these natural practices which had led him to the conclusion in 1946 that it was healthy for the American people to become aware of the real differences with the Soviet Union—differences which were prudently downplayed or understated during the war—for awareness "*may* shock" the country "into doing what needs to be done." [43] Privately, however, he agreed with Walter Lippmann that there was a great question as to whether "the American people can see the truth and not react foolishly."

Dulles had pondered this problem before publishing his 1946 articles describing the nature of the power struggle presented by the Soviet Union.[44] His statements in the post-World War II years reflected both his concern that Americans not underact or once again retreat from international responsibilities and his awareness of the danger of American overreaction. One of the main problems, as he saw it, was how to achieve that "resolution needed for large scale action" without, in the process, generating "such hates and fears as may themselves lead to war." [45]

In his 1946 articles on the nature of the Soviet challenge, after reiterating his counsel that "successful programs are those which are constructive and creative in their own right" and not merely against something such as communism, Dulles perceived some auspicious beginnings in the Western response:

We can demonstrate that our political and religious faith is a curative thing, able to heal the sores in our body politic.

There is encouraging evidence that free societies have not lost the capacity to advance the general welfare. . . . The abuses against which Soviet propaganda tilts are much the ghosts of a dead past. Political imperialism and cold-blooded *laissez-faire* economics are on their way out.[46]

The United States had done much to "humanize its order" as religious groups and some political leaders moved to eradicate "the blight of bigotry." Although progress was "slow," it was nonetheless "real." [47] But progress was not rapid enough for his liking from an international point of view and, a year later, he maintained that the "Russian appeal" was still helped by the American "assumption of racial superiority, particularly as regards negroes." [48] There continued to persist "many great blots and many deficiencies" in the United States and elsewhere in the so-called Free World. These "inequalities of many kinds, economic, social, political," weakened the position and appeal of the United States and the West.[49]

Dulles strongly believed in a vital link and broad interface between the internal or domestic life of a nation and its foreign policies. Success or failure in American foreign policy would, to a considerable extent, depend upon the recognition and resolution of the social, political, and economic problems in the United States. The solution of one's own ills required a connection between belief and practice. Agreeing with and often quoting Arnold Toynbee's observation that "practice unsupported by belief is a wasting asset," Dulles found a dangerous disconnection between America's ideology and American realities. The country had become conventional and ritualistic much like the churches had become before World War II: "But communists too profess to believe in 'democracy' and they

use the word *even more glibly than we do*. . . . While we have been
brought up to say that we believe in democracy, our statement has
become ritualistic." [50] (Emphasis added.) The challenge to freedom
derived "its greatest power from the weaknesses which have developed in our society of freedom and which have caused a widespread
lack of faith in it." [51]

American foreign relations were, by Dulles' account in 1946, pervaded by this "lack of faith," a loss of the American "sense of purpose and . . . capacity to inspire." [52] This was a cause for serious
concern:

It ought to dismay us to discover that the Western democracies, after ten
centuries of unchallenged economic and military supremacy in the world,
have so slight a spiritual hold on the masses of mankind that they eagerly
listen to those who have not even shown that they can establish a good society at home. What is happening is not a measure of Soviet communist
capacity. That is still an unproved factor. What is happening is a measure of Western inadequacy.[53]

He considered the reversal of this trend as no mean task. First, the
past motives of the West had "been sufficiently selfish so that," in
the postwar period, other races and cultures were naturally "fearful
lest the West take advantage of this crisis and use its superior economic and military power to regain world mastery." This fear could
be overcome only if the United States practiced the equality and fellowship, which it preached, in its dealings with other nations.[54] Second, it would be "impossible to prevent communism from
penetrating into and breeding in societies where there" existed "repression, misery and injustice on a large scale." [55] Constructive domestic and foreign policy programs were required to get at the
problems and, Dulles declared in 1947, the time had "come when
we shall have to put up or shut up." [56]

Much of Dulles' emphasis on moral power, righteous faith, sense
of mission, and spiritual and psychological offensives derived from a
conscious effort to revive what can perhaps best be termed "faith in
the American experiment" as a dynamic, growing, and changing experiment. What he had described as one of the most fundamental
and difficult problems for American foreign policy before the war
continued to concern him after the war: "The United States is . . .

a *status quo* nation." [57] From Versailles through the interwar years, he had consistently cast his appeals in terms of national or self-interests, supporting his positions with what he considered to be the political, economic, social, and security aspects of the case at hand. Also, he had consistently deprecated appeals to man's emotional side while recognizing that such appeals were often more potent. Religious references, ideological overtones, moral appeals, and any crusading aspects were noticeably absent from his writings and speeches during this long period. His uses of such terms, during and after the war, did not result mainly from an unconscious political habit of identifying particular positions with universal principles. The new terminology and appeals were largely products of his conclusion that a static, affluent, self-satisfied nation needed to be jarred from artless complacency into acceptance of some international realities and responsibilities. Thus, in 1948, he maintained that "there are times and conditions when the most effective appeal is to self-interest" and other times "when the most effective appeal *may be* to men's sacrificial spirit." [58] (Emphasis added.)

Without an inherent dynamism in its own right, Dulles was convinced that the long-range prospect for American foreign policy was gloomy. He was equally convinced that probably "the most fatal" of the several defects in the American approach was, as described by one student of power politics, "the lack of moral determination." [59] Late in his secretaryship, in 1957, Dulles was still concerned that neither the Americans nor other peoples were meeting the challenges of the cold war effectively on the political, economic, social, psychological, and spiritual levels while becoming too wrapped up in material security and military defense. Without more vigorous actions on the nonmilitary and nonmaterial fronts, success would not be in the offing.[60] If the great question of his time and of his own phrasing in 1950 was "whether . . . Western civilization had become so old and decadent that it was bound to pass away, giving place to the younger, dynamic, and barbarian society born out of the unholy union of Marx's communism and Russia's imperialism," [61] without compromising his democratic beliefs and beliefs in America, he was never really quite sure how the scales would ultimately tip.

⎯⎯⎯⎯⎯

CHAPTER SEVEN

INTERPRETING THE COLD WAR

Several of Dulles' statements, during the partisan years 1949–1953, imparted the image that he had to some degree, after all, become a victim of the nation-villain complex which he had so severely censured earlier. On a few occasions he spoke of the "black plague of Soviet Communism" and referred to this phenomenon as having "slimy, octopus-like tenacles." [1] Besides such descriptions, there were his habitual references to "atheistic, materialistic communism," his not infrequent description of the "faith" as "evil," and a rare reference to that "which we hate." [2]

Also, his perspective appears to have been distorted when he asserted that the United States was "not interested in opinions which derive from this atheistic view of our world." [3] Had he forgotten his dictum that actions reveal purposes more than words when he maintained that "the actual purposes of Soviet Communism are to be judged in the light of its official creed"? [4] Was the conflict in Korea and elsewhere at mid-century really explained away somewhat simplistically in terms of an international or world-wide, monolithic communist plot? "It is all part of a single pattern . . . of violence planned and plotted for 25 years and finally brought to a consummation of fighting and disorder in the whole vast area extending from Korea . . . into Indochina, Malaya, the Philippines . . . Tibet and the borders of Burma, India and Pakistan." [5]

Such items as the "octopus" simile, "hating" Soviet communism, and disinterest in Soviet opinions were not only overstatements but irresponsible statements, particularly in the sense that they aimed at his audiences to such an extent that they no longer accurately reflected his own thinking much less reality. His criticisms of the moral position of dialectical materialism and dogmatic atheism were neither necessarily inaccurate nor unexpected in light of the incompatibility of individualist democracy with the Stalinist ideal. Moreover, the phrase was habitually used not so much in the fashion of a man seduced by his own free world ideology, but rather in the manner of propaganda or competition on the ideological level. In most of his statements regarding the difference between words and deeds in the cold war, the latter always spoke louder to Dulles than the former. On the other hand, he was not averse to describing Soviet actions in terms of its creed or a dogmatic bent toward expansionism when it could be used to buttress the will of the West or for propaganda purposes.

Most importantly, Dulles was not, in his own mind, inclined to simplify the problems of the cold war even though he would, on occasion, simplify problems and explanations for public consumption. When the temperature of the cold war rose substantially, during the Korean War, stopping Russian imperialism was to be no easy matter: "We must, in all honesty, admit that we are up against one of the most complicated tasks the world has even known." [6] He found that there persisted, at times, "a tendency to underestimate the complexities and difficulties of the problem" which was "by no means a simple problem." [7] With no simple problems, there could be no black and white answers, and his insight into the ways of both American foreign policy and the American public was reflected when he chose "to present the problem in terms of what, to the American temperament, is its most baffling aspect, namely, indecisiveness." [8] These insights were, if anything, sharpened during his years at the foreign policy helm. In a major 1957 article, he advised that United States power and policy were "but one significant factor in the world" which, in "combination with other factors" was "able to influence importantly the course of events. *But we cannot deal in absolutes. This, to many Americans, is a source of worriment.*" [9] (Emphasis added.)

It is, in fact, doubtful that Dulles ever really denied his past or that his perceptions began to suffer from nation-villain or diabolical enemy images. There exists but a handful of such exaggerated and somewhat irresponsible remarks, all of which were apparently uttered during the politically partisan years from 1949–1953, a most difficult period for Dulles as an internationally minded, liberal Republican. Apart from the international considerations discussed later, such as possible miscalculation and self-deception on the part of the Soviet Union, there were domestic reasons for establishing an unquestionable anticommunist image. Dulles needed to dissociate himself from the Democrats and their policies in order to retain a position for his views in the Republican party. More importantly, avid "anticommunism" and "right-wingism," in one form or another, spread through both parties and many segments of American society to the extent that, at mid-century, a firm anticommunist image was requisite to function as an effective political agent. Political necessity and political appeals best explain some of Dulles' hyperbole and some of his statements which would have been better left unsaid. His political predicaments, partisan requirements, and the politician's affinity for catchy phrases aside, his reactions toward and estimation of the Soviet challenge actually mirrored his early pragmatic realism.

FROM COOPERATION TO THE COLD WAR

There was an element of surprise behind both the official and to a greater degree, because of insufficient preparation for possible Soviet obstructions, the public reaction to Soviet foreign policy and its so-called spearhead of communist ideology after the combined allied effort against the Axis powers. For his part, throughout the war and at least until the middle of 1946, Dulles believed that while there would certainly be complications and differences with this wartime ally, the Soviets would still tend more toward some form of cooperation or coexistence, however coolish, than toward confrontation.

In 1941, shortly before the United States entered World War II, Dulles wrote of America's dilemma as "quasi-partners of Russia." Unless there were some sort of internal change in the Soviet Union, the United States would "be faced with a very serious problem, as a highly armed Russia facing a disarmed and socially chaotic Europe would be a grave menace." [10] Two years later, in the course of discussing the possible sources of future disharmony among the allies, he prognosticated that the "greatest problems will arise with the Soviet Union." At this time he also recognized the need for some decisions relating to Eastern Europe which would probably contradict national aspirations in the area. His preference was that the forces of narrow nationalism and shortsighted sovereignty, which had their sway in the Balkans during and after the Versailles peace conferences, not be loosed again prematurely. But he asserted that the agreements or decisions relating to Eastern Europe would not be generally acceptable if viewed as permanent solutions rather than as temporary, necessary adjustments. [11] This assertion contained the seed to his later ideas on "peaceful liberation."

Dulles' recognition of future difficulties in American-Soviet postwar relations apparently diminished neither his belief that the Soviets would prefer some form of cooperative relationship nor his hopes that a workable relationship could be achieved. His statements concerning the possibility of Soviet obstruction were utilized to emphasize the idea that means had to be established whereby the conflict of interests would be mitigated and kept within reasonable bounds. If "only the ignorant or the sentimentalists" could believe that the Allies would "automatically remain friends," only the cynic would maintain that any cooperation and relatively stable coexistence were impossible. [12] Dulles found himself in neither camp. Since some natural antagonism between the two countries was likely to develop, he concluded that efforts should be concentrated on decreasing the intensity of any encounter. His reasoning near the end of the war ran as follows:

I do not say, and did not say, that we *ought* to trust the Soviet Union or that they *ought* to trust us. There are doubtless reasons on both sides for mistrust. A task of the future will be to clear up such mistrust. [13]

The situation in 1945 called for "intensified and carefully planned effort" in clearing up the mutual distrust. [14]

Two important realities influenced Dulles' thinking at this time.

He recognized the "special" interest of the Soviet Union in keeping the powder keg of Eastern Europe dry and friendly. Also, one could not ignore the fact that the Soviet's forces in effect controlled the power balance in the Balkans. In January of 1945, somewhat as though he were preparing the American people for the decisions which soon emerged from the Yalta Conference, he mentioned that territorial propinquity creates special relations and, in rejecting noncooperation, the United States "must not go to the other extreme of assuming that all nations have an equal interest everywhere." In this same vein, the United States "must not be dogmatic" in seeking cooperation, but rather "conciliatory and understanding of the ideals and vital needs of others" for American "ideals and sense of vital interest are not the only ones in the world." [15]

His reaction to the Yalta Conference, in February of 1945, dealt not as much with mistakes or shortcomings in the decisions taken as with the necessary give-and-take in the situation and the need for continued consultations:

The actual decisions taken at the Crimea Conference are not yet fully reported and to the extent that they are reported will not satisfy everyone. But more important than the substance of the decisions is the procedure by which they were reached. For if the procedure of consultation is kept going, mistakes of the past can be remedied in the future.[16]

In fact, it was encouraging to him that the United States government realized it "should get down into the arena and battle for its ideals 'even under conditions such that partial and temporary defeat is inevitable.' " [17]

Dulles was concerned with, but not hasty to judge, some of the decisions taken at Yalta. Since Russia would take part of Poland and Poland part of Germany, the decisions did not "stand up very well" against the principle, proclaimed in the 1941 Atlantic Charter, that peoples everywhere have the right of self-determination. However, he pointed out that the Atlantic Charter itself probably was too static, idealistic, and "not perfect preachment." Therefore, one could expect some "constant and unnecessary embarrassment" until it was "remolded into a better statement of our long-range objectives." One could likewise expect that "decisions taken in the heat of war" would necessarily fall short of high principles and long-range goals.[18] It was also shortly after Yalta that he recalled that American expansion had generally "been through war or the threat of war" and wondered what the rebirth and dynamism of Russia would mean for matters in Poland. There were, to be sure, no easy principles of solution to the Polish boundary question.[19]

Dulles highlighted what he considered the two most encouraging signs at Yalta: First, the United States would not remain aloof and withdrawn as it had done after World War I; and second, Russia was willing to meet, discuss, and consult on postwar problems. The fact of collaboration was more important to him than the details or deals which fell short of United States desires. He drew upon the example of the Yalta Conference as evidence of the need for an active and effective international organization to work out the inevitable problems and differences.

Half a decade later, when it became popular in the United States to condemn Yalta as a disastrous mistake at best and a "sell out" bordering on treason at worst, Dulles did not really turn his back on his earlier judgments. Although he would agree that some mistakes had been made, particularly regarding the Far East, he was strongly against the United States formally denouncing the agreements and opposed such a move both in the formulation of the 1952 Republican campaign platform and in his dealing with Congress during the first years of his secretaryship. In 1953 he found it "quite natural" that those in charge of American foreign policy during Yalta assumed, as he admittedly had assumed, that an era of cooperation was on hand and that the Soviet Union would not threaten this cooperation.[20] The fact was, at the time of Yalta, that "we still had the hope that the Russians would cooperate with us." Additionally, "since the Russians were already in occupation of the Balkans, all we could hope for was their promise that the peoples of the Eastern European countries could have the governments of their own choosing." [21]

The evidence of an era of cooperation, which Dulles found in early 1945, was not long in continuing. Invited by Secretary of State Byrnes to attend the London Council of Foreign Ministers in late

1945, Dulles concluded that United States rejection of Soviet demands signaled the end of appeasement and the beginning of a "no
appeasement" policy.[22] Reporting to the nation upon his return, he
advised that the London Conference, far from creating difficulties,
"merely revealed difficulties of long standing" which had been obscured by the war. It was "healthier that we now know the facts." [23]

After the 1945 meeting of the British, French, Russian, and
American ministers, Dulles questioned more seriously Soviet policy
and motives, familiarized himself with Stalin's *Problems of Lenin-
ism,* pondered the problems for American foreign policy and of the
action-reaction syndrome. He did not quickly discard his earlier
judgment that the postwar era would be characterized by at least a
tendency more toward cooperation, with some inevitable conflicting
interests, than toward confrontation, with intermittent cooperative
measures when both side's interests so demanded. In the spring of
1946 he thought there would be ways to stem the drift apart and,
though by no means easy, to strengthen unity and fellowship for the
future.[24] By the summer, however, he decided it best to reveal that
the Soviet actions and plans "were incompatible with the American
hope to restore normal relations with the Soviet Union and establish a peaceful, secure world." [25] His *Life* articles appeared in June,
describing what he conceived as the difficulties and fundamental
disagreements between the United States and the Soviet Union. As
mentioned previously, he took this step with some hesitancy, pon-
dering whether the American people would react "foolishly" or exercise "self-restraint." On balance he figured that if the United
States did not exercise self-restraint, "then we are not entitled to
freedom, and, in fact, cannot keep it long." [26]

It was with such an idea that he accepted the challenges of the
cold war. The difficulties with the Soviet Union seemed to be exceeding those which he had anticipated. In 1947 "the most difficult
international problem" was that of establishing "working relations
with the Soviet Union." [27] Throughout this period of re-examina-
tion and questioning, he arrived at several principles and conclusions regarding the nature of the conflict and the parts of the two
main players. The operational emphasis and effectiveness of some of
these principles changed over the years with changing circum-

stances. Some were also affirmed or arrived at later than others, and appeared to overtake certain aspects of earlier positions. (These facts are reflected in the ordering of the ensuing discussion.) Other assumptions, such as his concern regarding competition on the psychological, moral, and ideological levels, have been reviewed already; and still others, including his belief in allied cooperation and collective security, are reserved for the examination of his secretaryship. But his early principles regarding the nature of the conflict *per se* remained generally intact for the remainder of his career, although some were admittedly not very visible during the partisan years of the early 1950s and during certain issues of his term as Secretary of State.

Principle 1. The Soviet challenge is neither unnatural nor demonical. On several occasions and perhaps culminating in *War or Peace* (1950), Dulles defined what he considered to be the worldwide quest of Soviet foreign policy. Although sometimes, particularly in the partisan years of 1950–1953, condemning the "evil" methods of the communist "faith," and the aggressive, world-wide scope of Soviet foreign policy, for the main part he did not assign "evil" or perverse motives to Soviet policy. Soviet leaders sought "world-wide acceptance of their system" partly "because of a nationalistic desire to enlarge their domain and protect it," and also because of an honest belief that individual "freedom is a basic cause of human discord and inefficiency" and should be taken away to "increase men's material welfare" and "promote world-wide peace and security." [28] But he thought the principal reason for the Soviet program resulted from a combination of fear and national security: "Soviet leaders feel compelled to seek a world-wide extension of their system as the only way to prevent their labors at home from being undone." Since the Soviet system could "not be kept purged of freedoms if elsewhere those freedoms are rife," the Soviets not unnaturally felt "it necessary to try to bring others to join in the purge." [29]

Soviet foreign policy also had an inherent dynamism and attraction for others by its revolutionary nature: "Change is the law of life and those who seek change have the exhilaration of seeming to move with an irresistible current of history." The revolutionary dy-

namism of Soviet foreign policy attracted "those who think that radical change is needed to make the world better . . . those who think
they can gain personal advantage from overturning the existing
order," and "the many who are discontented with their lot." [30]

Dulles believed that the problem of the cold war was compounded by its ideological twist. The United States had to contend
not only with "nationalistic goals" which reflected "the fears and
the ambitions of the Czars," but also with the "far-flung goals" of
the Soviet Communist party. He was inclined in 1948 to think that
Russia's traditional, nationalist ambitions had, in large part, already been achieved in Eastern Europe and the Far East, though
probably not in the Middle East. Those national goals which remained unattained were a cause for concern, but presented no excessive or insuperable difficulties.[31] The problem, as he saw it, was
that the Russian government was "to an extent a tool of the Communist Party." While the line between ideologically rooted and na-
tionally rooted ambitions was not always clear, he believed the
party introduced a doctrinal world-wide scope and ambitions wider
and not always in harmony with the strictly national interests of the
Soviet Union.[32]

If the Russian political personality was a product of both histori-
cal-national circumstances and ideology, the extent to which these
forces were either contending with or merely reinforcing each other
within the Soviet system was not obvious to Dulles. He believed
that most of the Soviet leaders were realistic, shrewd politicians
whose foreign policy was, ultimately, derived from national interests
and security. But this belief did not warrant the assumption that
they were motivated purely by what the United States considered
traditional national considerations. Inclined toward the conclusion
that the Russian leaders used "ideology as an instrument of power"
and were not themselves "the instruments of ideology," Dulles recognized that this distinction was "not an easy one to make with confidence" since "most people are apt to believe in what advances
their own power and position." [33] In spite of any lingering doubts,
he did not accept the idea that the Russian rulers were "true believers," "idealists," or "instruments of ideology." The Russian leadership was, above all, sober, shrewd, and realistic, and, one might

add, the more formidable opponents because of it. Dulles did not
fail to take note of the expertise and diplomatic skill of such men as
Molotov and Vyshinsky.

Dulles, like the Sovietologist George Kennan, concluded that the
Soviet leaders would avoid military adventures and not endanger
national security, or, as it were, the citadel of communism, for the
chimera of the universalization of the communist creed. In fact, he
maintained that the chosen course for Soviet foreign policy was
"neither war nor peace," a course which he recognized as difficult
for the American people to understand.[34] Soviet foreign policy, in
the final analysis, was chiefly concerned with national security,
largely reflecting the historical ambitions of Russia, and then with
extending its power or influence and communist ideology.

Although Dulles sometimes exaggerated the "demonry" of the Soviet threat and its coercive methods after the communist success in
China and the outbreak of war in Korea in 1950, either for propaganda purposes internationally or to rally support for international
programs at home, he hardly presented distorted pictures prior to
these events in the Far East, particularly when speaking outside the
domestic context:

It is not contended that Soviet communism is wholly bad. . . . Certainly,
there was so much imperfection under the Czars that any change . . .
could readily work some improvement. Also, Soviet leaders do not rely
wholly or continuously on means of violence and there have been some
good, peaceful developments. Also, the very fact that there is a Soviet
challenge has had a stimulating effect upon the Western democracies
which, for their own good, needed the spur of competition.[35]

He described himself as having "no sense of personal animosity
whatever as regards Soviet foreign policy" and as trying "to treat it
realistically. . . . Their bid for world leadership is not unnatural,
and if kept within bounds could be a stimulating thing for the
whole world." [36]

*Principle 2. If war is avoided, the Soviet challenge could exert a
salutary effect on the status quo Western powers.* Before the spring
of 1946, in the days when Dulles had thought there could well be a
degree of friendly collaboration between Russia and the United
States, or at least keen but nonviolent competition between the sys-

tems, he expressed a type of convergence theory in rather rosy terms, probably rosier than usual because of the war going on: "There will be friendly competition which will lead one country to adopt the better features of the other's system with the result that the difference between the two will constantly diminish. . . . It is good for the world to have that kind of friendly yet keen competition to find the best forms of society." [37]

Late in 1946, convinced that any friendly collaboration was a long way off and that the keen competition tended toward confrontation, a long-term balance of power theory appeared in his analyses of the Soviet challenge. Accordingly, unsettlements "will go on until a new equilibrium is established . . . between the faith and institutions of Soviet Communism and the faith and institutions of the Western world." This *equilibrium* would "be established by the weight of facts. It must first be determined how much constructive influence each society can exert in the world. That will take time." [38] An important key in this viewpoint was Dulles' emphasis upon a "new equilibrium" process as contrasted to a zero sum game approach, and the fact that this emphasis reappeared throughout the 1940s.

Much of his analysis of the situation, as he admitted on several occasions, was likened to Arnold Toynbee's "challenge and response" view of history and civilizations. The Soviet challenge could prove to be a useful event if kept within peaceful bounds and if it led "to the invigoration of the worthy features of our historic faith and an elimination of the unworthy features which have accumulated largely because the Western white democracies have enjoyed, perhaps over-long, unchallenged leadership in the world." [39] It became clear to him, in 1950–1951, that the Russian and American definitions of "peaceful bounds" differed substantially. What was earlier described as the "Soviet challenge" now became more the "Soviet threat" or the "Soviet menace." Even then, this outside threat put the United States "much more on our metal to do the right thing than we might do otherwise." [40]

Principle 3. Since the primary challenge of the cold war is not military, but political, economic, psychological, and spiritual, the United States or Western democracies could not hope to succeed without putting their own houses and foreign policies in order. As detailed in the discussion of "The United States and Moral Power," Dulles was convinced that an effective response to the Soviet challenge required the manifestation of one's own ability to promote the general welfare, to advance human understanding, to right injustices, to eradicate inequalities, and to demonstrate that freedom can not only inspire but also produce "good works." His "sense of mission" and "righteous faith" were essentially the same as George Kennan's "greater sense of national purpose" or what another observer described as a "power of attraction" without which American power becomes "a dynamo without transmission lines." [41]

Dulles constantly returned to or "preached" on this subject, not only because the inherent dynamism of Soviet foreign policy operated more effectively in areas where there existed inequalities and discontentment but also because of his belief that the United States was, as before, inherently a wealthy and satisfied *status quo* power. Moreover, there was a general tendency to react defensively:

Whenever a system is challenged, there is a tendency to rally to support the system "as is." The world becomes divided between those who would maintain the *status quo* and those who would change the *status quo*. . . . Those who would sustain the *status quo* inevitably are defeated. The result may not be the particular changes desired by the dynamic powers, but equally, it does not maintain the status which their opponents sought to preserve. So it is that in the face of the Soviet challenge we must not ally to the defense of our institutions just as they are, but we must seek even more ardently to make them better than they now are.[42]

Principle 4. Military power is necessary insurance in containing Russian imperialism or Soviet expansionism, but this power has to be carefully bought and balanced against other interests.

Principle 5. War with the Soviet Union can and must be avoided without compromise of basic convictions. Dulles considered it a crucial "mistake to assume that" the "most serious menace" came "from the Russian State and its army and that military preparedness" constituted sufficient response to the Soviet challenge. But the possibility of Russian attack, and the likely miscalculation on the part of the Soviets if the United States were to disarm, necessitated organizing to meet such a possibility—that is, an effective military power in being.[43]

The primary purpose of military power was, therefore, to serve notice beforehand that aggression would not succeed and, thereby, diminish the likelihood of military adventures being undertaken. In this sense, as noted in Chapter V, Dulles considered the rapid demobilization after the war as both dangerous and signaling the old American longing for nonparticipation and isolationism. He considered the tendencies toward military solutions—either giving military considerations precedence over political-economic considerations or encouraging an Atomic Maginot Line posture and mentality—as equally dangerous. At the same time that the United States should organize to deter and, if necessary, to meet power, Dulles was confident that the Soviet leaders did not want war and that even if war were the communists' preferred method, which it was not, the Soviet leadership "could not wholly disregard the sentiment of the Russian people." [44]

The maintenance of a sufficient military establishment and the implied will to use it if necessary entailed, as Dulles recognized, a host of domestic and international balancing problems. At home, care had to be taken to avoid encouraging a Fortress America mentality and actually altering the traditional American character: "We must make certain that our military establishment is not bought at the price of impairing the moral and educational development of our youth." [45] To regain moral influence abroad, the "United States must make it clear, clear beyond a doubt, that it has no thought of using economic or military might to impose on others its particular way of life." Unless the United States made such clear, it would "be shunned and dangerously isolated." [46]

This prescription applied just as forcefully, if not more so, to the Soviet Union. Shortly after the war, he maintained that it was "necessary to make clear to the Soviet Union that the United States" did "not intend to use violence . . . to crush out the Soviet experiment." [47] Even if it were possible to crush this experiment by military and economic coercion, it constituted a completely absurd consideration not only on strictly humanitarian grounds but also on practical grounds. Annihilation of one of the "great faiths" would merely be "a display of our own might and make a martyr of the Soviet Union." [48] Dulles was unalterably opposed to the so-called preventive war concept as going against all reason, humanity, and all American traditions: "War has become so pregnant with evil that no sane person would invoke it as a means of achieving good ends." [49] When, during the Korean War, a certain explosive frustration among some Americans sought outlet in a get it over with quickly and bigly approach, he counseled that Americans "must have patience and steadiness of will, even when no sure solution has yet emerged. . . . It is hard to go on walking with . . . no safe end in sight. But to plunge, merely to find an end, is no acceptable solution." [50]

Principle 6. Relatively peaceful coexistence, not the eradication of communism, constitutes the primary goal of American foreign policy. When asked, in 1946, if democracy and communism could exist together, Dulles expressed "no doubt that we can get along in a world that is partly communistic," but questioned whether the Soviet "leaders think that their society can exist" alongside democracies.[51] He was convinced that "strong, conflicting and dynamic faiths can exist side by side in peace" if violence were renounced as a means of imposing one's beliefs and if channels were opened for nonviolent change.[52]

Having long accepted the principle of the inevitability of conflicting interests, continuing tensions were neither unnatural nor avoidable. Just as the United States should not give up its "right to preach in the world," neither could it expect the Soviet Union "to give up the right to propagate communist beliefs in the world." [53] Although the free societies "may not like the Soviet experiment in state socialism and its dynamic world-wide program," they "must recognize that a free world is a world of difference and that any society has a right to experiment and compete." [54] Accepting struggle, challenge, and response as part of a normal situation, Dulles could sincerely counsel that peace did not depend upon or imply the forcible ironing out of differences, but "should permit people to respond in their own distinctive ways to their own distinctive needs and aspirations and, for example, to practice socialism, private enterprise, or even communism if they desire." [55] Aggressively disposed forces opposing "religious freedom and democracy . . . always have been, and always will be . . . in the world," and peace did not depend upon the total eradication of these forces.[56]

Dulles never conceived of unlimited goals in the diplomatic sense. The goal of his diplomacy was diversity, a mode of coexistence encompassing even irreconcilable beliefs, a pattern for competition and conflicts of interests where coercion, violence, and terrorism were renounced or, at least, avoided as counterproductive. Actually, the renunciation of violence was all that was hoped for in the situation.[57] In the same vein as George Kennan, Dulles concluded that foreign policy should be concerned with balances of power and establishing an equilibrium between East and West whereby the balance would ultimately be determined by how much constructive influence each system could exert in the world.

Principle 7. The proper exercise of United States power could contribute to change both in the Soviet system and in its international objectives. Although this principle inhered in Dulles' previously mentioned convergence theory, it was not really clarified until a few years later. According to this thesis, the successful containment of Soviet expansionist tendencies combined with the free societies' setting their own domestic houses and foreign policies in order "would stimulate an evolution inside the Soviet Union toward more individual freedom and economic betterment and toward national objectives." These changes demanded not an "overthrow of the Soviet Government, but a gradual evolution in a better direction." [58]

He believed in a vital link between domestic situations and foreign policy in the Soviet Union much as he did with regard to the United States. If the Soviet leaders could not easily point to "foreign devils" or "outside threats," they would necessarily have to concern themselves more with the resolution of problems at home. Likewise, containment meant that military adventure could not be utilized to distract attention from domestic ills or to consolidate personal power, whereas the demonstration of the "vigor and worth" of free societies could, over the long run, erode the Soviet's thesis of "outside threats" and, internationally speaking, lead them to alter their methods and techniques even if just "as a matter of expediency." [59] But, in a rather ironic sense, if the Soviets proved capable of adjusting to circumstances and effectively adopting the more respectable diplomatic, political, and economic methods of dealing with the outside world, this manifestation of the viability of the Soviet experiment would present an even more poignant challenge to the free societies to do "what is right."

An explicit skepticism regarding the actual power of the United States to bring the Soviets voluntarily to alter their foreign program entered Dulles' thoughts. He concluded that the United States had to act on the assumption that its actions could contribute to change within the Soviet Union, even though there was no assurance that alterations would take place, because failure to act on such a premise would mean defeat by default or a "drift into surrender or war." [60] Recognizing that the ability of the United States to apply pressures was very limited, he maintained that effective pressure for change, in the final analysis, had to come from within the Soviet Union. Even then there existed no guarantee that the rulers would be greatly influenced by the subjective feelings of the populace; but, on the other hand, neither could they simply ignore these feelings. Thus, there could be "some signs that the Soviet rulers" were "bending to some of the human desires of their people," but this did not necessarily mean that the leaders "had been converted." [61]

He agreed with Kennan that, because of the nature of the Soviet power structure, the important alterations would be those which took place within the ruling circles and, perhaps because of the nature of power itself, change in the attitudes of the Soviet leadership was a long-term affair. But the Soviet structure did not represent, in the words of Kennan, "a completed inhuman robot . . . that has overcome all the internal contradictions and can defy with impunity the laws of change and evolution." [62] Dulles knew and acted upon the assumption that the Soviet structure was "not impervious to the erosion of time and circumstance." [63] Although he was always wary of self-advertised changes as mere strategems and watched for the weight of actions rather than words, his belief in Soviet change was nonetheless real as evidenced by a 1956 statement on the possibility of arms control:

The time must come when the Soviet rulers, *if only as a matter of expediency* and in deference to what should be incessant demands of world opinion, will be prepared to take steps to assure that the new power of modern weapons is in fact subjected to the will of the community. It may seem that this prospect is remote. *But when we consider the many startling changes which from time to time have occurred within the Soviet Union,* we need not regard this particular prospect as wholly visionary.[64] (Emphasis added.)

As in his earlier philosophy and approach, the inevitability of change was a fundamental principle: "Nothing is 'inevitable' with respect to Communism, except that it too is bound to change." [65] Practically speaking, Dulles' scheme or goal of his diplomacy required no so-called moral regeneration of the "enemy" but acceptance of nonviolent coexistence. The overall strategy for the West was, therefore, to create the circumstances whereby the Soviets would find it in their own interest to accept less tension or more normal relations. To Dulles, this meant combining "military, economic and moral assets to meet Soviet strength," for this course would lead in time—"one year, five years, ten years, twenty years. I do not know"—to some alterations in the Soviet attitude.[66]

Principle 8. The cold war is an historical challenge to which there exists no panaceas or simple solutions. This principle has, of course, either been implied or explicit in some of the other guidelines which he followed in interpreting the nature of the cold war's conflict of forces and national players. His basic approach to politics and international relations, as noted in previous chapters, was undergirded by an acceptance of struggle and conflicts of interest as inextricably woven into the human situation. The intensity of these conflicts could be mitigated by reason; also reason could reveal that some conflicts were really unnecessary. But the fact of disagreement and differing interests could not be avoided. Although Dulles sometimes held out the idea that the *basic* conflict between the two cold war protagonists would disappear if only the communists changed their nature and accepted the right of other "faiths" to exist,[67] it is fair to assume, in the light of most of his statements and background, that this meant only the intensity of the conflict would subside, not that conflicts of interest would become nonexistent. If "these huge concentrations" were "in conflict because each reflects differing aims, aspirations, and social, political, and economic philosophies," [68] one could expect the persistence of divergent national-historical aims and aspirations even if the "philosophies" were happily to converge.

Dulles was not a protagonist for reckless change, but approached the problems of the cold war in terms of the long-run and with far more patience than was sometimes reflected in some of his more partisan statements. His proposal, in 1951, that the United States move quickly in the Far East while there remained contacts on the mainland and friends on Formosa, was qualified with the idea that there was needed "long vision and endurance." One could not undo overnight what had "been accomplished by the best brains and skills of the Soviet Communist Party . . . over a span of 30 years."

In the campaign year of 1952, he stated that nothing happened "terribly fast in Asia" and what had been constructed in thirty years could not, practically speaking, be undone in the next thirty years.[69] Moreover, the gradual breaking away of China from Soviet domination was a more immediate goal of American foreign policy than any dissolution of communism in China. His major 1952 campaign statement suggested that there surely existed "a vast range of possible China policies between the one *extreme* of liquidating the loyal representation . . . on Formosa and the other *extreme* of now escorting them to the military reconquest of the mainland." [70] Also, during the 1952 campaign, patience and long-term planning were woven into his doctrine of "peaceful liberation" whether applied to the Far East or Eastern Europe. The international situation in 1953 did "not hold out the prospect of any quick change." [71]

Principle 9. The possibility of successfully negotiating differences with the Soviets is limited in the near term and any agreements should have self-enforcing provisions. A long-standing principle in Dulles' approach to international politics had been that treaties or other agreements would be effective only if they reflected reality, rather than wishful thinking, and a genuine convergence of interests between the parties. He was a careful and cautious negotiator by nature, but these qualities seemed to come more to the fore within the context of the cold war than before.

While always keeping the traditional lines of diplomacy open for negotiation, the fact is that Dulles—like Acheson, Kennan, and Kissinger—held out no large hope for successful negotiation, in the short-term, of outstanding issues between East and West. The series of ministerial level meetings, between 1945 and 1948, convinced most of the American foreign policy elite that the foreseeable future would be characterized more by a test of wills and confrontation rather than serious negotiations and open cooperation. What Dulles distrusted was not the process of negotiations, but dealing in generalizations which would be interpreted by the West as Russia's abandonment of its objectives and strategy. It was in 1950 "hardly reasonable to expect such abandonment or deviation at a time when past adherence has brought great victories." [72]

A skepticism regarding successful negotiation of outstanding issues was expressed in Dulles' opposition to "summitry," in his position or briefing papers for the 1955 Big Four meeting in Geneva—describing the aims of the United States at the conference and the likelihood of achieving them, the Soviet aims at the conference and the likelihood of their achieving them, and the positions of Great Britain and France on each of the issues [73]—and in his reactions to the Foreign Ministers Conference following the summit gathering. Nearing the end of the conference in November, he questioned whether the United States should wind up on a note of optimism and some progress or on a note of pessimism with the Soviets unwilling to follow through on their summit commitments. To some extent, the tone would be determined by the wishes of the British and French, but he thought that the two notes could be combined. [74] At the conclusion of the conference, he did indeed combine the two by expressing that major progress had not been achieved because of the Soviet attitude but some progress had been made and some barriers lowered. Most important to understanding his position on negotiations, he believed "that the process thus begun cannot easily be reversed. Perhaps it will proceed *more surely through a living process than by dependence upon negotiation.*" [75] (Emphasis added.)

Dulles' statements on the limited prospects for negotiation were normally followed and balanced, however, by advice that to say "the possibilities of negotiation are limited" was "not to say 'non-existent'." He did not wish "to be misunderstood as opposing any and all agreements with the Russians" for some could "usefully be made" when they registered an actual confluence of interests or existing fact.[76] To say that the basic issues between Russia and the United States could not be compromised did not mean that nothing could be negotiated or that many useful agreements did not already exist.[77] These slightly more positive aspects of his skeptical statements on negotiations served not only to notify the Soviet Union and others that the United States was willing to negotiate in self-enforcing terms, but also to counter the tendency in the United States to reject all intercourse and even renounce past agreements with the communists. When approaching the 1954 Geneva Conference on Indochina, to offset the arguments of those who viewed commerce with the communists as "sell out," he warned that the United States must not abandon the tools of diplomacy out of fear or any other reason.[78]

Recognizing this American impulse against intercourse and negotiations with communists, it is fair to question why Dulles emphasized the limited play for negotiations. Even while stressing that the United States should carefully avoid trading any concessions for promises, he was aware that this was essentially "a negative policy" and "not of itself sufficient." [79] The answer to his expressed skepticism and appearance of inflexibility dated back to the post-Versailles period. The emphasis in 1950 on his unalterable opposition "to any deals with Soviet leaders which we would interpret as meaning 'peace in our time' when there is no peace" [80] derived less from his view that the Soviets had little reason to negotiate what appeared to them to be a successful program and approach than from the haunting fear of a recrudescent American isolationism. He was in effect aiming to counter the tendency in democratic, satisfied nations, particularly the United States, to accept generalities for substance so they could retire unto themselves and remain indifferent —at least until the force of circumstance brought them forth, not unusually in a quest for "total victory." While World War II and the Korean conflict were proof to Dulles that these attitudes could not be afforded, there was no guarantee that the lessons had been learned: "The longing of our people for peace is so intense that there is danger of accepting illusion for reality." [81]

Dulles' aversion to "summitry" and his preference for the less spectacular, traditional methods of diplomacy derived from this same concern. Several years before the summit issue of 1955, he maintained that the United States should not "delude" itself "into thinking that the basic differences are of a kind that can be resolved by Truman and Stalin chatting . . . over a cup of tea." [82] His skepticism on the question of "summitry" was a product of his belief that a grand meeting of the heads of state could have serious international and domestic consequences if it created unreal expectations or promoted a false euphoria. Internationally, he believed the West could be seduced into prematurely dropping its guard. Domestically, "unfortunate though it be," he not unreasonably believed programs such as mutual security and assistance "would be decimated" in Congress without the Soviet threat.[83]

Principle 10. The greatest danger of war comes from Soviet miscalculation abetted by United States action and/or inaction. After the defeat of Germany and Japan, as after all tremendous efforts, Dulles found that "none of us likes to face up to a new major international problem" or "to admit of danger coming from a nation which made an outstanding contribution to . . . victory." But, if the United States were to disarm and rely upon the proclaimed good ends of the Soviets or once again stay out of international affairs, "these are attitudes which contribute to war. They make possible the miscalculation out of which major wars arise." [84] Although he had himself seriously misjudged the dangers of the German threat in the late 1930's, he became convinced that the courses leading to World War I and World War II might have been altered had the United States expressed its determination earlier rather than later, and had it assumed its international responsibilities in the interwar years.

American postwar policy to Dulles had to ply a path between the extremes of inaction or default and the unthinkable prospect of "preventive war." Both these extremes, perhaps particularly the former, gave rise to miscalculation. Convinced that neither side wanted war, he concluded that "the greatest danger of war is from possible Soviet miscalculation." [85] Whether or not the Soviets miscalculated would depend largely on the United States. Since "war is neither useful nor inevitable . . . whether or not it comes depends most of all on the quality of United States leadership. . . . The old alibis have been swept away and if, today, the world passes into the blackness of another war, our leadership cannot escape a large measure of responsibility." [86]

Also in 1949 Dulles maintained that subject to accident or stupidity, the year would possibly and probably bring a "gradual lessening of tension" with the Soviet Union. This would occur primarily because "their rough methods may be reaching the end of their usefulness" and "because the internal problems of the Communist states require urgently more attention." [87] On the other hand, he saw no evidence of a Russian change of heart and predicted that they would "try to go elsewhere where they can get more results for their efforts, perhaps in the Far East." [88]

The outbreak of war in Korea, one year later, confirmed Dulles' suspicion that the greatest danger of war resided in Soviet miscalculation abetted by American actions. Basing its decision almost entirely on military considerations and the judgments of the military principals that the United States could not stretch to defend Korea, the Truman Administration had at worst "written off" Korea without accepting the full implications of what this policy meant, or at best failed to re-examine the established policy of "writing off" Korea. Secretary Acheson's delineation of an American defense perimeter which excluded South Korea, in January of 1950, was retrospectively untimely and imprudent to the extent that it strengthened Soviet calculations that the United States was not really interested in defending the area. To be sure, however, the speech was not the precipitating or even a seriously consequential factor contributing to Soviet and North Korean plans. As later recalled by General Ridgway, Acheson "was merely voicing an already accepted United States policy. Korea had always been outside our defense perimeter and we had written her off several times in the history of our dealings with her." [89] Dulles did not fail to read a message regarding miscalculation: "Communist leaders may understandably have doubted our devotion to the principles we verbally espouse

when we have seemed so negligent of the means to defend them."
The task now was "to correct that miscalculation before the consequences are irreparable" and that was "a matter of deeds, not words
alone." [90]

Despite his understanding of how American actions would have
contributed to Soviet miscalculation, the Korean War marked a
turning point in some of Dulles' thinking about the Soviets. Up to
this time he had believed, as did American foreign policy experts
generally, that the Soviets would "limit themselves to violence of an
internal character such as strikes, sabotages, and possibly guerrilla
and civil warfare" and preferred to avoid open warfare.[91] Korea did
not mean that the Russians were bent either on war or war by
proxy as the means for advancing their interests. The conflict
meant, however, that the Soviet Union was "willing to take increased risks of war." [92] If the world did nothing and allowed the
attack to succeed, one could expect aggression in other areas of the
world when it was to Soviet advantage. This, in its broadest form,
was the "domino theory."

To avoid or at least to minimize the possibility of other Korean-
type conflicts, Dulles concluded that the aggressors should be
stopped at the thirty-eighth parallel—not "rolled back" in the name
of Korean unification—and measures should be taken to strengthen
the free world against the possibility of sudden, armed attack: "If
we do that, we can close the most dangerous remaining loophole for
war." [93] Closing this loophole, as will be noted in Chapter X, did
not imply an American policeman in every corner of the world, but
did imply contributions to build effective local forces. The whole
affair made Dulles more suspicious of Soviet aggressiveness and willingness to take risks and, in this sense, had a definite hardening effect upon his "line."

There was another aspect, as discussed earlier, to this concern for
miscalculation: The United States had to communicate effectively
that it had no intention of crushing the Soviet experiment or undertaking so-called preventive war. This aspect was highlighted in
1949 in his attitude toward the proposed North Atlantic Treaty Organization. Emphasizing the idea that the defensive nature of the
organization had to be communicated to the Soviet Union, he real-

ized that effective communication was no simple task. Not to mention the Soviet ideological prejudice, the Russians inherited age-old suspicions of the West. In this light, Dulles asserted that peace could not be won merely by being right or by an inner consciousness of good intentions, for intentions had to be successfully communicated.[94]

This was not a new problem for him. While supporting the North Atlantic Treaty Organization idea in 1949, he recalled part of a statement prepared by the Federal Council of Churches' Commission on a Just and Durable Peace, which he had chaired, over two years earlier. This statement contained a similar sensitivity to the problems of communication and possible miscalculation, although in the different context of October 1946 or before the cold war tension lines had become so taut:

The United States should not seek military bases so close to the Soviet Union as to carry an offensive threat that is disproportionate to defensive value. . . . It would, indeed, involve a high tribute to Soviet leaders to assume that, under these circumstances, they would exercise more self-control than would our people under comparable circumstances, as, for example, if the Soviet Union had military arrangements with a country at our border.[95]

The problem of miscalculation, whether Soviet self-deception abetted by American action or American self-deception abetted by Soviet action, was a consistent Dullesian theme from 1946 through his secretaryship. His deep concern with this problem meant he was unwilling to relax the tension lines beyond a certain point, at least until one was quite sure of the probable outcome of any easement. He was unquestionably "inflexible" on the subject of symbolic measures. As another observer noted in the mid-1960s, "symbolic measures designed to reduce tensions, but having nothing to do with the substance of our conflicting concerns, may prove to be worse than useless, for they lead to self-deception and miscalculation."[96] These problems were equally vital in the early 1950s, if not far more vital in view of the relative instability of the West and the comparative absence of substantive dialogue between East and West. Much of Dulles' concentration on and, at times, exaggeration of the East-West encounter constituted a means of buttressing the will of the West, communication to the Soviet Union of United

States interests and the will to defend them, and a necessary tool in the process of obtaining congressional approval for various international programs such as mutual security and economic assistance.

Dulles, of course, accepted some relaxation in the tension between East and West and the temperature of the cold war had dropped during the later years of his secretaryship. He supported measures, such as cultural and other exchanges, which he thought would contribute to a lowering of the barriers and easing of the tension. Although this lowering of the temperature took place more through a "living process" than the process of negotiation, the communication between the two sides was nonetheless real. All in all, however, his secretaryship would be characterized by his conviction that an appearance of inflexibility was a better bargain than either miscalculation or self-deception. If the choice were between a tendency toward overstatement or toward understatement of American determination, he would normally select the former.

Principle 11. In dealing with the Soviets one has to consider their interests and predicaments. The need to express one's interests or determination beforehand in order to avoid war logically led to the idea that risks sometimes had to be taken to avoid war. Although Dulles neither coined nor liked the phrase "brinkmanship" or "going to the brink," such an idea inevitably followed from his concern with miscalculation and self-deception. Mere mention of "a brink" in the nuclear age, particularly the comparatively "nervous nuclear age" of the 1950s, naturally was a source of worriment. For example, considering the events leading to World War I, unraveling themselves with some sort of fate of their own, how could one determine the edge beyond which one slipped into a position of no return. This problem was also not new to Dulles. As early as *War, Peace and Change* in 1939, he had manifested a keen insight into the nature and dangers of "the brink." [97]

This insight did not escape him during the cold war as evidenced by his understanding, temperament, and attitude toward the Soviet Union during the 1948 Berlin blockade. After the Soviets announced their intention to blockade Berlin, cutting the city off from traffic and supply from the West, Secretary of State Marshall consulted with Dulles on a personal basis. One of the latter's main concerns was the need to understand the difficulties of the Soviet leaders. He expressed "some doubts about our note sent to Moscow," for it "seemed . . . that Soviet prestige was deeply engaged, particularly in view of set-backs in [the] Finland and Holland elections, the Tito quarrel and unrest in Czechoslovakia, and that they could hardly afford a public diplomatic back-down about Berlin." Therefore, "there was danger that diplomatic argument might force them to crystallize publicly a stronger position than they had yet taken and one which would preclude their backing down in fact at the working level." He "observed that even their reply note had referred to their obstructive measures as 'temporary.' " [98]

After this meeting with Secretary Marshall and Under Secretary of State Robert Lovett, Dulles met with a high level State Department working group which included Charles Bohlen, George Kennan, Dean Rusk, and a few other State officials. Dulles reiterated his view that "the Soviet leaders did not want war but . . . their prestige was so engaged that they could not retreat unless we eased it. . . . It was not merely a question of national prestige, but of the individual standing of members of the Politburo for whom failure in policy . . . was almost literally fatal." The first step, Dulles thought, was to "quickly let the Soviet realize the seriousness of our intentions." A diplomatic note should inform the Soviets that the United States was prepared to negotiate at Berlin about Berlin or other German questions, as suggested by the Soviets, and that supply trucks would continue unless stopped by force. He would not, however, ask for Soviet agreement "to lift the blockade or concede our rights prior to negotiating." These steps had to be taken before Soviet "prestige was further committed by legal positions formulated at a high level and publicly announced."

But Dulles also believed these steps had to be taken carefully. The United States would not, for example, demand a formal lifting of the blockade before negotiations. Moreover, after clearance with Great Britain and France and "prior to any formal diplomatic note, we should . . . tell our intentions *informally* to the Soviet . . . so that they would react soberly and not hastily and, if they wanted, have an opportunity *themselves* to announce first that the 'repairs' had been effected." This informal exchange "should be had, if possible, with Stalin rather than Molotov." [99]

Dulles did not want to exhaust the negotiating time and possibilities before either the United States or the Soviet Union had made its "determination clear by acts." [100] When informed a few days later that trucks had been stopped by physical force, he replied that he "assumed that this was the case, but that the whole problem of the diplomatic discussion was to create new conditions which would enable the Soviet without loss of prestige to end the 'temporary difficulties'." He "had no idea of trying to shoot our way through, and . . . was not willing to envisage the possibility of hostilities on account of the Berlin situation." In this vein, Dulles also thought that an appeal to the United Nations would be premature and dangerous. It would "force the Soviets to take an official position more uncompromising than any yet taken and close the 'way of retreat,' so far kept open, before efforts have been exhausted to bring them to use it." In addition, it seemed the most the United Nations could do would be to give some moral sanction to the use of force which was not what the United States wanted: "We want peace, not a legal basis for war." [101]

As far as Dulles' later dealings with the Soviet Union as Secretary of State, one still looks through a glass darkly to find his personal reactions and estimations of such problems. It appears, however, that his insight into the nature of the so-called brink and his respect for the predicaments of the Soviet leaders—to avoid placing them in an untenable corner—was perhaps recognized by one of his harshest and by no means unbiased critics. According to *Khrushchev Remembers,* "Dulles knew how far he could push us, and he never pushed . . . too far." Khrushchev reportedly told his friends in 1959 that the American Secretary "had never stepped over that brink . . . and for that reason alone we should lament his passing." [102]

DULLES AND KENNAN

Dulles' many postwar pronouncements on the nature of the Soviet challenge, beginning in 1946, were apparently designed both to bring home the realities of international difficulties and the need for the United States to bear some responsibility in the international arena and to counter tendencies toward hysterical anti-Sovietism in the United States. The general tone of his many articles and speeches was one of a man disinclined to exaggerate either the challenge itself or the motivation behind Soviet actions. For example, when asked to comment on the Department of State's draft report on German and Austrian settlement problems in 1948, he replied to Secretary Marshall that the report seemed "to be weakened by an apparent lack of objectivity. Instead of merely reporting the facts of what took place, it frequently uses adjectives to characterize unfavorably Soviet action and favorably United States action. Also it attributes motives to Soviet action rather than letting the action speak for itself." [103] Although his own reports were not always without some exaggerations, whether for political effect or whatever, the overall tone of his works was one of describing a rather classical and not unexpected power struggle with an important ideological twist.

Dulles' various principles regarding his interpretations of the cold war remained essentially intact over the years. But they did not, of course, remain immutable, particularly as to emphasis and tone. The "Soviet challenge" of the mid-1940s became the "Soviet threat" or the "Soviet menace" a few years later, and he became much less inclined to remind his audiences after mid-century that this phenomenon had at least the constructive influence of jolting the West out of a certain, selfish complacence. His more understanding approach of the early postwar period was clearly supplanted by a more partisan approach at mid-century. As noted early in this chapter, this led to some exaggerated statements and definitely imparted the image of a man seduced, to some extent, by his own preaching of the free world's cause.

On the other hand, the changes in tone and emphasis can more accurately be explained and understood in terms of both the international and domestic situation. (Interestingly, there also appeared a real contrast between Acheson's views of 1945–1946 and his positions in 1947–1952.) [104] Some inflexibility had, to Dulles, always seemed a better bargain than miscalculation, but this point and the problems of applying containment in Asia were driven home more forcefully by the Korean conflict. Also, as he moved from a compar-

atively "apolitical" approach under the Federal Council of
Churches to a more "political" approach with the Republican
party, some changes in presentational style could be expected.
When promoted from "a" spokesman to "the" spokesman on international affairs for the United States, both political considerations
and the nature and demands of authority itself would impinge
upon the content and presentation of his positions.

After examining Kennan's and Dulles' respective positions toward
the Soviet Union, summitry, coalition diplomacy, and the United
Nations, one observer has concluded that "the queerest thing about
the world of George Kennan is its similarity to that of John Foster
Dulles." The fact is that the two men's views were much alike "once
all the Dullesian make-up is washed off." [105] This does not mean
that both statesmen had a similar style and agreed always on policy
tactics, for such was not the case. Nor does it imply that style in diplomacy is unimportant. But the differences in style probably
stemmed more from the fact that Kennan and Dulles often played
disparate roles.

Kennan also proposed a vigorous policy, but was never really confronted with the problem of rallying public and congressional support.
As a career Foreign Service Officer, he was comparatively insulated
from the dilemma of political limitations and considerations. Much
like Dulles, he proclaimed that United States foreign policy should
be a manifestation of the "inner development of our civilization."
But, as another student of American foreign policy observed, "the
problem is not only to lay the course, but to survive and master the
course on the way." [106] Kennan twice resigned from positions in the
State Department largely because of political complications. Upon
leaving his ambassadorship in Yugoslavia, he concluded that "Congress has jealous and narrow ways" and he would not have accepted
the appointment if he "had known . . . how little value Congress
would assign to my own judgment." [107]

Whatever the "ways" of Congress, Dulles had to cope with and
consider them in the formulation of policy. To be sure, the Congress he encountered at mid-century was as much, if not more, over-
bearing in its views than the one Kennan encountered a decade
later. Inheriting a dual role of statesman and politician, the Ameri-

can Secretary of State operates under constant pressure for daily decisions and policy formulation, plus the need to explain and garner
support for decisions. Rightly or wrongly, the option of "packing
one's bags" generally and particularly because of hardships with
Congress is not, in the American system, considered a very effective
course for a Secretary of State. In spite of his yen for long-range
planning, Dulles was soon to discover that the daily demands effectually and unfortunately shoved such exercises onto the back-
burner. On yet another level, how could he implement his belief
that foreign aid should be granted on a five-year basis when powerful members of the Cabinet team, not to mention the prevailing
powers in Congress, opposed such a move? Dulles' foreign policy
moves and, equally, the way he presented them cannot be understood without a view of him as "political man."

CHAPTER EIGHT

POLITICAL ADJUSTMENT
AT MID-CENTURY

Before assuming office in 1953, Dulles had served the United States, the Democrats, and the Republicans. His close association with the policies and personalities of the Truman Administration placed him in an awkward position in the early 1950s. He had to dissociate himself politically from one of his past masters in order to retain a position of influence within his own party. More than any other factors, political necessity and acceptability accounted for the typical overstatement during election seasons at mid-century.

Surprisingly, however, one of the most enduring images of Dulles stems from the period between 1951 and 1954 and, particularly, from the national campaign of 1952. This image has not only discolored analyses of his career both before and during his secretaryship, but continues to lead a life of its own abstracted from the political realities and environment. Before delving into some of the problems of Dulles' secretaryship and diplomacy, a review of his parts in the political drama is in order.

During the national campaign of 1944, Dulles had acted as a principal adviser in Dewey's extremely mild campaign for the presidency. It was during this campaign and the development of the Republican foreign policy plank that the former's close and continuing association with Senator Vandenberg began. The unusual moderation of the 1944 election resulted primarily from the fact that the nation was at war. There was also a recognized need for bipartisan cooperation on such projects as the United Nations. By 1948, however, there existed no obviously impelling reasons to conduct a "soft" campaign. But Dewey and his advisers—Elliott Bell, McGeorge Bundy, Dulles, and others—with the polls increasingly in Dewey's favor, decided not to disturb the placid surface of bipartisanship in foreign affairs. Senator Vandenberg was, according to Dulles, "particularly anxious to avoid anything in the nature of attack." Although Dulles considered the Senator "a little too dispassionate," there was no question that "there must not be any 'break' between him [Vandenberg] and Dewey." [1] In many respects, the 1948 campaign was similar to the previous gentlemen's debate of 1944.

The Truman Administration made available special cable arrangements between Dewey and Dulles, as the latter was attending the meetings of the United Nations General Assembly in Paris. Dulles conscientiously abided by his proclaimed principles of bipartisanship. Ernest Gross, working with Dulles in the 1948 General Assembly, later recalled that the prospective Secretary of State "conducted himself under those somewhat trying circumstances with objectivity." It appeared "almost as if he were prepared to lean over backwards to avoid any imputation of partisan advantage, of anything in the nature of tactical position taking, that might have a bearing upon the campaign." Another colleague, Robert D. Murphy, observed that he "might as well have been a career Foreign Service Officer." [2] Comparing the 1948 campaign to the usual "uninhibited flamboyance of American campaign behavior," it has been noted that the "exclusion of foreign affairs seemed so complete as to indicate nothing less than a major change in the conduct of presidential campaigns." [3]

Truman's surprise victory in 1948 had many effects besides that of demoralizing the Republican party which, for the first time in almost twenty years, had seriously anticipated once again moving into the White House and taking hold of the reins of power. The decision "not to rock the boat" resulted in increasing charges of "metooism" against the Dewey camp, and many rank-in-file members of the party concluded that the nominee should have "slugged it out." Dewey and the so-called me-tooism philosophy became anathema to various elements in the Republican party, most noticeably to the conservatives. The more extreme forms of dissatisfaction and disillusionment, in both parties, represented the inchoate stages of "McCarthyism." Most important, Senator Taft and other Republican leaders, including the moderates, began seriously to wonder if the party had virtually become a type of permanent opposition which had seen the last of the White House. As one of Dewey's advisers recorded, it appeared as though the Republicans would "never elect a President again." [4]

The defeat for the Republicans in 1948, combined with the Truman Administration's lack of sufficient strategic, bipartisan, and public planning for its China policy and the repercussions of this oversight, also moved Senator Taft "in most unfortunate ways. It seemed even to some of his friends and admirers that he began, if unconsciously, to adopt the notion that almost *any* way to defeat or discredit the Truman plans was acceptable. There was, in the intellectual sense, a blood-in-the-nostrils approach, and no mistake about it." [5] Prior to the 1952 campaign, all indicators pointed to a return to at least the normal, if not more than the normal, flamboyancy of American presidential contests.

A year after Dewey's second defeat, Dulles was supporting Truman's policy toward the North Atlantic Treaty Organization against a dozen or so fellow Republicans in the Senate, including Senator Taft, while the President campaigned against Dulles in the New York senatorial contest. Senator Vandenberg had encouraged Dulles to run for the Senate in 1949, reportedly to strengthen the "internationalist" position of the Republican party. Three years later, President Truman remarked that Dulles had refused an ambassadorship to Japan on the grounds that he felt it necessary to remain in the country and help prevent the Republican party's becoming "isolationist." Although the Republican foreign policy adviser naturally denied the remarks attributed to him by the President over nationwide television, the Taft forces undeniably occupied a position of strength by 1952.

On September 4, 1951, Senator Henry Cabot Lodge visited General Eisenhower at his SHAPE headquarters in Paris to encourage the General to run for the presidency: "The Republican party, Cabot said, must now seek to nominate one who, supporting basic Republican convictions . . . could be elected and achieve at least a partial reversal of the trend toward centralization in government, irresponsible spending, and catering to pressure groups, *and at the same time avoid the fatal errors of isolationism.*" [6] (Emphasis added.) The General had already received other visitors bringing with them the theme that he should run for the presidency, but it was Lodge's exhortations which weighed heavily and marked a "turning point" in Eisenhower's thinking toward the proposition. [7]

In viewing Dulles' activities during this period, attention must be focused upon such factors as his own political adjustment at mid-century and Republican in-fighting. Referring to the 1949 campaign between Dulles and Lehman for a senate seat from New York, the then vice-chairman of the Republican State Committee noted that many New York Republicans thought the party had "gone very liberal" with Dulles. [8] Although incomplete, the following list illustrates the awkwardness of his position in the party at least in terms of why he was frequently no "friend" of the Old Guard and why he was anathematized by more extreme elements on the Right. Dulles was intimately associated with the foreign policies and personalities of the Truman Administration. He had association with, stood by for some time, and refused really to condemn Alger Hiss. His closest party relationship was with Thomas Dewey and the liberal Easterners who, it was claimed, brought the party twice to defeat. He was, furthermore, consistently representative of the internationalist school. He had, for example, supported the inclusion of a human rights statement in the Japanese Peace Treaty, and supported the Genocide Convention and the United Nations Declaration of Human Rights. He had advocated a limited war in Korea conducted only for the preservation of South Korea's integrity and not for the unification of the country. Lastly, for over three years, Dulles had offered trenchant criticism of the military influence and military thinking in foreign affairs.

When the more extreme Right found itself still dispossessed of power in the late 1950s and early 1960s, supposedly "cheated" by and disillusioned with the Eisenhower Administration, the attacks upon Dulles became more intense and even more absurd.[9] While the electoral success of Eisenhower in 1952 tended to overshadow the conflict between the diverse power centers in the Republican party, an appreciation of this encounter is necessary to an understanding of Dulles' struggle for power and a position of influence for his views.

In 1949, Dulles had openly opposed Senator Taft on the question of the North Atlantic Treaty Organization. Moreover, while Dulles had high regard for Taft as a politician, the former's views toward international affairs and American involvement varied considerably by any measure from the views of the conservative Senator from Ohio. Since Taft was probably the most powerful individual in the party by 1952, some fence-mending appeared in order. Mutual respect, developed over a period of years and stemming back to Dulles' law school days in Washington, could prevent an unpleasant dispute between him and Mr. Republican. But there was no guarantee that the Senator could control his followers, and he was naturally not at all inclined to weaken his own position of strength. The prospective Secretary of State's ability to sow unity, especially in light of his support for the candidacy of General Eisenhower, was reflected in Taft's announcement of June 2, 1952: "It is reassuring to find that Mr. Dulles' *present* position is so close to my own." [10] (Emphasis added.) However, no Republican could easily ignore other parts of Taft's June statement:

First of all, in the Republican campaign of 1952 there must be no hesitation about attacking the foreign policy of Mr. Truman and Mr. Acheson. That policy from 1944 to 1952 has been the most disastrous period in the entire history of American policy.

Some Republicans would avoid mention of the subject in the campaign and they criticize me because I am not being sufficiently bipartisan.[11]

Was not Dulles one of the principal advocates and architects of the bipartisan approach? In 1950 he wrote:

There have been sharp differences of opinion as to the wisdom of this practice of bipartisanship which has grown up during the five years since August 1944.

There is a question as to its wisdom from the standpoint of the nation, and also from the standpoint of the Republican Party.

As to its wisdom from the standpoint of the country, I have no doubts.

It has, in my opinion, made an indispensable contribution at a critical period. In the area where there has been this kind of bipartisanship, the Administration has been able to proceed with confidence. . . . In that way we have avoided the spectacle of a nation sharply divided at a time when our own peace and safety and the safety of friendly peoples were dependent upon presenting a united and resolute front to potential enemies.[12]

After praising the practice of bipartisanship during the campaigns of 1944 and 1948, Dulles recognized that there had always been powerful elements within the Republican party which opposed bipartisanship as a matter of principle, and still other members of the party were beginning to consider bipartisanship a political mistake. Indeed, he realized that bipartisanship was "equally problematic and beset with political difficulties" from the Democratic viewpoint as a party in power was not naturally inclined to share credit with the opposition. Recognizing that bipartisanship in foreign policy had a precarious future, in *War or Peace* Dulles concluded with an unqualified recommendation that the trend away from interparty cooperation be reversed.[13]

The prospective Secretary of State was, intentionally or otherwise, a target of Senator Taft's comment against bipartisanship. He was also intimately associated with several of the policies and personalities which were under fire by the Senator. As will be noted, his campaign statements were, in the main, reflections of the to-be-expected turgidity of American elections. Paradoxically, while his active participation in the campaign served clearly to dissociate him from the Truman Administration, he was to accomplish this dissociation without breaking with the basic principle of continuity in foreign policy.

PRE-CAMPAIGN INTRAPARTY DIFFERENCES

In May of 1952, Dulles accepted an invitation to address the French National Political Science Institute. The primary purpose of the journey was to call upon General Eisenhower, who had already declared his candidacy for the Republican nomination. Reportedly, the prospective Secretary of State wanted to ensure his future position less than he wanted "to convince General Eisenhower that there was a great danger of isolationist sentiment becoming predominant in the Republican Party." [14]

One of the first contests between the Republican factions revolved around the formulation of a platform which would sufficiently unite the diverse elements of the party and still be acceptable to Eisenhower. In a letter to Dulles on June 20, the General expressed some strong opposition to many of the conservative views and to all isolationist tendencies. He also declared confidence in Dulles' concurrence on such issues as strategy for deterrence, free trade, and access to raw materials. The General concluded on the following note:

I realize that it will not be easy to write a statement that will accommodate some of the widely divergent views I have heard expressed on these vast subjects. I am certain, also, that your understanding and determination are equal to the burden of carrying forward the fight to include these essentials.[15]

Three days before this letter, after consultations with Senators Taft, Wiley, Smith, Knowland, and Millikin, Dulles had written the General that he believed it possible to get an acceptable foreign policy plank without an irreparable breach in the party. This could not be achieved, however, without concessions.

Dulles' first draft outlines of a campaign platform included no denunciations of Teheran and Yalta, for he considered such denunciations negative, senseless, and, in many respects, irresponsible. His drafts concentrated on the more positive aspects of foreign policy rather than attacking weaknesses; they also contained no mention of drastically cutting the public payroll, getting men "of proven loyalty," and eliminating many from the State Department. A note on the draft of June 5 stated that Governor Warren and Dulles objected to the inclusion of these ideas—"But Millikin adamant!" Penciled in the same margin was the remark that Eisenhower and Dulles' ideas on free trade—namely, to press for the elimination of practices such as preferential tariffs, monetary license restrictions, and other arbitrary protective devices which hampered the mutually advantageous flow of goods—were also rejected by Senator Millikin and others.

But Dulles continued to press for the inclusion of the idea that

policies which had evolved through the bipartisan approach—
policies on the United Nations, peace with Japan and Germany, security arrangements, and other commitments to Europe—would
not be questioned.[16] Even in the heat of the campaign, he was not
to swerve from this course and, in no instance, to censure a policy
of the Democrats which had been developed after consultation with
Republican leaders. To be sure, he would suggest that some policies
could have been applied more vigorously, especially those pertaining to European cooperation or integration. But, in the campaign
as in the struggle for the platform, he asserted that the broad lines
of American policy should not be altered.

When asked later how he could reconcile the views in the platform with his earlier opinions and actions, Dulles is reported to
have replied: "As an individual he could not do so but . . . as a
platform writer he was merely stating the Republican case against
the Democratic Party, which was committed to the principle of liberation by the Atlantic Charter." [17] While there was a good dosage
of candor in the reply, the report mistakenly assumed that Dulles
was able to influence greatly the final statement. Campaigning for a
Republican victory, Dulles surely could not have replied that he
simply did not find himself in total agreement with some of the
views and much of the tone which found expression in the platform. He was, nonetheless, unquestionably uncomfortable when
confronted with any negative and purely denunciatory tactics with
respect to foreign policy. The platform, as to be expected, emerged
only after a series of concessions and compromises, and a statement
not unacceptable to Eisenhower was produced.

Although Averell Harriman later exaggerated the case for campaign effect, producing a platform around which diverse Republicans could rally was no easy political task:

Harriman: Let me compliment you, Foster, for having written a document that got the approval of the two Republican generals, General
MacArthur and General Eisenhower. . . .

Dulles: And the Democrats too!

Harriman: And Taft . . . I think that was one of the greatest achieve-
ments in your life.[18]

There was more than a modicum of truth in Dulles' retort. Both parties, for example, adhered to the idea of "liberation" and something more than mere containment. However, judging from Dulles' writings and actions both before and after the 1952 campaign, it is difficult to avoid the conclusion that his hand did not show through very strongly in the 1952 Republican platform. The document simply did not reflect his order of preferences and priorities.

CONVENTION AND CAMPAIGN

Republicans of all shades had an excellent reason for avoiding a glaring conflict over specific issues and ideologies. They were naturally more concerned with winning an election than with the details of a campaign manifesto. An intraparty feud, broadcast over nationwide television, could have hindered the chances of a minority party. However, the surface appearance of coming together and perhaps also the increasing popularity of Eisenhower resulted in a tendency on the part of outside observers to overlook the real struggle for power reflected in the 1952 Republican convention.

The General's greatest advantage was that the delegates viewed him as a "winner," whereas his greatest disadvantage was the fact that he was not a party man, as it were, and had little control over the party machinery. In their proverbial "heart of hearts," a majority of the convention delegates supported Senator Taft. The day before the convention was convened, Mr. Republican needed fewer than 100 votes to reach the victory mark of 604, while Eisenhower was anywhere from 52 to 103 votes behind the Senator from Ohio.[19] But the latter was still a more unqualified "vote getter" outside the convention halls. Although Taft received 500 votes on the first ballot, Eisenhower received the Republican nomination when the Minnesota delegation changed its ballots from a favorite son. Nevertheless, the General was still considered somewhat of an intruder by many, and he surely represented a shade of gray rather than a dyed-in-the-wool Republican. The man who had once praised the "long, unbroken friendship" between the United States and Russia [20] represented the "internationalists." He was never, in politi-

cal jargon, a "darling" of the conservatives or the Taft segment of
the party.

Listed among the General's reasons for selecting Senator Nixon as
his running mate, there was a telling comment: "Aside from this,
the question of Communist infiltration and proper methods for defeating it in our country had become a burning and widespread
issue." [21] Of course, there were several excellent reasons for the selection of Richard Nixon. He was young, a vigorous campaigner, and
a Californian. He had also conducted the relatively orderly investigations of Alger Hiss; and he had not failed to keep his political
party lines open and sweet. In short, he was palatable to the Taft
elements in the 1950s.

With the Eisenhower-Nixon team nominated, the convention did
not end altogether on an auspicious note. Eisenhower was lifted
somewhat reluctantly onto the Republican shoulders. Senator Taft
departed for Canada as the Eisenhower camp geared itself for the
dual task of defeating the Democrats and pulling the Republican
party together by sowing party unity. Success in the former largely
depended upon success in the latter. The second phase of the struggle, the campaign, was beginning. The first phase has been summed
up in the following terms: "If a playwright had tried to contrive a
pair of characters to dramatize the isolationist-internationalist cleav-
age in the Republican party he could not have found two better
prototypes." [22]

Eisenhower's nomination did not give him the hold the Taft
forces had on the grass-roots organizations, nor did it alter the fact
that many Taft followers occupied influential positions in the party
structure. The General could have perhaps enhanced his standing
among liberals, independents, and disenchanted Democrats by dis-
sociating himself further from the conservatives and from the rightist elements during the campaign. Such a move, however, would
have damaged his standing with the party organizations, and "by
most calculations the organizations are still the more worthwhile allies in a hard fight." [23]

By September of 1952, the idea of a "shoe in" against Adlai Stevenson of Illinois and Senator John J. Sparkman of Alabama
quickly vanished. The election seemed to take on the appearance of

a close contest. If this appearance of a narrow contest represented miscalculation or underestimation on the part of Eisenhower and his political advisers, their reading and cautious estimations had a solid basis in past experience—Dewey's surprise defeat in 1948. At any rate, the General and his advisers believed there was an increased need to mend party fences. McCarthy's overwhelming victory in the Wisconsin primary was an indication of the strength and appeal of those who believed the "Communist-in-Government" issue to be of overriding importance.

The Eisenhower camp did not ignore the results in Wisconsin, particularly since it appeared that a considerable number of Democrats had voted for "Joe." *Time* noted that the only answer to "McCarthyism" was for "other and far better men . . . to prove that they are more effectively against Communist infiltration than McCarthy." [24] During this period, the Republican presidential candidate began to talk more on the subject of "red penetration" and proper methods for dealing with infiltration. At this stage the problem was not one of avoiding a public dispute between fellow Republicans, for by September the General believed he needed the wholehearted support of the Taft faction for victory. Gaining such support called for compromise, concession, and cooperation.

While Truman had successfully ignored the wings of the Democratic party in 1948, several factors precluded a comparison with Eisenhower's situation in 1952. First, Truman was the majority party's candidate. Second, he controlled most of the Democratic party machinery. Third, besides being the minority party's candidate and not in firm control of its machinery, Eisenhower was not so much confronted with a Taft "faction" or "wing" but with a very substantial bloc of Taft supporters. Like Dulles, Eisenhower was probably uncomfortable in situations of hard political compromise. But a degree of discomfort was perceived as a far better proposition than another Republican defeat at the polls. On September 9, the General endorsed the re-election campaign of the cantankerous Senator Jenner, the man who referred to General Marshall as a "living lie" and characterized the Truman Administration as an assortment of "Communist fellow-travelling appeasers." [25]

Three days later, Eisenhower and Taft met at the former's residence in Morningside Heights. After the meeting the Senator declared: "I cannot say that I agree with all of General Eisenhower's views on . . . foreign policy . . . but I think it is fair to say that our differences are differences of degree." Taft's main concern was keeping down expenditures on armament and foreign aid.[26] He began a vigorous campaign against the "mess in Washington," and his followers shifted the machinery into gear. Differences of "degree" and "methods" became the catchwords pasting together a better semblance of party unity and agreement. In early October Eisenhower declared that he and Senator McCarthy shared a similar purpose in seeking to purge the government of "subversives." The General qualified his endorsement of the misguided Senator from Wisconsin only by pointing out that the differences between them applied to "methods."

ISSUES AND LIBERATION

During the campaign Dulles concentrated on areas where there existed ample room for constructive criticism. He criticized the lack of attention given to Asia and a Far Eastern policy; the unclear definition of America's interests in Asia, as even President Truman asserted that the Russians began hostilities mainly because they thought they would be unopposed; the inclination to present foreign policy issues and moves in terms of "cures"; and, lastly, after twenty years of one-party rule, one could expect a bit of a "mess in Washington." Dulles' campaign statements, while including some instances of campaign exaggeration, contained no instances of crossing the line of proper and responsible criticism on foreign policy matters. Besides the general appeal to a "positive" foreign policy and "peaceful liberation," he concentrated his efforts on legitimate issues and was wont to point out agreement with Democratic policies which had evolved through the bipartisan process. He questioned, however, the Truman Administration's "soft" approach to European unification.

The other foreign policy themes of his campaign utterances were: first, the duration of the East-West encounter or the fact that it would last for a generation or several; second, the need for an effective retaliatory force for deterrence; third, the need for a policy of deterrence, planning and utilizing power as a political weapon; fourth, the need for better organization for policy development at a high level (Dulles believed that Acheson had been so encumbered with duties and tasks that he hardly had time to concentrate on policy *per se*); and, fifth, the need for a broader perspective, a view which realized the United States as a world power and not merely an ally of Europe. Although he stressed the need for increased attention to Asia and an Asian policy, he was not at all inclined to de-emphasize the importance of Europe. In 1950 he had warned: "Now that the problem of Asia hits us with a violence that compels attention, let us not go wholly into reverse gear and neglect Europe." [27] There were no indications during the campaign that Dulles wanted to pursue a course either radically or even substantially different from the policies of Acheson, Marshall, or Byrnes. He emphasized the need for improvement and more attention to underdeveloped areas, but most of the campaign statements were designed to give a "new face" and emphasis to ongoing policies and trends.

Dulles was fully aware of campaign gamesmanship and the problems it presented for foreign policy. He had noted in *War or Peace* that should two presidential candidates "compete in making novel and unseasoned proposals, designed primarily to win votes, the end of that campaign would leave our foreign relations in shambles." [28] In 1951 he observed that "because elections come so frequently, there is a tendency on the part of government to seek short cuts which can bear quick political fruit. There is a tendency to evade the long, hard tasks." [29] While cognizant of the need to produce "political fruit" in the 1952 campaign, Dulles did not compromise his viewpoints on basic foreign policy matters. Although as a politician he would hint that certain problems of the East-West confrontation could be settled within "two, five or ten" years, he presented no illusory hopes of any simple or near solutions.

Early in the election year he observed that there existed a temptation for those in official positions to buttress specific programs with the idea that such proposals solved, as compared to settled, prob-

lems of international conflict. Realizing that the nature and complexities of international conflicts of interest precluded "solutions"
as such, he was still not inclined to be hypercritical of those who relied upon such arguments: "Perhaps if I were in a position of authority I might be saying the same thing because that is a very useful technique to use." [30] Does it, in some respects, represent an
indispensable technique?

Perhaps no other single foreign policy issue of the 1952 campaign
has been as long remembered and misinterpreted as the so-called
liberation debate. Dulles undeniably emphasized proposals for
peaceful liberation. The issue was surely, in part, a deliberate com-
ponent of the campaign strategy with the aim of making inroads on
the Democrat's strength in Slavic-ethnic communities. It was also a
generalized issue upon which diverse elements of the Republican
party could agree and come together, though possibly with substantially different operational interpretations. But the concept of "liberation" cannot be viewed as just another technique to gain votes
from various blocs. Nor can it be interpreted simply as a proposal
utilized to placate the Right. Peaceful liberation was in fact a standing principle with both parties, and Dulles had enunciated the idea
ever since 1949.

The concept was an integral part of the domestic change thesis
and his conception of a political and psychological offensive. In
War or Peace, he defined liberation in the following manner:

"Activation" does not mean armed revolt. . . . Violent revolt would be
futile. Indeed, it would be worse than futile, for it would precipitate mas-
sacre.

After several pages dedicated to a discussion of informational programs, propaganda, and psychological appeals, and other nonmilitary aspects of the cold war, he continued:

Some suggest that, if we took a moral offensive in the "cold war," we
should precipitate a shooting war. I believe, on the contrary, that peace
depends upon the growing internal difficulties of Soviet Communism and
its inability to consolidate its present and prospective areas of conquest.[31]

He characterized the Soviet communist structure as "over-ex-
tended, over-rigid, and ill-founded." It could be "shaken" if its la-

tent difficulties "were activated." There were recognized risks involved in any program designed to keep alive latent difficulties, for he had always assumed, as described in his 1935 analysis of "The Road to Peace," that "the most deep-rooted instinct is the instinct to relinquish only when compelled to do so." [32] Like Kennan, however, Dulles believed that conditions could be established in the long-run whereby the Soviet Union would be compelled by the dictates of self-interest to alter its position and mode of operation in Eastern Europe. In the words of Kennan:

The United States has it in its power to increase enormously the strains under which Soviet policy must operate, to force upon the Kremlin a far greater degree of moderation and circumspection than it has had to observe in recent years, and in this way to promote the tendencies which must eventually find their outlet in either the break-up or the gradual mellowing of Soviet power.[33]

Dulles' view of the decentralization of control and power in the Soviet "bloc" is best understood in combination with his interpretation of the nature of the Soviet-American encounter: namely, an historical encounter lasting for a generation or several generations. He was under no illusions concerning the prospects of greater freedom or independence for the satellite countries. The goal of "liberation" was not the uprooting of the Soviet power structure, but a gradual evolution away from Soviet domination and toward greater national independence. Moreover, in Dulles' conception of the East-West encounter, as noted previously, relatively peaceful coexistence between the superpowers did not demand peaceful liberation or the dissolution of Soviet power in Eastern Europe as a prerequisite.

The concept of "liberation" represented a natural evolution in Dulles' ideas on the inevitability of change and on the dynamic always prevailing over the static elements. In 1946 he warned that "no program is adequate if it is merely against something." [34] and similar exhortations continued throughout the postwar years. He disapproved of "containment" as the "be-all" and "end-all" of policy, not because it was "immoral" in itself, but because it was essentially static. He became wary of the concept of containment, as the fundamental principle of foreign policy, in terms of the extent to which a pure containment approach could encourage strictly military interpretations of the Soviet challenge, neo-isolationism in the United States, or Fortress America impulses. While adhering to the policy of containment insofar as the military arm of the Soviet Union was concerned, his "positive" or "dynamic" approach did not at all relate to the military aspects of the cold war.

Before, during, and after the campaign, he consistently defined the processes of "liberation" as a political and psychological offensive. In the emerging nations, it meant the challenge was to "capture the imagination and enlist the support of the multitudes whose interest in battling political, economic and racial injustice is greater than their interest in defending injustice merely because Communism attacks it." [35] In Eastern Europe it meant following Churchill's proclamation: "We must never cease to proclaim in fearless tones the great principles of freedom and the rights of man." [36] Much like, but in more emphatic tones than, the Truman-Acheson-Kennan team, Dulles maintained that a purely defensive, anticommunist stance was bound to fail.

Dulles labeled as "immoral" that interpretation of "containment" which meant that the United States would "call it quits with the Russians if they" would "be satisfied with six hundred million captives *and let us alone.*" [37] (Emphasis added.) The misunderstanding, both at home and abroad, derived largely from failure to recognize the fact that such a policy of "containment" had never been adhered to by the Truman Administration. Secretary Acheson, speaking "about those points of greatest difference which must be identified and sooner or later reconciled," had made the following declaration in 1950: "What concerns us is that they (satellite governments) should be truly independent national regimes with a will of their own and with a decent foundation in popular feeling." [38] In 1952 Acheson spoke of "the surge of the human spirit" bringing freedom "just as surely as a truth will push its way up through solid rock." [39] Kennan had described the process thusly: "But in actuality the possibilities for American policy are by no means limited to holding the line and hoping for the best." He asserted further that the satellite states . . . must, and will, recover their full independence." [40] As stated in the Democratic platform of 1952, the goal of the Democrats' policy with respect to the "victims of Soviet imperialism" was "peaceful liberation."

The goal of Dulles' approach was also "peaceful liberation" and, interestingly, his methods did not differ substantially from those pursued by the Truman Administration. Yet his major campaign article, "A Policy of Boldness," tended to communicate a greater sense of urgency than his previous writings. In this article he mentioned wooing the satellites, setting up task forces, aiding escape, and coordinating economic, commercial, and cultural relations with "freedom programs." Nevertheless, he specifically precluded the idea of violent uprisings and reprisals and continued to emphasize peaceful separation as exemplified by Tito's Yugoslavia.[41] Furthermore, "wooing," "task forces," and "freedom programs" had been accepted aspects of American foreign policy long before the campaign of 1952. During the campaign Dulles took these aspects and attempted to make the concept of "liberation" more real, as it were, something capable of bearing political fruit. At the same time, however, he warned of the dangers in conceiving the struggle in military terms, and deprecated any illusions of a panacea or quick solutions.

His descriptions of a "bolder" approach during the campaign resulted partially, if not mainly, from perceived political necessity. The two parties essentially supported the same principle. The Republicans utilized and, to a large degree, inherited a "bold" stance to separate themselves from the Democrats and to avoid charges of "me-tooism." Rather than echo the same tune, the Democrats decided that more political advantage could be gained by representing the Republican position as "war-mongering" and incitement to "armed revolt." President Truman took the so-called low road for the Democratic candidate, Adlai Stevenson. The President, in heated campaign style, referred to Eisenhower's programs as possibly leading to a third world war, thereby making "atomic battlefields of the Soviet satellites."

Dulles was portrayed by the President as one of the group of "master minds" playing "cruel gutter politics" and risking atomic warfare by influencing Eisenhower to pledge liberation to the nations enslaved by Russia.[42] Although thus depicted as a "nonpeace-

ful liberator," Dulles' campaign writings contained only the most
tenuous evidence to support such an image. His proposals were by
no means alarming. Actually, the Democrats' program to label "liberation" Republican-style as "war-mongering" or incitement to revolt could have been the cause of more worriment than Dulles' own
presentations.

More important than the campaign presentations and misrepre-
sentations was the fact that both parties saw disadvantages in not
actively supporting the idea of "liberation." There was a noteworthy exchange during the Dulles-Harriman debate:

Dulles: I was interested . . . that the Democratic platform . . . saying
they didn't want to deviate from their present policies did almost copy
the Republican platform with reference to this liberation policy, so much
so that the Moscow *New Times* claimed that I had written both planks
on the subject.

Harriman: Well, the only constructive part in the Republican platform
was the part . . . cribbed from the Democratic policies.[43]

Harriman further stated that the Democratic Administration had
pursued a "dynamic policy," one which had "rolled-back Communism," and hoped to field enough strength to begin the "disintegration" behind the Iron Curtain: "Russia is losing. . . . We . . . have
the initiative. . . . We must press forward with our plans and
programs."[44]

Not only was neither party prepared to assume an "antilibera-
tion" stance, but Harriman here appeared as much the "ambitious
liberator" as Dulles. Yet neither Harriman nor Dulles was an ambitious or reckless "liberator." Once one washed away all of the campaign rhetoric, the common ground of agreement behind the different political appeals became obvious. While the Democrats
purposely misrepresented Dulles' "peaceful liberation" and the Republican tactics involved misrepresenting the Truman Administration's concept of "containment," the campaign attacks upon generalized straw men paradoxically left intact the fundamental agreement
among the leaders of both parties on the basic principles of United
States foreign policy.

On the other hand, Dulles purposely obscured one significant aspect of peaceful liberation both during and after the campaign. Did

liberation necessarily mean more democratic freedoms for the peoples of Eastern Europe and genuine independence, or did it merely mean a loosening of Soviet control over the satellite countries? Since he emphasized the psychological and political aspects of the cold war, it followed that this issue was obscured for propaganda purposes with the view that pressures from the people would give the satellite governments more reason to assert themselves for some loosening of Soviet control. If there was deliberate ambiguity on this particular point, it likely resulted from the judgment that a detailed delineation of the meaning of liberation would only muddle the issue at home and reduce its appeal abroad. Dulles was surely aware of and calculated this ambiguity. It was generally understood at the time:

The true line of our policy, as I feel reasonably sure Mr. Dulles knows as well as I do, is not in the rebellion of the masses against the satellite governments, but in the rebellion of the satellite governments against the U.S.S.R. In a word, Tito-ism.[45]

The facts that Dulles consistently referred to Yugoslavia as the prime example of a liberated country and denounced the idea of inciting violent uprisings corroborated this view.

POST-CAMPAIGN LIBERATION

If, during the campaign, Dulles at first appeared to whisper the qualification that "liberation" meant "peaceful evolution," the qualification became louder and louder when the opposition began the attacks upon Republican-styled "liberation." As the campaign drew to a close, he was placing even more emphasis on peaceful, gradual developments and long-range results. However, these same qualifications and reservations had been present explicitly or implicitly in all, but perhaps one extemporaneous remark, of his statements from 1949 to 1953. After the controversy in 1952, he continued to accentuate the peaceful aspects of liberation. Thus, his so-called inaction in East Germany (1953) and Hungary (1956) can be described as "failures" to follow through with pronounced policy only by completely misreading his own proposals. The process had always been defined as a psychological and political offensive, not as a process of armed intervention in Soviet-held territories.

No episode of Dulles' career suggests that he supported a policy of "liberation" in the manner charged by political opponents during the 1952 campaign. One day after Poland declared its determination to pursue a Polish way, as compared to the Soviet way, toward socialism and democratization, and very shortly before the rumblings of discontent in Hungary, in October of 1956, the Secretary maintained that the contribution of the United States was not "one of actual intervening and meddling, because that kind of thing . . . often is counter-productive." The task of the United States was "to keep alive the concept of freedom." This represented the traditional theme of "conduct and example"—George Kennan's "spirtual vitality" or "spirit and purpose of American national life," and Dulles' "sense of mission" or "dynamic faith." The Secretary also noted, while praising Tito, that there were no "particular measuring rods" or litmus tests by which the United States judged whether or not a country was "liberated." [46]

There was still the question of what "liberation" actually meant at the operational level of American foreign policy. In 1957 the Secretary defined liberation as the time when the satellite nations would have regimes which, "whatever their label," would in fact "serve their own nations and their own peoples rather than the insatiable world-wide ambitions of an international Party." [47] Such statements were still designed for public consumption and, in good part, for propaganda purposes. Nearer the working level, at a NATO meeting in 1957, the Secretary referred to the "cautious encouragement of greater satellite independence." [48]

In a series of position papers for the Big Four Heads of State Conference in 1955, Dulles outlined one of the goals of the United States as "increased independence and growth of self-determination on the part of the satellites, so that they will not be, in effect, an extension of the Soviet empire into Europe." Noting that Great Britain favored raising the subject while France was probably indifferent (although it was later reported to him that both Macmillan and Pinay supported bringing up the "satellite liberation" issue, the latter against the counsel of his advisers), Dulles recognized that there were difficulties in any mention of the subject. It should not, therefore, be treated as a "big issue" but handled more in private conversation. Nevertheless, the United States should impress upon the Soviets the importance attached to developments in Eastern Europe, particularly as a "rod for measuring" extending cooperation with the Soviets in other areas: *"After all, what we ask for is less than what the Soviets gave Tito."* [49] (Emphasis added.)

His ideas on and operational approach to liberation hardly appeared ambitious or careless here. Quite the contrary, his conception represented the same policy lines he had developed during the 1945–1948 period and which were not dissimilar to the line adopted by the Truman Administration. When asked some questions about a "positive approach to foreign policy" statement on the Far East, statement before the Foreign Relations Committee in 1952, Dulles replied that the statement had been approved by the Truman Administration. He further responded: "I am rather appalled at the way in which the above viewpoint is misrepresented in the British press and sought to be dismissed as 'war mongering'. . . . With reference to your suggestion that I come to England . . . I question the wisdom of a foreigner coming to your shores to try to influence your public opinion." [50]

If there existed reason for doubts and some distrust during the campaign, Secretary-designate Dulles amply clarified his position on liberation and on the transition of foreign policy under a Republican Administration during the nomination hearings before the Senate Foreign Relations Committee in January of 1953:

But all of this can be done and must be done in ways which will not provoke a general war, or in ways which will not provoke an insurrection. . . .

It must be and can be a peaceful process. . . .

Surely, if they (Soviets) can use moral and psychological force, we can use it; and, to take a negative defeatist attitude is not an approach which is conducive to our own welfare, or in conformity with our own historical ideas.[51]

Nonetheless, in spite of the clarity of Dulles' statements on peaceful liberation and his sometimes shouting the qualifications, the impression was created of a more active "liberation" role for the United States.

On another series of questions, the Secretary-designate admitted that the language of the 1952 Republican platform was not all which he would have chosen nor which he desired to use as Secretary. While supporting the process of partisan advocacy and controversy during national elections, he expressed his hope for continued bipartisan cooperation in foreign policy. To allay any fears, both abroad and at home, of possible abrupt changes in United States foreign policy, he stated that the first year would be devoted basically to review and reappraisal of the present policies and how these policies should be adjusted to the changing world and state of affairs. He hoped that, within a year or so, the new administration would "be able to come up with either fresh policies or with a conviction" in the correctness of existing policies.[52]

Indeed, there appeared no indications of a substantial shift in American policy. At his first press conference as Secretary of State, both the questions and the answers sounded familiar. One broadcaster concluded: "Except for the fact that he doesn't have a moustache, you hardly would have known it wasn't Secretary Acheson." [53] If the signs clearly pointed toward continuity in terms of the broad lines of foreign policy and commitments, there were equally significant signals that, besides somewhat similar international issues, similar domestic problems continued to confront United States foreign policy.

❧

CHAPTER NINE

THE POLITICS AND DIPLOMACY
OF SECRETARYSHIP
PART I: INDICATIONS OF LIMITATIONS

The mere fact of a new administration and the necessary reorientation was enough to cause concern in allied capitals, particularly in London where Prime Minister Churchill and Foreign Secretary Eden hardly enjoyed the prospect of working with Dulles. Eden had approached Eisenhower earlier in the year with the request not to appoint Dulles Secretary of State in the event of a Republican victory at the polls. Eden's attitude toward Dulles probably stemmed from a number of experiences and impressions, the most important being the Foreign Secretary's lingering doubts about Dulles' handling of the negotiation and political problems surrounding ratification of the Japanese Peace Treaty and Great Britain's difficult adjustment to a substantially subordinate position of power. Eden's attitude may or may not have extended as far back as his discussions with Dulles in 1942 on the subject of colonialism.[1]

There were indeed differences of personality and temperament between the two men which, although not determining policy of their respective governments, often got in the way of sympathetic understanding of their positions and the working relationships in carrying them out. Whatever the source of Eden's and Churchill's opinion that they could not work well with Dulles, the latter began to mend fences immediately after the 1952 election.

Dulles met with Eden on November 13. In the course of the discussion, Dulles assured the Foreign Secretary of the standing pledges of the United States to Europe, mentioned the poor press coverage during the campaign—that is, how the Republican positions had been distorted both at home and abroad—and suggested a concert of British, French, and American action in parts of the world other than the North Atlantic Treaty region. Both statesmen expressed their concern for closer cooperation among the countries of Western Europe. Reporting to the President-elect, Dulles also mentioned that Eden considered ratification of the German Peace Contract as the most urgent problem of Western Europe. One of Britain's primary concerns was that the creation of a German military force would naturally divert part of Germany's economic activity into rearmament or away from competition with the United Kingdom. Dulles concluded that the meeting "throughout was most cordial and Eden seemed unusually relaxed." [2]

While reassurances and pledges to allies constituted one of the Secretary's first concerns in foreign affairs, a first order of business for the new administration as a whole inevitably centered about the domestic power struggle, the arduous task of adjusting the questionable reins of power. In January of 1953, President Eisenhower inherited a most tenuous position. The Korean War, growing unrest and war in Indochina, and the future of closer cooperation in Europe were vital international considerations to the President. Equally vital on a different scale, however, was the factious state of the domestic political situation. Eisenhower's overwhelming personal victory at the polls meant neither that his camp had gained control over the party machinery and over party leaders in Congress, nor that Republicans were united. Popularity and prestige carried weight, but were not necessarily the decisive factors in the political game. The Taft wing still controlled a significant portion of the party organization. More important, the combined power of Senator Taft and his followers as part of a conservative, neo-isolationist coalition of Republicans and Democrats in Congress could rival that of the President. Then, of course, there was Senator McCarthy in full swing mostly with Taft's blessing.

The new Chief Executive encountered a Congress which was very jealous of its own powers. Viewing itself as the protector of the Constitution and the people against the encroachment of such items as the Genocide Convention, Republicans and several Democrats were ready and armed with the Bricker Amendment to set the hatchet to the powers of the executive in international affairs. The amendment was cosponsored by nearly the necessary two-thirds for its passage. Moreover, the Republicans had gained very narrow majorities in Congress—a majority of one in the Senate and of nine in the House of Representatives. This narrow balance enhanced the leverage of the conservative and isolationist members, who also controlled several of the key congressional positions. In the words of one observer, the "die-hard Republican Old Guard" was "firmly entrenched in the 83rd Congress." [3] Of the many inheritances from the Truman Administration, including both domestic and international circumstances, a jealous Congress, "McCarthyism," and a pervasive security issue were perhaps the most unwelcome.

As President, Eisenhower required Democratic support for his policies. As party leader, he would have to gain Democratic support without splitting the Republican party wide open. While the election had temporarily united Republicans, the struggle for power recommenced after victory. The President soon began to invite congressional committee chairmen to White House luncheons, and ended up inviting all the members of Congress. Nonetheless, there were limits to what such amenities could accomplish and "even in the midst of them the gap between the President and the extreme right-wing Republicans not only persisted but began to widen ominously." [4] Believers in martyrdom and the Democrats would, of course, have thoroughly approved of an irreparable breach in the opposition. The party leader, however, set out to cement some semblance of party unity in order not to endanger his most effective form of organizing the electorate in the limited warfare of the democratic processes.

Dulles had indirectly forecast the difficulties with Congress before the election victory when answering the charge that Eisenhower was surrounded by men like Senators Kem, Jenner, Dirksen, and McCarthy. The prospective Secretary of State found that accusation "quite fantastic." He estimated approximately nine or ten senators who would consistently vote the "Jenner line." But, to Dulles, the future still rested on a delicate bipartisan balance—only if the "Democrats would give a Republican Administration the same kind of support the Republicans have given the Democrat Administration" could Eisenhower effectuate policies "without having to compromise with the small minority" in the Republican party.[5] As it turned out, often to the Secretary's chagrin, the nine or ten had many more sympathizers on particular issues.

Dulles was naturally less concerned with Republican unity than Eisenhower. But the Secretary was, by necessity, continually occupied with the problem of securing congressional support for his policies. Some have asserted that the price paid for congressional consent was too high and resulted in the stagnation of American foreign policy. Others closer to the action, however, have agreed with the Secretary's efforts to cultivate support for a bipartisan foreign policy without breaking the party organization.[6] While the cost of consent always remains debatable, certain factors remain indisputable. First, consent is indispensable. Congressional approval and at least public acquiescence, if not support, are vitally necessary to function effectively. In short, "Congress represents the most important part of the political setting within which the foreign policy machinery of the executive branch must operate." [7] Second, regardless of the extent to which the Truman Administration's troubles were self-wrought, Secretary Acheson's great difficulties with Congress became representative of the times and were inherited by his successor. With Acheson's lesson vividly in mind, and with perhaps subconscious memories of the lesson of President Wilson's disastrous failure vis-à-vis the Senate and the League of Nations, Dulles assiduously cultivated congressional support from the outset. During the first three years of his tenure, he was to meet with committees or subcommittees over one hundred times, not to mention the numerous private meetings with senators and congressmen.

Garnering congressional and public support for particular foreign policies was by no means the entire political chessboard of the Secretary of State. There were, of course, the politics of the White House. Almost every observer concerned with the Eisenhower Administration has, at some time, noted the remarkable working relationship between the President and his Secretary of State. Eisenhower indubitably granted Dulles a generous latitude both in the formulation and in the presentation of policy. But neither did Eisenhower ever abdicate his power of final decision, nor did Dulles fail to protect the relationship which was carefully cultivated. Protection of the relationship meant not only constantly taking into consideration the President's views and predicaments—intraparty, interparty, congressional, and public pressures—but also not interfering or issuing serious challenges in areas, such as military requirements, where Eisenhower and other advisers held the upper hand.

White House politics included the diverse viewpoints, which were beginning to feel their way, within the Cabinet room. The existence of an essentially harmonious working relationship between Eisenhower and Dulles did not preclude the possibility of other special relationships with the President. Henry Cabot Lodge, for example, was twice to defy State Department instructions at the United Nations and, in at least one of the instances, with the expressed authorization of the President. When informed of Lodge's direct line to the White House, during the Korean debates, Dulles advised Ambassador Robert Murphy that this was "one of those awkward situations which require special consideration." [8] While the "internationalist" members of Eisenhower's Cabinet were on the same general ground, this did not mean agreement on specific issues or tactics. If the "internationalists" of the Cabinet occupied the same general territory, there was a significantly different approach to international affairs among Secretaries Humphrey (Treasury), Wilson (Defense), and Benson (Agriculture). Between Dulles and Humphrey, for example, there always existed differences which led "to a lot of talk and harmonizing of views." [9] The Secretary of the Treasury always fought Dulles' attempts to get congressional commitments for economic assistance to developing countries on a long-term basis.

The basic problems of the Eisenhower Administration and Dulles were not, however, to be found in the divergent viewpoints around the Cabinet table. There were no insurmountable differences, and the Secretary of State was truly a formidable member of the board. On top of the international problems of European cooperation, war in Korea, and troubles in Indochina, the fundamental political problems facing the Secretary at home were establishing a working relationship with Congress and protecting his own domain by avoiding congressional wrath or, at least, the wrath of those obsessed with the all-pervasive security issue. His methods of protecting his domain have been described as the "shabbiest" period of his secretaryship.[10] The period certainly had its unfair aspects; but it was overall probably less "shabby" than fraught with domestic and international nettles. Whether or not Dulles actually hesitated before accepting the nomination for Secretary of State is less important than the fact that there were excellent reasons for hesitation.

THE APPROACH TO SENATOR MCCARTHY

The question of relations with Congress and congressional investigations was discussed at the first two Cabinet meetings of the new administration. The President took a definite stand to cooperate as much as possible, making it quite clear that he had every intention of avoiding any type of showdown with Congress or an open dispute with the rabid Senator from Wisconsin, Joseph McCarthy. Eisenhower had already decided how he wished to handle McCarthy: "This was to ignore him. . . . I would give him no satisfaction. I would never defend anything." [11]

Several factors combined to convince the President of the prudence of this approach to McCarthy. First, there was danger in issuing any challenges to an established force which operated with the acquiescence and frequent support of Senator Taft, particularly when the President was just securing his own position of power and the administration's political roots. Second, there was a disinclination to widen the already broad gap between the executive and legislative branches, by challenging one of the dominant figures of the Senate at a time both when a solid majority of the Republicans and

several Democrats opposed the traditional exercise of executive powers in foreign affairs and when the administration had to choose its
battles carefully. Third, although probably of less concern to Eisenhower than to his political staff, the President could not dismiss the
issue of Republican unity either generally or for the congressional
elections of 1954. A vehement or open Eisenhower-McCarthy dispute would have involved high political costs in terms of party
unity, and endeared the General neither to the party organization
nor to large segments of the public with which the organization was
necessarily concerned.

On the other hand, the strictly political benefits to be gained by a
course of open challenge appeared meager and insubstantial. A
showdown might have endeared him with the liberal minority in
his party, but not necessarily with the moderates. A showdown
would have undoubtedly pleased the Democrats for a variety of reasons and would have encouraged large segments of the governmental bureaucracy, especially in the demoralized State Department and
the beleaguered Far Eastern Division. But a passing popularity with
the Democrats and going out on a limb for the bureaucracy were
not considered to outweigh the hard "stuff" of politics—executive-
legislative relations and party unity.

Although a source of disappointment to liberal and some moderate circles, Eisenhower's approach was clearly one of minimizing political problems and risk. Whether despite or partially because of
his approach, McCarthy's political demise came about, on Decem
ber 2, 1954, in the form of Senate Resolution 301 censuring the un-
becoming conduct of the Senator from Wisconsin. The vote on the
issue found the Republican senators splitting down the middle, 22
for and 22 against censure. The Democrats carried the day with a
44-0 vote in favor of the resolution.

"In fairness to Dulles," one observer noted, McCarthy was "too
strong politically for Dulles to try conclusions with independently
of Eisenhower and . . . Eisenhower himself had no wish for such an
encounter." [12] In fairness to Eisenhower, "right wingism" and
"McCarthyism" were powerful forces at mid-century. McCarthy—as
the symbol generally for the disillusioned, the disenchanted, and
the frustrated Americans, besides being a rallying point for fervid

anticommunist elements—represented a formidable force in American politics. Most Washington politicians found it imprudent at the time to risk political fortunes by opposing the Senator from Wisconsin in his heyday. Out of the mere handful who took the risks in challenging, some were repudiated at the polls. The self-proclaimed liberals, as well as many with genuine liberal inclinations, usually sat biding time quietly in the background. The "Red scare" was, indeed, a shabby season for Washington and the country.

Dulles, personally less concerned with party unity, but necessarily occupied with the problem of keeping the political lines sweet for his programs, concurred and probably agreed with the President's decision. But problems of congressional approval for foreign policy generally and for such items as appointments, not to mention congressional control over such matters as the budget for economic and military assistance, were not Dulles' only considerations. Whether exaggerated or not, it would not have been unnatural for Dulles to consider the insecurity of his own position. The Secretary of State was hardly a dyed-in-the-wool Republican to a fair portion of the party. The arguments which had been presented against Secretaries Acheson and Marshall could also be applied to Dulles if it ever became politically advantageous. The fact that Eisenhower would have gone to every length for his Secretary did not diminish his own potential for political liability.

While riding out the storm from the beginning, Dulles succumbed to neither the methods nor the arguments of the extreme Right. As evidenced by his reactions during the Alger Hiss affair in the mid-1940s, he had a natural aversion to anything bordering on unsubstantiated charges and witch-hunting methods. Shortly after Hiss was elected President of the Carnegie Endowment for International Peace—a position which Dulles had some hand in the making—the latter, as Chairman of the Endowment, began receiving letters charging Hiss with a "provable communist record." Dulles replied:

I have heard of the reports which you refer to, but I am confident that there is no reason to doubt Mr. Hiss' complete loyalty to our American institutions. I have been thrown in intimate contact with him at San Francisco, London and Washington and I doubt that the people you refer to

. . . know him any better than I do or have seen him actually at work meeting alien efforts.

Dulles recalled that, during the campaign of 1944, he too had been a victim of "so-called documentary proof." [13]

In February of 1948, in a reply to Representative Walter H. Judd, Republican from Minnesota then serving on a subcommittee on personnel in the State Department, Dulles asserted that Hiss did "not seem to be at all un-American in actions or sympathy" in spite of the "rumors" to the contrary. When informed that files other than the State Department records, presumably Federal Bureau of Investigation files, contained some evidence of suspicion, his judgment remained one of confidence in Hiss. [14] He refused to speak against or to dismiss Hiss as President of the Carnegie Endowment on the basis of hearsay and would rely on nothing but factual information.

Half a year later, Congressman Richard Nixon sought Dulles' views on the testimony of Whittaker Chambers before the House Committee on Un-American Activities. Although Hiss had denied ever knowing Chambers, the latter not only claimed that he had known Hiss in the Communist party in the mid-1930s but, upon questioning, added many details regarding both Hiss and his wife. Confronted with such conflicting evidence, Dulles did not, in good conscience, think the young Californian congressman could simply drop the matter. Nevertheless, in 1949, he stood by his conviction that the Carnegie Endowment should not "take any action that assumes Alger Hiss to be guilty" and remained "sympathetic from Hiss' standpoint with postponing decisive action" even though perhaps unfortunate from the standpoint of the Endowment's reputation. [15]

Some doubts regarding Hiss' complete veracity began to grow as the case unraveled and came out in Dulles' testimony during the former's trial for perjury. But this testimony contained neither an indictment of Alger Hiss nor, according to one legal expert, "any controversy between the evidence of Mr. Dulles and that of Hiss on any matter in the least relevant to this case." [16] Dulles' last recorded comment on the affair, after Hiss' conviction in 1951, was less an indictment of any individual than of the times and circumstances:

"The conviction of Alger Hiss is a human tragedy. It is tragic that so great promise should have come to so inglorious an end. But the greater tragedy is that seemingly our national ideals no longer inspire the loyal devotions needed for their defense." [17]

As to the favorite arguments of the Right, Senator Taft summarized the targets in his attack upon "the pro-Communist group in the State Department who surrendered to every demand of Russia at Yalta and Potsdam, and promoted at every opportunity the Communist cause in China." [18] On the other hand, Dulles continued to deprecate any type of "scapegoat" approach to international affairs. When asked in 1949 if he agreed with the charge by Senators Knowland and Bridges that the State Department had been responsible for the communist victory in China, he replied:

Undoubtedly, they have committed sins of commission and omission in China, *but the conditions in China themselves are far more responsible for what has happened than what anybody has done or failed to do in the State Department.*[19] (Emphasis added.)

Recognizing that Acheson had "inherited a task of exceeding difficulty and delicacy," Dulles' major conclusion, after the 1949 communist victory in China, was that the United States needed to proceed with care and a bipartisan policy: "Little can be accomplished without bipartisanship with respect to Far Eastern policies." [20] The Truman Administration's China policy had evolved without any of the interparty consultation and cooperation which characterized United States policy toward Europe and later toward Japan. To Dulles, the problems of America's China policy signaled an increasingly important requirement for bipartisanship on issues in this part of the world. To many other Republicans, the communist victory meant a "no holds barred" attack on the "China policy" of the Truman Administration.

Dulles was, of course, to criticize the Democrat's "China policy" in legitimate fashion, especially during the 1952 campaign. It seemed, after all, fair to point out that what a later student of Acheson described as the Truman Administration's "belief that the Far East was a secondary area," combined with the "relative lack of familiarity and time to learn," meant that it "misjudged the implications of what happened there for American policy" [21]—not to mention the implications for American politics. These were, for the most part, precisely the targets of Dulles' political jabs.

While Dulles' approach to the Hiss affair and to some of the favorite arguments of the Right are generally clear, his approach to McCarthy was clouded by political realities and considerations during both the campaign of 1952 and the beginning of his tenure as Secretary. When his sister, a professional diplomat in her own right, warned him in the last days of the campaign of the serious damage being done by McCarthy in Washington and that "a large number of sincere patriots would vote against General Eisenhower unless 'McCarthyism' was repudiated," her impression was that "he felt that his part in the campaign was highly specialized and limited to foreign affairs. He had . . . increasingly warm respect for the President-elect [sic] and thought he would do the right thing. In the heat of the campaign any attempt to inject himself into the formulation of political tactics seemed to him awkward and perhaps even futile. . . . He did not think he should become deeply involved in partisan politics." [22]

Eisenhower's political judgment resulted in making peace with Taft and his supporters and, while whispering some qualifications, in supporting both Senators McCarthy and Jenner. Political factors also produced the decision, from the outset of the new administration in 1953, not to engage in a showdown with McCarthy and to cooperate as much as possible with Congress. Rightly or wrongly, Dulles concurred for obvious and compelling political reasons. However, after McCarthy claimed to have worked out an agreement with Greek shippers not to carry goods to the Chinese mainland in March of 1953, Secretary Dulles met with the Senator and told him in effect to discontinue his meddling in the foreign affairs business of the State Department and the Executive. Precisely how Dulles got the message across is not known, but the Senator from Wisconsin apparently agreed with the Secretary's advice on how the United States should go about restricting trade with the People's Republic of China. [23]

There can be little doubt that Senator McCarthy's methods and attacks, pandering to and arousing fear and suspicion, ran directly contrary to Dulles' grain. On February 9, 1950, McCarthy commenced his crusade against "Communists in government." Eleven days later, in the first of several speeches and interviews, the Senator read into the Senate record his charges against Secretary Acheson and the Truman Administration and of "known card-carrying Communists in the Department of State." In the uproar which followed, the Senate directed that the Foreign Relations Committee establish a subcommittee to investigate McCarthy's charges. It was this subcommittee, as Acheson was later to describe, which "furnished McCarthy with a platform, loudspeaker, and full press coverage for his campaign of vilification. . . . McCarthy maneuvered the chairman into insisting on open and public hearings and bringing out the names of alleged Communists, thus providing a feast of privileged slander." [24]

In April of 1950, Dulles described the procedures of the subcommittee as contributing to the nation's "sense of frustrating confusion." Admitting that the present circumstances required greater vigilance than ever before, but not believing in public attacks and recriminations, he thought there should be "procedures which would operate without this public spreading of suspicion." [25] Clarifying his press conference remarks in subsequent correspondence, he made it clear that he approved of neither the form nor the substance of McCarthy's attacks and the subcommittee's procedures. Referring to the Senator from Wisconsin as "sincere and misguided," Dulles did not approve of much that the Senator had done. On the other hand, he perceived no advantage to his "getting down to the level of personal attack and abuse." [26]

The fact that McCarthy's "loose charges" were given such widespread attention in 1950 indicated to Dulles that the State Department had "to a very considerable extent lost public confidence." [27] This observation applied with equal accuracy to the situation he inherited in 1953. His attempt to retain control over his own household resulted in some unpleasant and unfair, even if politically prudent and effective, incidents with some high costs in terms of individual careers (such as that of John Carter Vincent) and overall morale (as evidenced by the reverberations in the State Department of the reference to "positive loyalty"). The dismissal of Vincent, in view of the almost simultaneous nomination of Charles E. Bohlen for the Moscow post, was a sign of a Secretary carefully choosing his battles. He would "cave" on the sides when deemed necessary to salvage the core—retaining executive control over the affairs of the department and regaining congressional and public confidence in the Foreign Service and the State Department. But, whenever matters appeared to strike near the quick of either the foreign policy processes or United States foreign policy, such as the Bohlen nomination and particularly the Bricker Amendment, the Secretary would remain steadfastly immovable under pressures.

POSITIVE LOYALTY AND THE STATE DEPARTMENT

Soon after the election in November, Dulles announced that the Federal Bureau of Investigation would be conducting a thorough review of his background and that there was "going to be no taint of suspicion about the new State Department" from the top to the bottom.[28] Shortly before taking office, he had attempted to assuage any fears in the State Department by declaring that the Foreign Service members were, on the whole, competent and ought to be protected as a nonpartisan career group dedicated to promoting the interests of the United States. However, an already demoralized department gained few positive assurances from the speech's qualified tone: "Insofar as it is sound and free of corruption, it should be protected and I believe will be protected by the new administration." [29]

In spite of the fact that the address was designed primarily as positive assurance to a very troubled State Department and Foreign Service, Dulles' own position appeared slightly equivocal in light of the qualifications. Also, had he not referred to "rooting out" the "termites" in the governmental bureaucracies and getting men with a "passionate devotion to their country" in a florid campaign utterance? [30] Considering the facts that this was his only real overstatement on internal security aspects, that he personally preferred no exaggeration of or emphasis on internal security aspects, and that he was speaking before a generally conservative, very strongly anticommunist group, it was reasonable to assume that this unfortunate description in an isolated campaign statement in no way reflected Dulles' approach to the security problem. His approach to gaining political acceptance was, however, still cause for concern among a harrassed Foreign Service and State bureaucracy which found insufficient solace in the fact that the Secretary-designate appreciated their problem.

During these sensitive times there were ample sensitive chords to be struck by any qualifications. None of Dulles' statements on this matter received more attention by more people than part of his address to the department immediately after his swearing in as Secretary:

The peril is of a kind which places a special responsibility on each and every member of the Department of State and the Foreign Service. It requires of us competence, discipline, and *positive loyalty* to the policies that our President and the Congress may prescribe.

Less than that is not tolerable at this time.

Lest any misunderstand, let me add that loyalty does not, of course, call for any one to practice intellectual dishonesty or to distort his reporting to please superiors. Our foreign policies will prevail only if they are based on honest evaluations of the facts.[31] (Emphasis added.)

Actually, anything less than such requirements should hardly be tolerable at any time. But the phrase inevitably aggravated several nerve endings. Security and loyalty were congressional preoccupations which had already thrown parts of the State Department into disorder. Moreover, confronted with a Republican Administration, after having comfortably settled in under twenty years of Democratic rule, the bureaucracy was naturally uneasy and uncertain.

In some earlier drafts of the speech, no references to "loyalty" appeared. In other drafts, there appeared such phrases as "unswerving loyalty" or "a special measure of discipline and loyalty." This concern for and emphasis on loyalty derived mostly from a political strategy designed to secure his and the administration's realm generally and to avoid further congressional inroads, investigations, and suspicions. During one of the first Cabinet meetings, the President and Henry Cabot Lodge proposed a need for self-investigations by the executive branch. Although the maneuver would not prevent congressional investigations, it could possibly "take some of the steam out of them." [32] With a similar strategy possibly in mind,

Dulles' statement served to notify Congress that he, as Secretary, fully intended to manage his own household. Was he not utilizing a type of reverse psychology when, one month later, he welcomed "disclosures resulting from Congressional inquiries" if they would contribute to making "the Department of State more competent, loyal and secure" ? [33]

Recognizing some of the unfortunate repercussions of his reference to "positive loyalty," the Secretary clarified his remarks, a week later, in a fashion which left little room for misinterpretation or any discomfort.[34] The initial reference had reverberated throughout the department, and there was a tinge of truth to the idea that the phrase tended to lower the morale of the department. Such a view, however, was only a partial view of the real landscape. The morale of the State Department and the Foreign Service was at its lowest point in twenty years when Dulles assumed office. Recruitment for the Foreign Service had been suspended during the war, and no vigorous recruitment program had since emerged to revitalize the Foreign Service or to correct the inept examination and appointment procedures. A hodgepodge of agencies and departments had accumulated with no clear lines of responsibility.

Above all, the spectre of congressional investigations had been hanging over the department nearly three years before Dulles arrived. In the words of the man most closely associated with reorganization of the department in the 1950s, Henry Wriston, all these factors combined to produce a Foreign Service Institute which had "fallen into total decay."[35] Many distinguished older Foreign Service hands, like George Kennan, were not only disappointed by what they considered the incompleteness of Dulles' and Wriston's reorganization proposals and programs but also were highly critical of the problems of the security system's operations and the manner in which some career personnel had been dismissed by Dulles. Nonetheless, the fact was well recognized that, before the Republicans assumed power, the Foreign Service "was weakened beyond real hope of recovery," lay in "administrative ruin," and had already been thoroughly "demoralized by anonymous security agents." Kennan lugubriously concluded that "the experiment of professional diplomacy . . . had failed."[36]

Confronted with the China affair, the Korean War, problems in

Indochina, and the beginning of pulling NATO together—not to mention the troubles on the Hill—Secretary Acheson understandably hesitated to put into effect a basic and far-reaching reorganization of the department. Equally understandable, faced with the disrepair in the State Department and Foreign Service, was Dulles' constructive support for reorganization programs [37] in spite of the fact that like most all Secretaries of State, with the possible exception of Charles Evans Hughes, he generally found little time or interest for administrative affairs.

This characteristic disinterest, combined with the administration's process of protecting its political flanks, produced results which were undoubtedly unpleasant and unhealthy for the department and probably displeased the Secretary as well on a number of occasions. Such was the case when the Under Secretary of State for Administration, Donald B. Lourie, hired Scott McLeod to head the Bureau of Security and Consular Affairs. Scott McLeod had been an assistant to the conservative and extremely partisan Senator from New Hampshire, H. Styles Bridges. He was also a McCarthy man, now provided with access to the personnel security files and other business of the State Department. While Under Secretary Lourie "had rather innocently supposed that" McLeod's "appointment might pacify and appease the inquisitors, the effect was the precise opposite." [38] This direct line to the investigators on the Hill was serviced, and the problems in the State Department increased. By the time Dulles effectively transferred McLeod to a less strategic position, the damage had already been done and the Secretary experienced a round of execration not only from liberal and intellectual circles but also from some moderate elements.

JOHN CARTER VINCENT AND AMBASSADOR BOHLEN

Dulles' departmental and administrative problems, in the early 1950s, clearly reflected the fact that his responsibility extended beyond the department and the Foreign Service. The Secretary operates directly in the political world, the realm of possibilities and limitations imposed by the nature of the system and by the prevailing moods in the various centers of power. Because of his wider interests and responsibilities, the Secretary has the prerogative of sacrificing a few for the benefit—perhaps, in the early 1950s, for the survival—of the whole. In short, "the basic truth is that" his "interests and concerns are not always those of the bureaucracy." [39]

Protection of the Foreign Service, however, was a delicate and precarious point as Dulles inherited a dozen or more pending security cases. Much attention was focused on the issue of "controversial loyalty cases" and the Secretary's handling of a department which had already been victimized by the politicians. Several career men either resigned or lost positions during the first months of the new administration. With the passing of time, it was apparent that the Secretary never set out to "clean house" in the McCarthy sense, nor did he simply wash his hands of all controversial political liabilities. Neither was he, however, inclined to go out on a political limb for "weak cases" as necessarily defined by the political climate at the time.

Although somewhat hypercritical of or biased against President Truman, the latter years of the Democratic Administration have been thusly summarized:

When belatedly made aware of a certain amount of Communist infiltration, Mr. Truman had at once sought to tighten up security by authoritarian methods. The manner in which the loyalty order of 1947 was carried out and revised in 1951 to make "reasonable doubt" sufficient ground for dismissal led to procedures wholly foreign to American principles of justice.

. . . . [This] left his political opponents free to make the most out of his laxity while depriving his would-be defenders of a principle to defend.[40]

Considering Truman's failure, regardless of its sources, to counter effectively the charges by the Right in both parties, while such charges were still in their inchoate stages, could one expect a Republican Administration to fare any better? Admittedly, the incoming Eisenhower Administration possessed certain advantages: first, less identification with past "mistakes" not only in foreign policy, but also in the security systems operations business; second, an ability, indeed a natural desire, to point out past errors; and, third, the capability to take some steam out of the right-wing balloon by establishing itself as a staunch anticommunist force of a nonauthoritarian variety. On the other hand, the new administration inherited distinct disadvantages such as a discreditable security system, a jealous Congress and, a right-wing force of Republicans and Democrats which had gained momentum since 1949. The disadvantages precluded any quick or easy solutions.

Some of the well-known controversial "security cases" which Dulles inherited were well advanced before he assumed office and concerned senior Foreign Service Officers. The case of John Carter Vincent fell in this category. The Loyalty Review Board, established by Truman's Executive Order 9835, had been charged with the task of considering loyalty cases arising in the various governmental departments. On December 12, 1952, the board concluded by a 3–2 vote that there existed "reasonable doubt" as to Vincent's loyalty, but did not find him guilty of disloyalty. Approximately ten months before this judgment of the Loyalty Review Board, Vincent had been cleared by the State Department's Loyalty and Security Board after investigating charges by Senator McCarthy. To many, this first finding now served mainly as an indication that the department could not manage its own household.

With the Loyalty Review Board's judgment of December 12, Vincent was suspended from active duty pending Secretary Acheson's further review. Rightfully pointing out that the findings were vague and, more important, brought into question the subject of objective reporting from Foreign Service Officers, Acheson requested the President to establish "a group of unimpeachable authority and reputation to review the record and the two conflicting recommendations." [41] Acheson then raised the matter with Secretary-designate Dulles:

It seemed to me that the opinion of the Loyalty Review Board had passed judgment not on Mr. Vincent's loyalty but on the soundness of the policy recommendations he had made. If disagreements on policy were to be equated with disloyalty, the Foreign Service would be destroyed.

Acheson then informed Dulles of the proposed committee and the committee's request as to whether its review would have to be completed within the month or before Dulles assumed office.

After some discussion, in which Mr. Dulles showed an appreciation of the dangers of the Foreign Service that I had suggested, he said that he would regard the work of the board as helpful and would be glad to talk with any members who might wish to talk with him. He stressed the fact that the appointment of the board and the whole procedure should be wholly my responsibility, and not a joint responsibility. I said I fully appreciated this.[42]

As of January 20, 1953, the final decision now rested with the incoming Secretary while an *ad hoc* review board selected by the previous administration was reviewing the findings of other review boards. Regardless of the findings of the review committee headed by Judge Learned B. Hand, Dulles would still be confronted with conflicting conclusions and recommendations. After studying the matter, he informed Judge Hand that it would not be necessary for him and his associates "to act as a special review group to consider this particular case." [43] On March 4, he announced the termination of Vincent's career in the Foreign Service. However, the Secretary based the action not on the Loyalty Review Board's findings, but on the grounds that Vincent's reporting, evaluation of facts, and policy advice had failed to meet the standards demanded of his position and responsibility. Dulles positively asserted that he did not consider Vincent a "security risk" and, overruling the findings of the Loyalty Review Board, that he did not find any "reasonable doubt as to the loyalty" of Mr. Vincent. Under Public Law 495 (July 10, 1952), the Secretary had "absolute discretion" to terminate the services of an officer whenever "necessary and advisable in the interests of the United States." [44]

Whether or not Vincent's reporting and evaluation were substandard, an opinion which other Secretaries had not shared, remained, unfortunately, to some degree irrelevant. Vincent was undeniably identified as part of the policy failure in China.[45] Truman's own established Loyalty Review Board, regardless of its competence, had found "reasonable doubt" as to the loyalty of Mr. Vincent. Vincent had incurred the suspicion of the investigators in Congress, and the blunt fact was that he had become a figure in a spotlight and a definite political liability. At least partly in this sense, Dulles concluded that Vincent's usefulness as a Foreign Service officer had reached an end. The conclusion did not lack foundations. Although it is very doubtful that Dulles actually told Vincent that he suffered from the fatal weakness of having more critics than supporters in the Senate,[46] the quality of such a weakness was, in a very real sense, "fatal."

While many liberals and moderates were discouraged and dismayed by the dismissal of Vincent, and while Democrats undoubtedly did not miss a chance to execrate the Secretary, some of the conservative elements did not fail to notice that Dulles had overruled the findings of the Loyalty Review Board by stating that there was no "reasonable doubt" as to Vincent's loyalty: "Without authority and in clear violation of the regulations of the federal loyalty program, Dulles reversed the findings of the Loyalty Review Board," and thereby was accused of throwing a "wrench into the security operation of the federal government." The eloquent spokesman for the conservative segments, William Buckley, found it "curious that Secretary Dulles was never censured for his cavalier disregard of the rules." [47]

The middle course was not a very happy position. The Secretary's decision was a compromise between principle and political demands in an attempt to protect not only his own position but also that of the department and Service and foreign policy generally. A few other cases involved more or less similar compromise whenever the political liabilities question was inseparable from the subject at hand which was, however, by no measure always the case.

On the other hand, also in March, the Secretary exemplified his stand for the Foreign Service and his own prerogatives in the matter of Ambassador Charles E. Bohlen, Dulles' nominee for the ambassadorial post in Moscow. (This post had been vacant ever since Ambassador Kennan was declared *persona non grata* by the Soviet Union in 1952.) In February of 1953, Eisenhower and Dulles learned that a number of senators were out to block the nomination of Bohlen. This time Dulles viewed his brief both as defensible and, more importantly, as providing an acid test for orderly governmental processes. Was it not, after all, the prerogative of the Secretary and the President to fill ambassadorial posts? The battle which took form was a test of the Eisenhower-Dulles team's ability to bring Republican conservatives in some sort of line and isolate those further out on the wing. It also related to some of the real sore spots between different party elements.

The 1952 Republican platform had stated that the "Government of the United States, under Republican leadership, will repudiate all commitments contained in secret understandings such as those of Yalta which aid Communist enslavements." Much to the chagrin of several Republican senators, the President and Dulles supported only a rather innocuous resolution stating that the United States recognized no commitment "contained in secret understandings of the past with foreign governments" which permit enslavement. The administration had no intention of raking over the past and surely none of repudiating the agreement which gave the United States rights in Berlin and Vienna.

While the administration successfully fended off the demand of the extremists—that is, outright repudiation of the Yalta and Potsdam agreements—McCarthy and his followers took up the bludgeon against the nomination of Ambassador Bohlen. Was not Bohlen part of the Acheson-Hiss-Truman sellout? Had he not served with President Roosevelt at Yalta? Had not Scott McLeod refused to clear Bohlen after reviewing the FBI files and had not Dulles overruled one of his security officers? So went the reasoning and charges of Senators McCarthy, Malone (Republican of Nevada), and McCarran (Democrat of Nevada) on the Senate floor after the Foreign Relations Committee had unanimously approved Bohlen's nomination. The Foreign Relations Committee's unanimous approval included the votes of Republican Senators Taft, Knowland, Hickenlooper, Langer, and Ferguson.

The distinguished Foreign Service Officer had served as chief interpreter at both the Yalta and Potsdam conferences. When Dulles initially recommended Bohlen for the Moscow post, there was complete awareness that some senators would oppose the nomination. Asserting the rights of the executive branch, both Eisenhower and Dulles wholeheartedly supported the nominee. After days of testimony and countering pressure to publish the FBI reports by permitting Senators Taft and Sparkman to review the FBI files on Bohlen, the nominee was approved by the Senate with only thirteen dissenting votes. Two Democrats and eleven Republicans voted against confirmation.[48] Senators Taft and Sparkman, after reviewing the FBI files, had reported that there was nothing which should stand in the way of Senate approval and both voted for confirmation. Nevertheless, Taft considered the administration's selection gauche. He reportedly passed word to the White House—"No more Bohlens!" [49]

The Ambassador's later testimony included mention of the Secretary's predicament with several Republican and Democratic senators. At the time the Secretary "really had one obsession: to remain Secretary of State." (In view of alternative options or aspirants, as well as in view of the difficulties surrounding the office, this could be considered a somewhat admirable obsession.) Dulles clearly never suspected Bohlen. But, after the normal assurances in discussing the matter, Dulles remarked: "I'm glad to hear this. I couldn't stand another Alger Hiss." [50] In fact, a few like Senator Jenner still referred to Dulles' association in the matter of Alger Hiss. Another such incident would have unquestionably reduced the Secretary's effectiveness and credibility in relations with Congress. Another such incident, depending upon the circumstances, could possibly have ended the career of John Foster Dulles.

THE BRICKER AMENDMENT

If Ambassador Bohlen's confirmation was an acid test for orderly governmental processes, as Dulles believed, his fight against the Bricker Amendment was a struggle for nothing less than the Executive's powers in the conduct of foreign relations. He was not in any way prepared to compromise on what he considered the fundamentals of foreign policy or the foreign policy processes. In 1937, for example, he had clearly opposed the restrictions which Congress was attempting to place upon the government's power in the form of the Ludlow Amendment. This amendment, reflecting a "peace at any price" sentiment, would have required a national referendum on any declaration of war except in the case of actual invasion. Dulles felt "very strongly" that the United States should play its "part in getting rid of the war system, and of force, as the method of world evolution. Until, however, this is accomplished and we remain part of a world which functions on a war system basis, then we must be prepared to function effectively, and I do not think that this is possible where the conduct of foreign affairs is sought to be turned over to popular plebiscite." [51] Dulles was, if anything, for increased presidential discretion in the operation of foreign affairs.[52] In no debate of the early period of his secretaryship did Dulles' consistency and inflexibility prove more an asset than in the struggle for power represented by the Bricker Amendment.

On January 7, 1953, Senator Bricker and sixty-three cosponsors— 45 of the 48 Republicans and 19 of the 47 Democrats—introduced Senate Resolution 1. This proposed amendment to the Constitution read in major part:

1. A provision of a treaty which denies or abridges any right enumerated in this Constitution shall not be of any force or effect.

2. No treaty shall authorize or permit any foreign power or any international organization to supervise, control or adjudicate rights of citizens of the United States . . . or any other matter essentially within the domestic jurisdiction of the United States.

3. A treaty shall become effective as internal law in the United States only through the enactment of appropriate legislation by the Congress.

4. All executive or other agreements between the President and any international organization, foreign power, or official thereof . . . shall be subject to the limitations imposed on treaties or the making of treaties by this article.

Shortly thereafter, Senator Watkins of Utah introduced a variation of the amendment which basically included everything but the second provision. Thus, the movement began to curb the role of the President as director-in-chief of foreign affairs by doubly and perhaps triply controlling both the President's treaty-making powers and the power to pledge his word, but not his successor's, in the form of executive agreements.

Article VI of the Constitution reads: "This Constitution, and the laws . . . which shall be made in pursuance thereof; and all treaties made . . . under the authority of the United States, shall be the supreme law of the land . . . anything in the constitution or laws of any State to the contrary notwithstanding." The misoneistic concern of Senator Bricker and many others was contained in their warnings of the imposition of "socialism by treaty" on the United States and of the dangerous influence of the United Nations, the UN Human Rights Commission, and the UN supporters in the State Department.[53]

The two most controversial points, to the administration as a whole, were the "which" clause and the restrictions upon the making of executive agreements. The "which" clause, in Section 2, provided that "a treaty shall become effective as internal law . . . only through legislation which would be valid in the absence of a treaty." Although the precise meaning of the clause was unclear, it could be interpreted to subordinate the treaty-making power of the President not only to both Houses of Congress but also to the various states. On January 25, 1954, President Eisenhower informed the Majority Leader of the Senate, William Knowland, that this provision would "shackle the federal government so that it is no longer sovereign in foreign affairs." [54] The restrictions upon the President's conduct of foreign affairs in the form of executive agreements were equally objectionable to the administration.

When confronted with the proposed amendment in 1953, Dulles did not hesitate to oppose the measure. In January he wrote Eisenhower's political adviser, Sherman Adams, that the amendment "might seriously impair the treaty-making power and the ability of the President to deal with current matters . . . through Administrative agreements. I think this whole matter needs to be carefully studied." [55] Opposing this proposed encroachment on executive powers in the conduct of foreign affairs, Dulles' recommendation to study the matter meant rallying his arguments and forces against the amendment. This was no easy matter in the beginning. He not only encountered large segments of public opinion supporting the resolution and nearly two-thirds of the Senate opposing his views on the subject but he also had to convince Eisenhower and his staff of the dangers in any proposal resembling the Bricker Amendment.

The White House had been approached several times by Republican leaders with warnings of serious splits in the party in the event of an uncompromising White House. During the initial phases of the struggle, Dulles was opposing many within the administration, including Sherman Adams.

The President's position, on the other hand, appeared less clear. Attempting to mollify dissenters on the Hill, he began to consider various compromise arrangements. On March 26, he stated that the Bricker Amendment, as it stood, would mean that the President could not effectively conduct the foreign affairs of the United States. After a meeting with the President in June, Bricker reported that the difference was only one of "wording." On July 1, the President announced that he would support a Constitutional amendment which would allay the current fears, and then directed Attorney General Herbert Brownell to work with Senator Knowland on a substitute resolution. When Knowland's relatively innocuous proposal was set forth, Eisenhower gave it his "unqualified support." Knowland's proposal "ruled out any assertions of Congressional power over executive agreements and carefully excluded any state role in validating treaties as internal law." [56] Senator Bricker rejected the proposed substitute and Congress adjourned on August 3.

During the Senate debates on the issue in March, Bricker had quoted several passages from a 1952 Dulles speech to buttress arguments on the dangers of the treaty-making powers. Addressing a regional meeting of the American Bar Association, in April of 1952, Dulles had described the "treaty-making power as an extraordinary power, liable to abuse." He then expounded upon the subject by stating not merely that treaties become the supreme law of the land, but that treaties were more supreme than ordinary laws which become invalid if they do not conform to the Constitution. Treaties, thus, could "override the Constitution":

Treaties . . . can take power from the States and give them to the Federal Government or to some international body, and they can cut across the rights given the people by their Constitutional Bill of Rights.

This extraordinary power seems to have been deliberately intended by our founders in order to give the Federal Government untrammeled authority to deal with international problems.[57]

While the speech included praise for Bricker's endeavor to "study" the matter, Dulles cautiously left room for his own disagreement. (As it turned out, a former President of the American Bar Association and the ABA's Committee on Peace and Law Through the United Nations were to become two of the most avid supporters of the Bricker Amendment.) The prospective Secretary of State, however, was far less concerned with theoretical possibilities of abuse than with the course proposed by Bricker.

If, as Senator Bricker was to state, these remarks acknowledged a need for a Constitutional amendment restricting the president's powers of treaty-making and executive agreements, Dulles quickly belied such a reading of his speech. In the hearings of the Judiciary Committee, he flatly stated his opposition to the proposed amendment, the operation of which would present "a far worse danger" to the Republic than the potential for abuse in the treaty-making power.[58] The Secretary later wrote the President:

I realize that action by the Senate is but the first of many steps in the process of constitutional amendment. *I would myself be confident that on reflection the further steps would not be taken because sober thought would convince the nation of the danger of a program which would, in large measure, reproduce the international impotence which marked the Confederation* during the period preceding the adoption of our Constitution. . . . If the Senate with its great influence and prestige should by a two-thirds vote adopt the proposed amendment, *this would be taken by our friends and by our enemies as foreshadowing a revolutionary change in the position of the United States.*[59] (Emphasis added.)

Dulles became anathema to Bricker and the pro-Bricker Amendment forces. Senators Knowland, Bricker, and Millikin were convinced that the Secretary would not budge. The Secretary and his legal adviser, Herman Phleger, "became well entrenched in their opposition to anything resembling the Bricker Amendment, no matter how harmless or well intentioned such a proposal might appear." [60]

When Congress reconvened in 1954, the political battleground was well gone over and prepared. The Senate Republican leadership put forward an amendment to delete the "which" clause and substitute a provision, amending Article VI of the Constitution, to the effect that "no treaty made after the establishment of this Constitution shall be the supreme law of the land unless made in pursuance of this Constitution." On February 17, the Senate agreed to this amendment by a slim vote of 44–43 (Republicans 38–4, Democrats 6–39). Reconciled to losing the "which" clause, Senator Bricker voted for its deletion. He then moved to support a strengthened version of a substitute amendment which included the following, rather strained, provision:

A treaty or other international agreement shall become effective as internal law in the United States only through legislation by the Congress, unless in advising and consenting to a treaty the Senate, by a vote of two-thirds of the Senators present and voting, shall provide that such treaty may become effective as internal law without legislation by the Congress.

Opposed by the administration, by Senator Knowland, and other Republican leaders, the Senate rejected this move by Bricker, on February 25, by a vote of 42–50 with a majority of the Republican senators going against the White House and the Senate leadership (Republicans 29–17, Democrats 13–32, Independent 0–1).

Two courses of action remained: first, a relatively innocuous, administration-endorsed version; and, second, a similar substitute, proposed earlier by Senator George, which differed very importantly in that it gave Congress the power to decide whether executive agreements would become effective as internal law. From the inception of the George proposal in January, the Eisenhower Administration had consistently opposed the provision on executive agreements on the grounds that it would "infringe on the President's war powers and his authority to extend recognition to foreign governments." [61] The latter half of the administration's argument surely had little effect upon a Senate which unanimously and adamantly opposed any form of recognition of Communist China.

On February 26, the Senate substituted the George proposal for the administration-endorsed version by a vote of 61–30 (Republicans 30–16, Democrats 31–13, Independent 0–1). Since precisely two-thirds supported substituting this proposal, victory for the amendment appeared imminent. Senator Knowland announced that he would vote for the amendment in spite of the opposition of the

White House. With two other Republicans switching their votes to "yea," and one Republican and four Democrats switching their votes to "nay," the proposed amendment was defeated by one vote. Sixty senators, 32 Republicans and 28 Democrats, voted against the White House. The Bricker Amendment was dead even though Bricker announced his intention to continue the battle in the next Congress: "The threat of treaty law has not abated. The treaty-making ambitions of the United Nations and its agencies continue to reflect a zeal to regulate the political, economic and social rights and duties of people everywhere." [62]

Such a view and fear were totally foreign to Dulles' entire approach. His staunch opposition to any form of a Bricker Amendment was not without some cost—although a very minor price in terms of what he saw at stake. In 1948, as acting chairman of the United States delegation to the United Nations, Dulles had strongly supported the General Assembly's adoption of the Universal Declaration of Human Rights and the Genocide Convention. The latter was in the form of treaty to be ratified by the member nations, whereas the former was a declaration of standards. Dulles also supported, however, the effort to draw up an International Convention on Human Rights. In *War or Peace* (1950) he wrote:

Thus there is some progress in making human rights a subject of international law.

The founders of our nation, who sought to make a union of the thirteen sovereign states, were emphatic that both federal laws and treaties should be the "laws of the land" and enforceable by and against individuals just like state laws. They felt that federal laws and treaties often would not work well if they only operated upon states and depended on intermediate state laws for enforcement.

However, the United States is drifting away from that point of view. We do not seem to be willing to permit international law defining individual rights and duties to become the law of our land. The Genocide Convention was deliberately drawn so that it would not be "the law of the land," but would call only for subsequent domestic legislation. . . . The same problem will arise in connection with any convention on human rights.

Obviously, respect for and observance of human rights depends largely upon community sentiment; and it would be foolish to ignore the fact.

But some basic rights are admitted by every civilized community and reflect the conscience of mankind. . . .

Those [referring to Soviet leaders] who operate a police state must always fight for the concept that there are no human rights except as governments choose to accord them. They cannot admit that human rights and fundamental freedoms exist irrespective of national laws or admit that international law should recognize those rights.

In the early days of the United States there was clear thinking and high purpose in these matters. There is again need for such qualities today.[63]

The Universal Declaration of Human Rights and Genocide Convention, not to mention Dulles' whole approach, was obviously anathema to a very considerable portion of the Bricker Amendment supporters. In fighting against the amendment, Dulles had attempted to weaken congressional arguments by stating that the administration had no intention to press for human rights covenants in general or for ratification of the Genocide Convention in particular. Without this concessive understanding the arguments against the White House and Dulles might have been more effective. To be sure, an understanding of any statesman "requires the appreciation of conditions and forces at work outside the Cabinet room which are often by no means what the responsible authorities would wish." [64]

CHAPTER TEN

THE POLITICS AND DIPLOMACY
OF SECRETARYSHIP
PART II: SAMPLES OF FOREIGN POLICY

While the preceding chapters set the political stage for a clearer understanding of Dulles and his secretaryship, they do not provide, nor attempt to provide, any simple framework from which his foreign policy moves can be deduced. If international circumstances, past policies, the political environment generally, and Washington politics all impinge upon the formulation and presentation of foreign policy, the actual impact of each of these factors varies widely from issue to issue. It remains to be seen, in a sampling of cases in decision and tactics, how diverse considerations and pressures interacted in Dulles' decision-making processes.

The different roles these factors played are illustrated in five case studies—"agonizing reappraisal," the "massive retaliation" debate, the 1954 Geneva Conference on Indochina, "neutralism," and the Suez crisis of 1956. In the first case, for example, domestic and congressional political considerations were not necessarily restricting factors upon the Secretary's policy preferences and options. He might have preferred to operate without the congressional concerns which were present and obvious; but, if anything, these concerns probably strengthened his hand in following his natural inclinations in the "agonizing reappraisal" statement. It was vintage and deliberate Dulles. At the other end of the spectrum, there was the 1954 Geneva Conference on Indochina where a host of international and internal political factors compounded to restrict United States policy options and flexibility.

The "massive retaliation" debate, the "off again, on again" attitude of the United States government toward the phenomenon of "neutralism," and the consistent but not always clear policy during the Suez episode are not as easily explained. Perceived international interests, international circumstances, past policies, and technological considerations provided the basic framework within which the substantive issues and related explanations were decided. Nonetheless, factors beyond the control of the Secretary or the President could significantly affect timing, tactics, and even the extent to which a policy was understood correctly or misunderstood. Why, for example, did Dulles' so-called massive retaliation speech cause so much concern in 1954 in view of the fact that the same thesis had been announced in much the same language several months earlier? What accounted for the inconsistencies and uncertainties in the United States policy toward "neutralism"? How could the United States hand be forced by the actions of others at different stages during the unraveling of events leading to the Suez crisis? Each of these three policy cases involved problems in balancing diverse interests and viewpoints.

AGONIZING REAPPRAISAL

United States postwar foreign policy has, to some extent, always contained evidence of an inherent tension between the United States commitment and interest in a broad "Atlantic community" concept and the American preference for European integration. Over the years this tension has learned to work itself more often than not in comparatively subtle, quiet ways both in Europe and in the United States. But, during the postwar process of defining the American commitment and aid to a war-ravaged Europe, it was a far more obvious and, at times, intrusive factor in Atlantic relations.

In 1947, testifying before the Senate Foreign Relations Committee on the subject of interim aid to Europe, Dulles asserted that the basic concept should not be "the rebuilding of the prewar Europe, but the building of a new . . . more unified . . . better Europe." [1] The statement reflected a generally accepted interpretation of American interests both in Congress and in the Truman Administration. The 1948 Marshall Plan for the reconstruction of Europe was purposely designed in a manner to encourage the idea of intra-European cooperation.

The concern for European integration was, to Dulles, not a product of the developing cold war even though the Soviet attitude and obstructions to postwar cooperation no doubt accentuated the desire for increased strength and unity. On several occasions during the war, he had expressed an American interest in a federated continental Europe, or some type of commonwealth, or some form of regional collaboration.[2] Although he most often referred to a federal-type approach, the actual political form for collaboration was apparently far less important than the idea that postwar European development be in the direction of increased economic and political unification rather than a return to the relatively unconnected and insulated national systems.

Throughout the early 1940s, prewar Europe was characterized by Dulles as a "firetrap" whose outdated political and economic mechanisms failed to reflect both the degree to which Europeans were interdependent and the need for resource and market coordination in maximum development. He believed that the United States, even "from a purely selfish standpoint," had a fundamental interest in European stability, independence, and maximum economic growth, and that these developments depended largely upon increased European integraton.[3] He was, moreover, inclined to view "self-seeking politicians" as the prime barrier to the movement for European untiy while both labor and business interests appeared willing to cooperate: "Because a lot of politicians want to hold on to the trappings of sovereignty, are we to allow a condition to persist which makes recurrent war inevitable and which . . . inevitably involves our being drawn into such wars." [4] Understanding that Prime Minister Churchill may prefer the policy of continued division and balance, he sided with the British Labor party leader's statement that "Europe must federate or perish." [5]

In the early postwar period, the interest in European integration was expressed by Dulles at the operational, policy-formulation level. When the subject of a regional military arrangement and a United States guarantee came up in the inner councils of the government in 1948, he questioned the soundness of a long-term, formalized agreement. Such an agreement, he thought, could easily be interpreted as a guarantee of the *status quo* and inculcate a sense of permanency which could well prove counterproductive to the American interest in increased European integration. He did not, however, question the necessity for some form of United States guarantee to Europe. Once the United States commitment began to take shape in the form of the North Atlantic Treaty Organization, he supported the proposal without reservation but emphasized its broad "community" aspects. The idea, once again, was to operate the organization in a manner which would stimulate rather than discourage European unity.[6]

Increased economic and political cooperation and integration in Europe remained a consistent postwar theme both in numerous statements and at private levels. Although Dulles, not to mention European leaders who were arguing for a similar direction, frequently drew upon the American experiment as an example, the "Americanization" of Europe was not the issue. The issue was his belief that certain basic principles of organization and coordination were required for both stability and maximum economic growth and that United States working relations would be easier and healthier with a stable and thriving Europe. The issue was compounded by the problem of Germany. Desiring a productive and revitalized Germany, which he had also pressed for after World War I, there remained the question of how this could be brought about in the least disturbing manner to France, the Soviet Union, and others concerned with the possibility of a revanchist Germany. European integration seemed to provide a workable solution to this dilemma.

Dulles was convinced that the evolution of postwar Europe could be influenced by United States policies and actions, and that the in-

terest in European integration should not and need not be short
shrifted by the equally vital interest in Atlantic alliance. In its sim-
plest form this meant that "if the United States . . . is going to take
a continuing interest in the affairs of Europe, it is imperative that
we have clear-cut policies. We need to know our own mind. Also,
the peoples of Europe are entitled to know our intentions, so that
they can judge them." [7] To many Europeans, although surely not
all, the price of American commitment and aid appeared to be
American meddling in their internal affairs. This suspicion and
concern was not without some basis as evidenced by the following
exchange in 1949, during the Senate Foreign Relation Committee's
hearings on NATO:

Senator Fulbright: That part . . . recalls to my mind a very excellent
statement you made. . . . You said that several of the leaders of the European countries had expressed to you the view that they needed a little
push toward European federation and European unity. Do you consider
that this Government is giving them an adequate push in that direction,
in this last year and three months?

Mr. Dulles: No, sir, I do not.

Senator Fulbright: I may say I agree with you. And I have the feeling
that that has been one of the principal failures of our foreign policy.[8]

One of the European leaders with whom Dulles apparently discussed problems of European integration over the years was a friend
of long standing who helped lead the way toward the European
Economic Commission in 1958, Jean Monnet.

The usually more subtle ways and quiet "sticks and carrots" of
the later 1960s and 1970s were not the ways or American political
"truth" at mid-century. In *War or Peace,* Dulles claimed that dis-
unity alone prevented "Western Europe from being a great—perhaps
the greatest—distinctive area of spiritual, intellectual, economic and
military power." But this carrot had a stick. Since European unity
would not be accomplished without "friendly but firm outside pressure," the "United States can and should take that opportunity and
exert that pressure." [9] At this time he also believed that time for
effective pressure was running short as increased socialization and
economic planning in Europe seemed to argue for insulation and
protection rather than adaptation to a larger community.[10]

Prior to his becoming Secretary, there was every indication that the tension between the United States interest in an Atlantic community and alliance and an interest in increased intra-European cooperation or European integration was a much livelier issue in Dulles' mind than in Acheson or Truman's. One could expect far more than lip service to the latter interest if or when Dulles came into power. Contrary to some appearances, however, he was not insensitive to the Europeans' feelings and the predicament for American foreign policy. In a broadcast interview during the campaign of 1952, Dulles expressed disappointment with the progress to date in the movement for European unity. On the other hand, he concluded:

It's not easy to put a time limit on and then give an ultimatum. . . . I think we need to work more effectively toward it than we have done. Part of the mistake to date is our mistake and not just the mistake of the Europeans. . . . I think the Administration [Truman] is behind it now to a degree that it has not been before.

There are many ways whereby persuasion and influence, if exerted in a skillful way, can help to bring about this result. But I don't think to wave a big stick and threaten is a way to deal with friendly sovereign countries.[11]

But, in the case of the European Defense Community, a type of "big stick" emerged as a live option.

The treaty for the European Defense Community was signed on May 27, 1952, by the governments of Germany, Belgium, France, Italy, Luxembourg, and the Netherlands, with the aim of establishing an integrated European army. It was hoped, by Dulles and many others, that the treaty would be ratified and become operative within six to nine months. In furthering this hope, he undertook a journey to seven European capitals almost immediately after assuming office in 1953. Reporting to the nation upon his return, his themes were European integration, military unity, and the firmness of the United States commitment. All three themes were aimed at both his domestic and international audience; and the third theme was particularly important by serving not only to remind Americans of their own interest in a commitment to Europe but also to meet the concerns of those many Europeans who not unnaturally suspected the United States interest in European integration derived from a longing to be able to dissociate itself once again from "entangling alliances."

The principal message to Europe was abundantly clear. While the United States had been "delighted that our European friends had taken this bold step" toward military unity, the delay in ratification of the treaty was now "somewhat disconcerting . . . because the plans for our own security are based on the assumption that the North Atlantic Treaty Organization . . . would be bolstered by the European Defense Community, which would draw on German military strength." Describing his mission as one of sounding out European positions, he concluded that the EDC "was not dead but only sleeping." Both the President and his Secretary of State had a keen interest in this project: "We hope that in the coming weeks this determination will be translated into concrete evidence that real progress is being made. *Without that, future planning will be difficult. Candor requires us to say this."* [12] (Emphasis added.)

A few weeks prior to this nationwide address, the Secretary had relied upon a slightly more diplomatic approach: "If . . . France, Germany and England should go their separate ways . . . certainly it would be necessary to give a *little rethinking* to America's own foreign policy in relation to Western Europe." [13] (Emphasis added.) Shortly after his return from Europe, EDC was the "most urgent matter" in European discussions, and a matter "which very vitally concerns the United States because our own planning as a member of the North Atlantic Treaty Organization has been proceeding on the assumption that that treaty . . . represents a course which they [Europeans] intended to follow." [14] Diplomatic niceties aside, the message was the same. The airing of these warnings, however, did nothing to remove the impasse to the treaty's coming into effect. France, as the key country, had neither ratified nor made moves to bring the matter to a vote in the National Assembly.

At the NATO ministerial meeting of April 23, 1953, it became apparent that the patience of the United States was running thin. While expressing encouragement about renewed European interest in EDC and its prospects for success, Dulles declared that it would be difficult to get funds for NATO through Congress unless the EDC came into effect soon.[15] The NATO meeting adopted a resolution attaching "paramount importance to the rapid entry into force" of the EDC treaty, and the American Secretary responded that the delay "strains our patience" but "should not break it." [16] Shortly thereafter, it was made clear that the United States viewed EDC as "necessary in itself" and "not linked up with existing international tensions," so that "a relaxation of tensions'. . . would not in any way detract from the importance of proceeding." [17]

But a series of announcements and private pressures proved ineffective in the sense that no French government—although apparently favoring EDC—brought the treaty before the National Assembly. The project remained in limbo and the policy of the United States and other allies was, for all practical purposes, stymied. The American interest was, by no means, the only concerned party. In his discussions with Dulles, in November of 1952, British Foreign Secretary Eden reportedly defined ratification of the German Peace Contract as the most urgent problem facing Western Europe. The economic advantages accruing to Germany by virtue of its remaining disarmed were only too obvious to the struggling postwar British economy.[18] Having stayed apart from the EDC project, however, the United Kingdom had comparatively little leverage to exercise in breaking the log jam at this stage.

The dilemma for Dulles and United States policy became less how to ensure ratification of the EDC, although this remained a principal aim, and more how to break the log jam in order either to attain ratification or to get on with working out possible alternatives. In this sense, French rejection of the treaty would present a far better situation than that created by French inaction, for the latter simply blocked possible renegotiation and held up the question of West Germany's future. With rejection emerging as a better bargain than inaction, and since normal diplomatic methods had failed, a stronger dosage of candor appeared a justified and reasonable tactic. At the December meeting of the NATO Council, after reassuring NATO allies that EDC would not mean United States abandonment of military support but would "insure intimate and durable cooperation," the American Secretary declared that

failure to move toward unification through the EDC and a settlement of the German question "would compel an *agonizing reappraisal* of *basic* United States policy." (Emphasis added.) Recognizing that the formula was not perfect and presented problems, he
was convinced that "the EDC Treaty . . . decisively poses a fateful
choice." [19]

The phrase "agonizing reappraisal," while perhaps strong diplomatically speaking and looking like a threatening stick which he
thought unwise earlier, cannot easily be considered a case of overstatement. Had not, as Dulles soon thereafter claimed, the "forward
strategy" of NATO been initiated "on the assumption that there
would soon be German participation in the common defense"? [20]
EDC seemed to provide the solution to a rearmed Germany without
unnecessarily disturbing France and the Soviet Union. Without
EDC, would the United States and other allies decide to go their
own ways in dealing with the German question? Meanwhile, where
did all of this leave Germany? More fundamentally, what would
this do to the American commitment? The Richards Amendment to
the foreign aid bill had stipulated that half of the appropriations
for the following year were to be disbursed by the EDC. Regardless
of whether the Secretary would or would not have preferred to operate without such Congressional action, congressional support for
European integration in general and EDC in particular existed and
in effect handed Dulles a "bigger stick."

In this light Dulles' earlier references to "difficult planning" or a
"little rethinking" if the EDC project aborted and each country
went its respective way appear as polite understatements. Continued French inaction and lack of cooperation would have necessitated serious rethinking of policy and, in view of the United States
postwar interests and hopes, this process would have been "agonizing." When the phrase hit the streets, "several usually anti-Ameri-
can papers as *Combat* and *Le Monde*" conceded that the warning
was justified but deplored certain aspects of the language. Vice-Pre-
mier Paul Reynaud reportedly had a similar reaction: "Perhaps
Dulles could have used more diplomatic language, but that is not
important. What is important is that Dulles spoke the truth." Belgian's Foreign Minister agreed that the time was on hand for a "yes

or no on European unity," and the British found the "warning timely and useful." [21] In the final analysis, "agonizing reappraisal" was a deliberately frank description of the American position designed to reach the European public and parliaments, particularly the French, as well as the government leaders.

Whether or not this calculated use of strong language or "bombshell" was justified is less important than the question whether it proved counterproductive in terms of policy preferences. To many, this seemed to be the case when, on August 30, 1954, the French National Assembly rejected the EDC treaty. Having issued, since December of 1953, United States assurances that EDC would not lessen the American interest in and commitment to Europe, the American Secretary described the French "negative action, without the provision of any alternative" as necessitating a review of United States policy vis-à-vis Europe. But the United States also stood "ready to support the many in Western Europe" who wished to move ahead as planned, and Dulles counseled against any hasty American reactions:

It is a tragedy that in one country nationalism, abetted by communism, has asserted itself so as to endanger the whole of Europe. That tragedy would be compounded if the United States was thereby led to conclude that it must turn to a course of narrow nationalism. *It is a matter of elementary prudence that the United States should review its dispositions and planning in the light of the new situation. . . . In doing so, we shall be governed by the realization that we cannot in isolation find safety for ourselves.*[22] (Emphasis added.)

But French rejection of EDC did not necessarily mean Dulles' earlier move was counterproductive. As noted earlier, rejection was the second best alternative in that it created conditions for renegotiation. Foreign Secretary Eden took the initiative and, on October 3, the Final Act of the Nine-Power London Conference was signed and European defense relationships were established within the 1948 Brussels Treaty structure. Dulles worked closely with Eden before and during the conference and, thereafter, concluded that "a large part of what was sought to be achieved by EDC" had been salvaged. He noted further that the agreements contained a "tremendous asset not present in EDC—the generous committal of the

United Kingdom to the defense of the Continent." While Dulles re-affirmed the American commitment and praised Eden's initiative, the latter commented on the American Secretary's "much valued frankness" during the meetings regarding the wave of disillusion-ment in America, especially in Congress, and the skepticism regarding long-term commitments to Europe.[23] Whatever effect the "agonizing reappraisal" statement may have had on Dulles' image, it was not counterproductive to United States policy and interests.

If "agonizing reappraisal" was neither a diplomatic blunder nor the work of an "angry man," it was the product of an impatient Sec-retary. There were, to be sure, not altogether unpowerful forces at work in the United States for pulling out in the event Europe would not gird itself for its own defense. These political forces would gain momentum as long as Europe's defense project drifted and, to Dulles, further drift was untenable. The whole episode could well have brought back the unpleasant memories of the drift after World War I with Great Britain and the United States re-maining disentangled while France sought guarantees. At that time he favored American participation in the League of Nations and utilizing the "carrot" of canceling or greatly easing the war debts owed the United States as leverage in working out an overall politi-cal-economic settlement in Europe. At mid century the United States perhaps had more leverage to exercise as this time its commit-ment was in the "pot." A repeat of the interwar experience was, to Dulles, totally unacceptable.

While risking some of the Atlantic community interest for the benefit of European integration, Dulles was not unaware of Euro-pean sensibilities. In fact, over the years of his secretaryship, his own commitment to the community concept appeared to become more firm, almost as though making up for his ruffling of European feathers in 1953. He attempted to expand the areas for political consultation and cooperation within NATO and defined its aim as the development of "the Atlantic Community . . . whose roots are far deeper than those necessary for the common defense." [24] The Secretary also remained particularly sensitive to the European side of the question regarding the forward deployment of United States divisions. While the President was also firmly committed to a strong

British Foreign Secretary Eden and Dulles, during consultations in Washington on the Geneva Conference and Indochina (1954)

Dulles and German Chancellor Konrad Adenauer

Soviet Foreign Minister Molotov, British Foreign Secretary Macmillan, Secretary Dulles, and Austrian Foreign Minister Figl at a reception following the signing of the Austrian State Treaty in Vienna (May 1955)

Secretary Dulles, Soviet Premier Bulganin, and Communist
Party First Secretary Nikita Khrushchev, at the Geneva Summit
(July 1955)

Soviet Foreign Minister Shepilov, left, addresses United Nations Security Council during Suez crisis debates with British Foreign Secretary Lloyd and Secretary Dulles listening. Henry Cabot Lodge at far right (October 1956)

RIGHT: With Indian Prime Minister
Nehru (1956)
BELOW: With Generalissimo Chiang
Kai-shek (1956)

Princeton University Library

General Eisenhower and Winston Churchill, with Dulles during his last days

Dulles sailing, a lifelong pleasure and challenge

Princeton University Library

NATO, how one attained strength and viability left room for differences of opinion. According to one involved observer, Dulles "consistently opposed Eisenhower's tendency to reduce the number of American divisions in Europe, a move which was supported by all the [Joint] Chiefs except the Army." [25] If the Europeans suspected the Secretary's motives in 1954, he left little room for any suspicion thereafter on the subject of the American commitment to Europe.

THE MASSIVE RETALIATION DEBATE

Soon after the "agonizing reappraisal" speech, another so-called Dulles bombshell exercised not only American allies but also the Americans themselves in a debate about "massive retaliation." Dulles' actual statement of policy—namely, that "local defenses must be reinforced by the further deterrent of massive retaliatory power" [26]—was obviously less journalistic. But the more popular phrase became so deeply embedded in the public mind that many considered the Secretary as a man who enjoyed brandishing nuclear weapons and who had lost his sense of selectivity and flexibility. Nonetheless, Dulles' address before the Council on Foreign Relations, on January 12, 1954, contained no passages which warranted such conclusions. An understanding of both Dulles' position and the issue involves several interrelated factors: first, his approach and thinking on the subject before 1954; second, the context of the Council speech setting forth the policy, plus the background and reasons for it; third, why the announcement caused so much concern in 1954 in view of the fact that the same thesis had been advanced in much the same language, by Dulles and others, several months earlier; and finally, the Secretary's thoughts and adjustments in the months and years following.

Much of the "massive retaliation" debate, of course, centered about whether the United States actually possessed adequate diversification of forces and whether it had, in fact if not in word, locked itself into the options of nuclear holocaust or inaction. In a few senses, this had already tended to be the case before Dulles entered office. The Korean experience found the United States ill-prepared for limited conflict. The Truman Administration had previously a sort of unstated "all or nothing" doctrine in its planning and presumptions. Moreover, both at this time and during the "massive retaliation" debate, military technology and planning themselves did not provide for many flexible response options unless one were willing to entertain very much higher defense budgets.

But the questions pertaining to military hardware and quantity of forces *per se* do not lie within the scope of a study dealing with Dulles' approach and frame of mind within his area of responsibility. The decisions relating to military hardware must be assigned to Eisenhower, the Joint Chiefs of Staff, Secretary of Defense Wilson, and Secretary of the Treasury Humphrey. As far as the so-called bigger bang for "lesser cost" was concerned, one observer noted Humphrey's advice was "determining." He was, with the exception of the President, "the strongest personality and had the strongest influence." [27] Respecting Eisenhower's background and position, which was not symptomatic of the "all or nothing" thesis, Dulles had no reason impoliticly to question the General's competence in his dealing with his military advisers. While his adherence to the broad outlines of the adopted strategy never dimmed his awareness of the need for conventional forces, local defenses, and some flexible response capabilities, the Secretary of State was assured by those responsible that adequate diversification existed.

Prelude to the Council Speech

The Secretary of State was, however, necessarily concerned with overall military posture and with the implications of this posture for diplomatic maneuverability and foreign policy. In 1946–1947 Dulles began to concentrate on the concept of deterrence. According to this idea, the United States had to maintain a credible military force capable of deterring war by making aggression appear an unprofitable business. In combination with this force, there had to be an expressed will and determination to meet aggression if it occurred and a rather clear definition of American interests. Convinced that any open Soviet aggression would probably be a product of miscalculation, he believed that official actions and utterances should leave no room for miscalculation in the minds of the Soviet leaders.

Dulles was convinced that deterrence could work, if the strategy was effectively organized and explained, primarily because the Soviet leaders neither wished nor were prepared for war, particularly one which could endanger the citadel of the communist experiment. They were not, according to Dulles, irrationally and ideologically bent on short-term programs. War was avoidable because a variety of United States and Soviet interests made it an unattractive option, not merely because the United States possessed a particular weapon of terrifying power. In 1949, when asked to what extent the atom bomb deterred the Soviet Union, Dulles responded: "I don't think it is a decisive factor—although that's only a guess." [28] During these years he also concentrated on the political, psychological, and economic aspects of the cold war challenge. Military power, to contain and deter possible Soviet adventures, was viewed as a necessary item to provide the "umbrella" under which the nonmilitary competition would take place.

In 1951–1952, after the outbreak of war in Korea, his statements concentrated more on the problem of deterrence and what he considered the general lessons of the commencement of hostilities in the Far East. Once the political rhetoric is washed off, it becomes apparent that nearly all the thoughts which formed the basis for his 1954 statement were developed during this time. The principle political-military lessons of Korea were, to Dulles, the following:

1. The strategy and power of deterrence had to be openly organized and more clearly defined to avoid miscalculation; and deterrence as a political-military-psychological concept must be developed.

2. Effective deterrence depended upon allied cooperation. American troops in Europe should be recognized as part of a deterrent power.

3. The United States should organize its deterrent power in a manner which would assure allies and potential adversaries that the United States would never take the military offensive.

4. There should be continued stress upon mobile air and sea power in deterring a major aggressive move by the Soviet or Chinese Red Armies.

5. Massive retaliatory power related only to aggression which itself constituted or would inevitably lead to general war.

6. Local defenses and conventional forces should not be abandoned, for limited conflicts would require limited responses.[29]

Believing that the miscalculation which led to the Korean conflict might possibly have been avoided, and recognizing that Truman had had to deal with a strong congressional and public sentiment for rapid demobilization to a minimum, Dulles' answer was that a willingness and appropriate means to defend interests must be made credible to minimize the prospect for a series of Korean-type wars.

To say that the United States could not be committed to a series of Koreas around the world was not to say that limited aggression would be met by an unlimited, general war response. Admitting that there were, indeed, "gray areas" of the world where United States interests were not vitally involved, he still thought that policy should be designed hopefully to keep the competition in these areas below the level of open, armed aggression across borders. Besides his broad strategy of deterrence against major attack by the Soviet Union or Communist China, discussed below, he therefore devised a related, but distinct, line in his approach to accomplish the purpose of avoiding war in the "testing ground" areas. This line meant first the establishment of a credible will and determination rather than "writing off" an area:

Is it not time that the Chinese Communists knew that if, for example, they sent their Red Armies *openly* into Vietnam, we will not be content merely to try to meet their armed forces at the point they select for their aggression, but by *retaliatory action* of our own fashioning.[30] (Emphasis added.)

"Retaliatory action" left room for a variety of possible responses. Since there existed in the Far East no clear demarcation line between reasonably establisished spheres, as there did in Europe, there was not precisely the same type of "trip wire" thesis for the former. Therefore, Dulles' line meant secondly that while possible responses could not always be clearly defined, it was "necessary to throw the aggressor off balance, to create doubts and uncertainties in his mind, and to deny him untroubled leisure to consolidate his gains." These doubts and uncertainties could work not only to limit conflict if it occurred, but also to deter its occurrence. This idea was qualified, however, by the statement that "we must not and will not take the military offensive of general war in which there could be no victory for anyone." [31]

In his major 1952 campaign article, "A Policy of Boldness," Dulles outlined his thoughts on deterrence at considerable length. Listing several reasons why the Soviet Union neither wished nor relied on military aggression—including, for example, harm to the communist image abroad, a preference for political methods, recognition of the industrial superiority of the West, and respect for atomic weapons—he concluded that:

The cumulative weight of these deterrents has proved great. It would be made overwhelming by the creation of a community punishing force known to be ready and resolute to retaliate, in the event of *any* armed aggression, with *weapons* of its choosing against *targets* of its choosing at *times* of its choosing.

Today atomic energy, coupled with strategic air and sea power, provides the community of free nations with vast new possibilities of organizing a community power to stop open aggression before it starts. . . . *In the hands of the statesmen, they [atomic weapons] could serve as effective political weapons in defense of the peace.*[32] (Some emphasis added.)

"Any armed aggression" did not imply that local conflicts and civil strifes would be turned into major battlefields, for the article referred to major aggressive moves by the Soviet Union and its satellites or China. Moreover, Dulles asserted that this did "not mean that old ways of defending the peace should be abandoned where they can still be efficacious. The United States should maintain a strong military force befitting our responsibilities." [33] As brought out in another 1952 piece, he was under no illusions regarding any military panacea to the problem of conflict control:

Even when we deter Soviet or Chinese Communists from open invasion with their Red Armies, there will still remain the problem of dealing with local revolts which may be stimulated and secretely aided from without. . . . Once that external menace is neutralized by a known will and capacity to retaliate, then the internal revolutionary problem will become more manageable.[34]

In several respects Dulles was merely reiterating the established policy of the Truman Administration which assumed that deterrence against any major move by the Soviet Union or China should be based upon nuclear weapons, air, and sea power. At the same time, however, he believed that one had to attempt to extend deterrence into the "gray areas." This was to be accomplished by establishing a will and determination not to ignore open aggression while leaving the nature of the possible response vague or uncertain. In fact, in view of the Korean experience, it was not unnatural that Dulles' explanations contained a clearer dosage of limited or flexible response ideas than the Truman Administration's earlier approach.

On the other hand, the prospective Secretary of State was at variance with the Truman Administration's approach in an important aspect. In 1952 he thought that there was only "a vague impression" that the United States would retaliate against the Soviet Union in the event of a major attack. Neither had the potential adversary "been given the kind of warning which is necessary for a deterrent to be fully effective," but strategic air power could not serve as an effective deterrent in the absence of political decisions with United States allies. He concluded thusly:

There is urgent need to clear up the present vagueness by a free world decision which the potential aggressors cannot misjudge, either as to its power or its certainty—and "certainty" means not only a statement of the circumstances of aggression under which punishing power would surely be invoked, but also certainty that it would never be invoked except under such circumstances.[35]

Dulles was perhaps the first postwar Secretary of State who, from the beginning, started to think in terms of overall strategy and posture and the implications for American foreign policy. This was a natural evolution, for his emergence as a national figure coincided with the developing dialogue on deterrence within the government and in academic circles. Upon entering office, he believed that the strategy of and power for deterrence had to be more openly organized and clearly defined.

When all was said and done before he became Secretary, however, Dulles reflected a tendency to rely primarily upon the air-sea argument. The first drafts of "A Policy of Boldness" in 1952 reflected the tendency more than the final product which defended the air-sea deterrent power in terms of economic necessity. (As noted below, economic considerations were not minor at mid-century. Such considerations had been highlighted in Dulles' writings on the subjects of war and armaments from 1924 through *War, Peace and Change.*) The air-sea impression was clear in 1952, and General Eisenhower wrote to his prospective Secretary of State that "exclusive reliance upon a mere power of retaliation" was "not a complete answer to the broad Soviet threat." [36] But Dulles needed no reminding. His thoughts on the question of primary reliance were clearly summarized in a memorandum prepared for a conversation with Hanson Baldwin a few weeks after "A Policy of Boldness" appeared in *Life:*

The United States . . . should maintain a strong, balanced force— including land, sea and air power—capable of expansion in any direction that seems wise. We should not put all of our eggs in one basket. But the abstract principle of "balance" should never be applied so rigorously as to impair emphasis on what is the practical need of particular circumstances, just as England, in the last century, did not allow the principle of balance to deny it preponderant sea power.

Since, for reasons of finance, the United States cannot have unlimited power of all kinds, let us not adopt the "meat axe" method of first cutting the appropriations and then mechanically dividing the resultant "pie" into three equal slices. . . . Rather, after providing for basic balanced strength, let us give priority to striking power which, by common consent, has the greatest deterrent influence.[37]

Dulles needed no reminding of Eisenhower's advice for yet other important reasons. Although the former's attempt to describe a policy of deterrence left some observers with the impression that he was too preoccupied with the military aspects of the cold war and too little concerned with the political-economic-psychological aspects, the truth was probably exactly the opposite. The nonmilitary aspects of the cold war challenge had always been, according to

Dulles, the most important area and the area where the United States was most lacking. There was also his belief that American security depended on a healthy economy and this demanded lower defense budgets. Also, he believed that a huge defense system could encourage a trend toward a "militaristic" approach to the cold war challenge and "militarism" in America.

He tended, therefore, toward the air-sea argument in order to make for a healthier American economy and to make room for increased political and economic programs. A defined and long-range approach to deterrent power would, he thought, leave money and efforts for military and economic assistance without either draining the American pocketbook or contributing to militarism in the United States:

As we stop fretting and start thinking, the first problem to tackle is the strictly military one. It comes in the form of a paradox: for we must seek a military formula more effective than any devised to date—that we may no longer be so overridingly preoccupied with purely military necessity.[38]

Announcement of the New Look

Dulles' famous Council on Foreign Relations speech—after which the phrase "massive retaliation" became notorious—first stressed the need for long-range policies, long-range budget planning, and a coordinated effort with America's allies. He not only discarded, but had earlier criticized, the "crisis year" concept which the Truman Administration had used, in the words of one observer, "to justify very large expenditures on the grounds that they would level off and be reduced after the . . year of great crisis" had passed. The "new look" aimed to justify "reduced expenditures on the grounds that they would be continued indefinitely." [39] Dulles had, over the years, emphasized the need for a selective approach to military power, a strategic force planned and maintained for the "long haul" without the waste of crash programs. Desiring a "maximum deterrent at a bearable cost" in 1954, he concluded that *more* but *not total* reliance should be placed on the air, sea, nuclear weapons aspects of deterrence:

Local defense will always be important. But there is no local defense which alone will *contain* the mighty land power of the Communist world.

Local defenses must be reinforced by the further deterrent of massive retaliatory power. A potential aggressor must know that he cannot always prescribe battle conditions that suit him.[40] (Emphasis added.)

He underlined that last sentence with the comments that to deter aggression the "free community" must "be willing and able to respond vigorously at places and with means of its own choosing," and the "basic decision" of the Eisenhower Administration "was to depend primarily upon a great capacity to retaliate." [41]

The so-called new look was "old Dulles." Moreover, with the exception of discarding the "crisis year" for a "long haul" approach, there was nothing drastically revisionist about Dulles' speech when compared to the latter years of the Truman Administration. Yet, as he mentioned, there were some basic decisions in the matter. To the military, it meant more emphasis upon air and sea power and tactical nuclear weapons, and there commenced the debate over the size of the Army and the proper "mix" of forces. To Dulles, the decision meant that the relatively unstated and underdeveloped strategy of deterrence in the previous administration should now be publicly declared and defined. Military power would no longer represent a silent partner in the event diplomacy failed, but would be conceived and utilized as a deterrent or "political weapon." Contrary to some interpretations, the decision did not mean that the United States intended to rely totally on strategic power and presumably some nuclear weapons as a sanction against not only major aggression from the Soviet Union or China, but virtually any form of aggression. A careful reading of the Council speech itself would have precluded such an interpretation. In addition, as will be noted, one has to differentiate between strategies of deterrence and strategies for fighting a war. The Secretary of State was concerned with and defining the former.

The Democrats naturally jumped on the statement as any professional politician would. Adlai Stevenson asserted that the policy presented the United States with "the grim choice of inaction or a thermonuclear holocaust." It, therefore, invited Moscow to "nibble us to death." Dean Acheson joined the chorus with the idea that the United States, indeed the world, could only afford Korean-type wars with strategic bombing being considered only as a last resort.[42] Although such political jabs could be beneficial, if they kept the administration on its toes in implementing policy and if they made the public more aware of the absurdity of an "all or nothing" thesis, the criticisms did not accurately portray Dulles' expressed approach.

A similar and more serious type of adverse criticism emerged from the academic world. Henry Kissinger found that "massive retaliation" contained a tendency toward a "Maginot mentality" or "Fortress America" posture. He rightfully concluded that an "all or nothing" military policy "makes for a paralysis of diplomacy." [43] This more serious criticism could also prove beneficial in keeping the administration on its toes and in contributing to the public and the foreign policy elite's awareness of the problems in this or any strategy. In this sense, some of the criticism could well have derived less from a concern about Dulles *per se* than from questions regarding how Eisenhower and his military advisers would implement this strategy in the absence of opposition from the Secretary of State. At any rate, the critics were reluctant to point out that the Secretary counseled against "all or nothing" thinking in the Council speech:

We do not, of course, claim to have found some magic formula that insures against all forms of Communist successes. *It is normal that at some times and at some places there may be setbacks to the cause of freedom.*[44] (Emphasis added.)

Also, the "new look" was designed to deter not all forms of aggression, but only "such aggression as would mean general war." [45] Such forms were not only generally defined but also well understood in the case of Europe where the Soviet Union could not issue marching orders without taking into account the firmness of the United States commitment. The situation in the Far East, as Dulles recognized, was less amenable to precise definition. He asserted that any "open Red Chinese army aggression" in Indochina "would have *grave consequences which might not* be confined to Indochina." [46] (Emphasis added.) China was being served notice that it could not count on sanctuary status if it openly invaded Indochina. This did not automatically or necessarily mean strategic, nuclear bombing— as the President had announced, the forces would feature "highly mobile naval, air and amphibious units" [47] —but a potential aggressor could not be certain that it did not. Equally important, Dulles' statement revealed no indications of a willingness or inclination to escalate local affairs into major encounters.

In the final analysis, the policy outlined in the Council speech presented the United States with neither Stevenson's "grim choice" nor Kissinger's "paralysis of diplomacy." With the important exceptions of the "long haul" approach and a clearer definition of will and determination, the policy did not differ radically from established policy and even contained more flexibility in terms of limited retaliation than the pre-Korea Truman posture. Why, then, did the Secretary find it necessary or advisable to present the "new look" in the fashion selected in 1954?

First, the address was concerned not primarily with the Far East, but with the general problems of deterrence, allies, NATO, and the proposed European Defense Community. He prefaced the "further deterrent of massive retaliatory power" statement with the idea that local defenses were necessary and "we need allies and collective security." [48] Although the announced strategy was to come under fire in Europe—for example, Arnold Toynbee's "no annihilation without representation"—the address was probably designed largely, if not mainly, as a reassurance of America's firm commitment to European allies.

Of course, in pre-ICBM days, allies were indispensable to a credible retaliatory deterrent even in strictly military terms. But this was not Dulles' major concern. Shortly before the Council speech, he had issued the warning that the United States would experience an "agonizing reappraisal" of basic policy were the Europeans to go their separate ways and leave unresolved the questions of their own defense and of Germany's sovereignty and contribution to the Western defense. Therefore, in the Council speech, Dulles reaffirmed that the United States meant business with Russia. While the United States did not view its major contribution as one of manpower and conventional forces, this did not lessen its commitment to the defense of Europe over the long haul. Also, the policy announcement carried the message that rather than attempt to "liberate" the heartland of Western Europe by nuclear weapons, should the Soviets attack, the United States would rather tend toward the heartland of the aggressor. The address caused some disturbances in allied capitals in 1954, but Dulles' approach was generally and genuinely accepted within half a decade at least by Britain and France.

Supportive of this assurance to allies was the "long haul" concept itself. First, the speech recognized that America's allies were also weighed down by heavy military expenditures and that this burden could be eased by less dependence on attempting to match Soviet manpower. Second, although the strategy was often referred to as a "bigger bang for lesser cost," this phrase was more a euphemism for developing a "bang" with high costs continuing over the years. The Council address established that the United States would not return to what, in the past, had been normal peacetime operations, but would persist in military preparedness and military cooperation with its allies. In short, the easing of tensions in Korea was not a signal "to return to normalcy" in the 1920 and 1946 senses. The President was proposing a military budget which was three times the amount of the proposed pre-Korea 1950 budget. When Senator Taft was shown the proposed military budget, in April of 1953, "he charged that the defense expenditures . . . were at least 50 per cent too large and represented only the thinking of jingoistic and ambitious men in the services." [49]

A second reason for Dulles' speech was his view that one of the primary tasks of his office was to strengthen the will and determination of the West and, as one observer described it, to convey effectively "to the other side the West's will to preserve its sphere of power." [50] This view of his responsibilities derived, in the main, from the danger of miscalculation which he described, three years before the Korean War, as the greatest possible source of war. Also he had since taken much note of the political implications of nuclear power and a temporary superiority before entering office. This led to his belief not only that an organized community power could be "effective political weapons" for statesmen, but further that war could be prevented "only if such power as we possess" were "used as a political weapon." [51]

A third reason for Dulles' address was that it served two important roles in the Far East situation and Indochina problem. At one level, as American ground forces departed from Asia, Eisenhower and Dulles did not want to leave any room for miscalculation of

American interest in Indochina. Since the Council address took place shortly before the opening of the Big Four (United States, Russia, Great Britain, and France) Foreign Ministers Conference at Berlin, it afforded a timely opportunity to communicate one's interests in Europe and elsewhere. The message was clear that any major aggressive move by the Soviet Union in Europe or China into Indochina would threaten United States interests and risk general war. He was, in a sense, relinquishing the initiative for general war. At another level with regard to Indochina, his speech and subsequent statements represented what he referred to as using power as "political weapons." This aspect belongs to the later discussion of the Indochina affair.

A fourth reason for the speech was its message to the American public. It contained the ideas that war could be avoided only if the United States assumed its responsibilities, cooperated with allies, remained militarily prepared so as to deter war, and girded itself for a "long haul." These were hardly new themes to Dulles. But the address also served to reassure the American public that the administration intended to preserve its sphere of power and defend United States interests. It was perhaps designed to gain some room for maneuverability in the Korean and Indochinese matters. Indeed, there was some degree of truth in Truman's reported comment later that he would have been hung for such a treaty as the Korean settlement. While the country as a whole remained staunchly opposed to any "sellouts" or a "Far East Munich," the Secretary's Council speech advised that some "setbacks to the cause of freedom" could be expected.[52] Lastly, in the domestic sense, the speech was possibly partially designed to calm a disquieted America. This was a period when many Americans genuinely feared a surprise attack which would leave the country "defenseless." [53]

Out of all the above domestic political factors, however, the key point was probably the message to the American public and, particularly, the United States Congress that there was to be no return to the pre-Korean War type of demobilization and general lack of preparedness. In the few years prior to the Korean conflict, the annual defense budgets had remained below fifteen billion dollars; after the commencement of hostilities in 1950, the annual budgets rose sharply to a peak of Truman's 1953 defense budget of about fifty billion dollars. The budget began to dip sharply until, in 1955, it was leveled off and then kept rather constant by the Eisenhower Administration. Dulles' Council speech was unmistakably designed in part to help "sell" the "new look" and its dollar implications and, thereby, avoid another sharp decline in American preparedness as occurred after World War II.

Since the late 1940s, Dulles' ideas on deterrence had evolved and been enunciated in much the same terms as the Council speech. Speaking for the North Atlantic Pact in 1949, he referred to a supreme deterrent to armed aggression as the "means to hit with shattering effectiveness the sources of power and lines of communication of the Sovietized world." The conclusion was that "the best deterrent to aggression is the *certainty* that *immediate* and *effective* countermeasures will be taken." [54] He had outlined a similar approach to deterring war in his major 1952 campaign article, and Eisenhower had used even stronger language.[55] Moreover, the basic policy announced in 1954 had been generally accepted since 1949 with the exception of the long haul approach. The doctrine of flexible response or limited retaliation was clear in the Council speech. As another official noted later, in August of 1954, "the capacity for retaliation by itself is not enough, nor . . . was it ever intended to supply the whole answer." [56] Nevertheless, there was a good deal of uproar and misunderstanding in 1954.

Much of the anxiety was probably unavoidable. If Dulles' speeches represented a commitment to an international role and defense of interests, there was a problem, as later defined by one military strategist, that "most commitments are ultimately ambiguous in detail." [57] Confusion arose from the fact that there was no strict delineation between the will to retaliate if necessary and the precise circumstances under which this massive retaliatory power would be utilized. In 1952 he had stated that "punishing power" did "not reliably deter unless it" was "known, in advance, that it would be used under clearly defined conditions." [58] But this general proposition was not without some intentional ambiguity:

Our deterrent striking power does not, today, have anywhere near the reassuring power of which it is capable because no one knows whether, when or where it would be used. *Complete precision on all of these matters is of course neither practical nor wise. There is reason for some calculated uncertainty and some flexibility.* . . .[59] (Emphasis added.)

This was particularly the case if laying out all the conditions meant, in effect, "writing off" gray areas where attacks might nonetheless bring an American response, such as in Indochina. Thus, his policy of deterrence contained degrees of uncertainty and ambiguity and a tendency to view overstatement as a better bargain than understatement, which may well have included a degree of bluff in some cases.

There was also a serious concern in 1954 that the strategy announced by Dulles inevitably tended toward the "all or nothing" thesis, otherwise known as limiting one's options to "nuclear holocaust or inaction." As far as Dulles was concerned, it should be clear that such an approach was alien to his entire understanding of international politics and his particular understanding of the cold war challenges. Two years before he assumed office he had spelled out his thoughts on deterrence and preparedness: "But total reliance should not be placed on any single form of warfare or any relatively untried type of weapons. . . . The arsenal of retaliation should include all forms of counter attack with maximum flexibility, mobility, and the possibility of surprise." [60] Nonetheless, there remained concern that the strategy itself contained a trend toward a "Maginot Line" mentality and "Fortress America" approach. Even if Dulles fully recognized this factor, it did not mean that military influence or some military advisers might not prevail in the implementation of American policy or place the United States in an "either/or" position in fact if not in word.

There were other causes for anxiety and concern. A large dosage derived from the interrelationship between "deterrence" and "a strategy for fighting a war." It was the former which lay largely within the domain of the Secretary of State, and Dulles was not presenting strategies for fighting in the event deterrence failed. But the inherent relationship or dilemma between the two concerned the more serious critics, such as Henry Kissinger, who were never quite sure that this dilemma was understood fully by those in power:

Obviously an overemphasis on destructiveness may paralyze the will. But an overconcern with developing a tolerable strategy for the conduct of war may reduce the risks of aggression to such a degree that it will be encouraged. . . . A course of action that increases the opponent's uncertainties about the nature of the conflict will generally discourage aggression. If war should break out, however, through accident or miscalculation, it may make limitation extremely difficult.[61]

The dialogue on strategies and deterrence, which is taken for granted today, did not exist in the early 1950s. There was finally the natural tendency, perhaps especially in allied capitals, of those "riding the nuclear train" to be wary of the "driver." This was further complicated by those who were inclined to misinterpret or distrust Dulles.

It appears overall, however, that one of the prime reasons for the widespread disturbance when "massive retaliation" hit the streets in 1954 was the fact of a tense situation in Indochina. Deterrence in action, so to speak, with the concomitant manipulation of risks, was a different affair than deterrence as a speculative theory. The utilization of power as a "political weapon" contained even more seeds of unrest.

Clarification and Further Developments

Dulles' process of clarification and qualification after the Council address appears repetitive since most, if not all, of the same ideas had been either expressed or implied in his earlier statements. The Secretary, nevertheless, found it prudent to reassure his audiences that "our" meant the free world; that consultation would normally take place before action; that there was absolutely no inclination to convert local conflicts into general wars; that concentration on a deterrent power did not exclude a flexible response capability; and that retaliatory action "would presumably be limited in scope with regards to the gravity of the offense." [62] There existed no illusion of a rigid formula, and he stressed the fact that deterrence meant the nonuse of military power.

The *Foreign Affairs* article by the Secretary, appearing a few months after the Council speech, concentrated on clarifying some of the then current questions regarding "massive retaliation." He again emphasized the need for "a collective system of defense" since no "single nation" could "develop for itself defensive power of adequate scope and flexibility." The necessity of allies and allied cooperation, as a two-way street, was stressed again as had been the case in nearly all of his statements: "Without the cooperation of allies, we would not even be in a position to retaliate massively." The article was most important for its emphasis on the idea that "massive atomic and thermonuclear retaliation" was "not the kind of power which could most usefully be evoked under all circumstances." Deterrence required the capability of flexible response:

To deter aggression, it is important to have the flexibility and the facilities which make various responses available. In many cases, any open assault by Communist forces could only result in . . . a general war. But the free world must have the means for responding effectively on a selective basis when it chooses. *It must not put itself in the position where the only response open to it is general war.*[63] (Emphasis added.)

Some flexibility of response options and allied cooperation had been consistent themes in his writings on the subject since 1949. It has even been suggested that the Secretary viewed the novelty in his 1954 presentation as the highlighting of "a sort of collective policeman— a collective mobile force which could be used wherever necessary." Perhaps, he did think that this would be a way "to avoid the necessity of proliferating forces all around the Soviet-Chinese." [64] At any rate, the *Foreign Affairs* article set out to reassure anxious publics and leaders both at home and abroad.

Recognizing the validity of limited retaliation, Dulles also began to perceive the probability of changing positions resulting from nuclear stalemate. The 1954 *Foreign Affairs* article noted that massive retaliatory power, although a "dominant factor" at the time, would perhaps "not have the same significance forever." His awareness of the differences between superiority and stalemate was brought out in the discussion in 1957 of "relinquishing the initiative":

In the future it may thus be feasible to place less reliance upon deterrence of vast retaliatory power. . . . Thus, in contrast to the 1950 decade, it may be that by the 1960 decade the nations which are around the Sino-Soviet perimeter can possess an effective defense against full-scale conventional attack and thus confront any aggressor with the choice between failing or himself initiating nuclear war against the defending country.

Thus, the tables may be turned, in the sense that instead of those who are non-aggressive having to rely upon all-out nuclear retaliatory power for their protection, would-be aggressors would be unable to count on a successful conventional aggression, but must themselves weigh the consequence of invoking nuclear war.[65]

From 1954 to 1959, the Secretary was adjusting and searching for the proper concept of deterrence and its application to the diplomatic struggle. When the balance of power began to be redressed in favor of the Soviet Union, one observer has noted that "Dulles was quick to perceive it and to start the slow retreat toward a different military and political posture." [66] He was also described as a man "beginning to change and seek new answers—earnestly seek them, beg almost, for people to come up with new ideas." [67]

Adjustments to the changing problems of deterrence were reflected in his draft outline of a speech prepared for an Armed Forces Policy Council conference at Quantico, Virginia on June 14, 1957. The Secretary outlined three fundamental areas of concern. First, the growth of the Soviet's nuclear capability tended to diminish the efficacy of the threat of all-out use of nuclear power as a deterrent to local Soviet attack. Second, the United States must devise a flexible strategy and maintain military flexibility which could deter war by convincing the Soviets that the West had the capability to counter local military action while, at the same time, convincing American allies that local attacks could be countered without necessarily inviting all-out nuclear war. This, it was thought, would decrease the possibility of local conflicts which might escalate into general war. Flexibility was defined, however, mostly as increased emphasis upon small yield nuclear weapons development. Third, besides containing expansionist ambitions, a flexible military force should be designed to strengthen the political cohesion of a collective security system, and to provide a better protective shield behind which the West could work to assist political and economic development of other countries.[68]

The last point was particularly important to Dulles over the years, and he apparently accepted the implications of collective security. In 1958 he was urging increased sharing of nuclear knowledge, a move dictated by the change in emphasis from retaliatory striking power to shield forces with tactical nuclear weapons in Europe: "Let me point out that unless our government is able to share its nuclear knowledge more fully with our allies grave consequences may result. Our NATO allies may either intensively seek to develop nuclear weapons capacity for themselves; or move toward neutrality, or at least non-participation, in what should be a common military effort." [69] During the meeting with General de Gaulle the same year, he declared "that it would be a mistake to give exclusive consideration to nuclear deterrents. There will be also an indispensable need for the means of limited war." [70] He simply never bought the arguments of those who tended to view massive retaliation as a deterrent to any kind of threat. The Secretary consistently opposed the President's tendency to go along with a reduction of forces in Europe. As long as the Europeans contributed significantly and meaningfully to their own defense, according to Dulles in 1954, "the United States would expect to maintain substantial forces . . . in Europe, both in support of the forward strategy of defense and for political reasons." [71]

INDOCHINA AND CONGRESSIONAL PRESSURES

One of the main reasons why the so-called massive retaliation speech struck so many sensitive chords, in January of 1954, probably related to the existence of a tense situation in Indochina and the Far East generally, combined with the necessary vagueness in Dulles' references to that area if deterrence was to mean anything. The emphasis was on the determination and willingness to counter open aggression or communicating one's interest in the area while leaving it uncertain as to what would constitute "retaliatory action of our own fashioning." Dulles was not presenting an "all or nothing" proposition, nor was he laying out a strategy for fighting a possible war. He was, however, setting out to "throw the aggressor off balance" and "to create doubts and uncertainties in his mind." [72] Above all, he was attempting to avoid another Korean situation. His statements on deterrence and retaliation, from 1952 to 1955, cannot be separated from the Korean and Indochina issues.

He had clearly outlined his thoughts on this subject in 1952. Once the external threat from China or Russia was "neutralized by a known will and capacity to retaliate . . . the internal revolutionary problem will become more manageable." Therefore, the United States "might consider whether open military aggression by Red Armies" in Indochina "could not best be prevented by the readiness to take retaliatory action, rather than by attempts to meet the aggression on the spot where it occurs." Obviously, along this line of reasoning, sanctuary status could not be guaranteed in the case of an openly aggressive move: "Is it not time that the Chinese Communists knew that, if . . . they sent their Red Armies openly into Vietnam, we will not be content merely to try to meet their armed forces at the point they select." [73] These statements, which appeared in other speeches during 1952, did not include any idea of converting local, limited, or civil wars into general encounters. In fact, the implications of his statements can be read as meaning that the United States would be willing to compete or accept conflict at the revolutionary level. He was, however, notifying China and Russia that any direct offensive would create a far different situation.

There was probably another message Dulles was communicating consciously or unconsciously to the Chinese and Russians to the effect that major aggression in Indochina could place an American government in a near impossible situation. The Truman Administration encountered significant pressures to widen the battle into North Korea or for pre-emptive strikes along the Chinese-North Korean border, particularly after China had moved into Korea. The concept of "limited war"—a unique concept both to the public, the administration, and especially the military—had been a difficult pill for some Americans to digest and, therefore, not an easy concept to apply. If China had then turned around and intervened in Indochina, who could have guaranteed a localization of the conflict was not a rhetorical question. Considering the high temperature of the American public and Congress, who would have recommended either inaction or sending more ground troops back to the Far East? Needless to say, the message should have been clear to China and Russia regardless of Dulles' added communication.

In his 1954 Council on Foreign Relations speech, the Secretary warned that "if the Communists renewed the aggression" in Korea, "the United Nations response would *not necessarily* be confined to Korea." He repeated his warning of September 1953 that "if there were *open* Red Chinese army aggression" in Indochina, it would have "grave consequences which *might* not be confined to Indochina.'" (Emphasis added.) The United States forces for the Far East would "now feature 'highly mobile naval, air and amphibious units.'" The determination to counter any major aggression was established without committing himself to any particular strategy for meeting aggression except, by unmistakable implication, that the United States had little inclination to get bogged down in any drawn out land war and, technologically speaking, there was not the range of response options which were developed later, including, by the way, nuclear options. The administration's concern that the other side not misread the withdrawal of American land forces from Korea was obvious in the Council address.[74]

On the eve of the Geneva Conference on Indochina (April–July, 1954), Dulles' approach was summed up in the words that "the chances for peace are usually bettered by letting a potential aggressor know in advance where his aggression could lead him." [75] As the conference opened, and in the process of clarifying his January speech, the Secretary's article in *Foreign Affairs* emphasized his earlier qualifications:

A would-be aggressor will hesitate to commit aggression if he knows in advance that he thereby not only exposes those particular forces which he chooses to use for his aggression, but also deprives his other assets of "sanctuary" status. That does not mean turning every local war into a world war. It does not mean that if there is a Communist attack somewhere in Asia, atom or hydrogen bombs will necessarily be dropped on the great industrial centers of China and Russia. It does mean that the free world must maintain the collective means and be willing to use them in a way which most effectively makes aggression too risky and expensive to be tempting.[76]

While setting forth a strategy of limited or calculated retaliation in the article, Dulles recognized the necessity for a different approach in various regions of the world. Some areas, such as Western Europe, were "so vital that a special guard should and can be put around them." [77] No such definition could be applied in the Far East, with the possible exception of Japan, because of less vital and less clearly defined interest in the "gray areas." So his dilemma was how not to "write off" an area as occurred in the case of Korea. He answered this dilemma in a draft of the article in the following manner: "Many wonder just where those consequences might occur, and just what they would be. It is better that the enemy should be left to wonder than that the path of aggression be cleared for him by eliminating his doubts." [78]

In the following draft, however, this section was revised to read that there were obviously areas where attacks would not indicate or lead to general war, and where threats to turn minor wars into general atomic wars would be "empty threats." The editor of *Foreign Affairs* questioned the approach: "Doesn't it give away too much? Might it not encourage the Soviets to aggress in areas where they think the free world would not resist?" [79] The Secretary handled the dilemma, in the final product, by stressing the need for a flexible response capability and the idea that the method of reinforcing local defensive strength would "vary according to the character of the various areas." Also, local defenses should be capable not only of maintaining order against subversion and resisting "other forms of indirect aggression," but also of meeting "minor satellite aggressions." [80]

The Four Power Foreign Ministers Conference in January–February, 1954, had cleared the way for the Geneva Conference on Indochina and Korea in late April, as the French fortress of Dien Bien Phu was under attack by the Vietminh. There were, from the beginning, clear differences between the approaches of Great Britain, France, and the United States to the conference and the situation in Indochina generally. According to Eden, the French would describe Dien Bien Phu as their "last battle" in the event it fell and, therefore, American assurances of aid in defending the rest of Indochina were not enough. Dulles made it clear "that there was no possibility of United States participation in the Dien Bien Phu battle, because the President had not the power to act with such speed and because . . . no intervention could now save the fortress." Admiral Radford, the Chairman of the Joint Chiefs of Staff, favored some other American action without delay to bolster the French fighting effort and to prevent what he thought would occur in the event the fortress fell: namely, the military situation getting completely out of control in favor of the communists. Eden seriously questioned whether any joint military action "could decisively alter the situation" and, in fact, whether or not it might not be counterproductive and escalate the conflict.[81]

Although all the details of Dulles' position and exactly what he said to the British and the French during this episode are still not available, both Dulles and Eisenhower apparently favored some type of military aid or relieving action (or perhaps symbolic action) to buttress the French effort in what was considered a desperate situation. This position had, however, important qualifications. The first was that while the United States would consider helping with air and sea power, the United States would certainly not get involved with land forces in Indochina. The second qualification was that any such action had to have a credible international flavor and, therefore, the United States would not act alone without *both* the French and the British and insisted that the French step up an independence program for the area. Finally, the battle at Dien Bien Phu should not be viewed as a "do or die" proposition. Implicit in such qualifications was the fact that the United States did not view Indochina as a strategic area of vital interest regardless of its political and psychological importance. All in all, the impression was clear to Eden and others that the United States was willing to "internationalize the struggle and protect South-East Asia as a whole" *if* the other allies desired it.[82]

It was equally apparent that the tactics of the British and the Americans would widely differ during the conference. Eden and Churchill recognized that the negotiating position of the French was not strong, but did not see the situation in Indochina so desperate and believed the best approach was "to keep the Chinese guessing as to what form of action France's allies intended *eventually* to pursue." [83] (Emphasis added.) The American point of view was that the situation was rather more desperate, the position of the French weaker, and a better approach was to keep the Chinese guessing what the United States might do soon if reasonable negotiations did not take place.

These different tactics were reflected in the question of a mutual security pact for the area. Although not necessarily bent on firming up a Southeast Asia Treaty Organization before the conference in Geneva had completed its work or had its chance, Dulles desired certain audible and visible motions toward its establishment. He believed this could be done outside the conference and would create a stronger negotiating position and effectively communicate the idea that French collapse did not mitigate the interests of the West in Indochina. The American Secretary also believed, as a result of his conversations with Eden on April 11–13 in London, that Britain supported the proposal both in substance and in timing.[84] According to Eden's later account, Dulles "did not think anybody was advocating military intervention in Indochina," although Admiral Radford had made remarks to the contrary.[85] Dulles did want to push ahead with the pact. But, very shortly after these conversations and contrary to what Dulles viewed as an agreement, Eden balked at the question of timing and at what he thought would be hasty arrangements in terms of composition of the organization. Eden's understanding was that he had agreed only to think over the proposition. At any rate, he decided it best not to move ahead on the matter before the conference had its full opportunity.

The differences between the two allies continued throughout the Geneva Conference. Eden wanted the Chinese guessing as to the consequences if the conference were to fail; Dulles wanted them guessing sooner with a view that this would strengthen the West's negotiating position. For their part, the French were exhausted and perhaps at times torn between the two. The American Secretary departed from Geneva after a few days, but not out of pique over differences with the British. The matter was prearranged, and he was perforce concerned with other problems in Washington, such as the crucial question of the future of the EDC, plus counter-revolution in Guatemala.[86] Moreover, the political gesture of sending General Bedell Smith to Geneva represented less a departure than a reassurance of American interest in the outcome.

While Eden assiduously stuck to the hard task of creating a meaningful dialogue and negotiating details, there were, from mid-May until early June, reports of bargaining between Paris and

Washington over the terms for the latter's intervention in Indochina. It was never quite clear whether this referred to action soon
or only in the event the conference failed to reach agreement. Nor
was one sure whether it involved only a gesture, or some substantive
move such as helping to train troops, or something more. On May
25, the Secretary described the situation in Indochina as "different
and more complex" than that in Korea. Conditions for intervention
were defined at least as congressional sanction plus allied cooperation and support, and perhaps as much as a United Nations sanction. Although there had been "some conversations to explore the
conditions" with the French under which intervention "might be
possible," he concluded that Paris had made no request for more
United States involvement.[87]

Eden simply did "not accept the United States argument that the
threat of intervention" would incline the Chinese and Russians to
compromise,[88] and his view was not without good logic. By mid-
June the conference appeared deadlocked, but the British Foreign
Secretary remained convinced that it provided the best channel for
the cessation of hostilities which would be in the interests of the
French and their allies. Another American threat, implying that
continuation of the hostilities would not be a bad deal under the
circumstances, came in the form of Eisenhower's instructions to Bedell Smith to bring "the conference to an end as rapidly as possible,
on the grounds that the communists were only spinning things out
to suit their own military purposes." [89] But the negotiations continued and the Americans did not sabotage them.

Prime Minister Churchill and Eden departed for Washington on
June 24. Talks with Dulles were "encouraging" as he "accepted that
nothing short of intervention with ground forces could restore the
situation . . . and also seemed ready to countenance the partition of
Vietnam." On the other hand, he believed "that partition would
only be effective if the French could be persuaded to abandon their
stranglehold on the Vietnamese economy" and thereby make the regime less vulnerable to internal subversion. Eden accepted this
judgment and outlined his dual system of guarantees. This meant
first a guarantee by all the parties involved, which could not really
be relied upon in an emergency because of the differences between

the West and the East and, second, a collective defense arrangement with commitments to military action in the event of renewed aggression. The second hand of this proposed dual system was in keeping with Washington's preference, but Dulles saw "little chance" in the United States guaranteeing the settlement although he himself could accept partition: "It would be difficult, he said, to persuade Congress to guarantee, in effect, the communist domination of North Vietnam." [90]

In this light, Dulles was not later convinced by Eden and the new Prime Minister of France, Pierre Mendes France—who came into power on June 18 and announced that he would undertake to reach a settlement by July 20—to return to Geneva: "After discussion with the President, it had been agreed that he should not return." [91] It is, by Eden's account, slightly unclear as to who was wanting what within the American government. Dulles announced the following day, July 14, that General Smith would be returning to the conference.

Armistice agreements were reached in Laos, Vietnam, and Cambodia, and the final settlement was in the offing. The line of demarcation and the composition of the advisory commission had been settled, as well as the stipulation that elections would be held in July of 1956—a stipulation which Dulles had said the United States would support if the conditions of genuinely free elections were met,[92] but which the American side no doubt would have preferred not specified in the agreements. The plenary session was held on July 21 and, since the United States would not formally associate itself with the agreement by signature, Molotov and Eden agreed "to eliminate the problem of signature" by having the declaration headed with a list of the participating countries.[93]

This dilemma for American statesmanship may not have appeared totally reasonable to Eden, but he surely understood the problem and its relationship to domestic politics. Although Eisenhower publicly announced that the United States was not itself "a party to or bound by the decisions taken by the Conference"—a statement mostly designed for domestic consumption against those who might argue "sellout" or recognition of Communist China against the unanimous sense of the Senate—he nevertheless accepted the agreements with minor reservations and declared that the United States would "not use force to disturb the settlement." [94] The Western allies then proceeded to the task of a collective defense arrangement, which did not include the associated states of Indochina. There was in Washington never any real plan to support elections because of the closed society in the North and the communist organization in the South.

While the complete details of policy and possible policy differences within the United States government remain relatively obscure, Dulles' manipulation of risks was undisguised and appeared very much like a planned part. Since the American military judgment was that the situation could become desperate or completely out of control with the fall of Dien Bien Phu, the Secretary's "crashingly audible maneuvers," the "loud stage-whispers," and the "bargaining over conditions for military intervention" [95] were likely attempts to avoid continuation or escalation of the conflict. There seemed to be, as one observer has noted, a deliberate and calculated effort to create a "threatening ambiguity," to enfold American policy in a "hectoring uncertainty, designed to induce the Communist bloc to forestall Ho Chi Minh's opportunity to control the whole of Viet Nam." [96]

Eden disagreed both with the tactics and with the view that the situation could easily become desperate. Given current evidence, he may well have felt further that the Americans were asking the British to sign off on a "blank check." As one of the ablest negotiators, he set about the task in a different manner, putting his hopes in the conference while leaving the future open. In the final analysis, regardless of whether the two sides understood or respected each other's tactics, the sharp differences between the Americans and the British were in effect complementary. Although considering Dulles' approach as basically unhelpful, even one of his harshest critics concludes:

Eden's flexible and versatile use of all these methods of diplomacy, coupled occasionally with hints at the alternative policy of joining Dulles' threatening posture achieved diplomacy's *raison d'etre*, avoidance of war, preservation of peace.[97]

Dulles' posture could add leverage to Eden's statesmanship, whether the latter wished it or not. Eden required no threats from his corner to keep the other side of the table guessing as to the possible consequences if the Geneva Conference failed. The disagreement in tactics was probably the more convincing because it was real.

Tactics aside, there remained the more serious question of United States policy. Dulles' slightly aloof manner toward the Vietnamese settlement seemed to derive from acceptance of the fact that the conference was virtually limited to recognizing the *status quo* in view of Ho Chi Minh's program to unify the country and Western opposition to this program. While the sides agreed upon a type of armistice, there was no common ground for fundamental agreement on basic questions. From this standpoint, the American Secretary accepted the seven points of agreement and basically supported the declaration of 1954. Leaving the future open, he concentrated on the Southeast Asia Treaty Organization. But, to American policy, a relatively permanent settlement to the conflicts of interests in Indochina did not appear to exist unless one were willing to countenance the idea of Ho Chi Minh's gaining control of all of Vietnam and this was entertained by no one at high levels in the American system.

Regardless of what some consider possible shortcomings in United States policy at the time, any failings cannot simply be attributed to Dulles or Eisenhower. Policy dealt with the possible and followed a logical and largely inherited middle course. For example, even if the prospect of "Titoism" in Vietnam had been perceptible in 1954, which is debatable, a move resembling concession to unification under Ho Chi Minh would have spelled political disaster at home on a scale not greatly different than the so-called China debate. Both large segments of the public and particularly the Congress remained absolutely firm in their opposition to even semblances of Soviet or communist expansionism. Senator John F. Kennedy had equated "partition or a coalition government" with "eventual domination by the Communists." [98] This warning shortly before the opening of the Geneva Conference was indicative of the congressional mood which could, in some respects, be even more inflexible on related questions.

There was the unanimous opposition to recognition of and dealings with Peking.[99] At the conclusion of the Four Power Conference in Berlin, which had cleared the way for Geneva, the Secretary announced that the United States would not refuse to deal with Communist China where occasion required. There existed no reason why America "should refuse to seek peacefully the results we want merely because of fear that we will be outmaneuvered at the conference table." He obviously found it necessary to justify and reassure the American public and Congress, with its vivid memories of Yalta, regarding his stand to meet indirectly with Chou En-lai:

We need not, out of fright, lay down the tools of diplomacy and the possibilities which they provide. Our cause is not so poor, and our capacity not so low, that our nation must seek security by sulking in its tent.[100]

The proposition of the United States as an Atlantic and Pacific power was accepted. Rejecting the arguments of Europeans who desired America to abandon interests in Asia, and the arguments of Asians who wanted America to lessen its interests in Europe, the Secretary counseled Americans in typical fashion not to "be critical of them, for they are subject to strains which we are spared by our fortunate material and geographical position Indeed, there are some Americans who would have us sacrifice our friends both in Asia and in Europe for some fancied benefit to ourselves." [101]

There persisted the old seeds of isolationism in American society, although sometimes dressed up in a new coat, combined with a strong impulse to have no commerce with the communists. There were considerable warnings from Congress that there should be no implicit recognition of the People's Republic of China and, indeed, Dulles studiously avoided any contacts with Chou En-lai at Geneva. (In fact, "neither the Americans nor the French had established any contacts with the communist representatives," which compelled Eden "to adopt the role of intermediary between the Western powers and the communists." [102]) Senate Majority Leader William F. Knowland warned that there had better not be a "Far East Munich" in Geneva. The Secretary's practicable policy options were, to be sure, severely limited if existing at all. On May 11, Senator Kefauver summed up the situation when he asserted that the senators had sent Dulles to Geneva "with his hands tied." [103]

Thus, in a real sense, Dulles' threatening posture must also be considered in terms of its domestic implications. With senators equating partition with eventual take-over by the communists, perhaps American policy was unsure whether continued limited hostilities would not be better than partition. Nevertheless, when the idea of partition emerged as the option to continued hostilities, it was not challenged but accepted by Dulles. The coupling of the domestic political and the international situations effectually forced him to ply a course without appearing to concede any ground to the communists. Assuming that another Korean-type episode would have presented a most unhealthy circumstance, both at home and abroad, he opted for defense of the Indochina area and the attainment of a reasonable, but fluid settlement. His tactics of threats mixed with some aloofness from the dealings in Geneva allowed him his decisions without the appearance of conceding or "selling out." Depending upon one's normally subjective judgment of the domestic problems, this appearance was either what the administration wanted, particularly Eisenhower and his political advisers, or what the country and Congress demanded.

There was yet another domestic factor contributing to the unraveling of the Geneva agreements: namely, Congress' indisposition to support or appropriate funds for what was viewed as French "colonialism" or "imperialism" in Indochina. Dulles also had an anticolonialist streak, but it was based on pragmatic rather than moralistic foundations. In 1951 Senator Kennedy had claimed that the United States had allied itself "to the desperate effort of a French regime to hang on to the remnants of empire," and forecast that success depended on satisfying the nationalistic aims of the Indochinese.[104] Before the settlement in Geneva, there were many more demands that France grant full independence to the peoples of Indochina and that the United States exert pressures in this direction.

After July 21, 1954, the anticolonialist sentiment in Congress did not subside. Senator Mike Mansfield of Montana, chairman of the special subcommittee on Indochina, promoted the unconditional support of Diem and the elimination of "colonialist" France. Congressman James Richards, soon to become chairman of the House Foreign Affairs Committee, insisted that "the task of building up an anti-communist force be assumed by the United States" in Vietnam.[105] When the Southeast Asia Treaty Organization came up for the Senate's advice and consent, there was only one dissenting vote. American involvement and actions in 1954 stemmed directly from the inherited and accepted position, at least since 1945, that control of Indochina by a potential or real adversary would be detrimental to the interests of the United States.

As the year neared its end, the Secretary had no more flexibility than earlier. When all is said and done, then, it appears that the fundamental weakness in American policy during the Truman and Eisenhower administrations was the lack of a systematic review of longer-range options and political-economic methods of conflict control. This would have been the slow, long, planned process which Dulles had often described as the goal of policy. But this process still seemed one of the least amenable to democratic statesmanship and the "system" of American foreign policy as long as there were no pressures for change. On the other hand, there were not insubstantial reasons for proceeding on an essentially *ad hoc* basis. Dulles was not convinced that the Diem experiment in the South would prevail in the long-run, and the area was not viewed as a vital strategic interest even though its political and psychological importance in the cold war contest could not be ignored. If and as Diem's experiment appeared to get off the ground, Washington would increase its aid and economic support. But, as long as North Vietnam refrained from overt aggression, there appeared no designed hurry to jump into the situation lest the administration be confronted with the choice of either sending in ground forces to avoid a failure, which Dulles and Eisenhower opposed doing, or accepting a failure which would reflect higher on United States prestige and power.

CHAPTER ELEVEN

BALANCING INTERESTS
AND VIEWPOINTS

THE RISE OF NEUTRALISM

Today, the various nuances of nonalignment and the subject of the "third world" are, if not always well understood, at least much studied. Fifteen years ago, however, the phenomena of neutral nations and the doctrine of neutralism were only beginning to emerge as forces in their own right on the international stage. In April of 1955, over 60 per cent of the world's population was represented at the Bandung Conference of African and Asian states. On the whole, the conference was far less negative and anticolonialist than positively proneutralism and nonalignment. The year 1955 also saw the membership of the United Nations leap from sixty to seventy-six countries. Six of the newly admitted members, in this package of sixteen, were Arab or Asian—Jordan, Libya, Cambodia, Ceylon, Laos, and Nepal. During meetings with President Eisenhower, in December of 1956, one of the most august proponents and practitioners of nonalignment, Prime Minister Jawaharlal Nehru, expounded upon the meaning and reasons for Indian neutrality.[1]

Neutrality or nonalignment *per se* were not, of course, unfamiliar phenomena. However, the doctrine of positive neutralism and the emerging Afro-Asian identity were new forces in what was still conceived as a largely bipolar environment. Moscow perceived neutralism—with or without, but preferably with, any anticolonialist or anti-West flavors—as consonant with the interests of the Soviet Union and, accordingly, encouraged this natural check upon Western influence or this potential opportunity for Eastern influence. As expected and as exemplified by the performance of Chou En-lai at the Bandung Conference, Peking set about attempting to place the Chinese People's Republic at the center of this Afro-Asian identity. Although having encouraged the dissolution or complete reorientation of the colonial empires, Washington was inclined to view the trend toward neutralism coolly while continuing to deal on a country-to-country basis. Thus, the general policy statements of the United States naturally appeared, at times, to conflict on the subject. The actual content of United States policy, however, reflected a more consistent line of pragmatic adjustment to an inevitable reality.

Dulles referred to neutrality, in general terms, in a 1955 address dealing with productivity, power, principles, and partnership as assets of the "free world": "The United States does not believe in practicing neutrality. Barring exceptional cases, neutrality is an obsolete conception. It is like asking each community to forego a police force." [2] The entire address was designed to accentuate advantages of partnership and collective security. The Secretary first explained to an American audience the reasons for "entangling alliances" and an interdependent approach. The address seemed to have been primarily, although perhaps not entirely, for domestic consumption.

Dulles also directed his argument against the Soviet appeals in the opposite direction. Refuting the Soviet Union's advocacy of "neutrality" for other nations, he maintained that the Soviet domain carved out of Eastern Europe and Asia was contrary to any genuine adherence to the concept and position of neutrality. As for the United States, according to the Secretary, it preferred neither to advocate nor to practice neutrality. In a literal sense, the address meant that the United States had certain responsibilities and interests in an interdependent world.

The question which the address opened up, however, related to the extent and scope of the responsibilities and interests of the United States. Was the Secretary under the illusion that the interests of every non-Soviet "bloc" country were so inextricably inter-related with American interests as practically to demand alignment? Was it the duty of every "free" state to align itself? Dulles continued, in the address, with the idea that "peoples who trust each other should freely draw together for their mutual security." [3] Did this mean that the African and Asian states had or should have such trust in the United States? Had the Secretary come to accept a type of "if you are not with me, you are against me" ethic rather than the more typical bourgeois and tolerant ethic—"if you are not against me, you are potentially with me"?

In fact, the 1955 pronouncement contained no indications of a blanket indictment of neutralism. In its design for domestic consumption, as an argument against isolationism, the statement served well. The statement probably also served some purpose in its reassurance to allies and to those obviously leaning toward the United States. To other parts of the world, to those particular areas caught between the two superpowers which preferred to remain nonaligned, the pronouncement no doubt appeared as an unnecessary extension of, for lack of a better term, the cold war psychology and contest. From this standpoint, the reference to "neutrality" as an "obsolete conception" could be considered unproductive if not unfortunate.

But from the standpoint of the interests and priorities of the United States, the statement portrayed America's dilemma in the mid-1950s. Committed to the idea of collective security, the United States could not very well advocate or encourage neutrality. The United States counter to the Soviet's advocacy of "neutrality" did not mean, however, that American policy was burdened by a rigid formula which dictated that there existed no salvation outside of the Western "bloc," nor was any such formula evident in 1955. Dulles concluded his address with the statement that the United States had "no desire and no mandate to run the world." [4] It was also evident that he possessed a list of exceptional cases where "neutrality" was not to be considered "obsolete."

A certain amount of confusion was occasioned by Dulles' failure to distinguish clearly between what was implied and what was not implied in his statements on neutrality. Even before his second pronouncement, in June of 1956, defining neutrality as not only increasingly "obsolete" but also, again barring exceptional cases, "immoral" and "shortsighted," it was apparent both that the list of exceptions was substantial and that Dulles was not inclined in practice to indict neutralism *per se*. His views on neutrality, for example, did not mean that the United States should assist only those countries which eschewed involvement with the Soviet Union. Neutrality was not considered "immoral" or "shortsighted" because it included dealings with the Soviet Union or other communist states. During congressional hearings on mutual security appropriations in 1954, the Secretary had asserted that there was a need for a pragmatic approach: "I think we cannot adopt a policy of not extending a certain amount of assistance to countries which also deal with the Soviet Union. For example, that would in effect involve writing off India. . . . As a matter of fact we all have some dealings with the Soviet Union, including the United States. Each case must be dealt with on its own facts." [5]

Shortly after Nasser confirmed the conclusion of a cotton-for-arms agreement between Egypt and Czechoslovakia, in September of 1955, the question arose as to what implications this agreement had for United States policy toward Egypt. Dulles observed that "the Arab countries were independent governments and free to do whatever they wished in the matter." He added that it was "difficult to be critical of countries which, feeling themselves endangered, seek the arms which they sincerely believe they need for defense." [6] After mentioning there was little likelihood of a cooperative arrangement between the Soviet Union and the United States in the building of a high dam for Egypt in May of 1956, the Secretary was asked whether the United States planned to take another look at economic and technical aid to countries which accepted assistance from the Soviets. His reply was direct—"No." Cooperation with the Soviet Union on a specific project was not only unlikely but also "something quite different from our assisting on one project while the country in question is obtaining assistance from the Soviet Union with respect to some other project." [7]

The increasing ties between neutralist countries and communist countries, along with the latter's advocacy of neutralism, led to expressions of alarm from some American circles, including the

United States Congress. Dulles responded to the situation in late 1955 thusly:

We need not become panicky because Soviet communism now disports itself in this new garb. We need not assume, as some seem to assume, that the leaders in the Asian countries are unaware of danger and easily duped by false promises. These leaders have, indeed, had much political experience and have helped to win great political successes for their countries.[8]

He added that the less developed areas of the world confronted the United States with new tasks, particularly in the sense of providing the necessary assistance to developing economies. While the flow of private capital partly met the need, government had an important role to play in providing economic aid, technical assistance, and scientific cooperation, and "a grudging response" would "not be enough." [9] In this sense, even if there were not the concern about the extension of Soviet influence and power, the "third world" posed a challenge to the United States.

There was, in this particular description of the challenge to the United States in the "third world," a noticeable absence of any reference to collective security or military arrangements. For the developing countries, Dulles considered military nonalignment itself neither obsolete nor necessarily impractical. He was well aware of the areas where there existed no real bases or justification, either from the point of view of the United States or of the area in question, for reciprocal military arrangements. He was equally aware that the interests of the United States were served by continuing and increasing economic and technical assistance to these areas. After his discussions with Nasser and other Arab leaders in 1953, he had reported that there existed no basis for an overall defensive arrangement in the Middle East: "We must . . . avoid becoming fascinated with concepts that have no reality. We should, rather, through measures such as the above (economic assistance and Point IV) seek to improve the general situation without demand for specific *quid pro quo* on our part." [10]

However, what was apparently not implied in Dulles' statements on neutrality was far easier to ascertain than just what he meant by the obsolescence, immorality, or shortsightedness of neutrality.

There resulted confusion or misunderstanding at home and abroad. This became more apparent on the occasion of his oft-quoted 1956 pronouncement on the subject.

On June 9, 1956, Dulles outlined the reasons for the United States proposed "peace insurance policy" for 1957, which included approximately $36 billion for the cost of the United States military establishment, both at home and abroad, and approximately $4.7 billion in the Mutual Security Program. The entire budget package was running into congressional opposition. Although roughly eighty per cent of the Mutual Security Program was planned for various military assistance programs, some of these requests, and especially the economic aid requests, were in serious trouble in Congress. Dulles first justified the whole $40 billion package in terms of the defense requirement for deterrence and of the moral equivalent of war. He deprecated the illusion that peace could be achieved by wishful thinking or by American isolationism and neutrality. He cited the Monroe Doctrine and membership in the United Nations as two examples of America's move away from isolationism. Pointing out that the United States, within ten years, had become a signatory to more than forty treaties in South America, Central America, Europe, and Asia, he maintained:

These treaties abolish, as between the parties, the principle of neutrality, which pretends that a nation can best gain safety for itself by being indifferent to the fate of others. *This has increasingly become an obsolete conception and, except under very exceptional circumstances, it is an immoral and shortsighted conception.*[11] (Emphasis added.)

After briefly describing the reasons why the "peace insurance policy" was "so expensive"—namely, the requirement for a retaliatory force and local defenses for deterrence and to prevent miscalculation—Dulles concentrated on justification of the proposed expenditures in the Mutual Security Program. The estimations in his address included about $1.5 billion for military aid and defense support in the Far East and Southeast Asia, about $800 million for military aid and defense support in the Middle East, about $1 billion for Europe—including some assistance to Yugoslavia, "a notable example of national independence in Eastern Europe"—and about $700 million for various economic aid programs to the developing countries. The military assistance programs were "de-signed to make secure, at minimum cost to us, countries whose safety is part of our own safety." He relied upon a broader justification in supporting the economic aid aspects of the program:

The United States has far and away the most highly developed economy of any nation in the world. Our productivity almost equals that of all the rest of the world put together.

Always the economically developed nations have helped less developed countries. . . . We were helped from Europe when we were beginning to develop this continent. That is a law of social life and we cannot violate it except at our peril.[12]

Of course, the economic aid aspects of the Mutual Security Program were justified as even more imperative in light of the recent Soviet efforts to push "its own interests by means of credits extended to other countries." Nothing seemed to move Congress more than actions of the Soviet Union.

In justifying the Mutual Security Program, the Secretary countered the usual arguments against foreign aid by maintaining that there was no "give-away" in the program, that the United States was not attempting to buy any gratitude, that the amounts were closely calculated, that the administration of the funds was efficient and, finally, that there was a requirement for local forces. The address concluded on the note that there already existed "signs that a new day may be dawning." The Soviet leaders no longer relied on the doctrine of force. The de-Stalinization process represented some genuine alterations, and the freedom of labor had been increased in Russia. There were greater pressures in the satellite countries for more independent roles in decision-making.

Out of all this there may come—not this year, or next year, but some year—a government which is responsive to the just aspirations of the people and which renounces expansionist goals.[13]

Even if this "new day" arrived, however, the United States would still have to "wage peace," to continue military and economic aid programs.

The speech, in its entirety, was designed as an elucidation of American interests which justified the Mutual Security Program then running into serious trouble in Congress. The administration had requested more for 1957, in terms of both military and economic assistance, than during the past two years. Several congressmen considered the extent of military assistance too extravagant and the economic assistance requests for some neutral countries came under particular fire. Aid to such countries as India, Yugoslavia, Indonesia, and Egypt did not at all sit well with many in Congress.[14] Congress set out overall to cut $1 billion from the $4.7 billion request and, as it turned out, succeeded in cutting approximately $900 million in spite of the efforts of the Secretary of State, in June of 1956, in taking the justification for the Mutual Security Program to the nation. The following year, the President himself decided to take the justification to the nation, but succeeded in fending off the attack on military assistance and economic aid only for the moment.

In the process of his justification, Dulles censured the tendencies toward wishful thinking, isolationism, and neutrality in the United States. In spite of the description of interlocking and widespread security arrangements, the address contained no implication that every "free" nation should align itself militarily with the United States. There was no such appeal for more allies. Nor was there any indication that everyone should "stand up and be counted." The Secretary was merely stating, although somewhat clumsily to some, that the United States had an interest in providing military and economic assistance to other countries. The address as a whole was directed by and large for domestic consumption and not for foreign audiences. The conclusion can hardly be avoided that his description of neutrality as "an obsolete conception and, except under very exceptional circumstances . . . an immoral and shortsighted conception" was likewise aimed at the American audience and surely not directly, if at all, at the neutralist countries. The Secretary was, after all, including justification for assistance programs to such countries as India, Yugoslavia, Indonesia, and Egypt. The statement, in context, resembled neither an attack on nor criticism of neutralist attitudes in the Afro-Asian world. It was by no means an expression of blanket disapproval of any and all forms of neutralism and nonalignment.

Nonetheless, regardless of the aims of the speech, the remarks of the Secretary of State automatically have foreign audiences. The speech in itself did constitute a reminder of the commitment of the United States to the idea of collective security. The United States did not advocate neutrality. Although the Secretary's remarks did not appear as a hint to neutralist nations, it was obvious and natural that defending assistance to allies was generally an easier political task than defending economic assistance to neutralists. At any rate, the media became attached to his description of neutrality with its unfortunate, even if unintended, connotations.

The fact that there was some misunderstanding became apparent within a few weeks after the address. On July 11, 1956, in response to a question on his earlier statement, the Secretary explained that he considered "immoral" only that kind of neutralism which was indifferent to the fate of others and sought security in complete isolationism. After mentioning that this kind of neutralism came to an end not only in collective security arrangements but also "in spirit" at the United Nations, the following exchange took place between the Secretary and the press:

Q. I think some of us had the impression from the statement you made that the standard which was in your mind, the standard of action or commitment, was the collective security system, that is, the willingness to take a position on some specific current issue during the past 10 years. Your definition here broadens neutrality to the point where, well, I now have the impression that hardly any country would be considered to be immoral in its neutral policy.

A. I think there are very few, *if any*, although I do believe this: I believe that countries which denounce genuine collective security pacts are seeking to promote a somewhat wrong view of neutrality.[15] (Emphasis added.)

Although left unsaid, it was abundantly clear, in the 1956 speech itself and in the clarification afterward, that Dulles would have surely considered one type of neutral policy as obsolete, immoral, and shortsighted—namely, any return to American neutrality and isolationism.

While Dulles' widely quoted pronouncements tended to obscure his awareness of the complexities and subtleties of nonalignment, there was no gainsaying the fact that neutralism or neutrality ran against his grain in two senses: whenever it represented what he considered moral indifference, and whenever it went against his views of United States interests. These two considerations were integral to his general approach to the subject.

First, in *War, Peace and Change* (1939), Dulles noted that there was coming a time when nations would no longer adhere to the procedure of declaring war, of fixing the moment when the employment of forces would constitute a status of war. The formal change of status, affected by a decision of the highest authority, had served as a type of safeguard. He concluded that one of the reasons for the trend toward undeclared war was that this procedure "renders awkward the invocation of sanctions, or of 'neutrality' measures which have a similar effect. Neutral states, as a matter of friendliness or of domestic expediency, may close their eyes to operations which to others seem clearly to evidence a state of war. The possibility of cooperative neutral action is thus minimized." [16] Surreptitious alignment with aggressors or complete indifference were considered by Dulles to be "immoral"—that is, impractical and contrary to enlightened self interest or the "general good."

In his press conference after the 1956 address, he stressed that neutrality was immoral only when it meant complete indifference to the fate of others.[17] His arguments against such indifference and lack of concern coincide with the general criticism by one student of that "pluralism and ethical relativism" which:

avoid judgment of the actions and purposes of other states at a time when the infractions of certain, necessary common-law principles of international behavior not only risk nuclear war, but sabotage the very rudimentary procedures . . . which might diminish its likelihood.[18]

Generally speaking, Dulles considered obsolete, immoral, and short-sighted only those varieties of neutralism which have been described as representing "escapism pure and simple," "moral indifference" to global issues, or "surreptitious alignment with the Soviet bloc." [19]

Second, at a more practical level, denouncements of the United States commitment to a program of collective security and related developments which worked against its implementation ran contrary to the Secretary's grain. This did not mean that he was either set against all expressions of neutralism or bent toward a grand world-wide alliance: "It is not necessary to bind all of the nations together in military pacts or political unions. . . . The form of co-operation suitable for the Americas or for Western Europe is not necessarily applicable to Finland or Sweden or India." [20] Nor did Dulles conceive of collective security in the sense that nonalignment *per se* generally implied an anti-West position or "surreptitious alignment" with the Soviet Union. The commitment of the United States to collective security did mean, however, that Dulles was often found disagreeing with certain policies of particular neutralist nations.

Between 1951 and 1954, for example, the United States and India strongly disagreed on such matters as the Japanese Peace Treaty, the Korean settlement, and the Southeast Asia Treaty Organization. The conflicts between Dulles and India, not to mention other neutralist countries, were products of different specific interests and varying interpretations of what best served the general interest. There was, broadly speaking, a natural conflict between the involvement of the United States in Asia and India's advocacy of no big-power entanglement in the political, economic, or military affairs of the developing countries. Dulles did not hide the fact that, at times, he found Indian policy perplexing and displeasing. On the other hand, although he sometimes thought Nehru naïve on certain foreign policy questions such as Korea, Dulles neither doubted the Indian leader's sincerity nor considered him neutral on the question of democracy versus totalitarianism.[21]

When viewed *in toto,* Dulles' attitudes and policies toward neutralism and neutrals were more understanding during the 1956–1959 period than during the first years of his secretaryship. In the early period from 1953–1956, he was inclined to express impatience with certain so-called neutrals and what he considered to be their naïveté in terms of the East-West struggle. There were occasionally overtones of a "one had to stand up and be counted" complexion. Neutralism in various parts of Asia, in the years and in light of the Korean War experience, did not go down easily with the Secretary.[22] Nor was he at all pleased with the fact that the foreign policies of India often appeared diametrically opposed to the interests and policies of the United States. By 1956, however, he appeared more flexible, showing increased interest in problems of economic development and more understanding of the neutrals' predicaments. He had, to be sure, accepted the inevitability of neutralist postures:

Some of these newly independent nations realized that their independence can best be assured through such collective security arrangements as we have described. We are proud to be associated with these nations and are determined to justify their confidence.

Other newly independent nations prefer not to adhere to collective security pacts. We acknowledge, of course, their freedom of choice.

We have a deep interest in the independence of all these new nations and we stand ready to contribute, from our store of skills and resources, to help them achieve a solid economic foundation for their freedom.

This is a challenging problem for the free world. For, in the long run, political independence and economic well-being are interdependent. Much has been done, and is being done, to meet the problem. But it is on a piecemeal basis. The search for adequate and dependable processes is still unfinished business.[23]

The thesis was beginning to be accepted that, if neutralist countries truly desired to safeguard and were capable of safeguarding their freedom, they were in effect "aligned philosophically and ideologically with the West."[24]

The acceptance of this thesis was not, however, entirely a late development in the last few years of Dulles' tenure. Before and soon after assuming office, he had expressed the idea that the interests of the United States were served by the maintenance of free or independent countries without reference as to whether or not they were militarily or politically aligned with the West.[25] Without denying that he came to a fuller understanding of neutralism through the years, there were several other factors which contributed to this development besides what might have been some personal maturation in his basic approach. During the 1956–1959 period, changes in the international and domestic environments slightly enlarged his field for operations. The slackening of the tension lines between East and West, combined with some increasing domestic or congressional awareness of and concern for international needs, problems, and responsibilities, produced an opportunity to explain programs more in terms of their own merits. Also, advancements in military technology and strategic planning to some extent altered alliance structures so that, by the late 1950s, the United States could afford more neutralism.

Finally, in fairness to Dulles during the early years, he had to deal with and adjust to a phenomenon for which there existed no criteria for identification and classification. He assumed office amid the revolution of the "third world." Judging from his overall performance, he neither adhered to nor operated under the burden of any rigid formula on the subject of neutralism. He adjusted from case to case, favoring or disfavoring any neutralist tendencies according to the circumstances and his perception of the interests of the United States. He accepted no absolute standard by which neutralism *per se* was to be measured. His reactions, throughout his secretaryship, represented a normal ambivalence, episodic adjustment, and pragmatic evaluation.

THE SUEZ CRISIS

As to the neutralists themselves, the theme of positive neutrality was variously played upon and utilized. The theme played well into the hands of the young Premier and later President of Egypt—Gamal Abdel Nasser. At the time Great Britain was adhering to the Baghdad Pact, and thereby becoming willy-nilly further embroiled in an inter-Arab conflict against Egypt, Colonel Nasser "was being induced" into neutralism at the Bandung Conference.[26] The nations and spirit of Bandung, in April of 1955, at least provided Nasser with a sympathetic audience, both in Africa and Asia, for his maneuvers in the Arab capitals and between London, Moscow, and Washington. In 1956 he "threw down the challenge to Britain in well-chosen circumstances" [27]—the Suez crisis.

The course of events leading up to Nasser's seizure of the Suez Canal Company, the Israeli-French-British invasion, the denunciations, and the withdrawal constitutes a multifaceted tale of diplomatic maneuver. At the time, the event was considered by some as "one of the most calamitous episodes in the history of United States diplomacy." [28] The luxury of hindsight, however, provides bases upon which one can question in what respects the episode was "calamitous" from the viewpoint of United States policy. The role of the United States before, during, and after the Suez crisis has been the subject of much conflicting interpretation.

The following analysis emphasizes merely two aspects of the complex Suez episode without in any way pretending to represent the complete picture. First, a review of the background to the proposed grants to aid Egypt in the construction of the Aswan Dam and Dulles' official retraction of the offer is in order. After the event, this move was not uncommonly considered abrupt and hasty at best and, at worst, an angry spur of the moment decision supposedly deriving from a fervid anti-Soviet or anticommunist sentiment on the part of the Secretary.[29] Actually, neither view was accurate. Second, no understanding of United States policy over Suez would be complete without examination of the restrictions upon the Secretary's freedom of action—restrictions arising not only from broad political and international considerations but also from the very obvious allied differences and conflicts of interest. In 1956 it was contended that America's market was replete with "tinsel" in the sense that legal and moral platitudes constituted the foreign policy of the United States.[30] Some platitudes were, of course, utilized by all sides in the dispute. But in retrospection, in spite of the legal and moral icing (which was actually not much), Dulles' moves followed a course of action consonant with perceived national interest based on hard political and power considerations.

The Aswan Dam Project

On September 27, 1955, Nasser announced that Egypt had concluded an arms agreement with Czechoslovakia. In mid-October, Prime Minister Eden, seriously concerned with the prospect of a Soviet foothold in the Middle East, approached the Americans with the idea of underwriting obligations to Egypt for the construction of the High Dam at Aswan.[31] Economic aid to Nasser's Egypt was not entirely new in Washington. On November 7, 1954, after the conclusion of an agreement between London and Cairo for the phased withdrawal of British forces from Egypt, the United States had announced a $40 million grant to Egypt. In fact, the United States had agreed to use economic aid as a sweetener or "incentive to induce the Egyptians to make and keep an agreement on acceptable terms." [32]

The Aswan Dam project, however, was a slightly different matter as American policy contained an inherent tendency to waver on the subject of identification with either Great Britain or France in the Middle East or, generally, in the "third world." Reporting on his Middle East trip in 1953, Dulles wrote that the "Israeli factor" and "the association of the United States in the minds of the people . . . with French and British colonial and imperialistic policies" were "millstones" around the American neck. While not insensitive to the viewpoint and concerns of Great Britain, he was equally not inclined toward an overall Anglo-American combine in this area:

The British interpret our policy as one which in fact hastens their loss of prestige in the area. To some extent, regardless of efforts to the contrary on our part, this may be true. However, this is, for the most part, due to natural evolution in the area, and altered world power relationships between the U.S. and the U.K., more than to specific action on our part.

Accordingly, from the outset of the Eisenhower Administration, the United States conceived of its position as having a "delicate role to play" in attempting to settle local problems in the Near East without excessively worsening relations with Great Britain.[33]

Besides this inherent tendency to waver on the subject of identification with the British or the French in the Middle East, there was also the consideration that Britain was already deeply entangled in the inter-Arab conflict between Nasser and the pro-Western Prime Minister of Iraq, Nuri Es-Said. On February 24, 1955, Turkey and Iraq signed the treaty of mutual defense, which became known as the Baghdad Pact. Nasser, having made known his opposition to the idea beforehand, immediately denounced Iraq and the pact. Less than two months later, Britain formally adhered to the pact and, not incidentally, thereby reassured the Royal Air Force's rights to use two air bases in the area. No other Western power followed suit. France, with concerns in Syria, remained aloof. Having, to some degree, supported and encouraged the idea of a pact, the United States still welcomed the idea, but remained cool on the subject of membership and did not join for a complex of reasons.[34] The Soviet Union denounced the agreement. Prime Minister Nehru of India, concerned both with tension in the Middle East and Pakistan's adherence to the pact, was even more denunciatory. In one observer's summation, the "immediate consequence of the Baghdad Pact was to inflame everybody against everybody," most particularly the Egyptians against the British and Iraqis.[35]

Moreover, the sheer scale of the Aswan Dam project itself was enough cause for some hesitation in Washington before embarking upon any plan of cooperation. The project was not only the most expensive development endeavor ever launched in the Middle East, but its completion was to stretch over a period of at least ten years. In spite of the political advantages to be gained by the United States in supporting the project, there were also political disadvantages in becoming a creditor nation on such a scale for several years. Although Dulles was inclined to support congressional commitments to foreign aid generally for upwards of five years for planning purposes, this idea was fought both by Congress and by the Secretary of the Treasury.[36] There were also possible political disadvantages vis-à-vis the debtor nation depending upon the state of relations.

The British, although no doubt sharing similar doubts and concerned with probable problems for Sudan, exhibited more enthusiasm for the project and continued to enlist the support of the United States. After two months of discussions, on December 17, 1955, it was announced that the United States and Great Britain would offset the foreign exchange costs of the first stages of the construction of the High Dam at Aswan by supplementing a $200 million loan from the World Bank with approximately $70 million in grants ($56 million from the United States and $14 million from Great Britain). While the first phases of the work were to take from four to five years, the Egyptians were assured that further support would be sympathetically considered—meaning approval given legislative authority. This support would run in the neighborhood of $130 million to finance the later stages of construction. The High Dam was a popular and symbolic project for the Egyptians. Among other considerations, the two Western allies had a common and obvious interest in countering Soviet influence in the Middle East. Final understandings on the project were to await the Egyptian Finance Minister's consultations with his government.

When Eugene Black, then President of the World Bank, presented the agreements to the Egyptians, Nasser "made some very strong statements that he could never accept the conditions imposed by the World Bank." [37] After reaching a settlement on the conditions established by the bank, the Egyptian negotiators signed an agreement "in principle" for a loan of $200 million. For all practical purposes, the matter reposed "in principle." Regardless of the specific points of contention, and whether genuinely wooed by tempting offers from the Soviet Union or attempting to improve his own bargaining position, Nasser held back rather than push forward with the agreements. In April, he asserted that Egypt was "still considering a Soviet offer to build the dam." [38]

If this were not ample cause for some consternation in Washington, the issue was compounded in May by Egypt's formal recognition of the Chinese People's Republic. Washington's official reaction to this step by Nasser was, nonetheless, a relatively mild expression of regret with no further comment. At the same time, Dulles made it clear that the United States was not adverse to aiding in a project when the country involved was also receiving Soviet aid for other purposes or projects. Thus, the Aswan Dam was still on the United States schedule.[39] But the matter evolved relatively quietly until brought to the fore by Nasser himself, not long after the British and the Americans had decided to allow the project to dwindle without any unceremonious cancellations.

In February of 1956, Eden had reported that Anglo-American policies toward Egypt were in close accord. After his first session in Washington, the Prime Minister cabled London that it was agreed that the future of United States and British policies in the Middle East depended considerably on Nasser: "If he showed himself willing to cooperate with us, we should reciprocate. . . . If his attitude on this [Aswan Dam] and other matters was that he would not cooperate, we would both have to reconsider our policy towards him." [40] As far as both allies were concerned, the process of reconsideration was neither long in the making nor discouraged by Nasser.

In mid-June, Soviet Foreign Minister Shepilov attended what was to be a celebration of the departure of the last British soldiers from the Suez base—although the British troops had departed earlier than scheduled. Rumors of yet another big arms agreement circulated in Washington.[41] By this time, from the point of view of the United States, the situation was hardly auspicious. Neither the President nor his Secretary of State had much zest to enlist legislative forces and exert pressures for a project which was daily becoming more unpopular. Secretary of the Treasury George Humphrey frowned upon Nasser's "shopping around" between Moscow and Washington and began to question Egypt's ability to sustain the Aswan Dam project along with other commitments.[42]

On June 20, Eugene Black departed for Cairo "to brief Nasser on a final offer, still with United States support." Nasser's counterproposals convinced the President and Dulles that Nasser "was not really interested in serious negotiations on the project." Negotiations halted and, not long thereafter, the President and Dulles considered "the matter dead for all practical purposes."[43] Egypt's financial conditions and continuous flirtations with the Soviet Union, plus the growing congressional opposition to the Aswan Dam project in particular and to aid for Egypt in general, were not the only ingredients in the policy-making process at this time. Egypt had made no effort to cooperate with Sudan, and there persisted the problem of Sudanese rights to Nile waters. On the contrary, Egypt appeared to be moving in the opposite direction by intensifying the dispute with Sudan and by increasing its anti-West activity in other Arab capitals.

For mostly similar reasons, especially those related to Nasser's activities with the Soviet Union and in other Arab capitals, the British were beginning to arrive at a tentative conclusion to back off the Aswan Dam project on their own. After establishing that the Department of State shared doubts regarding the advisability of following through with an offer which had not yet been accepted, in mid-July the British government decided not "to go on with a project likely to become increasingly onerous in finance and unsatisfactory in practice."[44] Eden "would have preferred to play this long and not to have forced the issue."[45] Whether the issue was to be played long or short, however, depended not only upon Dulles and Eden but also upon Nasser. Furthermore, a position of playing it long was not enhanced by the *London Times'* announcement on July 14: "The attempt to stabilise the Middle East in cooperation with Egypt is now over." [46] The proverbial cat was now, if not earlier, out of the bag.

Dulles later informed the President that the Egyptians had been advised on July 13, both that the United States was not prepared to deal with the Aswan matter at the time because congressional action could not be predicted, and that the views of the United States toward the project were not unchanged. The Egyptians were informed further that the United States would consult with them on the matter within a week.[47] The exact reasons for the full content of Dulles' message are still uncertain. The message appears, in some respects, as a logical warning that an Egyptian attempt to wrap up the agreement would be counterproductive and that salvaging of the project and offer, if there was to be any salvaging, would be found only in playing it very long.

It was at this juncture that Ambassador Ahmed Hussein played out the instructions to accept the offer and conditions of December 17, 1955. The Ambassador had been in Egypt for lengthy consultations since mid-May. Before departing for Washington in mid-July, he "announced that he was returning . . . to sign the Aswan Dam agreement and that he foresaw no serious problems." [48] On July 17 or 18 in Washington, Dulles met with British Ambassador Sir Roger Makins. The former apologized for not being able to notify the British more than two days in advance and, while desiring the luxury of more time, obviously felt his hand was being forced. There was virtually no time for consultation, and the British government accepted Dulles' decision with no substantial, if any, reservations at the time.[49] The Aswan Dam project was all but officially dead.

On July 19, 1956, Ambassador Hussein informed Secretary Dulles that Egypt was prepared to finalize an Aswan agreement under the conditions previously discussed with the offer. Egypt also wanted a commitment for the duration of the construction, or approximately ten years. Furthermore, "if the United States would not guarantee to foot practically all of the Aswan bill, the Soviet Union would do so." [50] Dulles replied with the official withdrawal of the United States offer to help finance the Aswan Dam. The move has been variously described as "sudden," "abrupt," or "spur of the moment." Yet, in the light of the preceding events, the withdrawal and the official press release represented a comparatively calm retraction of the offer. Although one line of the official statement alluded sharply to Egypt's affinity for Soviet arms agreements—". . . the ability of Egypt to devote adequate resources to assure the project's success has become more uncertain than at the time the offer was made" [51] —as a whole the release was matter-of-fact in tone. The retraction of the offer of aid for the Aswan Dam was combined with a statement of purpose to seek other areas of economic aid to Egypt.

With regard to the substance of the decision to retract the offer, Dulles' policy options were, practically speaking, narrowed to two courses of action at the time of the Hussein visit—retraction of the offer or postponement and dragging the issue out. Regardless of the reasons for the American and the British decisions to drop the Aswan plan, it is clear from these decisions, the former's apparently taken well before the Dulles-Hussein meeting, that granting Egypt's request to finalize an Aswan agreement was not considered a practicable policy option. If there was an error in policy, it related not to the timing of the official retraction, but to the earlier decision to drop the Aswan Dam project in the first place.

Thus, the policy options boiled down to a statement of fact that the United States no longer considered financing the project or some form of postponement—bluff, dragging out the issue, or a statement of intent to consider the matter carefully with the hope of finding common ground for the project. There was an implicit understanding between the British and the Americans, more understood than stated, simply to let the matter dwindle.[52] It was, at this stage, only a matter of timing and tactics. Yet, timing and tactics were not entirely within the control of Secretary Dulles or Prime Minister Eden as the former's hand was obviously being forced rather effectively by Egypt and, indirectly, by the United States Congress.

First, but of secondary importance, the political costs and benefits analysis of the policy options had to include the fact that Congress was in no mood to appropriate any funds for the Aswan project. While agreeing to maintain credits to Yugoslavia, only after some sharp disagreement with Dulles, the Senate "did nothing to hide its dislike of giving financial aid to Egypt." [53] Two days after Dulles had informed the Egyptians that the United States was not then prepared to deal with the Aswan matter because of the unpredictability of congressional action, on July 15, the Senate Appropriations Committee adopted a report on the Mutual Security Act which included the statement that the "Committee directs that none of the funds provided under this Act shall be used for assistance in connection with the construction of the Aswan Dam nor shall any of the funds heretofore provided under the Mutual Security Act, as amended, be used on this Dam without prior approval of the Committee on Appropriations." [54] While the report had no standing in law, the existence of an anti-Dam coalition had a standing in politics. Furthermore, there existed considerable pressure from this coalition to attach a rider specifically barring the use of any funds whatsoever for the construction of the Aswan Dam. The Dam was not the only United States aid project for Egypt, but it was the one under particular fire. While the mood of Congress and the future of the foreign aid bill were not the determining factors in reaching the decision to discontinue the project,[55] the Senate's attitude toward economic aid to "neutrals" in general and particularly to Egypt had to be addressed and carried some weight in practical and tactical terms. The issue was compounded from the administration's point of view by the long-term nature of the financing required for completion of the Dam.

Had there been less considerable anti-Dam feeling in Congress, Dulles would have had more room for maneuverability, and some form of postponement option might have looked more promising. As it was, however, any public declarations either supporting the scheme in principle or indicating a willingness to go on with financing the project would have only produced stronger reactions among the anti-Dam coalition, thereby increasing congressional pressures against the project and, above all, endangering other aspects of the foreign aid bill then before Congress. These considerations were necessarily on the Secretary's mind and were expressed during his meetings with the British Ambassador not long before the formal retraction of the American offer.[56]

As illustrated by the cases of Yugoslavia, India, and Indonesia, and by Dulles' writings on economic assistance, both Eisenhower and Dulles were willing to do battle with antiforeign aid forces. But legislative support for economic aid to nonallies was slim indeed. There was much to be said for selecting the time and places for confrontations on such issues and, thereby, retaining some Executive flexibility, if not at least a semblance of Executive authority: "If I had not announced our withdrawal when I did, the Congress would certainly have imposed it on us, almost unanimously. As it was, we retained some flexibility." [57] To do battle for an unpopular project which both the President and the Secretary had already considered dead naturally looked like a poor, if not insupportable, policy alternative.

While the attitude of the Senate constituted one reason against attempting to drag out the issue, postponement was made virtually impossible by another factor in the equation—Egypt. An important key was in Nasser's hands and, to a large degree, playing it long required his cooperation. On July 13 Dulles had advised the Egyptians that the United States was not in a position to deal with the matter. But, probably anticipating the logical outcome, the Egyptian President was afforded and readily utilized the opportunity to force the issue. The Egyptians did not entirely attempt "to clinch the business on their own terms," as Eden later claimed.[58] Actually, although the matter was not played out, it appeared that Nasser's maneuver involved acceptance of the terms previously established by the United States and Great Britain, combined with an appeal for a firm long-term commitment.

An American attempt at bluff, at this stage, would have been not only deliberately deceptive but, equally important, could hardly have succeeded. Delaying devices would have been readily recognized and, as far as Nasser was concerned, could have served the same purpose as cancellation of the offer. In making his bid, Nasser was apparently not prepared to accept an American response somewhere between a "yes" and a "no." As publicly announced, Ambassador Hussein was returning to Washington not to consult, but to sign an Aswan agreement. Carrying out his instructions from Cairo on July 19, Ambassador Hussein's demand "was in effect an ultimatum." Even if personally inclined toward collaboration with the West, the Ambassador was inescapably caught "in a chancery of circumstances." [59] To the degree that Nasser had decided to play the issue short was, practically speaking, the limit of Dulles' playing it long.

There were, of course, other secondary factors to be considered in arriving at the decision of how to handle the Egyptian demands of July 19. A willingness to reconsider the offer could have easily placed the United States in the position of appearing to be the hagglers. This appearance could have been used by Nasser at any time to similar effect as actual cancellation. Also, Nasser's tactics of openly playing Washington and London off against Moscow did not sit well at all in Washington. To encourage these attempts to play one side against the other was considered a poor proposition. Lastly, the Egyptian President had basically turned away from the West, in terms of both diplomacy and propaganda, months before the withdrawal of the American offer. Neither Washington nor London considered it in their interest to buttress his brand of so-called aggressive neutralism.

In totaling all the preceding considerations, withdrawal of the offer to help finance the Aswan Dam emerged as the most attractive course for the administration to follow. Although the move appeared somewhat ill-timed in retrospection, neither London nor Paris criticized the move in July of 1956. There existed hope in both capitals, now seen as unfounded, that the action would contribute to a demise of Nasser's political career.[60] London, Paris, and Washington gave little, if any, thought to the possible cards remaining in Nasser's hand.

Precisely why Nasser decided or consented to make a final bid for the Aswan agreement remains unclear. He was surely aware that Dulles would in all likelihood issue no positive assurances, that Washington and London no longer had any real interest in pursuing the plan, and that a request for a definitive reply would result in a negative. On September 15, Dulles informed the President that the "outcome was not in fact anything in the nature of a 'shock' or 'surprise' to the Egyptians." [61] One could have imagined that Washington would be reluctant to cancel the project outright had it not been for Dulles' note of July 13 stating that the United States was not prepared to deal with the matter and for the Senate Appropriations Committee's report shortly thereafter. If Nasser seriously wanted to do business with Washington, neither his timing nor his tactics indicated any such interest.

At any rate, even anticipating the outcome, Nasser could have perceived little, if anything, to lose by forcing the issue. The Soviet offer still seemed afloat. On July 15, Soviet Foreign Minister Shepilov denied reports that he had expressed a preference for financing projects other than the Aswan Dam.[62] This offer, however vague, was designed as an unconditional loan at 2 per cent, repayable in thirty years. The advance from the World Bank, on the other hand, was a conditional loan with budgetary controls at $3\frac{1}{2}$ per cent, redeemable in twenty years.[63] Eden later described the Soviet offer as "uneconomic and all the more attractive for being so." [64] Whatever the precise differences between the two offers, if Nasser had agreed to the Western advance, in many respects "the Egyptian economy would have been largely controlled from Washington." [65] Furthermore, nationalization of the Suez Canal Company could provide Egypt with a source of revenue, the supply of which was scarce, to help finance the Dam. Such a direct snub to the West would be a far less viable option under a Washington-London-World Bank financial agreement for the Aswan Dam than under an agreement with the Soviet Union. Although the Dam was indisputably Nasser's prize project, there exists insufficient basis to date for an assumption that he preferred to do business with the West.

With hindsight and second-guessing, considering Nasser's brand of independent Arab nationalism, the following scenario has some obvious attractions: first, rebuff by the West in mid-July, supplying a pretext for nationalization of the Canal Company; second, nationalization of the Canal Company in late July; and, third, journey to Moscow in early August, as previously scheduled, and possible agreement with the Soviet Union to finance the Aswan Dam. The second and third steps of such a scenario could be considered interchangeable. The plans for seizure of the Canal Company had been prepared well in advance of Ambassador Hussein's meeting with Dulles. Furthermore, the decision to nationalize the canal at some-time was likely already made before Dulles officially withdrew the offer of an American grant.[66]

Nevertheless, it cannot be established with any certainty that Nas-ser set out to force the issue simply to place himself in a better posi-tion regarding a scheme for taking over the Canal Company. In fair-ness to Nasser, he might have neither desired nor anticipated an official withdrawal of the offer by the United States. Ambassador Hussein's instructions to issue in effect an ultimatum could have been a play designed to gain an American commitment actively to reconsider the project, as it was becoming increasingly apparent that the United States and Great Britain had lost interest in an agreement. In fairness to the situation, however, such a commit-ment by the United States would have equally played into Nasser's hands. Scheduled to visit Moscow in August, he would have had a stronger bargaining position vis-à-vis the Russians while his options would still remain open with regard to the nationalization of the Canal Company.

If any such scenario as the above were contemplated, a fly entered the ointment between Dulles' withdrawal of the American offer and Nasser's nationalization of the Suez Canal Company. On July 22 Foreign Minister Shepilov expressed interest in weighing aid to in-dustries which were considered, from the Soviet viewpoint, more vital than the Aswan Dam.[67] The Soviet "offer," which Nasser had publicized as early as April and to which Ambassador Hussein re-ferred in his meeting with Dulles, was indeed far from firm. Shepi-lov's statement was not publicized in Egypt, and two years were to elapse before the Soviet Union actually began to help in the financ-ing of the Dam.

If some uncertainty surrounds Nasser's maneuvers up to this point, there also remains the question regarding Russian tactics. By his denial of reports that the Soviet Union preferred other projects over the Dam, on July 15 Shepilov encouraged the impression that the Russians were still interested in financing the Dam. Yet, three days after the Dulles-Hussein meeting, Shepilov essentially affirmed that the Soviet Union preferred other projects for the time being.

Of course, with the Soviet Union only beginning to feel its way in the Middle East, there may have been a natural tendency to move cautiously. There also appeared no need to move rapidly on the Aswan Dam. The Russians were, to some degree, in a position indirectly to force an issue in a manner which could contribute to increased Egyptian reliance upon the Soviet Union and, generally, to a stronger foothold in the Middle East without in any way endangering the prospect of their handling the Aswan deal in the longer-run.

Allied Conflicts Over Suez

While denouncing British and American policies, the Baghdad Pact and "imperialism" generally, on July 26, 1956, Nasser announced the nationalization and occupation of the properties of the Suez Canal Company. Martial law was declared in the Canal Zone, and foreign employees of the Canal Company were not to be allowed to leave their positions. He announced further, however, that shareholders would be adequately compensated.

From this date until November 6—when the cease-fire was accepted by Britain, France, and Israel—the policies of the United States and Great Britain, not to mention France, were at variance because of differing degrees of interests and concomitant disagreement over tactics. With a real vital concern in the flow of oil from the Middle East, a declining position in the area and high investments in the Suez Canal, the British had decided from the beginning "to go it alone" if necessary. With a developing and delicate position in the Middle East and negligible investments in the Suez Canal, the United States was prepared neither to support nor to approve armed intervention. The obvious differences were exacerbated by the fact that the allies were virtually unprepared or caught with no contingency plans for Nasser's move. Without attempting to inspect every nuance of diplomatic maneuvering, from July 26 to November 6, the conflicts of interest between the Atlantic partners became increasingly apparent, important and painful at each successive stage.

Both Great Britain and France desired urgent and decisive action against Egypt after Nasser seized the Suez Canal Company. Eden cabled Eisenhower: "My colleagues and I are convinced that we must be ready, in the last resort, to use force to bring Nasser to his senses. For our part we are prepared to do so. I have this morning instructed our Chiefs of Staff to prepare a military plan accordingly." [68] The French Foreign Minister, Christian Pineau, was due to arrive in London on July 29. Indeed, if the British and French had been capable of rapidly successful military operations, immediate intervention would have served their perceived interests far better than months of delay and conferences. However, receiving no intelligence warning that seizure of the canal was imminent and possessing no diplomatic or military contingency plans, the allied capitals were caught unawares and unprepared. In fact, Great Britain's military preparations were not completed until September. Naturally inclined toward a quick response, but with neither the military means nor the will to upset Atlantic relations abruptly, Britain followed a course favored by the United States during the early stages of the episode.

On July 28, with no instructions from the President except "to see what it's all about" and to "hold the fort," Ambassador Murphy arrived in London. The United States was feeling its way into the matter, observing more than participating. When the British Foreign Secretary, Selwyn Lloyd, confirmed Her Majesty's Government's decision to use force if necessary, Ambassador Murphy informed him that "of course the United States Government had made no such decision." During two days of discussions with Lloyd and Pineau, "there was no hint that the United States would be expected to join any military moves." But the British and the French assumed "that the United States would be involved in their plans." There was, according to Murphy, also a "confident assumption . . . that the United States would go along with anything Britain and France did." The British mood, in approaching the crisis at this stage, was adequately expressed in the Chancellor of the Exchequer's informal remarks to his old wartime associate, Ambassador Murphy. Britain, according to Macmillan, had no intentions of becoming another "Netherlands" by refusing to accept Egypt's challenge, and had every intention of chasing Nasser out of Egypt.

Summing up the situation, it seemed to Ambassador Murphy that the British were "laboring under the impression that a common identity of interest existed among the allies." This was not the American view, and the Ambassador "gave no encouragement to the idea." [69]

On July 31, informed that the British and French might employ force without delay and without attempting any intermediate steps, Dulles departed for London and President Eisenhower forwarded the first in a series of letters to Prime Minister Eden. While recognizing "the possibility that eventually the use of force might become necessary . . . to protect international rights," the President expressed his conviction, as well as that of his associates, "as to the unwisdom even of contemplating the use of military force at this moment." With somewhat extraneous references to American public opinion, world public opinion, and the United States Congress, the message that all possible peaceful methods should be exhausted was unmistakably clear: "If unfortunately the situation can finally be resolved only by drastic means, there should be no grounds for belief anywhere that corrective measures were undertaken merely to protect national or individual investors, or the legal rights of a sovereign nation were ruthlessly flouted." Eisenhower's letter also implied both that the United States had no interest in chasing Nasser out of Egypt by force and, most importantly, that the maximum demand of the United States was the efficient operation and freedom of passage through the Suez Canal.[70]

Dulles consulted with Eden and Pineau on August 1. During the meetings, it was perfectly understood that the United States was against intervention at any early stage and in favor of conferences, resolutions, and delays.[71] he American Secretary did not specifically rule out all possibilities of the use of force. As a matter of course, the United States did not preclude such means if all other methods failed. The following comment "rang in" Eden's "ears for months":

A way had to be found to make Nasser disgorge what he was attempting to swallow. . . . We must make a genuine effort to bring world opinion to favor the international operation of the canal. . . . It should be possible to create a world opinion so adverse to Nasser that he would be isolated. Then if a military operation had to be undertaken it would be more apt to succeed and have less grave repercussions than if it had been undertaken precipitately.[72]

In terms of possible American influence over British-French policy and sensitivities to the situation, perhaps even references to a last resort measure, in the event all other methods failed, should have been avoided. The entire context of all Dulles' remarks is not known. It became apparent, however, that Eden clung to Dulles' phrase "to disgorge" and even to Eisenhower's "absolutely firm position," notwithstanding the fact that this position was likewise to be "reasonable and conciliatory" and supported by public opinion both at home and abroad.

On the subject of force, Dulles simply included military intervention as a possible last resort. At this stage the Egyptian President's approach, intentions, and next steps, plus the Egyptian ability to operate the canal, were yet unknown. Serious open disagreement, at the outset, between the Western allies on the subject of force would have greatly diminished the West's chances of persuading Nasser to negotiate or, at least, to make an appearance at a conference table. At a time when so many questions remained unanswerable, the draftsman could not reasonably exclude the possibility of the use of some force or, at a minimum, the implicit threat of such use. Furthermore, the existing and recognized disagreement between Washington and London was an easy matter neither for Prime Minister Eden nor for President Eisenhower and Secretary Dulles. Mention of intervention as a possible last resort also served to notify Great Britain that her vital concern in the matter was recognized by the United States. Eden recorded that the British "were encouraged" by Dulles' words during the meetings of August 1.[73] Dulles' subsequent actions, however, were designed to discourage the British desire for intervention and to dispel the notion that the United States would approve of intervention.

During the consultations of August 1 and 2, the Secretary of State firmly established the idea that the United States would not directly participate in any military operations. Throughout the ensuing two and a half months, it was equally established that the United States would moreover not countenance resort to force. On August 16, twenty-two nations gathered at the London Conference on the Suez Canal. At the conclusion of the conference, on August 23, there emerged a set of proposals, largely along the lines sponsored by the United States, supported by eighteen nations. The proposals were based upon the establishment of "a definite system destined to guarantee at all times, and for all the Powers, the free use of the Suez Maritime Canal." The system, to be established with due regard to Egypt's sovereign rights, accordingly provided for the following assurances:

Efficient and dependable operations, maintenance and development of the Canal as a free, open and secure international waterway. . . .
Insulation of the operation of the Canal from the influence of the politics of any nation.
A fair and equitable return to Egypt for the use of the Canal, increasing with enlargements of its capacity and greater use.
Equitable Canal tolls with no profit except to Egypt.

Under this scheme, the operation, maintenance, and development of the canal were to be vested in a Suez Canal Board. Although represented on the board, Egypt was to grant this body all rights and facilities appropriate to its functioning.[74] The United States supported the proposals.[75] President Nasser indicated a willingness to discuss the program. But after less than a week of discussions, Egypt formally rejected the eighteen-nation proposals on September 9.[76]

Even before the chairman of the Suez Canal Committee, Prime Minister Menzies of Australia, met with Nasser, the British prepared a draft resolution for the Security Council which called upon Egypt to negotiate on the basis of the eighteen-nation proposals and which further declared "that a threat to the peace exists." On August 30, Dulles reviewed the British draft resolution. He guaranteed American support "on the understanding" that the "move was an honest attempt to reach a solution and not 'a device for obtaining cover.'" He maintained that the United States did not want to become committed to a proposition which implied force.[77]

Four days later, Eden received "a disquieting message" from President Eisenhower. The President, while admitting both a possible later appeal to the United Nations and that the present negotiations would probably not result in the setback Nasser deserved, declared that "American public opinion flatly rejected force." He expressed grave doubt that congressional authority could be obtained for even lesser support measures which the British might wish from the United States. On a personal and professional level, Eisenhower did "not see how a successful result could be achieved by forcible means." Above all, the United States wanted to play it long and did not combine the problems of the canal with the longer-term problem of Nasser and Soviet influence in the Middle East:

We have two problems, the first of which is the assurance of permanent and efficient operation of the Suez Canal with justice to all concerned. The second is to see that Nasser shall not grow as a menace to the peace and vital interests of the West. . . . These two problems need not and possibly cannot be solved simultaneously and by the same methods, although we are exploring further means to this end. . . . Above all, there must be no grounds for our several peoples to believe that anyone is using the Canal difficulty as an excuse to proceed forcibly against Nasser. . . . We have friends in the Middle East who tell us they would like to see Nasser's deflation brought about. But they seem unanimous in feeling that the Suez is not the issue on which to attempt to do this by force.

The letter [78] constituted notification that the United States would surely take exception to any military move.

Eden replied, in part, by comparing Nasser's designs to the schemes of both Hitler in the 1930s and Stalin in the 1940s. While admitting that there were risks in the use of force against Egypt, Eden clearly thought that military intervention would be necessary and that such intervention soon would be less costly and difficult than intervention after Nasser's revolutions erupted throughout the whole continent:

But if our assessment is correct, and if the only alternative is to allow Nasser's plans quietly to develop until this country and all Western Europe are held to ransom by Egypt acting at Russia's behest it seems to us that our duty is plain. We have many times led Europe in the fight for freedom. It would be an ignoble end to our long history if we accepted to perish by degrees. [79]

Both Dulles and Eisenhower disagreed with Eden's assessment of the situation and informed him of this disagreement. [80] The United States held back on approving the British draft resolution for the

Security Council and, on September 4, Dulles presented his proposition for a Suez Canal Users' Association to the British Ambassador in Washington. Dulles explained that the demand for a new convention with Egypt, which was part of the eighteen-nation proposals sponsored by Dulles, was neither necessary nor likely to succeed. The conflict between the British and the American positions, and the latter's opposition to force, were vividly illustrated in the approaches to the concept of a Users' Club. To Dulles, the scheme represented both an attempt to cooperate with Egypt and, in the event of noncooperation, a means of buying valuable time. If the Egyptian President remained disagreeable, the Eisenhower Administration would at least be afforded greater scope for maneuverability after the presidential contest then underway. Eden interpreted the plan as a means of depriving Nasser, by force if necessary, of revenues from the canal.

The British and French understood the American design behind the Canal Users' Association as a device to deflect the course of events, to prevent bringing matters to a head with Nasser.[81] This was indisputably and logically part of the United States position. It was abundantly evident that the gap between the allies was broad. The United States preference for slower and less dramatic processes was playing it long indeed, including such items as the Users' Club which "might work out a *de facto* 'coexistence,' " economic pressures, exploiting Arab rivalries, and even "alternatives to the present dependence upon the Canal." [82]

Eden, on the other hand, was determined to play it short along the lines of his own thoughts and programs. Responding to Dulles' statement that the Club was not designed to shoot its way through the canal, the British Prime Minister referred to Dulles as that "terrible man" who had consciously deceived the British.[83] Years later, in *Full Circle,* Eden still maintained that the American Secretary misled the British, and did not present the Users' Club as a means of cooperating with Egypt.[84] But cooperation with Egypt was implicit in the plan itself. A few weeks after the proposal was surfaced, on September 19, Dulles laid the position of the United States out for full view before the second London Conference of Maritime Powers. The United States did not exclude the possibility that the plan would fail to work as a provisional operating scheme. All that was required was *"de facto* operating cooperation at the local level":

Therefore, it does not require agreement with Egypt. I think I made clear that there is no thought on the part of the United States of trying to impose any of the facilities of this Association upon Egypt by force. . . . There is no thought in my mind whatever that this agency would attempt to supersede the Egyptian authorities as they handle the Canal equipment on land. . . .

Obviously if Egypt makes it obligatory to use only pilots that are chosen and assigned by it, then I do not see that the pilots of the Association would practically have very much to do, and that part of the plan would have collapsed.[85]

The Users' Club was envisaged by the Americans neither as a means of depriving Egypt of canal dues nor as a device for forcing the issue. During a press conference, on October 2, Dulles asserted: "There is talk about teeth being pulled out of the plan, but I know of no teeth; there were no teeth in it, so far as I am aware." [86] On October 15, he again communicated the position of the United States to Her Majesty's Government.[87]

If Eden continued to misunderstand Dulles' position, then the misunderstanding probably stemmed from what has been described as "wishful thinking," not from Dulles' statements and from the views expressed in the Eisenhower letters.[88] By October 16, if not months before, Eden was well aware of the position of the United States. Meaningful communication between Washington and London had dwindled and the actual blackout, from October 16 to October 30, represented a logical, even if unfortunate, consequence of the conflicting approaches. The fact was that the gap between the Atlantic partners, which was apparent from the outset of the episode, could not be bridged. For Eden and the French, both bent on delivering a critical blow to Nasser, continued contact would mean further attempts by Washington to delay the matter and perhaps increased pressures against the use of force. With the help of Israel, the British and the French chose to go it alone. On July 27, 1956, the day following Nasser's seizure of the waterway, the British Cabinet had decided that Britain "could not stop short of using force"

to internationalize the canal even if it meant acting without allies.[89]

As far as Washington was concerned, the blackout was not totally
contrary to its interests. The two sides had in effect agreed to disagree. An ephemeral consideration, but nonetheless a very important
one, was the fact that the Eisenhower Administration was necessarily preoccupied with the problem of winning the 1956 election.
After more than two months of diplomatic maneuvering, Washington had firmly established its position: "The British Government
had been told over and over again at the highest levels that we
wished to do everything possible to avoid the use of force." [90] To
pressure the British and French for more time on the basis of the
national campaign at this stage would have been fruitless without
either some change in policy toward intervention or an attempt at
deliberate deception.

Behind the absence of meaningful communication, however,
there were some serious misunderstandings or miscalculations. The
diplomatic moves, in many respects, had represented a type of "cat
and mouse" game. Eden was maneuvering into a position for intervention and hoped to ensure himself of American approval at best,
American silence at worst. Dulles was operating in exactly the opposite direction, attempting to avoid a showdown over the canal issue
—especially as the election neared—while seeking some acceptable
settlement. (The roles of the two statesmen had largely switched
from those of the 1954 Indochina problem.) While it was abundantly clear that the United States opposed military intervention
without some dramatic change in the issue itself, this position did
not necessarily imply automatic censorship of any military move by
Great Britain and France. The two European allies approved such
a move in early October when it was decided that a "peace-keeping"
force would take over the canal in the event Israel attacked Egypt.
The cover for intervention had been devised. But, at the time of
this decision, Eden and his advisers apparently assumed that Eisenhower and Dulles would "lie doggo" at least until the election was
over. Assurances to this effect were reportedly offered by one of
Eden's closest advisers, Chancellor of the Exchequer Harold Mac-

millan, who had recently returned from Washington where he conducted some business not related to the Suez affair and had a brief
meeting with the President.[91]

On the British side, this misunderstanding was compounded by a
more serious miscalculation. If a military move were well-timed and
geared to succeed within a very short time, Eisenhower and Dulles
might have time for some middle position instead of open censure
and, at least, Washington would be confronted with a *fait accompli*.
The British miscalculation related not so much to Washington as it
did to their own capabilities. As it turned out, the military move
was not only imprudent by American thinking but also ill-timed
and inadequate.

On the American side, there was also some room for misunderstanding and perhaps miscalculation. The Eisenhower Administration was deep in a national election, campaigning on a theme of
"peace and prosperity," and had already come under fire from the
Democrats, who maintained that the administration was attempting
to sweep the crisis under the rug until after the election. By mid-October, it was apparent that Israel was on the verge of taking some
action and that Britain and France were involved. Dulles and then
Eisenhower later warned Israel that Washington would censure any
military move. Timing was becoming more critical as the election
neared, and Eisenhower and Dulles would not unnaturally figure
that two of America's closest allies would refrain from bringing the
matter to a head so soon before Americans voted. Moreover, the
Secretary of State had reportedly been informed that London would
consult or notify Washington prior to any action.[92]

More important, from an international standpoint, in mid-October a revolt within the Communist party in Poland took power
from the Stalinists and seized control of the army and police from
the Russians. Moscow's conceding points to Warsaw not only har-
monized with the Eisenhower Administration's policy for Eastern
Europe but also had an important domestic political content. Less
than a week later, on October 22, a popular uprising broke out in
Hungary, and there were soon some indications that Moscow might
possibly consider concessions in this case also. To Washington's way
of thinking, it would be illogical at best for the West to divert at-

tention from these tumultuous events in Eastern Europe, to compli-
cate further the situation, and, particularly, to undermine the
West's position against the use of force to settle disputes at a time
when Moscow was considering whether or when to move in with
force. As one student of the crisis later concluded, the developments
between Moscow, Warsaw and Budapest "seemed of first importance" and "Eisenhower did not question that his nearest allies saw
it so." [93]

Behind it all, however, there persisted an unbridgeable disagreement between the Atlantic partners over Suez. The conflicts of interest were a cause for hesitation and not easily accepted in either
Washington or London. The variance in their respective policy positions derived from different interpretations of three factors: first,
Soviet influence in the Middle East; second, Nasser; and third, international control of the canal.

Although both Great Britain and the United States had a common interest in countering Soviet influence in the Middle East, the
latter could not accept the former's interpretation of this particular
issue. The British Prime Minister maintained that, if Nasser were
allowed to "get away" with seizing the Canal Company, he would
"be able to mount revolutions . . . in Saudi Arabia, Jordan, Syria
and Iraq." The "new Governments" would "in effect be Egyptian
satellites if not Russian ones." [94] He described Nasser as "effectively
in Russian hands, just as Mussolini was in Hitler's." He summed up
the wider dangers of the Middle East in one word—Russia.[95]
Eden's emphasis upon the dangers of Soviet control and his tendency to identify the issues as a juncture in the cold war were
means of stressing Britain's vital concern and of attempting to bring
in the Eisenhower Administration.

With substantial, but much less vital interests in the area at the
time, the Eisenhower Administration viewed the attempts of the Soviet Union to extend its power and influence in the Middle East as
a natural Russian tendency which presented a longer-term challenge
and problem. Moreover, the particular issue of the canal was not
considered so much an important aspect of the East-West confrontation, but basically a problem stemming from the seeds of colonialism and the general trend toward nationalism in the "third world."

On October 2, Dulles thusly described the American position between the two forces:

The United States cannot be expected to identify itself 100 per cent either with the colonial powers or the powers uniquely concerned with the problem of getting independence as rapidly and as fully as possible. There were . . . differences of approach by the three nations to the Suez dispute. . . . While we stand together, and I hope we shall always stand together in treaty relations covering the North Atlantic, any areas encroaching in some form or manner on the problem of so-called colonialism, find the United States playing a somewhat independent role.[96]

American interests could not always be expected to coincide with the interests of Western allies in other parts of the world. Both the interests and interpretations of the threat diverged over Suez.

A second variance in interpretation was that Dulles probably never understood Eden's evaluation of Nasser. Eden not only incessantly compared Nasser to Hitler and Mussolini but also portrayed the Egyptian President leading a semiunited Arab world, acting at Russia's behest and holding the West to ransom. Eisenhower and Dulles advised that Britain "should sharply separate the question of the canal from" her "general policy towards the Egyptian dictatorship and the menace under which Africa and the Middle East lay." The Eisenhower Administration viewed the latter as "a long-term problem." Eden found such advice "most disturbing." [97] The allies' estimations of Nasser were completely at odds, as evidenced by Eisenhower's reply to Eden on September 8:

You seem to believe that any long, drawn-out controversy either within the 18-nation group or in the United Nations will inevitably make Nasser an Arab hero and seriously damage the prestige of Western Europe, including the United Kingdom, and that of the United States. Further you apparently believe that there would soon result an upheaval in the Arab nations out of which Nasser would emerge as the acknowledged leader of Islam. This, I think, is a picture too dark and is severely distorted.[98]

(Interestingly, as Britain would not buy the American picture of desperation in Indochina in 1954, so the Americans did not buy the desperate Middle East landscape painted by Eden.)

Considering Nasser something less than a fatal threat to Western interests, the United States was willing to reach agreement with the

Egyptian President as long as passage through and operation and development of the canal were guaranteed. Great Britain would accept nothing short of a serious setback—if not in Egypt, at least in the other Arab countries—to Nasser's prestige and influence. Washington also wished to counter Nasser's influence in the Middle East and had no fondness for Nasser or his programs, but considered the use of force over the particular issue of nationalization of the Suez Canal as counterproductive to this interest.

It soon became apparent that international control of the canal was Dulles' maximum demand and that he was not averse to accepting something less than actual international operation and control. If the Egyptians were capable of operating the waterway, as they proved in mid-September, and guaranteed passage and maintenance, the United States would view any thought of using force under such circumstances as "almost ridiculous." [99] As long as the international rights of access were guaranteed, the United States actually accepted Egypt's nationalization of the canal. On the other hand, international control of some sort constituted Britain's minimum demand. If Egypt proved unwilling to accept international control and operation, force was to follow.

The American Reaction

On October 29, Israeli forces attacked Egypt across the Sinai Peninsula despite Eisenhower's messages to Prime Minister Ben Gurion, on October 27 and 28, warning that the United States would view any military action in the area as a matter of grave concern endangering the peace. Having already warned the Israelis of the seriousness which the United States would attach to any aggressive move, two weeks prior to Eisenhower's notes on the eve of the invasion, the United States had already decided to take the matter to the United Nations. On the evening of October 29, Ambassador Lodge met with the British Ambassador to the United Nations, Pierson Dixon, to request British participation in presenting the case to the United Nations. Eisenhower wrote to Eden, on October 30, that he was astonished to find the British Ambassador "completely unsympathetic, stating frankly that his government would not agree to any action whatsoever to be taken against Israel." The British Ambassador added that "the tripartite statement of May, 1950, was ancient history and without current validity." [100] The following morning, British Foreign Secretary Lloyd informed the American Ambassador to St. James, Winthrop Aldrich, that "he thought Her Majesty's Government would immediately cite Israel before the Security Council . . . as an aggressor against Egypt." [101] However, Lloyd concluded with the comment that his government could not issue a definitive statement until after consultations with France. Aldrich reported the information to Washington and kept a telephone line open for further communications.

Approximately seven hours after the Lloyd-Aldrich exchange, Sir Ivone Kirkpatrick, a Permanent Under Secretary of the Foreign Office, showed the American Ambassador the ultimatums which had already been served to Egypt and Israel. The news reached Washington through regular news services before it arrived through official channels. The plan was now in the open. The ultimatums stated that Anglo-French forces intended to occupy Port Said, Ismailia, and Suez even if the Egyptians and Israelis complied with the request to withdraw forces from the vicinity of the canal. The ultimatum went so far as to request Israel to withdraw from a position which it did not yet hold. Egypt was requested to retreat and surrender the canal. Nasser naturally and expectedly considered the demands unacceptable.[102] The cat was out of the bag and the British and French were now on their way to attempt to deliver the blow which they believed Nasser deserved.

Before the ultimatums were served, on October 30, the State Department had prepared a draft resolution to be put before the Security Council wherein Israel was accused of "aggression." At Lloyd's request, the charge was modified so that Israel's action was described as a "violation of the armistice agreements." [103] At eleven in the morning, American time, Ambassador Henry Cabot Lodge concluded his statement before the Security Council with the following words:

No one, certainly, should take advantage of this situation for any selfish interest. Each of us here . . . has a clear-cut responsibility to see that the peace and stability of the Palestine area is restored forthwith. Anything less is an invitation to disaster in that part of the world.[104]

The resolution of the United States, which was vetoed by Britain and France, urged member nations to refrain from both force and the threat of force in the area. On the night of October 30, Eden received a telegram from Eisenhower, wherein the President "expressed the belief that peaceful processes could and should prevail." [105]

On October 31, British planes began the attack on Egyptian air bases, ports, and communications centers and troop carriers were on their way from Malta's ports. Eden explained to the House of Commons that, because of different approaches, agreement could not be reached with the United States. Furthermore, Britain could not wait to secure agreement when acting in her own vital interest.[106] The next day, at the request of Eisenhower, Dulles addressed an emergency session of the General Assembly with a "heavy heart." The Secretary outlined the disagreement with America's two "oldest, most trusted and reliable allies" in sober language. The speech contained neither harsh denunciations nor exaggerated criticism. While Dulles referred to the Israeli-British-French invasion as "a grave error inconsistent with the principles and purposes of the Charter," he also placed "part of the responsibility of present events" at the doorstep of the United Nations and, indirectly, of the United States.[107]

The move was not only expected by Britain, but had little, if any, effect upon Anglo-French plans. The decision to accept the cease-fire on November 6, or shortly after troops reached Egypt, was based upon other considerations. There was the adverse reaction of world opinion generally and, more important, large segments of British opinion rejected the move, particularly as it dragged on without a clear conclusion. The fact that the financial and oil condition of Great Britain was at best grim and would continue to worsen without the wholehearted and unqualified support of the United States probably weighed equally heavy in the decision process leading to acceptance of the cease-fire.

The common assumption that Dulles had a "free hand" in the formulation of United States postintervention moves tended to overlook the President's role and reaction. Eisenhower, for understandable reasons, was considerably more irritated by the whole affair.

Lloyd and Abba Eban, Israel's Ambassador to Washington, viewed
Dulles as a possible "agent for some salvage operation," while Eisenhower "was in a mood of someone betrayed." [108] The statements by
the President and other members of the Cabinet, including the actions of the United States in pressuring its allies to comply with
Washington's view by withholding financial and oil support, cannot
necessarily be assumed as reflecting the subtleties of Dulles' frame of
mind. Within the day following his address before the General Assembly, the Secretary was taken to the hospital for an operation and
was out of the thick of the conflict for the next few weeks.

The actions of Henry Cabot Lodge in the United Nations were
also not necessarily indicative of the Secretary's reaction. On November 23, an Afro-Asian United Nations resolution, led by India's
Krishna Menon, demanded that British forces be withdrawn "forthwith." Belgium introduced an amendment which, by eliminating
the word "forthwith," would have allowed the Anglo-French forces
to withdraw in an orderly manner without undue humiliation. On
November 22, the State Department had instructed the United
States delegation to vote in favor of the Belgian amendment and, if
it were not adopted, to abstain from voting on the Afro-Asian resolution. Lodge acted exactly opposite to the instructions. He ab-
stained from voting on the Belgian amendment, and voted in favor
of the Afro-Asian proposal. The Secretary and the State Department
were "not responsible for the action taken by Lodge on November
23." [109] As at least once before, during the Korean debates, Lodge
utilized his own clout with and access to the President rather than
accept State's instructions.

The American postattack, public policy followed from its preattack stances. But could the United States, while opposing the action, have remained relatively quiet or, at least, refrained from leading the charges? Other factors came into play, rightly or wrongly,
on this point. Staunch opposition placed the United States in a better position both to condemn the Soviet action in Hungary and to
counter any Soviet designs or threats over Suez. Also, the fact that
the military operations began only one week before the presidential
election effectually ruled out any desirability of reacting with a "no
comment." Silence would have likely been interpreted either as ac-

quiescence or as indecisiveness, and either appearance was not to the liking of the administration in the heat of a national election. Regardless of the reasons for commencing the attack in late October, the allies were either not at all concerned with lessening the expected adverse reaction of the United States or tragically inaccurate in their calculations. Israel had been specifically warned that the conduct of the campaign and some possible domestic support for Israel would not prevent the Eisenhower Administration from taking a strong stand against any attack.[110]

Shortly after Britain's decision to withdraw, Secretary Dulles reportedly commented to Lloyd and Sir Harold Caccia as follows: "Why on earth didn't you push through with it." [111] Whether or not the United States would have acquiesced in a *fait accompli* remains conjecture since, as one observer put it, "the *fait* was only half *accompli*." [112] Although Ambassador Aldrich has maintained that the United States was not prepared to acquiesce in any *fait accompli,* and that he did "everything" in his power "to prevent Eden from misunderstanding Dulles' position," [113] there is reason to expect that the United States could have taken a much "softer" approach if Britain and France had been capable of quick results or if the adventure had been timed a fair while after the election. The Eisenhower Administration had "assumed that if the three nations did attack, they would all move at one time, and it would be over in almost twenty-four hours." [114] To Eisenhower, "even by the doctrine of expediency the invasion could not be judged as soundly conceived and skillfully executed." [115]

From the beginning, it was apparent that the Anglo-French operation would last days, if not a few weeks, depending upon the desired goals. It was only to be expected that Eisenhower and Dulles would oppose the move publicly. In their preattack planning, Great Britain and France could accurately gauge the probable reaction of the United States. It seemed to Dulles that only a few more days would have been necessary for the British and French to occupy the canal. A few more days might have meant little or nothing with regard to Secretary of the Treasury Humphrey's threats on the British pound and the supply of oil if the British had reacted forcefully. Although it remains questionable whether or not Dulles was actually so blunt in his conversation with Lloyd and Caccia, the American Secretary may well have been slightly puzzled as to why the European allies did not push through a little further. But, from London's standpoint, calculations regarding the approximate costs, the effects on the pound and the economy, and the force of British opinion were not so susceptible to easy measurement before the attack. There was also the matter of Eden's colleagues reversing their positions once the repercussions began, not to mention the matter of Eden's failing health.

CHAPTER TWELVE

ADJUSTING TO THE END

The statements and actions by which Dulles is most frequently remembered generally occurred during the period from 1952 through 1956. The common, although less than accurate, impression was one of a rather dogmatic "cold war warrior" at the helm of American foreign policy. It can fairly be said that some of Dulles' own rhetoric and style of presenting policies, as distinct from the actual content of the policies themselves,[1] oftentimes and not necessarily always unintentionally served to encourage such an impression.

By 1958, however, there appeared to many, including a few of his detractors, to be a slightly "new," a less rigid or more flexible, Secretary of State in search of broader alternatives and an increased lessening of the degree of tension between East and West which had characterized the last years of the Truman Administration and President Eisenhower's first term. A notable example in this development were Dulles' increasing hints toward possible rapprochement with the People's Republic of China and his handling of the 1958 crisis in the Taiwan Straits.

During the course of a background press conference for British correspondents, following Eisenhower and Dulles' conferences with Macmillan and Lloyd at Bermuda in March of 1957, the American Secretary was asked why there was no mention of the Far East in the annex to the official press release describing the topics discussed at Bermuda. Dulles replied that the absence of any reference to the

Far East or China policy meant that there was "not yet a sufficient rapprochement [between Washington and London] to allow anything to be registered in that respect." While describing his brief summary of the reasons behind the United States policy of nonrecognition as oversimplified, he explained that policy in terms of power politics and of not adding to Peking's national prestige and influence. Noticeably absent in this summary were any moralistic reasons. In addition, the Secretary stated that the United States would re-study the question of trade with the People's Republic of China in non-strategic goods, looking particularly at the matter of trade between Tokyo, London, and Peking. Dulles cautioned that such a review should be understood within a context "which does not seem to suggest . . . that anything we do in the commercial field is a preview of steps comparable to softening our position in the political field." [2]

The question of the variance in policies of the United States and Great Britain toward the People's Republic of China had come up more than once in the discussions between Eisenhower, Macmillan, Lloyd, and Dulles at Bermuda. The American side wanted the British to support United States political policy on China, while noting that this would "make it easier to meet the British views on some of the trade matters and the alignment of the Cocom and Chicom lists." In fact, the President spoke "at length" on the reasons why Washington was unwilling to recognize Peking or bring the People's Republic of China into the United Nations "under present circumstances." According to Dulles' memorandum of the conversations, Macmillan stated that the American approach "might be considered." [3]

Early in 1958 Dulles stated that "any time it will serve the interest of the United States to recognize the Communist Chinese regime, we will do it." [4] On at least three other occasions, he repeated the idea that the United States did and would continue to deal with Peking whenever it was expedient to do so.[5] In March, he indicated that renegotiation of the Japanese Peace Treaty was in order. Although the treaty had been successfully negotiated less than seven years earlier, with Dulles himself having made a major contribution to its achievement, it was becoming "obsolete in this new era which may be opening up." He also indicated that any new settlements would have to recognize the need for an expansion of trade between Japan and the Chinese mainland.[6] By September, when asked if "there is a possibility of *some important changes* [in United States policy], provided there is *some give* on the Chinese Communist side," Dulles responded: *"Yes, I would say so.* Our policy in these respects is flexible and adapted to the situation that we have to meet. If the situation we have to meet changes, our policies change with it." [7] (Emphasis added.)

Throughout the 1958 crisis in the Taiwan Straits, beginning with the Chinese communists heavy artillery attacks against the Quemoy Islands in August, until an implicit reversion to the preattack *status quo* in early November, Dulles did not bend from his conclusion that a forceful communist take-over of the Offshore Islands was not in the interests of the United States and that the best assurance against such a take-over was a display of United States willingness to come to their defense. But his approach in this episode was not without some obvious flexibility and room for accommodation.

While communicating to Peking the seriousness of United States intentions neither to stand by if the islands were taken by force nor to encourage the Nationalists to withdraw forces from the islands under the threat of a gun, it was equally clear that the United States was not unequivocally committed, as the Nationalist Chinese desired, to the defense of the Offshore Islands for their own sake. This refusal to become unambiguously committed was, of course, due in part to the significant opposition both in Congress and from many United States allies, including Great Britain and Canada, to hazarding real hostilities over the islands. It was also a product of the administration's natural desire not to lock itself into a position whereby its own options or freedom to respond as Washington determined necessary could be restricted. But, in addition, Dulles apparently considered the foreign policy and security significance of the Offshore Islands more in terms of a symbolic and psychological line of defense which could conceivably be neutralized, if not ultimately conceded, under certain circumstances.

In his press conference on September 30, the Secretary expressed the desirability of a reduction in the Nationalist forces on the islands on the basis of a reciprocal and *de facto* renunciation of force by both sides in the area: "If there were a cease-fire in the area which seemed to be *reasonably dependable,* I think it would be foolish to keep these large forces on these islands. We thought that it was rather foolish to put them there, and . . . if there were a cease-fire . . . it would not be wise or prudent to keep them there." (Emphasis added.) Of particular significance, in the course of the queries from the press, Dulles made it clear that Peking could not be expected to renounce the use of force unless Taipei reciprocated with a similar renunciation and that he was referring to a *de facto* cease-fire, not a negotiated formal agreement.[8] It was also during this press conference that he noted the possibility "of some important changes" in the United States position if there were "some give" by Peking. Although admittedly somewhat elusive, "this intimation echoed his public hints of September 9 when he implied that new, constructive, and significant consequences—including a Foreign Ministers' conference—could result from any first-stage agreement . . . on a dependable cease-fire." [9]

Dulles stated that a reciprocal renunciation of the use of force in the area did not mean the renunciation of the claims of both sides. But the proposed exit necessarily reflected some acceptance of a "two Chinas" approach which Washington no doubt recognized would require more than "some give" in Peking's position and, therefore, had little chance of getting off the ground. For its part, the Soviet Union seemed inclined toward some such exit, regardless of any "Two China's" overtones, as evidenced by its disinclination to provide a nuclear guarantee to Peking. Peking had been diplomatically and militarily checkmated and, for a variety of reasons not yet fully evident, "Peking now recoiled from further negotiation" at the Ambassadorial Talks in Warsaw and sought "Washington's capitulation." [10] While vehemently denouncing anything bordering on a "two Chinas" approach, the Chinese communists demanded unconditional American withdrawal from the area and the "liberation" of the Offshore Islands and Taiwan by any means necessary.

Washington's decision to come to the defense of the islands if necessary and not to seek the withdrawal of any Nationalist forces under pressure or without some sort of tacit agreement with Peking had been predicated, from the outset, on an assumption that the Offshore Islands were primarily important to Peking in terms of their relationship—regardless of whether political, symbolic, psychological, or military—to the Communist Chinese "campaigns" for the "liberation" of Taiwan or its return to mainland control and for "Asia without American presence." Dulles and others claimed that any giving in under pressure would bring into question the firmness of United States commitments to other Asian countries and risk aggressive moves in other parts of Asia. The first aspect of such claims was not without a large dosage of logic.

But the latter generalized claim, while probably considered necessary to underline the importance of the issue at hand to the United States, internationally and domestically, and to counter any American tendencies toward nonparticipation, did not really reflect the more immediate and determining factors in Washington's policy decisions. Of more immediate significance was Dulles' and Eisenhower's belief that to give in under the gun, and a comparatively empty one at that, by attempting to convince Chiang to withdraw the Nationalist forces then and there or simply to step aside and accept what may, would naturally lead Taipei to question the firmness of the American commitment to the Republic of China. Chiang was already made uneasy by what he considered a substantial shift in United States policy: namely, Dulles' call for a reciprocal renunciation of force and a *de facto* cease-fire. If the islands were taken, which seemed probable and was surely within Peking's capabilities in the absence of American willingness to assist in their defense, Washington judged that the psychological process of questioning the determination and intentions of the United States would not be limited to Taipei but extend as well to other Asian nations which relied on some form of American commitment. At the same time, a "standing aside" posture risked, if not increased harrassment of or actual aggression against the Nationalists, at least an intensification in Peking's political and propaganda pressures against Taipei and against American presence in Asia.

This combination of circumstances was patently unpalatable to Dulles and Eisenhower and not merely because of their perceptions of probable international consequences adverse to the position of the United States. In addition, and in spite of the fact that many Americans considered it imprudent to hazard hostilities over the Offshore Islands, no administration at the time could lose Taiwan or, as it were, "lose the rest of China" without at least incurring very high domestic, political costs bordering on political suicide and at worst risking another severe reaction in congressional and public opinion, generally such as resulted from the "loss" of the mainland. Given these political conditions and the determination that an expression of some willingness to assist in the defense of the area offered the best possibility of avoiding real clash over Taiwan, Dulles considered the least cost line of defense at the Offshore Islands—as long as they were under the threat of a gun and as long as Peking insisted on connecting them with its broader campaign for the "liberation" of Taiwan and the Pescadores.

On the other hand, Dulles clearly did not consider this line the most defensible in either political or military respects. This had already become abundantly clear to both Eisenhower and Dulles during the 1955 crisis in the Taiwan Straits. (The 1955 episode, among other aspects, resulted in the United States encouraging and helping Chiang evacuate Nationalist forces from the Tachens but at a price of becoming more entangled, even if only implicitly, with the remaining Nationalist outposts on Quemoy and Matsu.) Shortly before the communists resumed firing on the islands, in October of 1958, the American Secretary arrived in Taiwan and privately advised Chiang Kai-shek that the Nationalists would lose the support of the "free world" unless they abandoned the civil war complex. Convinced that Chiang should be willing to conclude an armistice along the current lines of division, Dulles pressed for both an open renunciation of the use of force to return to the mainland and a reduction in the Nationalist forces on the Offshore Islands. In the Secretary's words: "Such evolutions, when responsive to the needs of the time, are not retreats, but advances. They assure continuing vitality, or the alternative to extinction." [11]

He succeeded to the extent that Chiang accepted a communiqué with a slightly watered down renunciation of force which stated that the "mission" of the Nationalist Chinese would be achieved in several ways and "not necessarily" in "the use of force." The situation with respect to the Offshore Islands remained relatively intact. Dulles succeeded only in obtaining a limited reduction in the Nationalist forces on Quemoy. Upon returning from Taiwan, he continued to advocate the type of settlement he had outlined earlier, although it is unlikely that Chiang ever blessed such an approach because of its inherent tendencies toward "two Chinas."

Dulles' more conciliatory approach was designed to provide at best a reasonably graceful exit for both Washington and Peking out of the dilemma of the Offshore Islands and at worst a more viable diplomatic and public posture for United States policy. As it turned out, the episode never reached a stage where all the aspects and ramifications of the American position were spelled out in detail. In 1955, for example, Eisenhower and Dulles had concluded that it was absurd to garrison large forces on these islands as this tied the specific issue of the islands too closely to the broader questions in the area. Eisenhower's view was that, if anything, Chiang should maintain relatively small but highly fortified outpost positions on the islands.[12] If, in 1958, the United States ever hoped to legitimize such outpost positions with Peking, the former was indeed heading down a dead end.

But, even in 1955, Dulles' idea that the United States should declare a willingness to "assist in holding Quemoy and possibly the Matsus," while helping evacuate Nationalists from the Tachens, was conditioned on Peking's professed intention to take Taiwan.[13] The converse would seem obvious: Namely, if there were some sort of *de facto* cease-fire or renunciation of force in the area, Quemoy and Matsu may be expendable. In 1958 Dulles' statements on this aspect were sufficiently direct as to suggest that, in its broad effects, Washington's proposed settlement not only did not preclude but also served to encourage some sort of neutralization of the Taiwan Straits area. This would undoubtedly provide a better political and military buffer for Taiwan or at least for the American position that Taiwan should not be taken by force. Chiang never bought the idea. During his discussions with Dulles in October, it was apparent that the goal of the American Secretary's exercise was ultimately neutralization of the Offshore Islands sore spot or, in effect, "two Chinas" preceded by a *de facto* cease-fire, the cessation of harrassments from both sides, and a mutual renunciation of the use of force.

Peking, for its own international and internal reasons, had no interest in becoming involved in any implicit recognition of the *status quo* or of the possibility of an essentially "two Chinas" settlement, even if it ultimately meant the withdrawal of all the Nationalist forces from the Offshore Islands and neutralization of the straits area. Peking would entertain no separation of the question of these islands from the issue of Taiwan. The Ambassadorial Talks in Warsaw had already become ritualistic and, for all practical purposes, "Peking and Washington reverted to the *status quo*" in early November.[14]

Throughout 1958 there were other indications of some turn toward more flexibility and restraint besides the Secretary's hints at a possible accommodation with the People's Republic of China and his handling of the crisis in the Taiwan Straits. The year also marked the signing of an agreement between Moscow and Washington, which Dulles had long supported, on cultural, technical, and educational exchanges. When a crisis erupted over Berlin in late 1958, as Khrushchev demanded that France, Great Britain, and the United States withdraw from the city and then threatened to turn over Soviet responsibility and obligations in Berlin to the East Germans, United States policy to assure access to the city and not to deal with the East Germans as substitutes for the Soviet Union remained firm. The Secretary indicated, however, that there may be some minor flexibility in the degree to which the United States "might deal" with the East Germans "as agents of the Soviet Union." [15] In January of 1959, after noting that free, all-German elections remained the agreed formula for German reunification, the Secretary added that that particular formula was not "the only method by which reunification could be accomplished." [16] Such statements struck some sensitive chords in Europe, particularly in the Federal Republic of Germany. On January 30, Dulles departed for Paris, Bonn, and London to assure America's allies and to show Moscow that basic United States policy was intact.

Before 1958, as noted in Chapter X, Dulles' thoughts on a strategy for deterrence were adjusting to the changing circumstances, es-

pecially Soviet advancements in atomic weaponry. He had begun to
focus more on the need for better local defenses and tactical capabilities as a credible deterrent against and, if deterrence failed, an
effective counter to possible limited Soviet moves. On the other
hand, having considered the feasibility of adequate verification, he
accepted the desirability of pursuing serious arms control measures
based on the premise of building in an American atomic superiority
while granting the other side superiority in other areas. Less widely
known was the fact that "in the spring of 1958 he advocated a suspension of [nuclear] testing, despite objections from the Defense
Department and the Atomic Energy Commission." [17] Recognizing
that there was, in many countries, already a substantial public opinion favoring an end to nuclear testing, Dulles' support for a suspension derived primarily from his belief that the United States should
take a lead or could not afford to be morally, politically, and psy-
chologically behind on this issue. Since Great Britain and France desired further testing in their developing nuclear programs, the Secretary did not push publicly. However, his support for amending
the 1954 Atomic Energy Act to allow the United States to share
more nuclear information with its allies was designed in large part
to resolve this dilemma. Resolution required congressional approval, and such approval for France was not in the offing.[18]

The Secretary unquestionably grew in office and became more familiar both with the intricacies and complexities of the problems he
confronted and with the personalities and sensitivities of the diverse
actors in the international arena. Yet, the evolution of his thinking
on specific subjects and the mellower style generally derived far less,
if at all, from a personal maturation or mellowing process than
from pragmatic adjustment to changing structures, patterns, policies, and politics which affect the formulation and presentation of
foreign policy. A good case exists that, in the later years, Dulles was
more the "real" or less encumbered Dulles. The prescription he set
forth for a proper approach to foreign policy in 1957 was of vintage
stock:

Sound policy cannot be derived from *a priori* concepts. . . . It must always have a wholesome infusion of the pragmatic. Our national interest
requires that we relate our policies to the actual conditions of the world

about us. This means that we must understand both the realities we confront and the limitations on our power.[19]

The international and domestic climates of the last years of his secretaryship were, among other things, less restricting and less fraught with nettles and crisis issues than the early years. In broad, but by no means inclusive, respects, there were four obvious alterations in the overall climate.

The American public and, more specifically, the Congress began to adjust to the idea of United States participation in foreign affairs at least to the extent that acute isolationist or neo-isolationist impulses subsided as a serious challenge to various aspects of American foreign policy. Although sometimes grudging and always limited in scope, there developed an increasing awareness of and concern for international needs, problems, and responsibilities. Even the battles for economic assistance were not the same uphill struggle they presented in the first five years of the Eisenhower Administration. Looking back on the 1950s, one observer noted that the decade was marked by three favorable trends, including "a trend toward the maturation of mass opinion . . . an increase in the size of the attentive public . . . [and] a trend toward increasing homogeneity in American foreign policy opinion." There appeared some hopeful evidence suggesting "that the era of great fluctuations in American opinion may have passed, that some balance between the poles of American moods on foreign affairs may have been approximated." [20]

Part of this development was the reversion of the relationship between the executive and legislative branches to a more normal level of mixed distrust, bargaining, and cooperation. "McCarthyism" and fervid forms of "right wingism" had gradually faded into the background as a political force in its own right. But "McCarthyism's" running of its course, in diverse forms, left a sensitive scar in the American fabric which went deeper than the ignominious train of personal smears and tragedies in many fields and the demoralization of the professional Foreign Service and the State Department. The scar represented further a reminder to American policy-makers of the existence of such potentially powerful forces not always far enough below the normal political surface.

Internationally speaking, in spite of the persistence of basic differences and conflicts of interest, the tension lines between East and West had slackened in the aftermath of such developments as the 1955 Austrian Peace Treaty and the 1955 Heads of Government Conference at Geneva, including the leaders of Great Britain, France, the United States, and the Soviet Union. Also, after the Hungarian and Suez crises of 1956, it became more apparent that neither side was willing to risk nuclear holocaust for anything other than visibly vital interests. Spheres of interest and modes of competing within and beyond these spheres were, for the most part, tacitly recognized.

Finally, advancements in military technology had begun to alter strategic thinking and political approaches by the late 1950s. The rapid Soviet advances in weaponry constituted a balancing force as well as a cause for concern, and the concept of nuclear stalemate and mutual deterrence through a "delicate balance of terror" [21] came into the forefront. American advances in long-range ballistic missilery implied slightly less United States dependence upon allies in strictly military terms. Other technological developments, in areas such as aerial reconnaissance and photography, played an essential role in opening the door to meaningful arms control discussions. In addition to advancing technology, the fund of serious and sophisticated thinking about problems of deterrence, strategic policy, and related war-fighting capabilities markedly increased outside and within the government. The impact of these technological developments upon the political and diplomatic fields became manifest not only in the achievement of agreement between Washington and Moscow on a treaty banning nuclear weapon tests in the atmosphere, outer space, and underwater, in 1963, but also in the Khrushchev-Kennedy encounter in the 1962 Cuban missile crisis.

Such changes in both the international and domestic environments combined slightly to enlarge Dulles' field for operations. The climate in the latter half of the 1950s and Dulles' more secure position in power were conducive to a less strident style of leadership more similar to his practice before the 1952 campaign and the comparatively tumultuous first years of his secretaryship. Although this evolution in the international and domestic environments was a slow, living process, it was nonetheless real. President Kennedy inherited not only the continuing policy predicaments but also the developments which contributed to Dulles' "mellower" approach.

There has been, in fact, a continuum in the broad lines of American postwar foreign policy, from 1946 at least through the mid-1960s, with no sharp breaks or discontinuities resulting from personality differences or the unusual impact of a particular President or Secretary upon the process. The evolution of Eisenhower's and Dulles' strategy for deterrence, as discussed in Chapter X, was a clear illustration of this continuum or this process of refining upon given circumstances. Moreover, the "flexible response" side of the coin had already gained increased attention before the Kennedy Administration refined it and officially blessed it and a limited warfare strategy as doctrine. As evidenced in the 1962 Cuban missile crisis, the "massive retaliation" side of the coin remained to be used in deterrence either explicitly whenever policy-makers considered it useful or necessary, as Kennedy did, or just implicitly as the existence of such capabilities could not be excluded from political-military calculations of risks.

The continuity of United States postwar foreign policy was further exemplified in the relations between Washington and Peking where, in spite of the widespread impression that Kennedy would devise a new policy toward China, the "new image" was not matched by any distinct signs of greater flexibility or by a substantially different approach to the problems. In fact, in 1961 Kennedy moved to strengthen the United States position against Peking's admission to the United Nations. Shortly thereafter, in the 1962 Taiwan Straits crisis, he adopted the same position as Eisenhower and Dulles had in 1958 while suggesting that he would have preferred it otherwise.[22]

Both administrations would, of course, have preferred a reasonable exit from the Offshore Islands dilemma. But, in the absence of "some give" on the part of Peking, the international risks and domestic political costs of any other course were considered too high by both administrations. Neither these political costs nor Peking's attitude appeared to change until much later when, in 1968, both Richard Nixon and Hubert Humphrey found it politically advantageous or, at least, not disadvantageous to advocate rapprochement with the People's Republic of China. In the previous decade, both men had firmly opposed recognition of Peking and its admission to the United Nations. The 1968 campaign statements reflected adjustment to changing conditions and attitudes, especially internationally but also domestically, which provided the opportunity for more maneuverability in United States policy.

The continuum in American postwar foreign policy, in its broad aspects, represents a product of the largely determining effect of political, military, economic, and social circumstances, both abroad and at home, over which policy-makers have only varying degrees of influence ranging from insignificant to consequential depending upon the issue and its related circumstances. The interplay of international and internal conditions generally set boundaries on the number of practicable alternatives and define the advantages and disadvantages of the options within these boundaries. Nonetheless, to recognize that the President and his Secretary of State are hemmed in on various sides is not to conclude that they are caught in an ineluctable current of history which is unresponsive to individual attempts to divert, speed up, or slow down the course. There remains the important personal element in interpreting the conditions, in weighing the benefits and costs, in deciding on tactics and day-to-day operations, and, thereby, in creating some of his own circumstances which may or may not affect the basic course. It is in these processes that Presidents and Secretaries leave unmistakable impressions of their own as they exercise different sets of balancing scales, of motivations, and of perspectives.

Dulles, to be sure, stands out as one of the most powerful postwar Secretaries of State. He brought to the task a few basic, inextricably interrelated convictions and operational principles which, although each was shared to some degree by Acheson before him and Rusk after him, were uniquely blended in Dulles. The interreaction of such convictions and operational principles with the peculiar and complex set of circumstances with which he had to deal formed the spring from which emerged personal policy preferences and his style of leadership.

First, Dulles believed that the United States was basically a self-satisfied, *status quo* nation which had to be jarred from its tendency to return to "normalcy" or from a cycle of nonparticipation and then overreaction in international affairs. Having unhappily experienced and fought against the American yearning to stand apart from the world's problems after both major wars, but particularly the pronounced and disastrous return to "normalcy" in the 1920s, he viewed the challenge as nothing less than reversing a natural and deep-seated inclination and altering many aspects of the so-called common American approach to foreign affairs. The task included the cultivation of patience, the avoidance of absolutes, the acceptance of the indecisiveness of the cold war, and the understanding of a condition of "not war, not peace." To Dulles, the Soviet Union's professed aim of becoming the dominant world power or influence was "fantastic" except insofar as United States "lethargy gives it scope." [23] Given the size of the challenge, he was never quite confident that the United States would become accustomed to responsible participation and regain some political, psychological, and spiritual dynamism or "anti-*status quoism*" which he considered so necessary in this process, and which he considered essential to the American tradition.

Second, foreign policy had to be broadly understood and accepted or, at a minimum, acquiesced in by the American people. Having long since concluded that statesmen are always to some degree "the inevitable prisoners of their environment" and that even ingenious political formulas could not last without popular understanding, the dilemma for statesmanship was how to broaden public understanding while simultaneously having to rely on policies which did not greatly outdistance the existing understanding.[24] The operational influence of this second principle did not mean foreign policy by public opinion, as Dulles made clear during his confrontation with an adverse opinion during the 1958 crisis in the Taiwan Straits:

It is essential that a policy which involves grave decision . . . should so far as practical, have the support of the American people. But . . . elements which go into making final decisions are so delicate, oftentimes not subject to public appraisal, that there lies a responsibility upon the President and his principal advisers which cannot be shared with the general public.[25]

When the first two principles are considered together, however, they go a substantial distance toward explaining much of Dulles' political style, his so-called preaching, and his "grass roots" approach to foreign policy presentations as contrasted, for example, with Acheson's more subtle style and more "elitist" approach.

Third, foreign policy had to have reliable, substantial support in Congress, and Congress had to be placated as viewed necessary to this end. This was the most lasting lesson Dulles learned from President Wilson's losing battle for the Versailles Treaty and United States membership in the League of Nations. The operational implications of this principle were neither easily nor rapidly digested by Dulles. On the occasions of Senate consideration of the 1922 Four Power Treaties and the 1924 Treaty with Turkey, he objected strongly to what he considered the Senate's attempt to become negotiator through the use of reservations and concluded that whenever a treaty served the overall interests of the United States, even though it may contain political compromises which one would have preferred without, it should be accepted "rather than delay indefinitely in favor of some theoretical treaty which will never have existence other than in the mental conceptions of a few extremists." [26]

Acheson's mounting difficulties with Congress and, specifically, the unjustly severe reaction to the "loss of China," which continued to impact upon United States policy in Asia generally for some time to come, served to reinforce the impressions gained from Wilson's failure. The former's close cooperation with key senators during the negotiation of the Japanese Peace Treaty was a prime example of a lesson well learned. The unfortunate "sacrificing" of some career Foreign Service officials was, in the eyes of many, a lesson too well learned. At any rate, as Secretary, Dulles assiduously cultivated better relations with Congress in the belief that the stability of American foreign policy required the broadest possible support and the avoidance of both sharp fluctuations in congressional or public moods and even relatively moderate fluctuations which could seriously impact on United States foreign policy. The stress on and costs of bipartisanship to the grandest possible consensus were viewed as necessary to maintaining a responsible and active American role in world affairs.

Finally, several of Dulles' principles and conclusions regarding his interpretations of and approach to international politics in the cold war context were detailed in Chapter VII. The operational influence of any one or a combination of these naturally varied from issue to issue, depending on the circumstances and the overall temperature of the East-West encounter. One of the most dominant principles during his secretaryship, however, was apparently that the greatest danger of war comes from possible Soviet or Chinese miscalculation and, therefore, the United States should leave no doubt regarding its determination and willingness to come to the defense of its perceived interests. The problem of miscalculation concerned Dulles from 1946 until his death in 1959 and was sharply underlined by the outbreak of war in Korea. The problem included both Soviet self-deception abetted by American action and American self-deception abetted by Soviet action.

The operation of this principle meant, among other things, that Dulles was unwilling to relax the tension lines beyond a certain point, at least until one could predict the probable effects of any easement with reasonable assurance. When in doubt, it was considered best to keep some pressures and tension on Moscow and Peking. This principle was compounded by his belief that the easement of pressure merely for its own sake would give the Soviets and Chinese little incentive to modify or moderate their approaches and, at the same time, serve to encourage a premature dropping of the West's guard. Yet another aspect of this principle was his belief that "no trespassing" or "thin ice" signs in the form of defense commitments, however qualified and limited, could usefully serve to signal United States interests and determination. Dulles, of course, accepted and sometimes encouraged a relaxation of the situation. All in all, however, his secretaryship was characterized by his conviction that an appearance of inflexibility was a better bargain than miscalculation encouraged by "atmospherics." If the choice were between a tendency toward overstatement or toward understatement of American determination, he would normally select the former.

Another most dominant principle in Dulles' interpretation of and approach to international politics in the cold war context was that the cold war presented an historical challenge to which there existed no panaceas or simple solutions. Upon entering office, a major concern of Eisenhower and Dulles was how to devise a more effective policy of containment and deterrence, for Asia as well as Europe, at a moderate economic level which would be sustained politically and economically by the American people and Congress over the long haul. The Secretary believed that more effective and efficient containment would lead to gradual détente. His acceptance of many aspects of détente in the mid-1950s included, for example, his adjustments to neutralism and the "third world" and to the loosening of the cold war tension lines. But the balance between containment and détente, built up by Dulles and Eisenhower and based on the premise of moderate costs over the long haul, was upset when the Soviet Union launched the first man-made satellite on October 4, 1957. Sputnik presented a picture of the Soviets surging ahead in outer space and missilery and, therefore, called into question the stability of the established balance and the validity of the premise upon which it was founded.

Eisenhower and Dulles did not believe that the established balance was really upset. The President's response to Sputnik was to counsel the country not to panic or exaggerate the importance of the event. One observer later described Eisenhower's reaction as one "of a busy man reluctantly looking up from his evening newspaper, glancing around with an expression of studied disinterest, and finally shrugging his shoulders as he returned to more absorbing matter." [27] Dulles' reaction was in a slightly different but ultimately similar vein:

I think that this satellite coming along as it did is a very useful thing to have happened, so as to avoid any possible complacency on our part with our present superiority. It arouses the whole country, I think, and the Congress to the importance of pushing forward actively in this field which may be the field where superiority will be militarily decisive perhaps 5 or 10 years from now.[28]

However, the Secretary maintained that there had been no complacency within the administration and that the military power of the United States actually was and potentially would be markedly superior for some years to come. He carefully noted that the United States needed "a balanced society, with balanced teaching and balanced training," which seemed to mean that it should not surge ahead with more scientists and defense to the detriment of other areas in American society.[29]

But the country reacted differently and, in this sense, the balance was upset. President Kennedy rode into power on a "new image" for America which included not only the impression of some more flexibility and maneuverability in United States policy but also a more active role for the United States in various parts of the world and a concerted effort to close the alleged "missile gap" and "defense gap" generally. Some aspects of this more active approach were called into question rather soon by studies on whether there existed a serious missile gap and by the absence of room for significantly greater flexibility in basic United States policies given the international circumstances. (In the longer-run, the more active approach would come into question through, *inter alia,* the experiences with the Vietnam war and concerns regarding the military-industrial complex.)

The preceding general principles by no means represent all of the facets and the more subtle reflections of the spectacles through which Secretary Dulles viewed the world. Nor can decisions and policy preferences be simply deduced from any one or a combination of them. But the operational influence of the combined effect of such principles—whether complementing, contradicting, or not affecting each other—was nonetheless widespreading as they came into contact with the international and internal political realities with which the Secretary had to deal. Far from a simple picture, the product often represented an intricate web of changing considerations and patterns. Much of Dulles' concentration on the East-West encounter, for example, merely reflected the fact that this encounter was the primary backdrop for much of the activity, policy questions, issues, and crises during his secretaryship. At the same time, much of the same concentration and, at times, the exaggeration or oversimplification of this contest in his public presentations constituted a means of buttressing the will of the West, communicating United States interests and the will to defend them to the Soviet Union, obtaining the approval of Congress for various international programs and policy decisions, and warning the American people against any false sense of complacency.

There were, in the process of interpreting circumstances and weighing the real and probable advantages and disadvantages in policy alternatives, surely some errors of judgment of varying degrees of importance. Throughout the 1950s and into the 1960s there apparently persisted a less than correct reading of the motivation behind Communist Chinese participation in the Korean War and perhaps of Communist China's actual power. The common view that Peking acted essentially as an extension of a comparatively monolithic communist drive may have had ramifications for United States policy in the Far East generally. Also, while admitting that the following course would have entailed domestic political costs, perhaps the negotiation of the mutual defense treaty with Taiwan in the mid-1950s presented a real opportunity to press harder for at least a modified Nationalist Chinese position regarding the Offshore Islands if not for the withdrawal of forces from these islands. Although the details of Dulles' position are not yet known, a few of his contemporaries believed that the Secretary could have exhibited more flexibility in testing the sincerity of Peking's overtures regarding the possible exchange of newsmen in 1955–1957 and that he should have designed a program with less emphasis on cold war pressures as tactics in spite of obvious political costs. In yet another part of the world, the Middle East, questions later arose as to whether or not Nasser would have turned so much to the East for arms in 1955 had the West treated his requests for arms more sympathetically. Then there were some "lesser" but nonetheless important issues, such as Latin America, which seemed to receive very little of Dulles' attention (much like the fate of the "lesser" issues in the times of Secretaries before and after him).

The probabilities of success in different courses and the consequences of any tactical errors on the broader picture of overall relations, outstanding issues, and conflicts of interest remain elusive. But the consequences of basic policies, such as the commitment (even though limited) to prevent the spread of communism in Southeast Asia, are more widespread. At such junctures, however, one butts into the broad lines of American foreign policy which are not defined by any single policy-maker. A commitment inherited, shared, and perpetuated by an administration was fully shared and ardently encouraged by Congress and embodied the stiff American opposition to any communist expansion.

Analysis of such issues and Dulles' time will, of course, continue and more evidence will provide a better light for such analysis. But any realistic appraisal of foreign policy must take into account the fact that the Secretary of State remains, to varying degrees, a prisoner of Washington politics, of the prevailing congressional and national moods, of past policies, of international circumstances, and, in a real sense, of the very complexities of the issues themselves and of the immediate demands and crises which normally take precedence over an issue which may or may not erupt in the future. Only by understanding the dilemmas of democratic statesmanship does one avoid what Dulles considered "the error of assuming that . . . foreign policy . . . is due to the personal views and idiosyncrasies of some . . . politician who may have temporarily secured an ascendancy over his fellows." [30] Since his personality colored almost every major facet of American foreign policy during the Eisenhower Administration, John Foster Dulles represented a very important ingredient in the overall policy process—but only one.

Extracts from the Digest *of the Sixth and
Final Meeting of the Study Group on Japanese
Peace Treaty Problems* (*May 25, 1951*)

"When Mr. Dulles went out to the Pacific he had received
approval for a general security scheme which envisaged the linking
of Japan, the Ryukyu Islands, the Philippines, Australia, New Zealand, and possibly Indonesia, if it wishes, into a security pact. Before leaving Washington, Mr. Dulles had discussed the plan with
the British Ambassador, Sir Oliver Franks. In Tokyo the British
Ambassador . . . registered with Mr. Dulles the very unfavorable reaction of his government to the plan. . . . The British Government
felt that so grandiose a scheme must, for reasons of prestige, include
British participation. But Great Britain could not participate if
Hong Kong and Malaya were not included within the scope of the
plan. . . . Yet it was realized that the inclusion of Hong Kong and
Malaya within the scope of the proposed pact was out of the question. Hence Great Britain adopted an unfavorable attitude toward
the whole plan."

"In consequence the United States has readjusted its thinking on
the security problem, and now proposes the following: first, a bilateral security arrangement between the United States and Japan; second, the strengthening of relations between the United States and
the Philippines by the issuance of a declaration akin in purport to

the Monroe Doctrine; third, a triangular security pact among the United States, Australia, and New Zealand. The British are agreeable to this program."

"Comments on the draft treaty were asked for by May 1. Great Britain replied quickly and completely. The British had, in fact, been preparing their own draft treaty, and the American draft was completed only a week before theirs. . . . Soon after . . . Mr. Dulles informed Sir Oliver Franks that the United States was not in agreement with the British draft, and that if any progress were to be made on the treaty it had to be in terms of the American draft."

"It was then arranged that Great Britain would send a delegation to Washington to negotiate with the United States. . . . Negotiations were carried on with it for about ten days. In the result, the United States did give way to the British on some things, but the concessions made did not essentially spoil the treaty as envisaged by the United States. Many things have now been put into the treaty which, in the American view, would be better if the Japanese did voluntarily, and which . . . they would probably do anyway. For example, a clause has been inserted obligating Japan to resume service on outstanding prewar bonds. From the American point of view such a clause is unnecessary since Japan is quite willing to do this on its own. Indeed, the only result of the clause will be to give an aura of compulsion to a matter that the Japanese are quite willing to effect voluntarily. The British have insisted on many clauses such as this."

"The British eventually dropped the majority of their demands, but we accepted about twenty-five per cent. . . . These negotiations did not deal with the major issues that divide the United States and Great Britain . . . those stemming from the different attitudes of the two governments regarding the Chinese Communists and the island of Formosa. In respect of these matters the British presented a very brief *aide-memoire* to Mr. Dulles on about March 15 stating, first, that in their view the Chinese Communists should be brought into the . . . negotiations, and second, that Formosa should be restored to China by the peace treaty."

"Mr. Dulles said that he was anxious to build up British prestige in the Orient, and that hence he was quite willing that Great Britain should be a co-sponsor of the treaty. He noted, however, that anti-British feeling is growing in this country, and that agreement with the British may now be a liability."

"Mr. Dulles said that aside from the major issues mentioned above, the principal questions that have arisen between the British and ourselves in respect to the treaty have been economic ones. Great Britain wished to impose many economic obligations on Japan without reciprocity, and to eliminate any treaty obligations which precluded discrimination against Japan in future world trade. The British wished to limit Japanese shipbuilding, and also proposed informally a limit on the number of Japanese textile spindles. . . . It is clear . . . that Great Britain fears Japan as a commercial competitor. On the other hand, the British have made no proposals for enforcing armaments limitation upon the Japanese. This, however, is not the view of Australia or New Zealand in this matter."

"Mr. Dulles said that the British did not officially propose the limitation of textile spindles; the idea was only advanced informally. It is true, however, that Great Britain does want to confiscate Japan's reserves of gold and other precious metals, and also to seize Japanese assets in neutral countries. The United States has agreed that the Allies should keep Japanese assets within their own boundaries. In respect of Japanese assets in neutral countries the American position is that there are not enough of them to justify either the effort of getting them or the inevitable squabble that would arise in deciding the question of what to do with them. . . . We also oppose the British position on gold. We feel that Japan should keep its gold as a future monetary reserve. Had we wished to, we obviously would have used the gold before, but we preferred to conserve it. But we did not conserve it for others.

". . . . Mr. Dulles replied that the British have apparently given little thought to the problem of how Japan is to survive. In view of their own economic difficulties, they want Japan frozen out of India, Malaya and Indonesia, and also excluded from the Congo Basin Treaty. They probably will not succeed in the case of Indonesia.

"The British may be adamant in their determination to put economic restrictions in the treaty. But their attempt to do so would be costly. It is true that Great Britain fears Japan as a commercial competitor. But it also wishes to maintain British prestige and good will. . . ."

"In any case, Japan could in theory develop a viable economy without dependence on Communist Asia, but whether this will actually happen is dubious."

"Mr. Dulles replied that their governments (Australia and New Zealand) are committed to press for limitations on Japan, but that his impression was that they will not press to the breaking point. They must continue to press for limitations, however, for domestic political reasons."

"Mr. Dulles cited . . . main obstacles in the way of long-term success of the Japanese peace treaty. In the first place, it will be difficult for Japan to remain non-communist while the bulk of the Asiatic mainland is communist-dominated. Japan can hold out for five or ten years, but in the long run the mainland has many attractions of so strong a character that it is hard to visualize Japan and the communist mainland living indefinitely in separate orbits."

As the meeting neared its end, Dulles proposed that there was need for more cultural ties with Japan, and that the discrimination against the Japanese in American immigration laws should be ended.

〜

Paper I: US Goals at Geneva
(With probable attitudes of UK and France)

1. Progress toward unification of Germany, under conditions which will neither "neutralize" nor "demilitarize" united Germany, nor subtract it from NATO. [UK and France for.]

2. "European security" in terms of a reduction and control of forces in the Soviet area, comparable to that effected in the West by the Brussels Treaty, but without consolidating the Soviet grip on Eastern Europe. [UK and France for.]

3. Impetus toward a leveling and control of armaments, which will build-in US atomic superiority and protect against evasions and surprise by carefully planned and implemented supervision of critical and controllable factors. [UK for. France less clear.]

4. Increased independence and growth of self-determination on the part of the satellites, so that they will not be, in effect, an extension of the Soviet empire into Europe. [UK for. France indifferent.]

5. An end to Soviet support of international communism as a hostile, revolutionary body. [France for. UK indifferent.]

6. Opportunity to reach the people of the Soviet bloc with knowledge and ideas. [UK and France mildly for.]

7. (Marginal) Soviet participation in Eisenhower "atoms for peace" plan. [UK and US mildly for.]

Paper II: Soviet Goals at Geneva

These goals are listed in an order which suggests, very roughly, the relative importance which the Soviets may attach to each item at Geneva. This order does not attempt to reflect Soviet tactics, which often involve pushing hard for something which they know to be unobtainable so that their "concession" in this respect may enable them to invoke persuasively a corresponding "concession" in terms of another topic to which they actually attach much importance. Opposite each item is an indication of the probable real attitude of the UK and France toward the Soviet goals. This appraisal does not attempt to reflect official positions which may be taken to preserve Western unity.

1. An appearance that the West concede the Soviet rulers a moral and social equality which will help the Soviets maintain their satellite rule by disheartening potential resistance, and help them increase neutralism by spreading the impression that only "power" rivalries, and not basic principles, create present tensions. [US against. UK and France indifferent.]

2. A general relaxing of the military and cold-war activities of the Western nations, providing the Soviets with a needed "moratorium" to use for bettering their internal position, economically and governmentally. [US and UK against. France for.]

3. Impetus toward disarmament, with emphasis on "ban the bomb" and under "world conference" conditions which will subject the Western negotiators to powerful emotional pressures which are intolerant of the painstaking procedures needed to assure adequate safeguards. [US and UK against. France indifferent.]

4. Impetus toward freer trade, which will enable the Soviets to get strategic and specialty goods on a cash or barter basis, and get

consumer goods (e.g., agricultural products) on easy terms. [US moderately against. UK and France for.]

5. Agreement on a "Statement of Principles" or "Geneva Charter" which, like Chou En-lai's "Five Principles," can be given a communist trademark and used in Soviet propaganda as implying that Soviet communism has assumed a moral leadership which even the non-communists accept. [US and UK against. France indifferent.]

6. Acceptance of the principle of an All-Europe security system, which will tend to eliminate US "bases" and US troops in Europe. [US, UK, and France against.]

7. Agreement on some Far Eastern Conference which will advance the status of Communist China as one of the "great powers" and incidentally demonstrate to Communist China that the Soviet Union is a loyal and useful ally. [US against. UK and France for.]

8. A discussion of "war propaganda" which will give the world the impression that the US admits that it harbors a "preventive war" psychology. [US and UK against. France indifferent.]

9. A weakening of the political unity of US, UK, and France by straining their governmental unity, and dividing their public opinions, on one or more of the above matters. [US, UK, and France against "in principle," but see above.]

Paper III: Estimate of Prospect of US Achieving Its Goals

1. *Unification of Germany.* It will probably be possible to have this topic remitted to a future Four Power Foreign Ministers' meeting with participation of the Federal Republic through the Western powers and of GDR through the USSR. However, the Soviets will probably want to go slowly on this, and may use their invitation to Adenauer as a tactic of delay. Also, the progress here suggested depends upon progress under Item 2.

2. *European security.* (See also Soviet Item 6) It will probably be

possible to get agreement that, concurrently with study of German unification, there will be negotiations between a group representing the NATO powers and a group representing the Warsaw powers designed to achieve a degree of demilitarization in Central Europe, and a level of European forces, within the context of which German unification might take place. Care must be taken lest this arrangement operate in effect to accept and consolidate the Soviet control over the satellites.

3. *Global level of armament.* It will probably be possible to have the present UN Disarmament Subcommittee (Canada, France, UK, USSR, and US) continue as the nucleus for discussion. It will be difficult, but not impossible, to have Big Four delegates instructed to concentrate in the first instance upon the machinery of supervision. It will probably not be possible or even desirable to exclude the concept of a world disarmament conference *after* sufficient progress has been made during the initial phase above described.

4. *Liberation of satellites.* It will be difficult to get any formal undertaking from the Soviet Union with reference to the topic or even their acceptance of it as a proper topic for discussion. However, they may in fact move in that direction if we impress the Soviets deeply with the importance which the United States attaches to this subject and with the fact that we shall watch vigilantly to see what the developments are and use that as a rod for measuring the degree of cooperation which we can extend to the Soviet Union in other respects. After all, what we ask for is less than what the Soviets gave Tito.

5. *International Communism.* Best progress may be made privately, as suggested above with reference to the satellites. However, preliminary talks with Molotov indicate that the Soviets may be willing at least to discuss this topic and perhaps to agree to go through certain motions, as ending the Cominform. A Soviet statement, as in the Bulganin-Tito communique, may be possible. But real progress will have to be judged by what happens, not by what is said.

6. *Ideas across the Iron Curtain.* Probably some progress could be made here, although it may be conditioned upon reciprocal agreements to eliminate radio broadcasts, balloon flights and the

like into the Soviet area. The net value of any possible reciprocal agreement would have to be carefully appraised.

7. *Atoms for peace.* It is possible that if pressed the Soviets might be willing to agree to put up some small amount of fissionable material for this plan. The value of this result to the United States is chiefly psychological in seeming to have "put across" a plan much of the free world identifies with President Eisenhower.

Paper IV: Estimate of Prospect of Soviet Union Achieving Its Goals

1. *Moral and social equality.* The Soviets will probably make considerable gains in this respect. These gains can be minimized by the President avoiding social meetings where he will be photographed with Bulganin, Khrushchev, etc., and by maintaining an austere countenance on occasions where photographing together is inevitable. Also, the extent of Soviet gain could be limited by public knowledge that the occasion was being used by the US to push for satellite liberation and liquidation of international communism. Here we run into a conflict between a desire not to make the meeting into a propaganda forum and the fact that unless our position on these two topics is known, the Soviets will automatically gain very considerable advantage under this heading.

2. *Western relaxing.* Unless the conference ends on a note of open discord, the Soviets will probably gain a considerable degree of relaxing on the part of the West, particularly in terms of NATO level of forces and German rearmament.

3. *"Ban the Bomb."* It will probably be possible to prevent appreciable Soviet gains under this item by achieving the US goal 3.

4. *Trade.* Again, unless the conference ends on a note of open discord, the result will probably be to ease gradually the scope of control now exerted by the Cocom Committee.

5. *Statement of principles.* It will be possible to prevent any

statement of principles lending itself to communist propaganda either through (a) opposing any statement whatever or (b) having a statement of our own which avoids the communist "cliches" which, although unobjectionable on their face, portray communist origin. In this connection, see JFD speech at San Francisco, where he opposed Molotov's "seven principles" by saying that only one principle is needed, that is live up to the spirit of the UN Charter.

6. *All-Europe security system.* It will be possible to prevent acceptance in principle of any plan which would tend to eliminate US presence from Europe. The outcome of this discussion could be as indicated in the discussion of Item 2 of US goals.

7. *Great power status to Communist China.* It will be possible to prevent any agreement on a Far Eastern conference, including Communist China and excluding Nationalist China. However, the United States cannot safely take a purely negative position in relation to this area where obviously tension is most acute. Probably the best solution is for the US to have some direct talks with the Chinese Communists which will slightly increase the scope and the level of the talks now being held at Geneva with reference to citizens of the two countries held by the other.

8. *US propaganda for war.* By the very fact of bringing up this subject—if they do—the Soviets will gain some advantage. However, that can be minimized if we knock it down hard.

9. *Dividing the West.* It will probably be impossible to prevent some slight increase within Germany of neutralism and demilitarization and within France of the public nostalgia for a resumption of special relations between France and Russia to contain Germany. However, if we handle our case rightly, this increase should not be substantial and it should be possible to offset it by a demonstration of the value to our three countries of standing together.

The above drafts of background papers were prepared by Dulles on July 1, 1955.

〰️

Extracts from Dulles Memorandum of Washington Conference on the Berlin Blockade (July 19, 1948)

"I said I had had some doubts about our note sent to Moscow. It seemed to me that Soviet prestige was deeply engaged, particularly in view of set-backs in Finland and Holland elections, the Tito quarrel and unrest in Czechoslovakia, and that they could hardly afford a public diplomatic backdown about Berlin, and there was danger that diplomatic argument might force them to crystalize publicly a stronger position than they had yet taken and one which would preclude their backing down in fact at the working level. I observed that even their reply note had referred to their obstructive measures as 'temporary.' "

Secretary Marshall asked Dulles to meet with the working group and give an opinion afterwards. Dulles had only a few hours to formulate his opinions, and a position was to be taken that day. Dulles was not being consulted on behalf of Dewey, for Secretary Marshall wanted his "personal judgment." After the first meeting with Lovett and Marshall, Dulles then met with Bohlen, Kennan, Reber, Saltzman, and Rusk.

"I expressed it as my view that (1) the Soviet leaders did not want war but (2) their prestige was so engaged that they could not retreat unless we eased it. I mentioned that in Soviet circles it was not merely a question of *national* prestige, but of the *individual* standing of members of the Politburo for whom failure in policy they espoused was almost literally fatal.

"(A) We should notify the Soviet (1) that we were prepared through the Council of Foreign Ministers to negotiate at Berlin about Berlin and any other phases of the German problem, as the Soviet had suggested, and (2) that we were sending through to Berlin supply trucks, which could be stopped only by . . . force. We would not, however, ask for any *agreement* by the Soviet to lift the blockade or concede our rights prior to negotiating. This I thought would be unobtainable.

"(B) Prior to any formal diplomatic note, we should first tell our intentions *informally* to the Soviet, after clearance with Great Britain and France, so that they would react soberly and not hastily and, if they wanted, have the opportunity *themselves* to announce first that the 'repairs' had been effected. This exchange should be had, if possible, with Stalin rather than Molotov.

"(C) If the sending in of trucks resulted in an incident, then that could be referred to the Security Council or arbitrated or negotiated, and if thought wise, the Four Power negotiations could be suspended on the ground that new circumstances had arisen."

(Dulles hoped his program would achieve the following purposes):

"1. Quickly let the Soviet realize the seriousness of our intentions;

"2. Do so before their prestige was further committed by legal positions formulated at a high level and publicly announced;

"3. Leave time for negotiating *after* an incident—if there were to be one—instead of exhausting the negotiating time and possibilities *before* either we or the Soviets had made our determination clear by acts."

Dulles also reports that, in the meeting, some of the advisers were not too sure about their facts.)

~~~

Extracts from Memorandum of Telephone
Call with Robert Lovett (July 22, 1948)

Lovett was "not clear on the point of how much force would be used to test out the Soviet position. . . . He said that already trucks had been stopped by physical road blocks. I said I assumed that this was the case, but that the whole problem of the diplomatic discussion was to create new conditions which would enable the Soviet without loss of prestige to end the 'temporary difficulties'. . . . Of course, I had no idea of trying to shoot our way through, and, indeed, was not willing to envisage the possibility of hostilities on account of the Berlin situation."

Rather than press the issue or force the Soviets to "lose face," Dulles was again concerned with altering the conditions in fact, although not necessarily in words, in a manner that would not involve Soviet prestige.

"However, it is a prevalent view that the Soviets do not want war; they have carefully kept open, so far, a face-saving 'line of retreat'; even their latest note referred to the present obstructions as 'temporary measures'; they would not want to be held before the U.N. under a charge of actually using violence; and the procedure suggested would give them the cover of what they could call a diplomatic success to save their prestige."

"U. N. appeal can come later, if necessary, but it seems that at best the United Nations could give moral sanction to a large scale use of force which, however, is not what we want. We want peace, not a legal basis for war." Going directly to the United Nations would be a mistake, for it would "force the Soviets to take an official position more uncompromising than any yet taken and close the 'way of retreat,' so far kept open, before efforts have been exhausted to bring them to use it."

NOTES TO THE TEXT

Introduction: In Search of Dulles

1. See Hans J. Morgenthau, *Politics Among Nations* (3d ed.; New York: Alfred A. Knopf, 1963), pp. 4–15.

2. For a description of these categories, see respectively: John H. Herz, *Political Realism and Political Idealism: A Study in Theories and Realities* (Chicago: University of Chicago Press, 1951), pp. 226–27; and Reinhold Niebuhr, *Christian Realism and Political Problems* (New York: Charles Scribner's Sons, 1953), pp. 1–14. Dulles cannot be neatly placed in either category as specifically delineated in these works; but as far as such descriptive phrases go, "realistic liberalism" and, to a lesser degree, "Christian realism" best describe the tendencies in his basic approach.

3. The major exceptions are Coral Bell, *Negotiation from Strength: A Study in the Politics of Power* (London: Chatto & Windus, 1962); Richard Goold-Adams, *The Time of Power: A Reappraisal of John Foster Dulles* (London: Weidenfeld & Nicolson, 1962); Louis L. Gerson, *John Foster Dulles* (New York: Cooper Square, 1967); and E. Raymond Platig, "John Foster Dulles: A Study of His Political and Moral Thought Prior to 1953," unpublished doctoral dissertation, University of Chicago (November 26, 1957).

4. See respectively: Forrest Davis, "The G.O.P.'s Mr. Hull," *Saturday Evening Post*, CCXVII (September 16, 1944), 94; J. Remak, Review of *John Foster Dulles: A Reappraisal*, by Richard Goold-Adams, *Saturday Review*, XLV (November 17, 1962), 27; Max Lerner, Review of *War or Peace*, by John Foster Dulles, *New Republic*, CXXII (May 15, 1950), 18; and Platig, "John Foster Dulles," pp. 21, 23, 24, and 52–53.

5. See respectively: Coral Bell, *Negotiation from Strength*, p. 93; and Henry P. Van Dusen, ed., *The Spiritual Legacy of John Foster Dulles* (Philadelphia: Westminster Press, 1960), p. xxi.

6. Anthony Nutting and Heinrich von Brentano, as quoted in Roscoe Drummond and Gaston Coblentz, *Duel at the Brink: John Foster Dulles'*

Command of American Power (London: Weidenfeld & Nicolson, 1961), pp. 16–17.

7. Dulles essay or speech written in the 1920s, "The Relation of France to a Program of World Reconstruction," in *The Collected Papers of John Foster Dulles* (Princeton University), pp. 2–3, hereafter referred to as *Papers*.

8. Dulles, "Thoughts on Soviet Foreign Policy and What to do About It," *Life*, XX (June 3, 1946), 113. Dulles' wariness toward words unsupported by deeds was not a product of the East-West encounter after World War II and his growing skepticism regarding Soviet intentions and motivation. He had much earlier, in fact, been very wary of the official camouflage or the inconsistencies between words and deeds in American foreign policy (see Chapter V, note 77).

9. Kenneth W. Thompson, *Political Realism and the Crisis of World Politics: An American Approach to Foreign Policy* (Princeton: Princeton University Press, 1960), p. 212.

10. Gabriel A. Almond, *The American People and Foreign Policy* (New York: Frederick A. Praeger, 1960), p. 71.

11. Reinhold Niebuhr, *The Irony of American History* (New York: Charles Scribner's Sons, 1952), p. 101.

12. Louis J. Halle, *American Foreign Policy: Theory and Reality* (London: Allen & Unwin, 1960), pp. 150–51.

13. A "moralistic" approach to international affairs involves the transplantation of individual or national moral principles and rules to the international political sphere and the identification of one's particular standards with general rules which govern the world. Operationally, the "moralist" looks to differences in morality rather than conflicts of interest and power in approaching problems of international politics. For a discussion of the "legalistic" approach and the "legalistic-moralistic" approach, see Chapters IV and V and George F. Kennan, *American Diplomacy 1900–1950* (London: Secker & Warburg, 1952), pp. 91–103.

14. Dulles, "Where are We? A Five-Year Record of America's Response to the Challenge of Communism," address before the American Association for the United Nations (December 29, 1950), in *Department of State Bulletin*, XXIV (Washington: Government Printing Office, 1951), 85, hereafter referred to as *DSB*.

15. Pietro Quaroni, as quoted in Drummond and Coblentz, *Duel at the Brink,* pp. 18–19.

16. Hans J. Morgenthau, "John Foster Dulles," in Norman A. Graebner, ed., *An Uncertain Tradition: American Secretaries of State in the Twentieth Century* (New York: McGraw-Hill, 1961), p. 308.

17. *Ibid.,* pp. 289–308.

18. Seyom Brown, "The Great Foreign Policy Debate," The RAND Corporation, P-3815 (April, 1968), 2.

19. Morgenthau, *Politics Among Nations,* p. 7.

20. Dulles, "The Relation of France to a Program of World Reconstruction," in *Papers* (1920s), p. 4.

21. *Ibid.*

22. See Alexander L. George, "The 'Operational Code': A Neglected Approach to the Study of Political Leaders and Decision-Making," The RAND Corporation, RM-5427-PR (September, 1967).

23. Ortega y Gasset, "In Search of Goethe from Within," in *The Dehumanization of Art and Other Writings* (New York: Doubleday, 1956), p. 131.

24. F.S. Northedge, *British Foreign Policy: The Process of Readjustment, 1945–1961* (London: Allen & Unwin, 1962), p. 8.

Chapter 1: Background Influences and Experiences

1. Goold-Adams, *The Time of Power*, p. 23.

2. Ralph Barton Perry, *Puritanism and Democracy* (New York: Vanguard Press, 1944), p. 81.

3. Allen Macy Dulles, *The True Church: A Historical and Scriptural Study* (New York: Fleming J. Revell, 1907).

4. *Ibid.,* p. 51.   5. *Ibid.,* p. 59.   6. *Ibid.,* p. 282.

7. *Ibid.,* p. 94.   8. *Ibid.,* pp. 52–53.

9. Letter from "Father" to "Foster," in *Papers* (April 29, 1924), p. 1.

10. *Ibid.,* pp. 4–5.   11. *Ibid.,* p. 5.   12. *Ibid.,* p. 3.

13. See letters from Dulles to William P. Finney, Jr. (April 17, 1924) and to "Father" (May 2, 1924), in *Papers*.

14. Letter from Dulles to Dr. Charles Wood, in *Papers* (May 3, 1924).

15. Letter from "Foster" to "Father," in *Papers* (June 2, 1924).

16. *Ibid.*   17. *Ibid.*

18. Letter from "Father" to "Foster," in *Papers* (June 3, 1924).

19. Legal Brief (1925): Memorandum on Behalf of the Presbytery of New York, Respondent in the Matter of Complaints of Walter D. Buchanan and Others against the Presbytery of New York with Reference to Receiving into its Membership Reverend Carlos G. Fuller and to Licensing to Preach the Gospel Mr. Cameron Parker Hall (prepared by Dulles, Henry Sloane Coffin, and William Adams Brown), in *Papers*. See also the legal brief prepared by Dulles in 1925 in the cases of Henry P. Van Dusen and Cedric C. Lehman, in *Papers*.

20. See letter from "Mother" to "Foster," in *Papers* (December, 1918).

21. Dulles, "As Seen by a Layman," *Religion in Life*, VII (Winter, 1938), 36.

22. Quoted in William Castle, Jr., "John Watson Foster," in Samuel Flagg Bemis, ed., *The American Secretaries of State*, VIII (New York: Alfred A. Knopf, 1928), 223.

23. Quoted in *ibid.,* p. 188.   24. *Ibid.,* p. 187.

25. See Allen Macy Dulles, *The True Church,* p. 204.

26. Dulles, *War, Peace and Change* (New York: Harper & Row, 1939), p. 40.

27. *Ibid.,* p. 139.

28. Dulles, address on "Economic Imperialism," in *Papers* (January 18, 1925), p. 20.

29. Letter from Dulles to Ambassador John W. Davis, in *Papers* (July 14, 1920).

30. Letter from "Foster" to his brother "Allen," in *Papers* (January 21, 1921).

31. Letter and memorandum from Dulles to Ambassador John W. Davis, in *Papers* (July 18, 1924), pp. 3, 14–16, 8–9, and 10–12, respectively of the memorandum.

32. *Ibid.,* pp. 17 and 19 respectively.   33. *Ibid.,* in letter to Davis.

34. Interview with Arthur Krock, in Princeton University's *John Foster Dulles Oral History Project* (February 20, 1965), p. 1 (hereafter referred to as *Oral History*).

35. John Watson Foster, *Diplomatic Memoirs,* II (London: Constable & Company, 1909), pp. 240 and 221.

36. Dulles essay written at Princeton on "Pragmatism," in *Papers* p. 61.

37. *Ibid.,* pp. 62–63.   38. *Ibid.,* p. 62.

39. Platig, "John Foster Dulles," p. 16.

40. Robert Lansing, *War Memoirs* (London: Rich & Cowan, 1935), p. 314.

41. See "Political and Economic Conditions in Costa Rica, As Bearing on the Question of Recognizing the Government of General Tinoco," Dulles confidential report to the Secretary of State (May 21, 1917), in *Papers;* and Dulles, "Conceptions and Misconceptions regarding Intervention," *American Academy of Political and Social Science Annals,* CXLIV (July, 1929), 103 (hereafter referred to as *Annals*).

42. Dulles confidential report to the Secretary of State, in *Papers* (May 21, 1917), pp. 9–10.

43. Dulles, *Annals,* CXLIV (1929), 103. See also Dulles address before the Western Section of the Alliance of Reformed Churches, in *Papers* (February 8, 1944), p. 8.

44. Dulles confidential report to the Secretary of State, in *Papers* (May 21, 1917), p. 9.

45. See Dulles, *Annals,* CXLIV (1929), 103; and Dulles, "Criticisms of Mr. Hatch's Report on 'War,'" essay written as member of the Presbyterian General Assembly's Committee on War, in *Papers* (1924), p. 3.

Chapter 2: Coming of Statesmanship

1. John Chamberlain, "John Foster Dulles: A Wilsonian at Versailles, This Famous Lawyer may be Dewey's Secretary of State," *Life,* XVII (August 21, 1944), 90.

2. See "The Reminiscences of William Wilson Cumberland," in Columbia University's Oral History Project, *The New York Election of 1949*, I, 53, 63–64.

3. Quoted in John Maynard Keynes, *A Revision of the Treaty* (London: Macmillan Company, 1922), p. 145.

4. Northedge, *The Troubled Giant: Britain Among the Great Powers, 1916–1939* (London: G. Bell & Sons, 1966), p. 93.

5. Keynes, *A Revision of the Treaty*, p. 104.

6. Quoted in Dulles memorandum on "Appointment to Reparation Commission," in *Papers* (December 19, 1920), p. 7.

7. See Dulles memorandum on "The Desirability of a Fixed Sum" (June 3, 1919), reprinted in Philip Mason Burnett, *Reparation at the Paris Peace Conference: From the Standpoint of the American Delegation*, II (New York: Columbia University Press, 1940), 108.

8. Keynes, *A Revision of the Treaty*, pp. 145–46.

9. See Burnett, *Reparation at the Paris Peace Conference*, I, 5–6.

10. Dulles address on behalf of the American Delegation (February 13, 1919), reprinted in Bernard Baruch, *The Making of the Reparation and Economic Sections of the Treaty* (New York: Harper & Row, 1920), p. 293.

11. *Ibid.*, p. 295.

12. Dulles memorandum on "The Desirability of a Fixed Sum" (June 3, 1919), in Burnett, *Reparation at the Paris Peace Conference*, II, 108.

13. See Thomas W. Lamont, "Reparations," in Edward M. House and Charles Seymour, editors, *What Really Happened at Paris: The Story of the Peace Conference 1918–1919* (London: Hodder & Stoughton, 1921), pp. 259–90.

14. Dulles first draft of economic liability clause (February 21, 1919), reprinted in Burnett, *Reparation at the Paris Peace Conference*, I, 26–27.

15. For expansion on this view, see Burnett, *Reparation at the Paris Peace Conference*, I, 66–70.

16. Dulles, "The Indemnity Terms: Justification of Allied Demands: A Reply to Mr. Keynes," letter to *The London Times* (February 16, 1920), p. 10.

17. Letter from Keynes to Dulles, in *Papers* (March 2, 1920).

18. Dulles, Introduction in Burnett, *Reparation at the Paris Peace Conference*, I, xi, xiv.

19. See André Tardieu, *The Truth About the Treaty* (Indianapolis: Bobbs-Merrill Company, 1921), p. 287; and Lamont, in House and Seymour, editors, *What Really Happened at Paris*, p. 270.

20. Dulles memorandum on "Wilson's Decision on Pensions" (April 1, 1919), in Burnett, *Reparation at the Paris Peace Conference*, II, 776.

21. See Forrest Davis, *Saturday Evening Post*, CCXVII, 93.

22. Robert Lansing, *The Peace Negotiations: A Personal Narrative* (New York: Houghton Mifflin Company, 1921), pp. 199–200.

23. *Ibid.*, pp. 211–12. While Wilson never really got along with Lan-

sing, it was not unusual for the President not to get along with his advisers for any length of time.

24. See Dulles address "The Christian Forces and a Stable Peace" (January 25, 1941), p. 4, and Dulles address at Madison Avenue Presbyterian Church (October 20, 1941), p. 20, in *Papers*.

25. Letter from Dulles to Norman H. Davis, Assistant Secretary of the Treasury, in *Papers* (April 1, 1920).

26. *Ibid*.

27. Letter from Dulles to Louis Loucheur, French Minister of Liberated Regions, in *Papers* (January 17, 1921). For a harsher description of the U.S. attitude, see Dulles address given in early 1920s on "An Economic Conference," in *Papers*.

28. Dulles, "The Reparation Problem," address reprinted in *The Foreign Policy Association Bulletin*, II, No. 2 (June, 1921), 4.

29. Dulles, "Allied Debts," *Foreign Affairs*, I (September, 1922), 132. See also Dulles, "Allied Indebtedness to the United States," *Annals*, XCVI (July, 1921), 173–77.

30. Letter from Dulles to Mrs. A. J. Boulton, in *Papers* (December 5, 1923).

31. See Dulles address on "An Economic Conference" (1920s), in *Papers*.

32. Letter from Dulles to Louis Cartier, in *Papers* (September 17, 1923). See also, Memorandum of Conference with Mr. Theunis (July 10, 1923), Memorandum of Conferences in Germany (July 12–17, 1923), letter to Dr. Carl Melchior (August 3, 1923), and letter to Max Warburg (November 30, 1942), in *Papers*.

33. Letter from Dulles to Louis Cartier, in *Papers* (September 17, 1923).

34. For the basic description of this "merry-go-round," see Thomas A. Bailey, *A Diplomatic History of the American People* (New York: F. S. Crofts & Company, 1940), pp. 661–64.

35. For Dulles' full comments on the 1924 Dawes Plan, see Dulles, "The Dawes Report and the Peace of Europe," *The Independent*, CXII (April 26, 1924), 218+.

36. *Ibid.*, p. 240.   37. *Ibid.*, p. 218.

38. Letter from Dulles to Ogden Mills, Under Secretary of the Treasury, in *Papers* (June 18, 1931). See also Dulles memorandum to President Hoover, in *Papers* (June 12, 1931).

39. Dulles, "Criticisms of Mr. Hatch's Report on 'War,'" in *Papers* (1924), pp. 4–5, 6. Dulles commented as follows on the subject of disarmament: "Some means must be found to break the deadlock. That way, I believe, consists in . . . proceeding directly toward disarmament without necessarily awaiting the final perfection of peaceful agencies of settlement. . . .

"Admittedly this program involves some risks. Some nation must be found to assume leadership. . . . Our risk would be slight. If our example be not generally followed, we can quickly revert to the present order of affairs."

40. *Ibid.,* p. 5.

41. Dulles address on "Economic Imperialism," in *Papers* (1925), p. 20.

42. Dulles, *War, Peace and Change* (New York: Harper & Row, 1939).

43. See Platig, "John Foster Dulles," p. 72. By Dulles' account, *War, Peace and Change* was largely an expansion of the theses presented in his 1935 *Atlantic Monthly* article entitled "The Road to Peace." See letter from Dulles to John D. Rockefeller, in *Papers* (October 11, 1938).

44. Dulles, *War, Peace and Change,* p. 170.

45. *Ibid.,* pp. 1–5.　　　46. See *ibid.,* pp. 106–167, 168.

47. *Ibid.,* pp. 169–70.　　　48. *Ibid.,* pp. ix–x.

49. See Dulles draft of *War, Peace and Change* entitled "A Study of the Conditions which Produce Totalitarian War and the Possibility of Altering Them through Procedures which Elsewhere Operate to Eliminate Force as the Solvent of Conflicting Desires," in *Papers* (September, 1938), p. 96.

50. Dulles, *War, Peace and Change,* p. x.

51. See respectively: Dulles address on "Peaceful Change within the Society of Nations" at Princeton University (March 19, 1936), p. 5; and Dulles, "The Church and World Affairs," reprint from *The Presbyterian Tribune* (October, 1947), p. 9, in *Papers.*

52. Dulles summary of remarks for Foreign Policy Association address, in *Papers* (March 18, 1939), p. 2.

53. Lansing quoted in respectively: Dulles address on "Foreign Policy —Ideals, Not Deals," in *Papers* (February 10, 1947), p. 10; and Dulles, "The Church's Contribution Toward a Warless World," *Religion in Life,* IX (Winter, 1940), 34.

54. See letter from Dulles to Norman H. Davis, Assistant Secretary of the Treasury, in *Papers* (April 1, 1920).

55. Letter from Dulles to Ambassador John W. Davis, in *Papers* (January 13, 1920).

56. Dulles, *Foreign Affairs,* I, 130.

57. Letter from Dulles to Herbert B. Swope, Executive Editor of *The New York World,* in *Papers* (October 25, 1923).

58. Dulles, "The Securities Act and Foreign Lending," *Foreign Affairs,* XII (October, 1933), 33.

59. Dulles address on "Leadership for Peace" before the National Study Conference on the Churches and World Order, in *Papers* (March 8, 1949), pp. 2–3.

60. Dulles, "The Aftermath of the World War," *International Conciliation,* No. 369 (April, 1941), 265.

61. Letter from Dulles to E. M. Friedman, in *Papers* (November 7, 1921).

62. Dulles, "The Treaty of Versailles," draft article for *Christianity and Crisis,* in *Papers* (1941), p. 3.

63. Dulles, "The Problem of Peace in a Dynamic World," *Religion in Life,* VI (Spring, 1937), 196.

64. Dulles address on "Economic Imperialism," in *Papers* (1925), pp. 7–8.

65. *Ibid.,* p. 11.

66. Dulles, "The Road to Peace," *The Atlantic Monthly,* CLVI (October, 1935), 496.

67. Preliminary draft of *ibid.,* in *Papers,* p. 8.

68. Dulles summary of remarks for Foreign Policy Association address, in *Papers* (March 18, 1939), p. 8.

69. Dulles address before the Foreign Policy Association, in *Papers* (March 18, 1939), pp. 7, 9.

70. *Ibid.,* p. 6.

71. For quote and supporting analysis, see Platig, "John Foster Dulles," p. 92.

72. See respectively in *Papers:* Dulles summary of remarks for Foreign Policy Association address (March 18, 1936), p. 2; and "The American Churches and the International Situation," statement adopted by the Federal Council of the Churches of Christ in America (1940) and basically a Dulles draft, p. 2.

73. *Ibid.*

74. Dulles address at Second Presbyterian Church, in *Papers* (March 12, 1941), pp. 17–18.

75. Dulles address on "Our Foreign Policy" before the Economic Club, in *Papers* (March 22, 1939), pp. 9, 12.

76. See Dulles address on "The U.S. and the World of Nations" before the National Study Conference on the Churches and the International Situation, in *Papers* (February 27, 1940), pp. 1–16; and Dulles, "The Church's Contribution toward a Warless World," *Religion in Life,* IX (Winter, 1940), 35.

77. *Ibid.,* p. 35.

78. Dulles, "Long Range Peace Objectives," statement submitted to the Commission to Study the Bases of a Just and Durable Peace (September 18, 1941), which includes analysis of the Roosevelt-Churchill Eight Point Declaration, in *Papers,* p. 8.

79. Dulles, "Peace Without Platitudes," *Fortune,* XXV (January, 1942), 42.

80. Quoted in John Robinson Beal, *John Foster Dulles: A Biography* (New York: Harper & Row, 1959), p. 91.

81. Quoted in Walter Millis, ed., *The Forrestal Diaries* (New York: Viking Press, 1951), p. 41.

82. See Dulles "Summary of Conclusions relating to England Trip (June 28–July 25, 1942)," and "Notes taken by Bob as Foster recounted His Trip to England—July, 1942," in *Papers*. Quotes from "Notes by Bob," p. 17 (on E. H. Carr) and pp. 5 and 16 (on Cripps).

83. See *ibid.*, pp. 9–10; and Dulles "Report on England Trip," in *Papers* (August, 1942).

84. Dulles, "A Righteous Faith," *Life*, XIII (December 28, 1942), 49.

85. See respectively: Dulles "Report on England Trip," p. 1, and "Summary of Conclusions on England Trip," p. 1, in *Papers*.

Chapter 3: Politics, Controversy, and Diplomacy

1. See Arthur H. Vandenberg, Jr., ed., *The Private Papers of Senator Vandenberg* (Boston: Houghton Mifflin, 1952), p. 112.

2. *Ibid.*, pp. 112–13.

3. See Cordell Hull, *Memoirs*, II (London: Hodder & Stoughton, 1948), 1689–93.

4. U.S. *Congressional Record*, 78th Cong., 2d Sess., 1944, XC, Part 6, pp. 8058–61. For articles in periodicals described in the text as questionable, see the following: "Hitler's Backers, U.S. Bankers, and Mr. Dewey's Mr. Dulles," *In Fact*, X (October 30, 1944), 1–2; "On Mr. Dulles and What To Do About Him," *Soviet Russia Today*, XV (July 1946), 6–7; "Pepper Links Dulles to Nazis," *In Fact*, XIV (March 24, 1947), 1–3; "U.S. Money Behind German Revival," *In Fact*, XV (August 18, 1947), 1–3; "Vishinsky Wasn't First," *New Masses*, LXV (October 14, 1947), 3–5; "Pro-Nazi Ties of Marshall's Adviser," *In Fact*, XVI (December 8, 1947), 3–4; "Schroeder Scandal," *In Fact*, XVII (March 22, 1948), 3; and "The Suppressed Dulles Story," *In Fact*, XX (October 24, 1949), 3–4. Other magazines utilized some of this material and the charges against Dulles, and then made retractions: "In Justice to Mr. Dulles," *New Republic*, CXI (November 20, 1944), 467; and Harold L. Ickes, "Looking Forward Backwards," *New Republic*, CXXI (November 21, 1949), 16.

For defense of Dulles, see the following: Senator Vandenberg in U.S. *Congressional Record*, 78th Cong., 2d Sess., 1944, XC, Part 6, 8061; John C. Bennett, Reinhold Niebuhr, Justin Wroe Nixon, and G. Bromley Oxnam, "Concerning Mr. Dulles," *The Christian Century*, LXI (October 25, 1944), 1231; and "John Foster Dulles," *The Christian Century*, LXI, 1224–25.

5. Senator Pepper in U.S. *Congressional Record*, 80th Cong., 1st Sess., 1947, XCIII, Part 1, 788–92; Representative Sabath in *ibid.*, Part 4, p. 4607.

POLITICS, CONTROVERSY, AND DIPLOMACY

6. See U.S. *Congressional Record,* 81st Cong., 2d Sess., 1950, XCVI, Part 4, 4387–88.

7. Dulles memorandum entitled "Comment on *Reporter* on American-Soviet Relations," in *Papers,* enclosed in a letter from Dulles to Reverend Robert Y. Johnson (October 8, 1946). Dulles had prepared this confutation in July of 1946. See also letter from Dulles to Joseph R. Dillinger (December 4, 1945), and Dulles memorandum on "The Bank of Spain Defense on the Purchase of Silver by Sullivan and Cromwell" (undated), in *Papers.*

8. Quoted in Millis, ed., *The Forrestal Diaries,* p. 132.

9. Interview with Robert D. Murphy, in *Oral History* (May 1965), p. 7.

10. Acheson and Dulles were against having the Soviet Union on the Collective Measures Committee, but were in favor of not opposing Soviet membership on the Peace Observation Commission. Lodge strongly opposed the idea of including the Soviet Union on the commission on grounds that such moves would ultimately lead the United States to drop its guard prematurely. See letter from Lodge to Acheson (October 19, 1950) and letter Dulles drafted for Acheson in favor of inclusion, in *Papers;* and Dulles statement before UN Committee I (October 9, 1950), in *DSB,* XXIII, 651.

11. Dulles address before the Senate, quoted in Beal, *John Foster Dulles,* p. 108.

12. See Dulles memorandum on Blair House meeting, in *Papers* (April 27, 1948).

13. See Dulles interview with Dean Albertson, in *Papers* (November 8, 1949).

14. See political sheet distributed by New York State Republican Committee (1949), in *Papers;* and political advertisement by New York Democratic State Committee, in U.S. *Congressional Record,* 81st Cong., 2d Sess., 1950, XCVI, Part 4, 4387–88.

15. Dulles, *War or Peace* (New York: Macmillan Company, 1950), p. 4.

16. *Ibid.,* pp. 17–18.

17. Frederick S. Dunn, *Peace-Making and the Settlement with Japan* (Princeton: Princeton University Press, 1963), p. 105. For a first-hand account of the opposition in the Pentagon and particularly of the Joint Chiefs of Staff to a peace treaty with Japan at this time, see Dean Acheson, *Present at the Creation: My Years in the State Department* (New York: W. W. Norton & Company, 1969), pp. 426–35.

18. See Dunn, *Peace-Making with Japan,* p. 104; and Dulles in *DSB,* XXII (July 10, 1950), 49–50.

19. For analysis of the British, American, and other positions, see "Digest of Sixth and Final Meeting (May 25, 1951) of the Study Group on Japanese Peace Treaty," printed by the Council on Foreign Relations, in *Papers,* particularly pp. 7–12 (excerpts at Appendix A).

20. *Ibid.*, p. 8.

21. See Harry S Truman, *Memoirs: Years of Trial and Hope,* II (New York: Doubleday, 1956), 396–413.

22. Letter from Dulles to Ferdinand Lathrop Mayer, in *Papers* (April 10, 1951).

23. Anthony Eden, *Memoirs: Full Circle* (London: Cassell & Company, 1960), p. 19.

24. Shigeru Yoshida, "Japan and the Crisis in Asia," *Foreign Affairs,* XXIX (January 1951), 179. See also Shigeru Yoshida, *The Yoshida Memoirs,* translated by Kenichi Yoshida (Boston: Houghton Mifflin Company, 1962), in which Yoshida notes that the friendship of the U.S. always formed the "keynote" of Japan's diplomatic policy (pp. 285–86).

25. Dunn, *Peace-Making with Japan,* pp. 141–43. In June of 1951 Dulles was asked if the British had agreed that the Nationalists were the ones to be consulted on the negotiation of the treaty. He replied: "No, I wouldn't say that they have agreed with that." Dulles on NBC's "Meet the Press," in *Papers* (June 24, 1951).

26. Smith memorandum of meeting with Prime Minister Yoshida, in *H. Alexander Smith Papers* at Princeton University (September 3, 1951), hereafter referred to as *Smith Papers*. For the introduction to this collection and for an excellent analysis of some aspects of the Japanese settlement from which the author has drawn, the author is indebted to William M. Leary, Jr., "Smith of New Jersey: A Biography of H. Alexander Smith, U.S. Senator from New Jersey 1944–1959," doctoral dissertation, Princeton University (1966), pp. 216–27.

27. Smith *Diary* (September 4, 1951), quoted in *ibid.*, p. 218.

28. *New York Times* (September 14, 1951), p. 3.

29. Dunn, *Peace-Making with Japan,* pp. 142–43. See also Bernard C. Cohen, *The Political Process and Foreign Policy: The Making of the Japanese Peace Settlement* (Princeton: Princeton University Press, 1957), p. 150.

30. Smith *Diary* (December 11, 1951), quoted in Leary, "Smith of New Jersey," pp. 220–21.

31. See exchange of correspondence between Prime Minister Yoshida and Dulles, in *DSB,* XXVI, 120.

32. See Smith memorandum of conversation with Dulles, in *Smith Papers* (January 17, 1952). See also Gerson, *John Foster Dulles,* pp. 93–95; and Acheson, *Present at the Creation,* pp. 603–606.

33. Acheson, *Present at the Creation,* pp. 603–604.

34. Eden, *Memoirs: Full Circle,* p. 19.

35. Smith memorandum on conference with Dulles, in *Smith Papers* (January 11, 1952).

36. Acheson, *Present at the Creation,* p. 604.

37. Eden, *Memoirs: Full Circle,* p. 20.

38. Acheson, *Present at the Creation,* p. 604.

39. Eden, *Memoirs: Full Circle,* p. 20.

40. See Dwight D. Eisenhower, *Mandate for Change: The White House Years 1953–1956* New York: William Heineman, 1963), p. 142.

41. See Leary, "Smith of New Jersey," p. 227.

42. U.S. *Congressional Record,* 82d Cong., 2d Sess., 1952, XCVIII, Part 2, 2331.

43. *Ibid.,* p. 2327.

Chapter 4: Thoughts on International Politics, Part I

1. Dulles, "Locarno: Business and Finance Will Benefit Most Quickly from Treaties," reprint from *League of Nations News,* in *Papers* II (November 1925), 3.

2. Dulles, *Fortune,* XXV (January 1942), 87.

3. Dulles, "Long Range Peace Objectives," in *Papers* (September 18, 1941), p. 5.

4. Dulles, *Fortune,* XXV (January 1942), 87.

5. See Dulles statement before House Ways and Means Committee (May 4, 1953) and his statement concerning World Trade Week (May 15, 1953), in *DSB,* XXVIII, 744 and 748 respectively; Dulles statement before Senate Appropriations Committee, in *Papers* (April 26, 1955), p. 6. Dulles, "Our Cause will Prevail," *Life,* XLIII (December 23, 1957), p. 13; and Dulles statement before House Ways and Means Committee, in *Papers* (February 24, 1958), pp. 2–3.

6. Dulles statement (May 15, 1953), in *DSB,* XXVIII, 748.

7. Dulles address before American section of the International Chamber of Commerce, in *Papers* (April 26, 1937), p. 8.

8. See letter from Dulles to Bishop Henry W. Hobson (February 2, 1949); and "The Power of International Financing," stenographic report of discussion by Dulles and Morriss Hillquit at Foreign Policy Association meeting (March 24, 1928), in *Papers.*

9. Dulles, *War, Peace and Change,* p. 52.

10. Dulles, *War or Peace,* p. 75; and Dulles, "America's Part in an Economic Conference," in *Papers* (January 19, 1922), p. 12.

11. See Dulles, Introduction in Burnett, *Reparation at the Paris Peace Conference,* I, xiv; *Life,* XIII (1942), 50; and "Peaceful Change within the Society of Nations," in *Papers* (1936), p. 18.

12. See respectively: Dulles, *War, Peace and Change,* pp. 55–56; and "Peaceful Change within the Society of Nations," in *Papers* (1936), p. 6.

13. Dulles, *War, Peace and Change,* p. 30.   14. *Ibid.,* p. 52.

15. Dulles, "Law Needed in an International World Order," reprint from *Post War World,* in *Papers* I (April 15, 1944), p. 1.

16. "The American Churches and the International Situation," in *Papers* (1940), p. 2.

17. Dulles address on "The Cooperation of Sovereign Equals" before American Chamber of Commerce in Japan and Japanese Chamber of Commerce and Industry, in *Papers* (December 4, 1951), p. 2.

18. Dulles, "Criticisms of Mr. Hatch's Report on 'War,'" in *Papers* (1924), p. 5.

19. Dulles, *War, Peace and Change*, p. 8.   20. *Ibid.*, p. 170.

21. Dulles, "Christianity—Solvent of World Conflict," reprint from *Social Progress*, in *Papers* (January, 1943), p. 4. This was also a primary underlying message in *War, Peace and Change*.

22. Dulles, "Peaceful Change within the Society of Nations," in *Papers* (1936), p. 5. See also *War, Peace and Change*, p. 138.

23. Dulles, *War or Peace*, p. 260.

24. See Dulles respectively: "The Relation of France to a Program of World Reconstruction," in *Papers* (1920s), p. 3; "Criticisms of Mr. Hatch's Report on 'War,'" in *Papers* (1924), p. 5; *Annals*, CXLIV (1929), 103–104; "The Church and World Affairs," reprint from *The Presbyterian Tribune*, in *Papers* (October 1947), p. 9; "Peaceful Change within the Society of Nations," in *Papers* (1936), p. 7; and "Toward World Order," in *A Basis for the Peace to Come: The Merrick-McDowell Lectures for 1942* (New York: Abingdon-Cikesbury Press, 1942), p. 37.

25. Dulles, *The Atlantic Monthly*, CLVI (1935), 496. See also Dulles, *International Conciliation*, No. 369 (April 1941), 265.

26. Dulles address on "Economic Imperialism," in *Papers* (January 18, 1925), p. 17.

27. Dulles, *War, Peace and Change*, p. 156.

28. See E. H. Carr, *The Twenty Years' Crisis 1919–1939* (London: Macmillan Company, 1962), pp. 208–23.

29. Dulles, *The London Times* (February 16, 1920), p. 10.

30. Dulles, "The Relation of France to a Program of World Reconstruction," in *Papers* (1920s), p. 4.

31. Dulles, "The Treaty of Versailles," in *Papers* (December 5, 1941), p. 1.

32. Dulles, "The Relation of France to a Program of World Reconstruction," in *Papers* (1920s), pp. 2–3.

33. Dulles, "A North American Contribution to World Order," address at Conference on Canadian-American Affairs, in *Papers* (June 20, 1939), p. 5.

34. Dulles, "The Relation of France to a Program of World Reconstruction," in *Papers* (1920s), p. 3.

35. See Charles A. Beard, *The Devil Theory of War* (New York: Vanguard Press, 1936). In this work Beard accused Robert Lansing of having gone "behind the back of the State Department's head" in approaching President Wilson on the subject of loans and credits to France on October 23, 1914. Beard in effect retracted the accusation in "New Light on Bryan and War Policies," *The New Republic*, LXXXVII (June 17, 1936),

177–78. For Dulles' correspondence relating to this matter, see the exchanges between Dulles, Maurice Leon of France, and William Phillips of the State Department, in *Papers* (May–July 1936).

36. Dulles address, in *Papers* (March 12, 1941), p. 10.

37. Dulles, *War, Peace and Change,* p. 112.

38. Dulles address on "American Foreign Policy," in *Papers* (March 18, 1939), p. 3.

39. Dulles, *War, Peace and Change,* pp. 120–21.

40. Letter from Dulles to L. L. Summers, in *Papers* (January 5, 1921).

41. Letter from Dulles to William R. Cotter of America First Committee, in *Papers* (November 8, 1940).

42. Dulles, *War, Peace and Change,* p. 118.

43. See, for example, Dulles, "As Seen by a Layman: An Interpretation of the Oxford Conference on 'Church, Community and State,' " *Religion in Life,* VII (Winter, 1938), 36–44; and Dulles address, in *Papers* (October 11, 1939), pp. 14–15.

44. Dulles, *War, Peace and Change,* p. 115.

45. *Ibid.,* pp. 123–24.   46. *Ibid.,* pp. 130–31.

47. This was a recurrent theme in Dulles' speeches from 1936 to 1942. See, for example, "Peaceful Change within the Society of Nations," in *Papers* (1936), pp. 9–11; "The Problem of Peace in a Dynamic World," *Religion in Life,* VI (Spring 1937), 194; "Christianity in this Hour," in *Papers* (April 21, 1941), p. 13; and address at Union Theological Seminary, in *Papers* (May 19, 1941), p. 7.

48. Dulles address, in *Papers* (March 12, 1941), p. 17.

49. Dulles, *Religion in Life,* VI (Spring 1937), 204.

50. Dulles, *War or Peace,* p. 70.

51. Quoted in Dulles, *Religion in Life,* IX (Winter 1940), 38.

52. Dulles, *The Independent,* CXII (April 26, 1924), 240.

53. Referring to the United Nations in 1945, Dulles asserted that to "consolidate that beginning requires first to keep them talking, and second to find ways of action which will confirm the vague impression that they can be better off if they regularly work together." Dulles, "Peaceful Settlement of International Disputes," address at United Nations Forum, in *Papers* (March 26, 1945), p. 1.

54. Coral Bell, *Negotiation from Strength,* p. 68.

55. Dulles, *The Atlantic Monthly,* CLVI, 496–97.

56. See Dulles, *Fortune,* XXV (January 1942), 90; and Dulles, "Long Range Peace Objectives," in *Papers* (September 18, 1941), pp. 17–18.

57. These ideas were recurrent themes in Dulles' writings during this period. See the following in *Papers:* "A Christian World Hope," reprint from *The Presbyterian Tribune* (November 1944); address at the *New York Times* Hall Symposium (March 18, 1943); and address at meeting of the Federal Council of Churches (November 28, 1944). For specific com-

ments on sanctions and weighted voting, see letter from Dulles to Professor Quincy Wright (December 19, 1939) and letter to Stuart C. Rand (January 30, 1945).

58. Dulles statement at *New York Times* Hall Symposium, in *Papers* (September 24, 1943), p. 4.

59. Letter from Dulles to Mr. S. L. W. Mellen, in *Papers* (January 6, 1942).

60. Inis L. Claude, Jr., "The United Nations and the Use of Force," *International Conciliation*, No. 532 (March 1961), 333.

61. Dulles address on "The Beginning of World Order" at the San Francisco Conference, in *Papers* (April 22, 1945), p. 3.

62. Quoted in Millis, ed., *The Forrestal Diaries,* p. 41.

63. Dulles, in *A Basis for the Peace to Come* (1942), pp. 45–46.

64. Letter from Dulles to Mrs. George D. Huntington, in *Papers* (June 27, 1951).

65. Dulles, *Religion in Life,* IX (Winter 1940), 40.

66. Dulles address on "The Ecumenical Mission of the Church Today" at the North American Ecumenical Conference, in *Papers* (June 4, 1941), p. 7.

67. See Dulles Memoranda of Conversations at Bermuda Conference, in *Papers* (March 24, 1957), pp. 1–2.

68. See George F. Kennan, *American Diplomacy 1900–1950* (Chicago: Chicago University Press, 1951), pp. 95–100.

69. Dulles address on "World Court" before Illinois Bar Association, in *Papers* (May 29, 1925), pp. 6–9.

70. See Dulles, "Peaceful Settlement of International Disputes," in *Papers* (March 26, 1945), p. 7; and *War or Peace,* p. 187.

71. Dulles, "The Future of the United Nations," *International Conciliation,* No. 445 (November 1948), 588.

72. Dulles, *War or Peace,* p. 199.

73. Dulles, "Should Economic Sanctions be Applied in International Disputes?," *Annals,* CLXII (July 1932), 104. See also Dulles, *War, Peace and Change,* pp. 94–98.

74. Letter from Dulles to Henry R. Luce on the subject of Jessup's article in *Life,* in *Papers* (September 29, 1943).

75. Letter from Dulles to Professor Thomas A. Bailey, in *Papers* (January 12, 1942).

76. Dulles, *Annals,* CXLIV (1929), 104.

77. Dulles, as quoted in Foreign Service Memorandum, from E. F. Drumwright, counselor of U.S. Embassy in Seoul, in *Papers* (June 23, 1950).

78. Dulles memorandum on Near East Trip, in *Papers* (May 1953), p. 4.

79. Dulles memorandum of Blair House meeting with Secretary Mar-

shall, Under Secretary Lovett, and Senator Vandenberg, in *Papers* (April 27, 1948), p. 5. For other expressions of Dulles' support of European union and his concern that the U.S. guarantee could affect or be couched so as to retard such union, see his letters to Senator Vandenberg, in *Papers* (April 8, 1948 and March 27, 1949). In the latter, Dulles defined what he considered to be the "principal grounds for honest doubt regarding the Atlantic Pact" and enclosed a draft Senate resolution to counter these doubts by clarifying that the proposed pact should not be interpreted so as to impede progress toward closer economic and political cooperation in Europe. See also Dulles, *War or Peace,* p. 96.

80. Dulles statement on "The Atlantic Pact" before the Senate Foreign Relations Committee, in *Papers* (May 4, 1949), pp. 6–11.

81. Dulles remarks on "College News Conference," in *Papers* (August 24, 1957), p. 2.

82. Quoted in Andrew H. Berding, *Dulles on Diplomacy* (Princeton: D. Van Nostrand, 1965), p. 78. See also, Dwight D. Eisenhower, *Waging Peace: The White House Years 1956–1961* (London: William Heinemann, 1965), pp. 424–30.

83. Dulles address before Women's National Republican Club, in *Papers* (January 25, 1947), p. 5.

84. Dulles address before American-Japan Society, in *Papers* (February 2, 1951), p. 8.

85. Dulles, "Peaceful Settlement of International Disputes," in *Papers* (March 26, 1945), p. 4.

Chapter 5: Thoughts on International Politics, Part II

1. Dulles confidential report to the Secretary of State, in *Papers* (May 21, 1917), pp. 9–10.

2. *Ibid.*   3. *Ibid.*

4. Hersch Lauterpacht, ed., *International Law,* I (8th ed.; New York: Longmans, Green & Company, 1955), quoted in Robert H. Ferrell, *American Diplomacy in the Great Depression: Hoover-Stimson Foreign Policy 1929–1933* (New Haven: Yale University Press, 1957), p. 166.

5. Dulles confidential report to the Secretary of State, in *Papers* (May 21, 1917), p. 11.

6. See Dulles, *Annals,* CXLIV (1929), 103–104; and "Criticisms of Mr. Hatch's Report on 'War,'" in *Papers* (1924), p. 3.

7. Dulles memorandum to Ambassador John W. Davis, for use in campaign against Coolidge, in *Papers* (July 1924), pp. 8–9.

8. Letter from Dulles to Miss Esther E. Lape of The American Foundation, in *Papers* (March 16, 1933).

9. For the account in this paragraph the author is indebted to Ferrell, *American Diplomacy in the Great Depression,* pp. 151–69, especially pp. 153–58.

10. Dulles, *The Atlantic Monthly*, CLVI (1935), 494–95.

11. See Dulles record of trip to Hankow and meeting with Ambassador Johnson, in *Papers* (March 6–9, 1938).

12. Dulles, *War, Peace and Change*, pp. 86, 87, 88.

13. Dulles statement to Mr. Angelopoulos, in *Papers* (December 30, 1949).

14. See Dulles, "Korean Attack opens New Chapter in History," in *DSB*, XXIII (1950), 210; and letter from Dulles to Henry R. Luce, in *Papers* (April 24, 1950).

15. For purposes of analysis in this section, the issues of diplomatic recognition and admission to the United Nations are frequently linked together. This is not to imply that these two closely related, but separate, matters are identical for all purposes or that there are not important differences between them.

16. Dulles, *War or Peace*, pp. 190–91.   17. *Ibid.*, p. 209.

18. Dulles, "How to Take the Offensive for Peace," *Life*, XXVIII (April 24, 1950), 128.

19. Dulles, in *DSB*, XXIII (1950), 210.

20. Richard P. Stebbins, *The United States in World Affairs 1949* (New York: Harper & Row for the Council on Foreign Relations, 1950), p. 436. (For the account given in this paragraph, the author is indebted to Stebbins' analysis.)

21. Dulles rough draft of responses to questions on the China situation and Formosa, in *Papers* (January 8, 1950), p. 1.

22. Letter from Dulles to Senator Vandenberg, in *Papers* (January 6, 1950). See also Dulles draft memorandum on Formosa (January 5, 1950) and draft statement (January 6, 1950), in *Papers*.

23. Dulles rough draft of responses to questions on the China situation and Formosa, in *Papers* (January 8, 1950), p. 4.

24. Letter from Dulles to Senator Vandenberg, in *Papers* (January 6, 1950).

25. See Truman, *Memoirs: Years of Trial and Hope*, pp. 396–413.

26. *New York Times* (January 31, 1951), p. 4.

27. *Ibid.* (October 6, 1951), p. 1.

28. See Dulles memorandum on Formosa, in *Papers* (March 31, 1952).

29. See Dulles memorandum of meeting with George Yeh, Chinese Nationalist Minister of Foreign Affairs, and Dr. Wellington Koo, Chinese Ambassador to Washington, in *Papers* (November 19, 1952).

30. Hans J. Morgenthau, *American Foreign Policy: A Critical Examination* (London: Methuen & Company, 1952), p. 208.

31. Richard Neustadt, *Presidential Power* (New York: John Wiley & Sons, 1960), p. 105.

32. See Michael A. Guhin, "The United States and the Chinese People's Republic: The Non-Recognition Policy Reviewed," *International Affairs* (London), XLV, No. 1 (January 1969), 44–45.

346 THOUGHTS ON INTERNATIONAL POLITICS, PART II

33. See J. W. Fulbright, *Old Myths and New Realities* (London: Jonathan Cape, 1965), pp. 38–39.

34. Northedge, *British Foreign Policy*, p. 193.

35. Dulles press conference (January 16, 1958), quoted in Eleanor Lansing Dulles, *John Foster Dulles: The Last Year* (New York: Harcourt Brace Jovanovich, 1963), p. 45.

36. See respectively: Dulles interview with Congressman Kenneth B. Keating on "Let's Look at Congress," in *Papers* (June 15, 1958), p. 2; Dulles interview with Edgar McInnis of the Canadian Institute of International Affairs, in *Papers* (June 23, 1958), p. 6; and Dulles address on "Policy for the Far East" (December 4, 1958), in *DSB*, XXXIX, 992.

37. See transcript of remarks at Opening Session of the Far East Chiefs of Mission Conference, in *Papers* (March 14, 1958).

38. Dulles notes for talk with Chiang Kai-shek, in *Papers* (October 21, 1958).

39. Dulles interview with Congressman Keating, in *Papers* (June 15, 1958), p. 2.

40. See Dulles radio and television address on "Report on Berlin" (February 24, 1954), in *DSB*, XXX, 345–46.

41. Morgenthau, *Politics Among Nations*, p. 13.

42. Niebuhr, *The Irony of American History*, p. 5.   43. *Ibid.*, p. 37.

44. Dulles, in *DSB*, XXIII (1950), 210. He continued thusly: "Equally, power is of little value unless it be the servant of wise policies."

45. See Dulles, "The Relation of France to a Program of World Reconstruction," in *Papers* (1920s), pp. 3, 6; and "We Have the Initiative," *Nation's Business*, XLII (January 1954), 25.

46. See Dulles, "The Treaty of Versailles," in *Papers* (1941).

47. Dulles radio broadcast, in *Papers* (January 16, 1945), p. 5.

48. Dulles, in *DSB*, XXIII (1950), 208.

49. See *Look* Forum Question, in *Papers* (December 10, 1945); and *New York Times* (June 11, 1946), p. 5.

50. Dulles, "The Christian Citizen in a Changing World," in *The Church and the International Disorder: Reports of the World Council of Churches* (London: SCM Press, 1948), p. 99.

51. For "military dictatorship" comment, see Dulles draft of "A Policy of Boldness," in *Papers* (March 8, 1952), p. 1. For his criticism of military influence, military thinking and its effects, see Dulles, "Peace with Russia," *The Christian Century*, LXV (August 25, 1948), 849; *War or Peace*, pp. 3, 176, 239–40; and "A Policy of Boldness," *Life*, XXXII (May 19, 1952), 146. Similar concerns appeared in some of Dulles' correspondence during this period.

52. Letter from Dulles to Christian Herter, in *Papers* (December 22, 1948).

53. Dulles, *Life*, XXXII (1952), 152.

54. Dulles, *War, Peace and Change,* pp. 89–91.

55. Dulles address on "Not War, Not Peace" before the Foreign Policy Association (January 17, 1948), in *Vital Speeches of the Day,* XIV (1948), 272–73.

56. Dulles, *War, Peace and Change,* p. 94.   57. *Ibid.*

58. Dulles address on "Economic Imperialism," in *Papers* (1925), p. 19.

59. Dulles, "Criticisms of Mr. Hatch's Report on 'War,'" in *Papers* (1924), pp. 4–5. See also Dulles, *Annals,* CLXII (1932), 103.

60. Dulles address at Assembly of the World Council of Churches at Amsterdam, in *Papers* (August 24, 1948), p. 2.

61. Dulles address, in *Papers* (October 14, 1952), p. 5.

62. Dulles, *War, Peace and Change,* p. 31.

63. William James, *The Will to Believe and Other Essays in Popular Philosophy* (New York: Longmans, Green & Company, 1897), pp. 258–59.

64. Letter from Dulles to Henry R. Luce, in *Papers* (September 29, 1943).

65. See Dulles address, in *Papers* (October 27, 1952), p. 2; "Long Range Peace Objectives," in *Papers* (September 18, 1941), p. 17; *War or Peace* (1950), p. 19; and Dulles statement at Plenary Session of Special Emergency Session of UN General Assembly (November 1, 1956), in *DSB,* XXXV, 755 respectively.

66. William James, "The Moral Equivalent of War," in *Memories and Studies* (New York: Longmans, Green & Company, 1912), p. 265 (written for and first published by *International Conciliation,* No. 27).

67. *Ibid.,* p. 288; and Dulles reprint from *The Presbyterian Tribune,* in *Papers* (October 1947), p. 9.

68. Dulles, in *Vital Speeches of the Day,* XIV (1948), 273.

69. James, in *Memories and Studies,* p. 292.

70. Dulles, *War, Peace and Change,* p. 170.

71. Dulles, *War or Peace,* p. 3.

72. Dulles address, in *Papers* (September 18, 1952), p. 22.

73. Dulles interview with Martin Agronsky over NBC, in *Papers* (September 15, 1957).

74. Dulles draft of "Challenge and Response in United States Policy," in *Papers* (August 9, 1957), p. 3. In the published article Dulles stated that American policies were "influenced and modified by changing world conditions in the effort to apply . . . basic concepts to actual conditions." But by judging right and wrong, it "does not mean that we are so closely wedded to doctrinaire concepts that we cannot adjust our policies to the demands of the hour." "Challenge and Response in United States Policy," *Foreign Affairs,* XXXVI (October 1957), 41–42.

75. Dulles address on "The Strength of Adversity," in *Papers* (May 18, 1950), p. 2.

76. Kenneth W. Thompson, "The Limits of Principle in International

Politics: Necessity and the New Balance of Power," *The Journal of Politics*, XX (August 1958), 466–67.

77. The following list of Dulles' views is taken from the excellent analysis of Platig, "John Foster Dulles," pp. 259–64: (1) How the ideology of peace masks the interests of the *status quo* powers, *The Atlantic Monthly*, CLVI (1935), 496; (2) How America uses ideological camouflage, "Our Foreign Loan Policy," *Foreign Affairs*, V (October 1926), 38–40; (3) The tendency to hide behind treaties as "sacred," *War, Peace and Change*, pp. 38–51; (4) How an ideology of world order based on Christian principles can be utilized as a "smug formula for advancing the national interest," *Religion in Life*, IX (Winter 1940), 39; and (5) How most political leaders speak alike in terms of social ends, in *The Church and the International Disorder* (1948), p. 76.

78. Dulles, *War, Peace and Change*, pp. 60–61.

79. Platig, "John Foster Dulles," p. 382.

Chapter 6: Religion and America

1. J. H. Oldham, ed., *The Churches Survey Their Task: The Report of the Conference at Oxford* (London: Allen & Unwin, 1937), p. 36. Dulles was one of 425 representatives at this August conference which included such personalities as R. H. Tawney, Max Huber, Ernest Barker, Emil Brunner, Paul Tillich, Reinhold Niebuhr, and T. S. Eliot.

2. Dulles radio address on the Oxford Conference, in *Papers* (May 20, 1937), p. 2.

3. "The American Churches and the International Situation," in *Papers* (1940), p. 8.

4. *Ibid.*, p. 6.

5. Dulles statement for Manual of Laymen's Missionary Movement, in *Papers* (April 4, 1945), p. 1.

6. See respectively: Dulles, *Religion in Life*, IX (Winter 1940), 40; address at the North American Ecumenical Conference, in *Papers* (June 4, 1941), p. 2; *Life*, XIII (1942), 50; and "The American Churches and the International Situation," in *Papers* (1940), p. 6.

7. Quotations from Dulles for John Hightower's article, in *Papers* (December 22, 1954).

8. Dulles address before meeting of the Western Section of the Alliance of the Reformed Churches, in *Papers* (February 8, 1944), p. 15.

9. Dulles, in *The Church and the International Disorder* (1948), p. 73.

10. Dulles, reprint from *Social Progress*, in *Papers* (January, 1943), p. 2.

11. See Dulles respectively in *Papers:* "The American Churches and the International Situation" (1940), p. 6; article sent to the International Council of Religious Education (April 29, 1942), p. 5; and address at Episcopalian Diocesan dinner (May 19, 1942), p. 4.

12. See Dulles, "Peace with Russia," *The Christian Century*, LXV (August 25, 1948), 849; and address at the Assembly of the World Council of Churches, in *Papers* (August 24, 1948), p. 11.

13. Dulles, *War, Peace and Change*, p. 21; and *Religion in Life*, IX (1940), 39.

14. Dulles, "Criticisms of Mr. Hatch's Report on 'War,'" in *Papers* (1924), p. 6.

15. Dulles draft article, in *Papers* (April 29, 1942), p. 5.

16. Dulles address at St. Lawrence University on "Can Freedom Win," in *Papers* (June 8, 1952), p. 7.

17. Dulles address upon receiving the Peace Medal of St. Francis, in *Papers* (February 20, 1952), p. 1. See also *War or Peace*, p. 187.

18. See Will Herberg, *Protestant-Catholic-Jew: An Essay in American Religious Sociology* (New York: Doubleday & Company, 1955), pp. 59, 63–64.

19. For comments by friends and associates in this regard, see the following in *Oral History:* General Lucius Clay, p. 30; Gerard B. Lambert, p. 18; George Murnane, p. 11; Senator H. Alexander Smith, p. 49; Sir Percy Spender, p. 26; and Felix von Eckhardt, p. 3.

20. Platig, "John Foster Dulles," p. 131.

21. Dulles draft of essay enclosed with letter to "Father," in *Papers* (August 18, 1911), p. 1.

22. Dulles, reprint from *Social Progress*, in *Papers* (January, 1943), p. 4. See also Dulles address, in *Papers* (May 19, 1942).

23. See statement adopted by the Federal Council of Churches (December 1942), and Dulles, reprint from *The Christian Century* (March 19, 1952), in Van Dusen, ed., *The Spiritual Legacy of John Foster Dulles*, pp. 102 and 36 respectively.

24. Dulles, "Statement of Political Propositions which Underlie a Just and Durable Peace," *International Conciliation*, No. 409 (March 1945), 170.

25. Dulles address (September 8, 1946), in Van Dusen, ed., *The Spiritual Legacy of John Foster Dulles*, p. 119.

26. Dulles, in *The Church and the International Disorder* (1948), p. 104.

27. Dulles address at the National Council of Presbyterian Men, in *Papers* (February 2, 1952), p. 11.

28. Dulles, "Peace is Possible," reprint from *Presbyterian Life*, in *Papers* (February 28, 1948), p. 3. See also Platig, "John Foster Dulles," pp. 296–97.

29. Dulles address at St. Lawrence University, in *Papers* (June 8, 1952), pp. 7–8. See also Platig, "John Foster Dulles," p. 141.

30. Dulles, reprint from *The Presbyterian Tribune*, in *Papers* (October 1947), p. 14. See also Dulles, in *The Church and the International Disorder* (1948), p. 106.

31. Dulles, "Moral Force in World Affairs," reprint from *Presbyterian Life,* in *Papers* I (April 10, 1948), 28–29.

32. Dulles, reprint from *The Presbyterian Tribune,* in *Papers* (February 8, 1947), p. 14.

33. Coral Bell, *Negotiation from Strength,* p. 84.

34. From a letter to Mrs. Henry Whitman in Henry James, ed., *The Letters of William James,* II (Boston: Atlantic Monthly Press, 1920), 90.

35. Dulles, in *The Church and the International Disorder* (1948), p. 106.

36. Dulles, *Life,* XIII (1942), 49.

37. Dulles address on "Leadership for Peace" at the National Study Conference on the Churches and the World Order, in *Papers* (March 8, 1949), p. 8.

38. Dulles address at opening of National Mission on World Order (October 28, 1943), in Van Dusen, ed., *The Spiritual Legacy of John Foster Dulles,* p. 60.

39. Dulles address, in *Papers* (November 4, 1943), p. 5.

40. Dulles address on "U.S. Foreign Policy" at the Economic Club of Detroit, in *Papers* (February 5, 1945), p. 6.

41. See, in *Papers,* Dulles address (January 9, 1950), p. 7; and address on "The Strategy of Soviet Communism" (March 14, 1950), p. 8.

42. Dulles address on "Peace Insurance" at International House (May 16, 1950), in *DSB,* XXII, 862.

43. Dulles script for broadcast, in *Papers* (March 1, 1946), p. 3.

44. Letter from Dulles to Walter Lippmann, in *Papers* (June 4, 1946).

45. Dulles draft of address on "Not War, Not Peace" for delivery before the Foreign Policy Association, in *Papers* (January 1, 1948), p. 13.

46. Dulles, "Thoughts on Soviet Foreign Policy and What to do About It," *Life,* XX (June 10, 1946), 120, 122.

47. *Ibid.,* p. 122.

48. Letter from Dulles to Edward C. Carter, in *Papers* (January 22, 1947).

49. Dulles, in *The Church and the International Disorder* (1948), p. 84.

50. Dulles address on "The Meaning of Freedom" at Union College (June 13, 1948), in *Vital Speeches of the Day,* XIV (July 1, 1948), 581.

51. Dulles address on "Freedom through Sacrifice" before the Presbyterian General Assembly, in *Papers* (May 24, 1946), p. 3.

52. Dulles address on "The United Nations" at Princeton University, in *Papers* (February 22, 1946).

53. Dulles, reprint from *The Presbyterian Tribune,* in *Papers* (February 8, 1947), p. 13.

54. Dulles address on "Leadership for Peace" at the National Study Conference on the Churches and World Order, in *Papers* (March 8, 1949), pp. 14–15.

55. Dulles address before American-Japan Society (February 2, 1951), in *DSB*, XXIV, 253. See also Dulles address at American Club in Tokyo, in *Papers* (June 22, 1950), p. 3.

56. Dulles address before the National Publishers' Association, in *Papers* (January 17, 1947), p. 12.

57. Dulles article for *The Argonaut*, in *Papers* (September 25, 1946), p. i.

58. Dulles, in *The Church and the International Disorder* (1948), p. 82.

59. Morgenthau, *American Foreign Policy: A Critical Examination*, p. 231.

60. See Dulles interview with Martin Agronsky over NBC, in *Papers* (September 15, 1957).

61. Dulles address (December 29, 1950), in *DSB*, XXIV, 85.

Chapter 7: Interpreting the Cold War

1. See Dulles, "New Aspects of American Foreign Policy," address before the American Society of International Law (April 27, 1950), in *DSB*, XXII, 717; and Dulles address on "Can We Stop Russian Imperialism?" before the Advertising Council at Detroit (November 27, 1951), in *DSB*, XXV, 941.

2. Dulles address on "The Power of Moral Forces" (October 11, 1953), in *DSB*, XXIX, 512.

3. Dulles summary of remarks before World Trade Committee (April 3, 1951), in *DSB*, XXIV, 617.

4. Dulles, *War or Peace*, p. 6.

5. Dulles address on "Strategy for the Pacific" (March 14, 1951), in *DSB*, XXIV, 484.

6. Dulles address (November 27, 1951), in *DSB*, XXV, 938.

7. Dulles statement before Committee I of the UN (October 20, 1950), in *DSB*, XXIII, 749.

8. Dulles address at University of Arizona (May 30, 1951), in *DSB*, XXIV, 936.

9. Dulles, *Foreign Affairs*, XXXVI (October 1957), 26.

10. Letter from Dulles to Henry P. Van Dusen, in *Papers* (November 17, 1941).

11. Dulles, "Six Pillars of Peace: Cement Unity now with Organized World Collaboration," in *Vital Speeches of the Day*, IX (April 15, 1943), 406.

12. *Ibid.*

13. Letter from Dulles to Eugene Lyons, in *Papers* (February 14, 1945).

14. Letter from Dulles to John C. Higgins, in *Papers* (December 4, 1945).

15. Dulles address, in *Papers* (January 16, 1945), pp. 10–11.

16. Dulles broadcast on Crimea Conference, in *Papers* (February 13, 1945).

17. Dulles, "A Personal Appraisal of the Crimea Conference," in *Papers* (February 26, 1945), p. 2.

18. *Ibid.*, pp. 2–3. See also Dulles address at Foreign Policy Association meeting, in *Papers* (March 17, 1945).

19. Dulles, "Peaceful Settlement of International Disputes," in *Papers* (March 26, 1945), p. 4.

20. See Dulles remarks in press conference (November 24, 1953) in response to question regarding his reaction to Vice President Nixon's statement that the U.S. erred in attempting to disarm Japan and Germany after the war, in *DSB*, XXIX, 788.

21. Dulles, as quoted in Berding, *Dulles on Diplomacy*, pp. 22–23.

22. Dulles, *War or Peace*, pp. 24–30. For a fuller discussion of this period, to which the author is indebted, see also Gerson, *John Foster Dulles*, pp. 30–53.

23. Quoted in Dulles, *War or Peace*, pp. 30–31.

24. Dulles, "A First Balance Sheet of the United Nations," *International Conciliation*, No. 420 (April 1946), 181.

25. Gerson, *John Foster Dulles*, p. 44.

26. Letter from Dulles to Walter Lippmann, in *Papers* (June 4, 1946).

27. "Cross-Roads of American Foreign Policy," statement of the Commission on a Just and Durable Peace adopted by the Federal Council of Churches, in *Papers* (July 1, 1947), p. 3.

28. See Dulles address (May 24, 1946), pp. 2–3, and Dulles address (June 19, 1946), p. 3, in *Papers*.

29. *Ibid.*

30. Dulles, "Thoughts on Soviet Foreign Policy and What to do About It," *Life*, XX (June 3, 1946), 124.

31. Dulles, "Not War, Not Peace," address before the Foreign Policy Association, in *Papers* (January 17, 1948), p. 4.

32. Dulles, "U.S. and Russia Could Agree," interview in *U.S. News and World Report*, XXVI (January 21, 1949), 35. See also, Dulles address (May 4, 1948), in Van Dusen, ed., *The Spiritual Legacy of John Foster Dulles*, p. 152.

33. Letter from Dulles to Merlyn S. Pitzele, in *Papers* (August 4, 1947).

34. See Dulles address on "Not War, Not Peace" (January 17, 1948), in *Vital Speeches of the Day*, XIV (February 15, 1948), 270–73.

35. Dulles, in *The Church and the International Disorder* (1948), p. 97.

36. Letter from Dulles to Edward C. Carter, in *Papers* (January 22, 1947).

37. Dulles interview with Mlle. Daumarie, in *Papers* (December 19, 1944), p. 2.

38. Dulles address (September 8, 1946), in Van Dusen, ed., *The Spiritual Legacy of John Foster Dulles*, p. 115.

39. Letter from Dulles to Joseph Barnes of *New York Herald Tribune*, in *Papers* (January 31, 1947).

40. Dulles press and radio conference, in *Papers* (July 11, 1951), p. 7.

41. See James P. Warburg, *Faith, Purpose and Power: A Plea for a Positive Policy* (New York: Farrar, Straus & Company, 1950), pp. 3, 12–13.

42. Dulles, in *The Church and the International Disorder* (1948), p. 101.

43. Dulles address on "The Defense of Freedom," in *Papers* (May 6, 1948), p. 3.

44. *Ibid.*, p. 4. See also Dulles broadcast on "A Report on the Moscow Meeting of the Council of Foreign Ministers," in *Papers* (April 29, 1947), p. 12.

45. Dulles address, in *Papers* (February 10, 1947), p. 8.

46. Dulles address at Northwestern University, in *Papers* (June 18, 1947), p. 3.

47. Dulles radio discussion with Senator Tom Connally, in *Papers* (November 2, 1946).

48. Dulles, *Life*, XX (June 10, 1946), 120. It should be noted that Dulles used the word "great" usually to mean "numerous," "large," or "of consequence" without the moral connotations of "noble," "lofty," "admirable," or "of merit."

49. Dulles address at Vanderbilt University on "Our International Responsibilities," in *Papers* (June 4, 1950), p. 4. See also, Dulles address on "The Strategy of Soviet Communism," in *Papers* (March 14, 1950), p. 5.

50. Dulles, in *DSB*, XXIV, 936.

51. Dulles broadcast discussion with John Scheuer, in *Papers* (March 1, 1946), p. 2.

52. Dulles address, in *Papers* (February 10, 1947), p. 7. See also "Soviet-American Relations," in *Papers* (October 11, 1946), p. 5.

53. *Ibid.*, p. 4.

54. Dulles, *The Christian Century*, LXV (August 25, 1948), 849.

55. Dulles address before UN General Assembly on "Uniting for Peace Resolution," in *Papers* (November 1, 1950), p. 11.

56. Dulles address on "Leadership for Peace," in *Papers* (March 8, 1949), pp. 1–2.

57. See Dulles, *Life*, XX (June 3, 1946), 113; and Dulles, in *Vital Speeches of the Day*, XIV (February 15, 1948), 272–73.

58. Dulles, as quoted in Berding, *Dulles on Diplomacy*, p. 31.

59. See Dulles, *Life*, XX (June 3, 1946, and June 10, 1946), 112+ and 118+ respectively.

60. Dulles, *Life*, XX (June 10, 1946), 119.

61. Dulles, "Policy for Security and Peace," *Foreign Affairs*, XXXII (April 1954), 364.

62. George F. Kennan, "Did Stalin's Death Change Anything?—Review of Isaac Deutscher's *Russia: What Next?*," *The Reporter*, IX (July 7, 1953), 34.

63. Dulles, *Foreign Affairs*, XXXVI (October 1957), 28.

64. Dulles, "The Institutionalizing of Peace," reprint from the *Proceedings of the American Society of International Law*, in *Papers* (1956), p. 23.

65. Dulles address on "Principles and Policies in a Changing World" (November 18, 1958), in *DSB*, XXXIX, 901.

66. Dulles comments after 1957 NATO meeting, as reported in *New York Times* (December 20, 1957), p. 14.

67. See Dulles address before the National War College (June 16, 1953), in *DSB*, XXVIII, 895.

68. *Ibid.*

69. See respectively: Dulles address before China Institute (May 18, 1951), in *DSB*, XXIV, 845; and Dulles broadcasts, in *Papers* (March, 1952).

70. Dulles, "A Policy of Boldness," *Life*, XXXII (May 19, 1952), 158.

71. Dulles address before the National War College (June 16, 1953), in *DSB*, XXVIII, 897.

72. Dulles address, in *Papers* (March 14, 1950), p. 6.

73. See Dulles draft position papers for Big Four Meeting, in *Papers* (June 1955), at Appendix B.

74. Letter from Dulles to Herbert Hoover, Jr., in *Papers* (November 5, 1955).

75. Dulles statement before Foreign Ministers Conference at Geneva, in *Papers* (November 14, 1955), pp. 17–18.

76. See respectively: Dulles address on "Uniting for Peace Resolution" (November 1, 1950), p. 10; and address (March 14, 1950), p. 6, in *Papers*. See also *War or Peace*, p. 31.

77. Dulles address at Vanderbilt University, in *Papers* (June 4, 1950), p. 3.

78. See Dulles, "Report on Berlin," in *DSB*, XXX, 346.

79. Dulles, *War or Peace*, p. 32.

80. Dulles address, in *Papers* (March 14, 1950), p. 7. See also Dulles address, in *Papers* (May 6, 1948), p. 13.

81. Dulles address on "Areas for Deeds, Not Words" at New York Republican dinner (May 7, 1953), in *DSB*, XXVIII, 707.

82. Dulles address at Vanderbilt University, in *Papers* (June 4, 1950), p. 3.

83. Dulles, as quoted in Berding, *Dulles on Diplomacy*, p. 23.

84. Dulles, *Life*, XX (June 10, 1946), 119.

85. Dulles address, in *Papers* (February 10, 1947), p. 7.

86. Dulles address (March 8, 1949), in Van Dusen, ed., *The Spiritual Legacy of John Foster Dulles*, p. 202.

87. See Dulles, *U.S. News and World Report*, XXVI (January 21, 1949), 32, 35; and Dulles, "What I've Learned About the Russians," *Colliers*, CXXIII (March 12, 1949), 57.

88. See "Capitol Cloakroom" with Dulles, Edward R. Murrow, Eric Sevareid and Griffing Bancroft, in *Papers* (June 29, 1949), p. 4.

89. Matthew B. Ridgway, *The Korean War* (New York: Doubleday & Company, 1967), p. 10.

90. Dulles, "To Save Humanity from the Deep Abyss," *New York Times Magazine* (July 30, 1950), p. 35.

91. Dulles prepared portion of radio interview on "A Militaristic Experiment" (July 1, 1950), in *DSB*, XXIII, 50. See also Dulles address on "Leadership for Peace," in *Papers* (March 8, 1949), p. 10.

92. See Dulles, *New York Times Magazine* (July 30, 1950), pp. 34–35.

93. Dulles address on "U.S. Military Actions in Korea" at Colgate University conference on American foreign policy (July 7, 1950), in *DSB*, XXIII, 91. See also Dulles on "Meet the Press," in *Papers* (June 24, 1951), p. 2.

94. See Dulles address on "Europe and the Atlantic Pact," in *Papers* (March 23, 1949).

95. Statement on "Soviet-American Relations" by the Commission on a Just and Durable Peace (October 11, 1946), as cited by Dulles in address on "Leadership for Peace," in *Papers* (March 8, 1949), pp. 10–11.

96. Marshall D. Shulman, " 'Europe' versus 'Detente'?," *Foreign Affairs*, XLV (April 1967), 398.

97. See Chapter VI, "The Problem of Power"; and Dulles, *War, Peace and Change*, pp. 89–93.

98. Dulles memorandum on Washington Conference on the Berlin Blockade, in *Papers* (July 19, 1948), p. 1. Excerpts at Appendix C.

99. *Ibid.*, pp. 4–5. 100. *Ibid.*, p. 5.

101. Dulles memorandum of conversation with Robert Lovett on the Berlin Blockade, in *Papers* (July 22, 1948). Excerpts at Appendix D.

102. Nikita Khrushchev, *Khrushchev Remembers*, Strobe Talbott, ed. (Boston: Little, Brown & Company, 1970), p. 398.

103. Letter from Dulles to Secretary Marshall, in *Papers* (July 19, 1948).

104. See David S. McLellan, "Comparative 'Operational Codes' of Recent U.S. Secretaries of State: Dean Acheson," paper prepared for the sixty-fifth annual meeting of the American Political Science Association (September 2–6, 1969), pp. 8–9.

105. Max Ascoli, "George Kennan Updates His Diplomacy," *The Reporter*, XVIII (January 23, 1958), 19, 20. For this and the following references on Kennan, the author is indebted to the work of Alan Stephen

Cross, "The Function of Theory in International Relations: A Comparative Analysis of John Foster Dulles and George Frost Kennan," senior thesis, Harvard College (1966).

106. A. A. Berle, Review of *Realities of American Foreign Policy*, by George F. Kennan, *New York Times* (September 12, 1954), vii, p. 1.

107. Quoted in Robert Moskin, "Our Foreign Policy is Paralyzed," *Look*, XXVII (November 19, 1963), 26.

Chapter 8: Political Adjustment at Mid-Century

1. Letter from Dulles to Ferdinand Lathrop Mayer, in *Papers* (September 7, 1948).

2. See respectively, in *Oral History*, interviews with Ernest Gross (November 1964), p. 3, and with Robert D. Murphy (May 1965), p. 7.

3. Robert A. Dahl, *Congress and Foreign Policy* (New York: Harcourt Brace Jovanovich, 1950), p. 227.

4. Interview with Herbert Brownell, in *Oral History* (March 5, 1965), p. 16.

5. William S. White, *The Taft Story* (New York: Harper & Row, 1954), pp. 84–85, as quoted in Acheson, *Present at the Creation*, p. 364.

6. Eisenhower, *Mandate for Change*, p. 18

7. *Ibid.*, pp. 16, 18.

8. Interview with Miss Jane Todd, in *New York Election of 1949* (December 20, 1949), p. 291.

9. See Daniel Bell, ed., *The Radical Right* (New York: Doubleday & Company, 1964), for several excellent analyses of the "rightist" movements in the United States. Although the editor takes a rather narrow view of Dulles' moves in "The Dispossessed," pp. 1–45, he nevertheless maintains that the "eight years of moderation proved more frustrating than twenty years of opposition" to the right-wing (p. 3).

10. Senator Taft's remarks in *New York Times* (June 2, 1952), p. 14.

11. *Ibid.*   12. Dulles, *War or Peace*, pp. 129–30.

13. See *ibid.*, pp. 136, 178–80.

14. Interview with Herbert Brownell, in *Oral History*, p. 18.

15. Letter from Eisenhower to Dulles, in *Papers* (June 20, 1952).

16. See papers relating to the Republican party, especially remarks on the discussion of the platform outline, in *Papers* (June 16, 1952).

17. Richard Rovere, *Affairs of State: The Eisenhower Years* (New York: Farrar, Straus & Cudahy, 1956), p. 62.

18. "Pick the Winner," transcript of television program with Dulles and Harriman and Walter Cronkite as moderator, in *Papers* (August 21, 1952), p. 15.

19. Eisenhower, *Mandate for Change*, pp. 42–43.

20. Eisenhower, *Crusade in Europe*, as quoted in Brian Gardner, *The Wasted Hour: The Tragedy of 1945* (London: Cassell & Company, 1963), p. 22.

21. Eisenhower, *Mandate for Change*, p. 46.

22. Samuel Lubell, *Revolt of the Moderates* (New York: Harper & Row, 1956), p. 16.

23. Rovere, *Affairs of State*, p. 44.

24. *Time*, LX (September 22, 1952), 8.

25. Senator Jenner, as quoted in Acheson, *Present at the Creation*, p. 363.

26. See *Time*, LX (September 22, 1952), 8.

27. Dulles address on "Korean Attack Opens New Chapter in History" (July 31, 1950), in *DSB*, XXIII, 208.

28. Dulles, *War or Peace*, p. 136.

29. Dulles address before the China Institute (May 18, 1951), in *DSB*, XXIV, 845.

30. Dulles address on "Russian Imperialism" before Illinois Bankers' Association, in *Papers* (January 24, 1952), pp. 3–4.

31. Dulles, *War or Peace*, pp. 247, 250–51.

32. Dulles, *The Atlantic Monthly*, CLVI (October 1935), 493.

33. Kennan, "The Sources of Soviet Conduct," in *American Diplomacy 1900–1950*, p. 124.

34. Dulles address before the Presbyterian General Assembly, in *Papers* (May 24, 1946), p. 7.

35. Dulles address on "Leadership for Peace," in *Papers* (March 8, 1949), p. 14.

36. Winston Churchill at Fulton, Missouri (March 5, 1946), in *Vital Speeches of the Day*, XII (March 15, 1946), 330.

37. "Pick the Winner" with Dulles and Harriman, in *Papers* (August 21, 1952), p. 8.

38. Acheson address at Berkeley, California (March 16, 1950), in Norman A. Graebner, ed., *Ideas and Diplomacy: Readings in the Intellectual Tradition of American Foreign Policy* (New York: Oxford University Press, 1964), p. 738.

39. Acheson speech in *New York Times* (September 12, 1952), p. 12. Defining his approach as more than "containment," Acheson stated that "containment" did not adequately describe the policies of the Truman Administration.

40. Kennan, "The Sources of Soviet Conduct" and "America and the Russian Future," in *American Diplomacy 1900–1950*, pp. 123, 135.

41. Dulles, *Life*, XXXII (May 19, 1952), 154, 157.

42. See Dulles statement in defense of his and Eisenhower's concept of peaceful liberation, *New York Times* (September 4, 1952), p. 1; and related material on Truman's remarks in the 1952 campaign, in *Papers* (September 1952).

43. "Pick the Winner" with Dulles and Harriman, in *Papers* (August 21, 1952), p. 8.

44. *Ibid.,* p. 5.

45. Walter Lippmann column on "Containment and Liberation," in *Papers* (September 9, 1952).

46. Dulles on "Face the Nation," in *Papers* (October 21, 1956), pp. 2, 6. The entire program dealt essentially with the idea of "liberation" and the Polish situation.

47. Dulles, *Foreign Affairs,* XXXVI (October 1957), 28.

48. Dulles talking paper for Chiefs of Mission meeting relating to the NATO Ministerial Conference in Paris, in *Papers* (May 2, 1957), p. 4.

49. See Dulles draft position papers, memorandum from Dulles to Eisenhower, and memorandum from Douglas MacArthur, II to Dulles regarding the Big Four Meeting, in *Papers* (June 1955).

50. Letter from Dulles to Kenneth de Courcy of the *Intelligence Digest,* in *Papers* (February 28, 1952).

51. Hearing before the Committee on Foreign Relations of the U.S. Senate, 83d Cong., 1st Sess., on the Nomination of John Foster Dulles, Secretary of State-Designate, January 15, 1953 (Washington: Government Printing Office, 1953), p. 6.

52. *Ibid.,* p. 8.

53. Griffing Bancroft on Eric Sevareid program, in *Papers* (February 18, 1953).

Chapter 9: The Politics and Diplomacy of Secretaryship, Part I

1. For a brief account of these discussions, see Chapter III, "The War Years."

2. Report of meeting with Eden in letter from Dulles to Eisenhower, in *Papers* (November 14, 1952).

3. James P. Warburg, *The United States in a Changing World* (New York: G. P. Putnam's Sons, 1954), p. 466.

4. Robert J. Donovan, *Eisenhower: The Inside Story* (New York: Harper & Row, 1956), p. 85.

5. Letter from Dulles to Donald Grant of the *St. Louis Post-Dispatch,* in *Papers* (August 21, 1952).

6. For such opposing views on this matter, see Morgenthau, "John Foster Dulles," in Graebner, ed., *An Uncertain Tradition,* p. 308; and interview with Robert D. Murphy, in *Oral History,* p. 15.

7. Burton M. Sapin, *The Making of United States Foreign Policy* (New York: Frederick A. Praeger, 1966), p. 34.

8. Robert Murphy, *Diplomat Among Warriors* (London: Collins, 1964), p. 447.

9. Interview with Herbert Hoover, Jr., and George M. Humphrey, in *Oral History* (May 5, 1964), p. 4.

10. Coral Bell, *Negotiation from Strength,* p. 67.

11. Interview with General Dwight D. Eisenhower, in *Oral History* (July 28, 1964), p. 11. See also, Donovan, *Eisenhower: The Inside Story,* pp. 85–95; and Beal, *John Foster Dulles,* p. 139.

12. Coral Bell, *Negotiation from Strength,* p. 79.

13. Letter from Dulles to Larry S. Davidow, in *Papers* (December 26, 1946). See also, in *Papers,* letter to Dulles from Alfred Kohlberg (December 31, 1946); and Dulles files on Carnegie Endowment and Alger Hiss (1946–1952).

14. See letters from Dulles to Walter H. Judd (February 2, 1948), Judd to Dulles (March 1, 1948), and Dulles reply (March 22, 1948), in *Papers.*

15. See letters from Dulles to Philip C. Jessup and John W. Davis, in *Papers* (February 7, 1949).

16. The Earl Jowitt, *The Strange Case of Alger Hiss* (New York: Doubleday & Company, 1953), p. 263.

17. Dulles statement on Hiss case, in *Papers* (January 22, 1950). Also quoted in Richard M. Nixon, *Six Crises* (New York: Doubleday & Company, 1962), p. 68. For the account of the Nixon-Dulles meeting, see p. 21.

18. Quoted in Acheson, *Present at the Creation,* p. 364.

19. "Capitol Cloakroom" discussion with Dulles, Murrow, Sevareid and Bancroft, in *Papers* (June 29, 1949), p. 7.

20. See Dulles, *War or Peace,* pp. 226–228, 232.

21. McLellan, "Comparative 'Operational Codes' of Recent U.S. Secretaries of State: Dean Acheson" (September 1969), p. 27.

22. Eleanor Lansing Dulles, *John Foster Dulles,* p. 88.

23. For this account of the Greek shippers issue, see Beal, *John Foster Dulles,* pp. 148–49; and Eleanor Lansing Dulles, *John Foster Dulles,* p. 90.

24. McCarthy quotes and Acheson, in Acheson, *Present at the Creation,* p. 363.

25. Dulles press conference at home, in *Papers* (April 6, 1950), p. 2.

26. See letters from Dulles to Elton M. Davies (May 10, 1950) and Mrs. William Healy (May 10, 1950), in *Papers.*

27. Letter from Dulles to Davies, in *Papers* (May 10, 1950).

28. See Dulles statement, in *Papers* (November 21, 1952).

29. Dulles statement on "Discussion of Transition Problems" (December 3, 1952), in *DSB,* XXVII, 949.

30. See Dulles address before the Annual Convention of the American Veterans of Foreign Wars, in *Papers* (August 29, 1952) p. 1.

31. Dulles address to the State Department and Foreign Service (January 21, 1953), in *DSB,* XXVIII, 170.

32. Donovan, *Eisenhower: The Inside Story,* pp. 86, 286, 290–91.

33. Dulles press conference, in *Papers* (February 27, 1953).

34. Dulles informal remarks to State Department (January 28, 1953), in

DSB, XXVIII, 239. Dulles stated: "I don't think anybody wants in any such group as this, or our Foreign Service, to have 'yes men' or 'yes women' who just try to guess what their superiors want to have done and then try to meet their wishes. We have got to have people . . . who have minds of their own and who have the courage to express their views. . . .

"On the other hand, we must also recognize that once the decisions are made and made finally by the President and the Congress then we must all turn in, loyally, to support those policies. They won't be 100 per cent what any of us like; they won't be 100 per cent what I like or what you like. But they will become the policies of our nation, and then our job is to carry out those policies and do our best to make them succeed. . . ."

35. Interview with Dr. Henry Wriston, in *Oral History* (June 29, 1964), p. 14.

36. Kennan, "The Future of our Professional Diplomacy," *Foreign Affairs,* XXXIII (July, 1955), 568–86, quotes from 568–69.

37. See interview with Henry Wriston, in *Oral History,* pp. 11–12. Robert Murphy also noted, in his *Oral History* interview, p. 76, that the Secretary "showed a very constructive interest when it came to basic problems of reorganization."

38. Goold-Adams, *The Time of Power,* p. 67.

39. Sapin, *The Making of United States Foreign Policy,* p. 20.

40. Warburg, *The United States in a Changing World,* pp. 462–63.

41. See Loyalty Board's Finding re Davies and Vincent Cases and Acheson memorandum to Truman, in *DSB,* XXVIII, 121, 122–123 respectively; and Acheson, *Present at the Creation,* p. 711.

42. Acheson, *Present at the Creation,* p. 712.

43. Letter from Dulles to Hand (February 9, 1953), in *DSB,* XXVIII, 241.

44. Dulles memorandum on John Carter Vincent case (March 23, 1953), in *ibid.,* pp. 454–55.

45. Vincent had held key positions in China from 1936 to 1947, and headed the Special Presidential Mission to China in 1945–1946.

46. See Joseph C. Harsch, "John Foster Dulles: A Very Complicated Man," *Harpers,* CCXIII (September, 1956), 30, for the unfounded claim that Dulles told Vincent he had such a "weakness."

47. William F. Buckley, Jr., and Brent L. Bozell, *McCarthy and His Enemies* (Chicago: Henry Regnery Company, 1954), pp. 199–200.

48. For an administration account of the Bohlen affair, see Eisenhower, *Mandate for Change,* pp. 211–213. It should be noted also that, in 1948, Dulles had served with Bohlen at the UN.

49. White, *The Taft Story,* p. 235.

50. Interview with Charles E. Bohlen, in *Oral History* (June 23, 1964), p. 13.

51. Letter from Dulles to Frederick J. Libby of the National Council

for the Prevention of War, in *Papers* (December 30, 1937). As it turned out, after considerable pressure from President Roosevelt, the Ludlow Amendment was shelved by a margin of 209–188.

52. See Dulles, *Fortune*, XXV, 87.

53. For analysis and comments, see Eisenhower, *Mandate for Change*, p. 278; and *Congress and the Nation 1945–1964*, Congressional Quarterly Service, pp. 111–12.

54. Quoted in *ibid.*, p. 112.

55. Sherman Adams, *Firsthand Report: The Story of the Eisenhower Administration* (New York: Harper & Brothers, 1961), p. 105.

56. For the recounting of the series of events in this section and particularly the votes in Congress described later, the author has borrowed freely from and is indebted to *Congress and the Nation 1945–1964*, pp. 111–12.

57. Dulles address on "Treaty Making and National Unity," in *Papers* (April 11, 1952), p. 1.

58. Quoted in Eisenhower, *Mandate for Change*, p. 280.

59. *Ibid.*   60. Sherman Adams, *Firsthand Report*, p. 106.

61. *Congress and the Nation 1945–1964*, p. 112.

62. Bricker statement of August 5, 1954, upon introducing a new amendment on treaty-making power, quoted in *Congress and the Nation 1945–1964*, p. 112.

63. Dulles, *War or Peace*, pp. 201–203.

64. Northedge, *British Foreign Policy*, p. 8.

Chapter 10: The Politics and Diplomacy of Secretaryship, Part II

1. Dulles statement (November 14, 1947), in *Documents on American Foreign Policy. 1950–1955*, I, Department of State publication (Washington: Government Printing Office, 1957), 1442 (hereafter referred to as *Documents*).

2. See Dulles, "Long Range Peace Objectives," in *Papers* (September 18, 1941), pp. 12–13; "Toward World Order," in *A Basis for the Peace to Come* (New York: Abingdon-Cokesbury Press, 1942), pp. 31–57; *Fortune*, XXV (January 1942), 87; and address on "American Foreign Policy," in *Papers* (January 17, 1945), p. 13.

3. "Long Range Peace Objectives," in *Papers* (1941), p. 13.

4. Letter from Dulles to Whitney H. Shepardson, in *Papers* (April 28, 1942).

5. Dulles, *Fortune*, XXV, 87.

6. See Dulles memorandum of Blair House meeting (April 27, 1948), letters to Senator Vandenberg (March 29 and April 8, 1949), and statement before Senate Foreign Relations Committee (May 4, 1949), in *Papers;* and Dulles, *War or Peace*, p. 96.

7. Dulles broadcast, "Report on the Moscow Meeting of the Council of Foreign Ministers," in *Papers* (April 29, 1947), p. 9.

8. Dulles statement before Senate Foreign Relations Committee, in *Papers* (May 4, 1949).

9. See Dulles, *War or Peace*, pp. 212–14.   10. *Ibid.*, p. 220.

11. Dulles, "A Changing World," a series of broadcasts recorded on March 18, 1952, with moderator Dwight Cooke, in *Papers*, pp. 2, 5.

12. Dulles radio and television address (February 23, 1953), in *Documents*, I, 282–89.

13. Dulles radio and television address on "A Survey of Foreign Policy" (January 27, 1953), in *DSB*, XXVIII, 214.

14. Dulles press conference at UN Headquarters, in *Papers* (March 9, 1953), p. 4.

15. Dulles press conference in Paris, in *Papers* (April 23, 1953), pp. 4–5.

16. Dulles radio and television address on "Results of North Atlantic Council's Eleventh Meeting" (April 29, 1953), in *DSB*, XXVIII, 672.

17. Dulles background press conference for no direct attribution, in *Papers* (July 14, 1953), p. 3.

18. See letter from Dulles to Eisenhower, in *Papers* (November 14, 1952).

19. Dulles statement before NATO Ministerial Conference, in *Papers* (December 14, 1953), p. 4.

20. Communiqué of the Fifth Session of the North Atlantic Council (September 26, 1950), quoted by Dulles in address before National Press Club (December 22, 1953), in *Documents*, I, 1454.

21. See C. A. Shoenbrun's notes to Edward R. Murrow, in *Papers* (December 15, 1953).

22. Dulles statement on EDC (Department of State Press Release No. 486), in *Papers* (August 31, 1954), p. 2.

23. See papers on London Conference, in *Papers* (September 28–October 3, 1954).

24. Dulles remarks on "College News Conference," in *Papers* (August 24, 1957), p. 2.

25. Interview with General Nathan F. Twining, in *Oral History* (March 16, 1965), p. 25.

26. Dulles address before the Council on Foreign Relations on "The Evolution of Foreign Policy" (January 12, 1954), in *DSB*, XXX, 108.

27. Interview with Robert Sprague, in *Oral History* (August 11, 1964), p. 41. Coral Bell, *Negotiation from Strength*, p. 67, notes that "on the question of negotiation from strength, one may say that his [Dulles'] most important difference from Acheson in terms of impact on Western decisions was probably in his concept of the nature of the strength that should be sought as a backing for American diplomacy. This was a field

in which not all the responsibility—or formally even the major part—can be assigned to him; it belonged to Eisenhower and his Cabinet generally, especially the Secretaries of Defense and the Treasury."

28. Dulles interview in *U.S. News and World Report*, XXVII (July 8, 1949), 30.

29. These principles are brought out in Dulles' statements or articles such as the following: "North Atlantic Pact," *Vital Speeches of the Day*, XV (August 1, 1949), 617–24; "The Challenge of Today," in *DSB*, XXIV (June 11, 1951), 935–37; "Security in the Pacific," *Foreign Affairs*, XXX (January 1952), 175–87; "A Policy of Boldness," *Life*, XXXII (May 1952), 146–160; and "Far Eastern Problems," *Vital Speeches of the Day*, XVIII (June 1, 1952), 493–95.

30. Dulles address before the French National Political Science Institute (May 5, 1952) on ".Far Eastern Problems," *Vital Speeches of the Day*, XVIII (June 1952), 494.

31. Dulles address (May 30, 1951), in *DSB*, XXIV, 936.

32. Dulles, *Life*, XXXII, 151–52.

33. *Ibid.* See also, letter from Dulles to Walter Millis, in *Papers* (June 9, 1952).

34. Dulles, *Vital Speeches of the Day*, XVIII, 494.

35. Dulles draft of "A Policy of Boldness," in *Papers* (March 8, 1952), pp. 29–30.

36. Letter from Eisenhower to Dulles, in *Papers* (June 20, 1952).

37. Memorandum for conversation with Hanson Baldwin on "A Policy of Boldness" article in *Life*, in *Papers* (June 23, 1952), pp. 3–5.

38. Dulles, *Life*, XXXII, 148.

39. Morton H. Halperin, *Contemporary Military Strategy* (Boston: Little, Brown & Company, 1967), p. 47. For an excellent summary to which the author is indebted, see "The Evolution of American Military Strategy," pp. 43–55.

40. Dulles, in *DSB*, XXX, 108.   41. *Ibid.*

42. Quoted in Coral Bell, "Atoms and Strategy," in F. C. Benham, ed., *Survey of International Affairs 1954* (London: Oxford University Press, 1957), p. 99. Stevenson and Acheson's remarks from *New York Times* (March 7, 1954), pp. 62–63, and (March 28, 1954), vi, p. 13 respectively.

43. Henry A. Kissinger, "Military Policy and Defense of the 'Grey Areas,'" *Foreign Affairs*, XXXIII (April 1955), 425.

44. Dulles, in *DSB*, XXX, 110.   45. *Ibid.*

46. *Ibid.*, p. 108.   47. See *ibid.*, p. 109.   48. *Ibid.*, p. 108.

49. Quoted in Eisenhower, *Mandate for Change*, p. 451.

50. Coral Bell, *Negotiation from Strength*, p. 91.

51. See respectively: Dulles, *Life*, XXXII (May 19, 1952), 152; and Dulles address, in *Papers* (May 20, 1952), p. 3.

52. Dulles, in *DSB*, XXX, 110.

53. A real concern for SAC vulnerability was also apparent in official quarters such as the National Security Council. See interview with Robert Sprague, in *Oral History*, pp. 8, 18.

54. Dulles statement before the Senate Foreign Relations Committee on "The Atlantic Pact," in *Papers* (May 4, 1949).

55. See Dulles, *Life*, XXXII, 148; and Eisenhower statement, in *Papers* (August 16, 1952). Eisenhower stated that the United States "must be committed to security forces of such mobility and offensive impact that their retaliatory readiness and the massive potential of their blows" would "haunt the Kremlin with nightmares of the punishment to be visited upon Russia should it violate the peace."

56. Robert Murphy, "The Interrelationship of Military Power and Foreign Policy," address before the Air Force Association (August 20, 1954), in *DSB*, XXXI, 293.

57. Thomas C. Schelling, *Arms and Influence* (New Haven: Yale University Press, 1966), p. 67.

58. Dulles address, in *Papers* (May 20, 1952), p. 3.

59. Dulles memorandum for conversation with Hanson Baldwin, in *Papers* (June 23, 1952), p. 5.

60. Dulles address on "Where Are We? A Five-Year Record of America's Response to the Challenge of Communism" (December 29, 1950) before the American Association for the United Nations, in *DSB*, XXIV, 88.

61. Henry A. Kissinger, *The Necessity for Choice: Prospects of American Foreign Policy* (New York: Harper & Row, 1960), p. 81.

62. See Dulles statement in *DSB*, XXX, 464–65; and Coral Bell, in *Survey of International Affairs 1954*, p. 101.

63. Dulles, "Policy for Security and Peace," *Foreign Affairs*, XXXII (April 1954), 354–55.

64. Interview with Robert R. Bowie, in *Oral History* (August 10, 1964), pp. 45–46.

65. Dulles, "Challenge and Response in United States Policy," *Foreign Affairs*, XXXVI (October 1957), 31, quoted in Thomas C. Schelling, *The Strategy of Conflict* (Cambridge: Harvard University Press, 1963), p. 138. (For preceding Dulles quote, see *Foreign Affairs*, XXXII, 356.)

66. Roberto Ducci, "The World Order in the Sixties," *Foreign Affairs*, XLII (April 1964), 383.

67. Interview with Thomas S. Gates, in *Oral History* (July, 1965), p. 18.

68. See draft outline (June 12, 1957) of a speech for the conference of the Armed Forces Policy Council on June 14, 1957, in *Papers*.

69. Dulles statement on "Sharing Nuclear Knowledge with Our NATO Allies" (April 17, 1958) before the Joint Committee on Atomic Energy's Subcommittee on Agreements for Cooperation, in *DSB*, XXXVIII, 741.

70. See memorandum of conversation with General de Gaulle, in *Papers* (June 30, 1958).

71. Dulles, *Foreign Affairs*, XXXII, 363.

72. See Dulles address (May 30, 1951), in *DSB*, XXIV, 936.

73. Dulles, *Vital Speeches of the Day*, XVIII, 494.

74. Dulles, in *DSB*, XXX, 108–10.

75. Dulles address before Overseas Press Club (March 29, 1954), in *Documents*, II, 2376.

76. Dulles, *Foreign Affairs*, XXXII, 359.

77. *Ibid.*, p. 358.

78. Dulles draft of "Policy for Security and Peace," in *Papers* (February 19, 1954), p. 32.

79. Memorandum from Hamilton Fish Armstrong to Dulles, in *Papers* (February 24, 1954).

80. Dulles, *Foreign Affairs*, XXXII, 358–59.

81. Eden, *Memoirs: Full Circle*, pp. 102–103, 104–105.

82. *Ibid.*, p. 104.   83. *Ibid.*, p. 105.

84. See Eleanor Lansing Dulles, "Time and Decisions," *Foreign Military Commitments: The Forensic Quarterly*, XLIII (August 1969), 277–281; Beal, *John Foster Dulles*, p. 210; and Eisenhower, *Mandate for Change*, p. 349.

85. Eden, *Memoirs: Full Circle*, pp. 109 and 108–11 for full discussion.

86. Schedule as noted by C. M. Woodhouse, *British Foreign Policy Since the Second World War* (New York: Frederick A. Praeger, 1962), p. 48.

87. Dulles news conference (May 25, 1954), in *Documents*, II, 2391–92.

88. Eden, *Memoirs: Full Circle*, p. 120.

89. Quoted in *ibid.*, p. 128.   90. *Ibid.*, pp. 131–32.

91. *Ibid.*, p. 139.

92. Dulles news conference (June 28, 1954), in *Documents*, II, 2404.

93. Eden, *Memoirs: Full Circle*, p. 142.

94. Statement by the President (July 21, 1954), in *Documents*, II, 2397.

95. Coral Bell, *Negotiation from Strength*, p. 92.   96. *Ibid.*, p. 91.

97. Victor Bator, *Vietnam: A Diplomatic Tragedy* (New York: Oceana Publications, 1965), p. 107. It should be noted that Bator does not accept the views either that Dulles' threatening posture was a deliberate deterrent tactic or that some political or negotiating leverage was thereby gained. However, Bator's arguments against these views (pp. 125–29) are generally unconvincing.

98. Kennedy speech in the Senate (April 16, 1954), in John F. Kennedy, *The Strategy of Peace* (London: Hamish Hamilton, 1960), p. 59.

99. See Chapter V.   100. Dulles, in *DSB*, XXX, 346.

101. *Ibid.*, p. 347.   102. Eden, *Memoirs: Full Circle*, p. 128.

103. *New York Times* (May 11, 1954), p. 2.

104. Kennedy, *The Strategy of Peace,* p. 60.

105. Senator Mansfield and Congressman Richards, as quoted in Bator, *Vietnam: A Diplomatic Tragedy,* p. 184.

Chapter 11: Balancing Interests and Viewpoints

1. See Eisenhower, *Waging Peace,* pp. 109–10.

2. Dulles speech before the American Legion (October 10, 1955), in *DSB,* XXXIII, 642.

3. *Ibid.*   4. *Ibid.,* p. 643.

5. *Hearings, Mutual Security Appropriations for 1954,* p. 101, quoted in Cecil V. Crabb, Jr., *The Elephants and the Grass: A Study of Non-Alignment* (New York: Frederick A. Praeger, 1956), pp. 168–69.

6. Dulles news conference (October 4, 1955), in Paul E. Zinner, ed., *Documents on American Foreign Relations 1955* (New York: Harper & Row, 1956), p. 355.

7. Dulles news conference (May 22, 1956), Department of State Press Release, No. 272, pp. 6–7.

8. Dulles address on "The New Phase of Struggle with International Communism" (December 8, 1955), in Zinner, ed., *Documents,* p. 18.

9. *Ibid.,* p. 19.

10. Dulles memorandum on Near East Trip, in *Papers* (May 1953), p. 4.

11. Dulles speech at Iowa State College (June 9, 1956), in *New York Times* (June 10, 1956), p. 24.

12. *Ibid.*   13. *Ibid.*

14. For example, the ranking Republican on the Senate Appropriations Committee, Senator Styles Bridges, referred to advocates of some aspects of the Mutual Security Program as "do-gooders." When the President called him to task on the statement, the Senator made it clear that he meant both that the United States "should exclude such countries as India, Yugoslavia, and Indonesia from the list of beneficiaries" and that the administration should cut more than half a billion out of its request. See Eisenhower, *Waging Peace,* pp. 134–35.

15. Dulles press conference (July 11, 1956), Department of State Press Release, No. 380, p. 6. See also, pp. 4–5.

16. Dulles, *War, Peace and Change,* pp. 98–99.

17. Dulles press conference (July 11, 1956), Department of State Press Release, No. 380, p. 4.

18. Paul Seabury, *Power, Freedom and Diplomacy* (New York: Random House, 1963), p. 378.

19. Hans J. Morgenthau, "Critical Look at the New Neutralism," *New York Times Magazine* (August 27, 1961), pp. 25, 76–77.

20. Dulles address on "New Aspects of American Foreign Policy" before

the American Society of International Law (April 27, 1950), in *DSB,* XXII, 720.

21. See Dulles notes on important points of Near East Trip in *Papers* (May, 1950), particularly p. 5.

22. See, for example, Dulles, *Life,* XXVIII, 122. Also, on "Capitol Cloakroom" with Murrow, Sevareid, and Bancroft, in *Papers* (June 29, 1949), p. 5, Dulles stated: "Well, I think that the first thing you must do in Asia is to bring the peoples . . . to realize that the struggle which is on in Asia is a struggle that primarily concerns them and is not just a struggle between Soviet communism and American capitalism. If they think that is the struggle they're going to stay neutral and if they stay neutral they will not be effective participants in the effort to stop communism and without their affirmative effort it will not be stopped. If they try to be neutral they will probably themselves be overrun. They must be active participants and they must realize that 'they' are in this struggle, it is their values that are at stake."

23. Dulles address before Council on World Affairs (October 27, 1956), in *New York Times* (October 28, 1956), p. 34.

24. Crabb, *The Elephants and the Grass,* p. 195.

25. Crabb, *supra,* states that it was only in the late 1950s that American policy-makers began to accept the idea of neutralist countries being ideologically and philosophically aligned with the West, and thereby indirectly serving the interests of the West, without being politically and/or militarily aligned. However, it appears that Dulles had accepted this idea, at least partially if not all of its implications, much earlier. See Dulles address on "New Aspects of American Foreign Policy" (April 27, 1950), in *DSB,* XXII, 720; *War or Peace,* p. 18; and address before the United Nations (September 17, 1954), in *New York Times* (September 18, 1954), p. 1.

26. Northedge, *British Foreign Policy,* p. 130.   27. *Ibid.,* p. 131.

28. Hans J. Morgenthau, "Letter to the *New York Times*" (November 13, 1956), quoted in Ernest W. Lefever, *Ethics and United States Foreign Policy* (New York: Meridan, 1957), p. 3.

29. For at best judgments on abruptness, see Murphy, *Diplomat Among Warriors,* p. 377; and Bailey, *A Diplomatic History of the American People,* p. 841. For at worst judgment on supposed ideological motivation, see Herman Finer, *Dulles Over Suez: The Theory and Practice of His Diplomacy* (London: William Heinemann, 1964), pp. 45–51. It should be noted, however, that by no account does Finer's work appear as an exercise in objectivity.

30. See Hans J. Morgenthau, "The Decline and Fall of American Foreign Policy," *New Republic,* CXXXV (December 10, 1956), 11–16; (December 17, 1956), 14–18; and CXXXVI (January 7, 1957), 15–16.

31. See Eden, *Memoirs: Full Circle,* p. 420; and Harold Macmillan,

Tides of Fortune: 1945–1955 (New York: Harper & Row, 1969), pp. 635–39, 657–58.

32. Eden, *Memoirs: Full Circle*, p. 260.

33. Dulles memorandum on Near East Trip, in *Papers* (May, 1953), p. 3.

34. As Eisenhower notes in *Waging Peace*, p. 26, Washington supported and encouraged the Baghdad Pact idea. However, taking into account Dulles' conclusion in 1953 that there existed no basis for an overall defensive arrangement in the Middle East and that the U.S. should "avoid becoming fascinated with concepts that have no reality" (Dulles memorandum on Near East Trip), there is some reason to suspect that he did not share "the inspiration for the unity of the northern tier" to the extent Eden believed he did (Eden, *Memoirs: Full Circle*, p. 64).

35. Northedge, *British Foreign Policy*, pp. 129–30, to whose analysis the author is indebted for various aspects of the Baghdad Pact in this paragraph.

36. Interview with George Humphrey and Herbert Hoover, Jr., in *Oral History*, p. 35.

37. Interview with Eugene Black, in *Oral History* (July 15, 1964), p. 6.

38. Quoted in Eisenhower, *Waging Peace*, p. 31.

39. Dulles news conference (May 22, 1956), Department of State Press Release, No. 272, pp. 1, 6–7.

40. Eden, *Memoirs: Full Circle*, p. 335.

41. See Eisenhower, *Waging Peace*, p. 32; and Murphy, *Diplomat Among Warriors*, p. 378.

42. Eisenhower, *Waging Peace*, p. 31.   43. *Ibid.*, p. 32.

44. Eden, *Memoirs: Full Circle*, p. 421.   45. *Ibid.*, p. 422.

46. Quoted in Hugh Thomas, *The Suez Affair* (London: Weidenfeld & Nicolson, 1967), p. 23.

47. Eisenhower, *Waging Peace*, p. 32.

48. Murphy, *Diplomat Among Warriors*, p. 376.

49. Interview with Sir Roger Makins, in *Oral History* (June 5, 1964), pp. 5–7.

50. Murphy, *Diplomat Among Warriors*, pp. 376–77. See also Thomas, *The Suez Affair*, p. 24.

51. For text of the communiqué, see *DSB*, XXXV, 188.

52. Interview with Sir Roger Makins, in *Oral History*, p. 5.

53. Jean and Simonne Lacouture, *Egypt in Transition* (London: Methuen & Company, 1958), p. 469.

54. Quoted in Eisenhower, *Waging Peace*, p. 32.

55. See interview with Robert R. Bowie, in *Oral History*, pp. 30–31.

56. See interview with Sir Roger Makins, in *Oral History*, p. 6.

57. Dulles letter to the President (September 15, 1956), in Eisenhower, *Waging Peace*, p. 33.

58. Eden, *Memoirs: Full Circle*, p. 422.

59. Murphy, *Diplomat Among Warriors*, pp. 376–77.

60. Lacouture, *Egypt in Transition*, p. 470.

61. Dulles letter to the President, in Eisenhower, *Waging Peace*, p. 33.

62. *New York Times* (July 15, 1956), p. 2.

63. Lacouture, *Egypt in Transition*, p. 268.

64. Eden, *Memoirs: Full Circle*, p. 420.

65. Thomas, *The Suez Affair*, p. 18.   66. See *ibid.*, p. 24.

67. *New York Times* (July 22, 1956), p. 1.

68. Eden cable quoted in Murphy, *Diplomat Among Warriors*, p. 378.

69. For the accounts and quotes in this paragraph, see *ibid.*, pp. 379–82.

70. Eisenhower letter to Eden, in *Waging Peace*, pp. 664–65.

71. See Eden, *Memoirs: Full Circle*, pp. 432–33.

72. Dulles remarks at meeting of British and French Foreign Secretaries (August 1, 1956), quoted in *ibid.*, p. 437.

73. *Ibid.*

74. For these proposals of the conference, see Zinner, ed. *Documents on American Foreign Policy 1956*, pp. 305–306.

75. See Eisenhower statement (August 29, 1956), in *ibid.*

76. See letter from Nasser to the chairman of the Suez Canal Committee (Sir Robert Menzies) on September 9, 1956, in *ibid.*, pp. 317–23.

77. Eden, *Memoirs: Full Circle*, p. 460.

78. Eisenhower letter to Eden (September 2, 1956), in Eisenhower, *Waging Peace*, pp. 666–68.

79. Eden letter to Eisenhower (September 6, 1956), in Eden, *Memoirs: Full Circle*, pp. 464–67.

80. See Eisenhower letter to Eden (September 8, 1956), in Eisenhower, *Waging Peace*, pp. 669–71. Of course, and as noted by Eisenhower, his Secretary of State helped with the writing of these letters.

81. Eden, *Memoirs: Full Circle*, pp. 462, 478.

82. See Eisenhower letter to Eden (September 8, 1956), in Eisenhower, *Waging Peace*, pp. 669–71.

83. Quoted in Hugh Thomas, *The Suez Affair*, p. 82.

84. Eden, *Memoirs: Full Circle*, p. 511.

85. Dulles transcript of extemporaneous remarks before Second Suez Canal Conference in London, in *Papers* (September 19, 1956), pp. 5–6.

86. Dulles press conference remarks, quoted in Eden, *Memoirs: Full Circle*, p. 499.

87. *Ibid.*, p. 511.

88. Interview with Herman Phleger, in *Oral History* (July 21, 1964), pp. 53–54.

89. Eden, *Memoirs: Full Circle*, p. 426.

90. Winthrop W. Aldrich, "The Suez Crisis: A Footnote to History,"

Foreign Affairs, XLV (April 1967), 545. Aldrich was the U.S. Ambassador in London throughout the crisis.

91. For this discussion of the British decision and Macmillan's role, the author has borrowed from and is indebted to Richard E. Neustadt, *Alliance Politics* (New York: Columbia University Press, 1970), pp. 20–21. See also, pp. 100–103.

92. *Ibid.,* p. 23.   93. *Ibid.,* p. 24.

94. Eden letter to Eisenhower (September 6, 1956), in Eden, *Memoirs: Full Circle,* p. 465.

95. Eden telegram to Eisenhower (October 1, 1956), in *ibid.,* p. 498.

96. Dulles press conference (October 2, 1956), quoted in *ibid.,* pp. 498–99.

97. See *ibid.,* p. 464.

98. Eisenhower letter to Eden (September 8, 1956), in Eisenhower, *Waging Peace,* p. 669.

99. *Ibid.,* pp. 44, 51.

100. See Eisenhower letter to Eden (October 30, 1956), in *ibid.,* pp. 678–79.

101. Aldrich, *Foreign Affairs,* XLV, 546.

102. For text of ultimatums, see Finer, *Dulles Over Suez,* pp. 362–63.

103. See *ibid.,* p. 367.

104. Lodge statement, in *DSB,* XXXV, 748–49.

105. Eden, *Memoirs: Full Circle,* p. 528. Full letter in Eisenhower, *Waging Peace,* pp. 678–79.

106. Eden, *Memoirs: Full Circle,* p. 533.

107. Dulles statement, in *DSB,* XXXV, 751–55.

108. Interview with Abba Eban, in *Oral History* (May 28, 1964), pp. 38–39.

109. For this account, see Aldrich, *Foreign Affairs,* XLV, 550–51, quote from p. 551. After a similar incident during the Korean debates in 1953, Lodge explained to Robert Murphy that he took instructions from the President and did not "feel bound by instructions from the State Department." Murphy, *Diplomat Among Warriors,* p. 447. In his *Oral History* interview, pp. 30–31, 33, Murphy again mentions that Lodge attempted to establish another department by virtue of his position in the UN: "Sometimes it was very difficult, too. The thought that Cabot Lodge had that he didn't take instructions from the Department of State was novel." As far as Dulles was concerned, he "carefully avoided anything in the way of an emotional approach."

110. See Eisenhower memorandum (October 15, 1956), in Eisenhower, *Waging Peace,* pp. 676–77. At this stage, the U.S. was inclined to think that if Israel took action, it would be against Jordan.

111. Coral Bell, "The Diplomacy of Mr. Dulles," Canadian Institute of International Affairs' *International Journal,* XX (Winter, 1964–1965), 92.

112. *Ibid.*   113. Aldrich, *Foreign Affairs,* XLV, 552.

114. Interview with Eisenhower, in *Oral History,* p. 38.

115. Eisenhower letter to Winston Churchill (November 27, 1956), in Eisenhower, *Waging Peace,* pp. 680–81.

Chapter 12: Adjusting to the End

1. In the unraveling of events, the idea that "peaceful liberation" meant what Dulles had said was illustrated by U.S. policy toward the East German uprising of 1953 and the Hungarian revolt in 1956; the administration's decision regarding the Seventh Fleet hardly "unleashed Chiang Kai-shek" and the American Ambassador in Taipei cautioned Chiang not to read the move as a change in policy [see Karl Lott Rankin, *China Assignment* (Seattle: University of Washington Press, 1964), pp. 154–55; Morton H. Halperin and Tang Tsou, "United States Policy toward the Offshore Islands," *Public Policy,* XV (1966), 122; and Dulles memorandum on Formosa, in *Papers* (March 31, 1952), pp. 2–3]; it became clear that the "massive retaliation" posture was not an "all or nothing proposition and did not obviate the need for some flexible response capabilities; and the inherited commitment in Southeast Asia was viewed as a "limited commitment" quite different, for example, from the U.S. commitment to Europe.

2. Dulles background press conference for British correspondents, in *Papers* (March 28, 1957), pp. 20–21.

3. Dulles memorandum of conversation at the Bermuda Conference, in *Papers* (March 20, 1957), pp. 2–4.

4. Dulles press conference (January 16, 1958), quoted in Eleanor Lansing Dulles, *John Foster Dulles,* p. 45.

5. See respectively in *Papers:* Dulles telecast interview with Congressman Keating (June 15, 1958), p. 2; Dulles telecast interview with Edgar McInnis of the Canadian Institute of International Affairs (June 23, 1958), p. 6; and Dulles address before the California Chamber of Commerce (December 4, 1958), p. 7.

6. See Dulles remarks at Opening Session of the Far East Chiefs of Mission Conference in Taipei, in *Papers* (March 14, 1958).

7. Dulles press conference (September 30, 1958), in Paul E. Zinner, ed., *Documents on American Foreign Relations 1958* (New York: Harper & Row for the Council on Foreign Relations, 1959), p. 470.

8. *Ibid.,* pp. 466–67.

9. Kenneth T. Young, *Negotiating with the Chinese Communists: The United States Experience, 1953–1967* (New York: McGraw-Hill for the Council on Foreign Relations, 1968), p. 187.

10. *Ibid.*

11. Dulles notes for talks with Chiang Kak-shek, in *Papers* (October 21, 1958).

12. See extracts from Eisenhower memorandum to Secretary of State Dulles (April 5, 1955), in Eisenhower, *Mandate for Change*, pp. 611–12.

13. Dulles quoted in *ibid.*, p. 467.

14. Young, *Negotiating with the Chinese Communists*, p. 197.

15. Dulles news conference (November 26, 1958), quoted in Eleanor Lansing Dulles, *John Foster Dulles*, pp. 211–12. For the points on U.S. policy on Berlin and Germany in this paragraph, the author has borrowed from and is indebted to Eleanor Lansing Dulles' work (pp. 211–24).

16. Dulles news conference (January 13, 1959), quoted in *ibid.*, p. 224.

17. Gerson, *John Foster Dulles*, p. 309. The author has borrowed from and is indebted to Gerson's points regarding Dulles' position on nuclear testing and related developments.

18. *Ibid.* See also, Dulles statement on "Sharing Nuclear Knowledge with Our NATO Allies" before the Joint Committee on Atomic Energy's Subcommittee on Agreements for Cooperation (April 17, 1958), in *DSB*, XXXVIII, 740–42.

19. Dulles draft (August 9, 1957) of "Challenge and Response in United States Policy," in *Papers*, p. 3.

20. Almond, *The American People and Foreign Policy*, pp. xvii, 239. Defining the "instability of mass moods" as "perhaps the gravest problem confronting policy-makers," Almond notes that "even moderate fluctuations of moods may have serious consequences" for United States foreign policy.

21. See Albert Wohlstetter, "The Delicate Balance of Terror," *Foreign Affairs*, XXXVII (January 1959), 211–34.

22. Kennedy press conference (June 27, 1962), as summarized in Halperin and Tsou, *Public Policy*, XV, 128–29. It is interesting that, in this article, Halperin and Tsou (much like other observers) conclude that Kennedy "was forced to commit himself to the defense of the Islands in the face of renewed military threat" (p. 129). The impression is imparted that different sets of circumstances in the 1950s meant there were alternative policy courses which the U.S. could have followed had it not been for the "personalities" involved. In the author's view, it remains highly doubtful that there were significantly different degrees of the "force of circumstances" and, if anything, the "force of circumstances" was probably somewhat less during Kennedy's time.

23. See respectively: Dulles, *Vital Speeches of the Day*, XIV (1948), 270–73; Dulles draft (March 8, 1952) of "A Policy of Boldness," in *Papers*, p. 38; Dulles, *Foreign Affairs*, XXXVI (October 1957), 26; Dulles address

(May 30, 1951), in *DSB*, XXIV, 935; and Dulles address at International House in New York (May 16, 1950), in *DSB*, XXII, 873.

24. See "The American Churches and the International Situation," in *Papers* (December 1940), p. 6; Dulles draft (1935) of "The Road to Peace," in *Papers*, p. 1; Dulles address, in *Papers* (June 4, 1941), p. 7; and Dulles, *International Conciliation*, No. 369 (April 1941), 498.

25. Dulles news conference (September 9, 1958), quoted in Eleanor Lansing Dulles, *John Foster Dulles*, p. 173.

26. Letters from Dulles to Van S. Merle-Smith (February 28, 1922) and Henry Goddard Leach (October 15, 1924), in *Papers*.

27. Emmett J. Hughes, *The Ordeal of Power: A Political Memoir of the Eisenhower Years* (New York: Atheneum, 1963), p. 246. See also Eisenhower statement in *New York Times* (October 10, 1957), pp. 1, 14.

28. Dulles news conference (October 16, 1957), in *DSB*, XXXVII, 708.

29. See *ibid.*, pp. 708, 710.

30. Dulles, "The Relation of France to a Program of World Reconstruction," in *Papers* (1920s), p. 3.

SELECT BIBLIOGRAPHY

Papers and Unpublished Materials

Collected Papers of John Foster Dulles. Princeton, Princeton University. Collection includes addresses, statements and testimony, articles and reports, press releases, diaries and journals, news conferences and interviews, correspondence, conference dossiers and special subjects (1950–1959), and papers relating to the policies, conventions, and campaigns of the Republican party (1948–1956).

Collected Papers of H. Alexander Smith, Senator from New Jersey 1944–1959. Princeton, Princeton University.

Cross, Alan Stephen. "The Function of Theory in International Relations: A Comparative Analysis of John Foster Dulles and George Frost Kennan." Senior Thesis. Cambridge, Harvard College, 1966.

Holsti, Ole R. "Comparative 'Operational Codes' of Recent U.S. Secretaries of State: John Foster Dulles." Paper prepared for the sixty-fifth annual meeting of the American Political Science Association (September 2–6, 1969).

John Foster Dulles Oral History Project. Princeton, Princeton University. Project includes interviews with, *inter alia,* Sherman Adams, Elliott V. Bell, Eugene Black, Charles E. Bohlen, Robert Richardson Bowie, Willy Brandt, Herbert Brownell, David K. E. Bruce, General Lucius Clay, Eleanor Lansing Dulles, Abba Eban, Felix von Eckardt, General Dwight David Eisenhower, Thomas S. Gates, Ernest Gross, Christian A. Herter, Herbert Hoover, Jr., George Humphrey, Arthur Krock, Donald B. Lourie, Sir Roger Makins, Robert D. Murphy, Maurice Couve de Murville, Herman Phleger, General Matthew B. Ridgway, H. Alexander Smith, and Henry Wriston.

Leary, William M., Jr. "Smith of New Jersey: A Biography of H. Alexander Smith, United States Senator from New Jersey 1944–1959." Ph.D. Dissertation. Princeton, Princeton University, 1966.

McLellan, David S. "Comparative 'Operational Codes' of Recent U.S. Secretaries of State: Dean Acheson." Paper prepared for the sixty-fifth annual meeting of the American Political Science Association (September 2–6, 1969).

New York Election of 1949. Oral History Research Office. New York, Columbia University.

Platig, E. Raymond. "John Foster Dulles: A Study of His Political and Moral Thought Prior to 1953." Ph.D. Dissertation. Chicago, University of Chicago, 1957.

Governmental and Official Publications

United Nations. *Official Record of the General Assembly Emergency and Ordinary Meetings.* 1947–1957.

United States. *American Foreign Policy 1950–1955.* Department of State.

United States. *American Foreign Policy: Current Documents.* Department of State, 1956–1959.

United States. *Conference for the Conclusion and Signature of the Treaty of Peace with Japan: A Record of Proceedings.* Department of State, December, 1951.

United States. *Congress and the Nation 1945–1964.* Congressional Quarterly Service, 1965.

United States. *Congressional Record.* 1944–1959.

United States. *Department of State Bulletin.* 1948–1959.

United States. *Papers of the Presidents.* 1948–1959.

Documentary Collections and Reports

Documents on American Foreign Relations. New York, Harper & Row for the Council on Foreign Relations. Volume for 1952 edited by Clarence W. Baier and Richard P. Stebbins; for 1953 and 1954 edited by Peter V. Curl; for 1955, 1956, 1957, 1958, and 1959 edited by Paul E. Zinner.

Lothian, Marquess of, et. al. *The Universal Church and the World of Nations.* Volume VII of *The Official Oxford Conference Books.* Chicago, Willett, Clark & Company, 1938.

Oldham, J. H., ed. *The Churches Survey Their Task: The Report of the Conference at Oxford, July, 1937, on Church, Community and State.* London, George Allen & Unwin, 1937.

Survey of International Affairs. London, Oxford University Press for the Royal Institute of International Affairs. Volume for 1952 and 1953 by Peter Calvocoressi; for 1954 by Coral Bell; for 1955 and 1956 by Geoffrey Barraclough and R. Wall.

The Church and the International Disorder: Reports of the World Council of Churches. London, SCM Press, 1948.

The United States in World Affairs. New York, Harper & Row for the Council on Foreign Relations. Volume for 1945–1947, 1947–1948, and 1948–1949 by John C. Campbell; for 1949, 1950, 1951, 1952, 1953, and 1954 by Richard P. Stebbins; for 1955 by Hollis W. Barber; for 1956, 1957, 1958, and 1959 by Richard P. Stebbins.

Memoirs and Diaries

Acheson, Dean. *Present at the Creation: My Years in the State Department*. New York, W. W. Norton & Company, 1969.

Adams, Sherman. *Firsthand Report: The Story of the Eisenhower Administration*. New York, Harper & Row, 1961.

Baruch, Bernard. *The Making of the Reparation and Economic Sections of the Treaty*. New York, Harper & Row, 1920.

Benson, Ezra Taft. *Cross Fire: The Eight Years with Eisenhower*. New York, Doubleday & Company, 1962.

Byrnes, James F. *Speaking Frankly*. New York, Harper & Row, 1947.

Eden, Sir Anthony. *Memoirs: Full Circle*. London, Cassell & Company, 1960.

Eisenhower, Dwight D. *Mandate for Change: The White House Years 1953–1956*. London, William Heinemann, 1963.

Eisenhower, Dwight D. *Waging Peace: The White House Years 1956–1961*. London, William Heinemann, 1966.

Foster, John Watson. *Diplomatic Memoirs*. 2 vols. London, Constable & Company, 1909.

House, Edward Mandell, and Charles Seymour, eds. *What Really Happened at Paris: The Story of the Peace Conference 1918–1919*. London, Hodder & Stoughton, 1921.

Hughes, Emmet J. *The Ordeal of Power: A Political Memoir of the Eisenhower Years*. New York, Atheneum, 1963.

Hull, Cordell. *Memoirs*. 2 vols. London, Hodder & Stoughton, 1948.

Kennan, George F. *Memoirs: 1925–1950*. Boston, Little, Brown & Company, 1967.

Lansing, Robert. *The Peace Negotiations: A Personal Narrative*. New York, Houghton Mifflin Company, 1921.

Lansing, Robert. *War Memoirs*. London, Rich & Cowan, 1935.

Macmillan, Harold. *Tides of Fortune: 1945–1955*. New York, Harper & Row, 1969.

Millis, Walter, ed. *The Forrestal Diaries*. New York, Viking Press, 1951.

Murphy, Robert. *Diplomat Among Warriors*. New York, Doubleday & Company, 1964.

Nixon, Richard. *Six Crises*. New York, Doubleday & Company, 1962.

Talbott, Strobe, ed. *Khrushchev Remembers*. Boston, Little, Brown & Company, 1970.

Truman, Harry S. *Memoirs: Years of Decision.* New York, Doubleday & Company, 1955.

Truman, Harry S. *Memoirs: Years of Trial and Hope.* New York, Doubleday & Company, 1956.

Vandenberg, Arthur H., Jr., ed. *The Private Papers of Senator Vandenberg.* Boston, Houghton Mifflin, 1952.

Warburg, Max M. *Aus meinen Aufzeichnungen.* Glueckstadt, 1952.

Welles, Sumner. *The Time for Decision.* New York, Harper & Row, 1944.

Welles, Sumner. *Where Are We Heading?* New York, Harper & Row, 1946.

Yoshida, Shigeru. *The Yoshida Memoirs: The Story of Japan in Crisis.* Translated by Kenichi Yoshida. Boston, Houghton Mifflin, 1962.

General Books

Adler, Selig. *The Isolationist Impulse: Its Twentieth-Century Reaction.* London, Abelard-Schuman, 1957.

Almond, Gabriel A. *The American People and Foreign Policy.* New York, Frederick A. Praeger, 1960.

Aron, Raymond. *The Century of Total War.* New York, Doubleday & Company, 1954.

Bailey, Thomas A. *A Diplomatic History of the American People.* New York, F. S. Crofts & Company, 1940.

Bator, Victor. *Vietnam: A Diplomatic Tragedy.* New York, Oceana Publications, 1965.

Beard, Charles Austin. *The Devil Theory of War: An Inquiry into the Nature of History and the Possibility of Keeping Out of War.* New York, Vanguard Press, 1936.

Beaufre, André. *Suez Expedition: 1956.* New York, Frederick A. Praeger, 1970.

Bell, Coral. *Negotiation from Strength: A Study in the Politics of Power.* London, Chatto & Windus, 1962.

Bell, Coral. *The Debatable Alliance: An Essay in Anglo-American Relations.* London, Oxford University Press, 1964.

Bell, Daniel, ed. *The Radical Right.* New York, Doubleday Anchor, 1964.

Beloff, Max. *Foreign Policy and the Democratic Process.* Baltimore, Johns Hopkins Press, 1955.

Bemis, Samuel Flagg, ed. *The American Secretaries of State.* Vol. VIII of "John Watson Foster" by William Castle, Jr. New York, Alfred A. Knopf, 1928.

Bentwick, Norman. *The Religious Foundations of Internationalism.* London, George Allen & Unwin, 1933.

Boorstin, Daniel J. *The Genius of American Politics.* Chicago, University of Chicago Press, 1953.

Brodie, Bernard. *Strategy in the Missile Age*. Princeton, Princeton University Press, 1959.

Brown, Seyom. *The Faces of Power: Constancy and Change in United States Foreign Policy from Truman to Johnson*. New York and London, Columbia University Press, 1968.

Buckley, William F., Jr., and L. Brent Bozell. *McCarthy and His Enemies: The Record and Its Meaning*. Chicago, Henry Regnery Company, 1954.

Bundy, McGeorge, ed. *The Pattern of Responsibility: The Record of Secretary of State Dean Acheson*. Boston, Houghton Mifflin, 1952.

Burnett, Philip Mason. *Reparation at the Paris Peace Conference: From the Standpoint of the American Delegation*. 2 vols., New York, Columbia University Press, 1940.

Butterfield, Herbert. *Christianity, Diplomacy and War*. London, Wyvern Books, 1962.

Carr, Edward Hallett. *The Twenty Years' Crisis 1919–1939*. London, Macmillan Company, 1962.

Churchill, Randolph S. *The Rise and Fall of Sir Anthony Eden*. London, MacGibbon & Kee, 1959.

Cohen, Bernard C. *The Political Process and Foreign Policy: The Making of the Japanese Peace Settlement*. Princeton, Princeton University Press, 1957.

Cook, Thomas I., and Malcolm Moos. *Power Through Purpose: The Realism of Idealism as a Basis for Foreign Policy*. Baltimore, Johns Hopkins Press, 1954.

Crabb, Cecil Van Meter, Jr. *American Foreign Policy in the Nuclear Age: Principles, Problems and Prospects*. 2d. ed. New York, Harper & Row, 1965.

Crabb, Cecil Van Meter, Jr. *Bipartisan Foreign Policy: Myth or Reality*. Evanston, Row, Peterson & Company, 1957.

Crabb, Cecil Van Meter, Jr. *The Elephants and the Grass: A Study of Non-Alignment*. New York, Frederick A. Praeger, 1965.

Dahl, Robert A. *Congress and Foreign Policy*. New York, Harcourt Brace Jovanovich, 1950.

DeConde, Alexander. *The American Secretary of State: An Interpretation*. New York, Frederick A. Praeger, 1962.

Donelan, Michael. *The Ideas of American Foreign Policy*. London, Chapman & Hall, 1963.

Donovan, Robert J. *Eisenhower: The Inside Story*. New York, Harper & Row, 1956.

Dulles, Allen Macy. *The True Church: A Historical and Scriptural Study*. New York, Fleming H. Revell Company, 1907.

Dulles, Allen W., and Hamilton Fish Armstrong. *Can We Be Neutral?* 2d. ed. New York, Harper & Row, 1936.

Dunn, Frederick Sherwood. *Peaceful Change: A Study of International Procedures.* New York, Council on Foreign Relations, 1937.

Dunn, Frederick Sherwood. *Peace-Making and Settlement with Japan.* Princeton, Princeton University Press, 1963.

Ferrell, Robert H. *American Diplomacy in the Great Depression: Hoover-Stimson Foreign Policy 1929–1933.* New Haven, Yale University Press, 1957.

Finer, Herman. *Dulles Over Suez: The Theory and Practice of His Diplomacy.* London, William Heinemann, 1964.

Freymond, Jacques. *Western Europe Since the War: A Short Political History.* New York, Frederick A. Praeger, 1964.

Fulbright, J. W. *Old Myths and New Realities.* London, Jonathan Cape, 1965.

Gardner, Brian. *The Wasted Hour: The Tragedy of 1945.* London, Cassell & Company, 1963.

Glueck, Sheldon, ed. *The Welfare State and the National Welfare: A Symposium of Some of the Threatening Tendencies of Our Times.* Cambridge, Addison-Wesley Press, 1952.

Graebner, Norman A., *The New Isolationism: A Study in Politics and Foreign Policy Since 1950.* New York, Ronald Press Company, 1956.

Graebner, Norman A., ed. *An Uncertain Tradition: American Secretaries of State in the Twentieth Century.* New York, McGraw-Hill, 1961.

Graebner, Norman A., ed. *Ideas and Diplomacy: Readings in the Intellectual Tradition of American Foreign Policy.* New York, Oxford University Press, 1964.

Halle, Louis J. *American Foreign Policy: Theory and Reality.* London, George Allen & Unwin, 1960.

Halperin, Morton H. *Contemporary Military Strategy.* Boston, Little, Brown & Company, 1967.

Herberg, Will. *Protestant—Catholic—Jew: An Essay in American Religious Sociology.* New York, Doubleday & Company, 1955.

Hertz, Frederick. *Nationality in History and Politics: A Study of the Psychology and Sociology of National Sentiment and Character.* London, Kegan Paul, Trench, Trubner & Company, 1944.

Herz, John H. *International Politics in the Atomic Age.* New York, Columbia University Press, 1959.

Herz, John H. *Political Realism and Political Idealism: A Study in Theories and Realities.* Chicago, University of Chicago Press, 1951.

Hofstadter, Richard. *Social Darwinism in American Thought.* Philadelphia, University of Pennsylvania Press, 1944.

James, Henry, ed. *Letters of William James.* 2 vols. Boston, Atlantic Monthly Press, 1920.

James, William. *Memories and Studies.* New York, Longmans, Green & Company, 1912.

James, William. *The Meaning of Truth: A Sequel to 'Pragmatism'*. New York, Longmans, Green & Company, 1910.

James, William. *The Will to Believe and Other Essays in Popular Philosophy*. New York, Longmans, Green & Company, 1897.

Jowitt, The Earl. *The Strange Case of Alger Hiss*. New York, Doubleday & Company, 1953.

Kennan, George F. *American Diplomacy 1900–1950*. London, Secker & Warburg, 1952.

Kennan, George F. *Realities of American Foreign Policy*. Princeton, Princeton University Press, 1954.

Kissinger, Henry A. *The Necessity for Choice*. New York, Harper & Row, 1960.

Kissinger, Henry A. *The Troubled Partnership: A Re-Appraisal of the Atlantic Alliance*. New York, McGraw-Hill, 1965.

Kennedy, John F. *The Strategy of Peace*. London, Hamish Hamilton, 1960.

Keynes, John Maynard. *A Revision of the Treaty*. London, Macmillan Company, 1922.

Lacouture, Jean and Simonne. *Egypt in Transition*. London, Methuen & Company, 1958.

Lefever, Ernest W. *Ethics and United States Foreign Policy*. New York, Meridan Books, 1957.

Lubell, Samuel. *Revolt of the Moderates*. New York, Harper & Row, 1956.

Merriam, Charles Edward and Harold Foote Gosnell. *The American Party System*. Rev. ed. New York, Macmillan Company, 1930.

Morgenthau, Hans J. *American Foreign Policy: A Critical Examination*. London, Methuen & Company, 1952. Published in the United States (1951) under the title *In Defense of the National Interest: A Critical Examination of the American Foreign Policy*.

Morgenthau, Hans J. *Politics Among Nations: The Struggle for Power and Peace*. 3d ed. New York, Alfred A. Knopf, 1963.

Neustadt, Richard E. *Alliance Politics*. New York and London, Columbia University Press, 1970.

Neustadt, Richard E. *Presidential Power: The Politics of Leadership*. New York, John Wiley & Sons, 1960.

Nicholas, Herbert. *Britain and the U.S.A.* Baltimore, Johns Hopkins Press, 1963.

Niebuhr, H. Richard. *The Kingdom of God in America*. New York, Harper & Row, 1937.

Niebuhr, Reinhold. *Christian Realism and Political Problems*. New York, Charles Scribner's Sons, 1953.

Niebuhr, Reinhold. *Moral Man and Immoral Society: A Study in Ethics and Politics*. New York, Charles Scribner's Sons, 1960.

Niebuhr, Reinhold. *The Irony of American History.* New York, Charles Scribner's Sons, 1952.

Northedge, F. S. *British Foreign Policy: The Process of Readjustment 1945–1961.* London, George Allen & Unwin, 1962.

Northedge, F. S. *The Troubled Giant: Britain Among the Great Powers 1916–1939.* London, G. Bell & Sons, 1966.

Nutting, Anthony. *I Saw for Myself: The Aftermath of Suez.* New York, Doubleday & Company, 1958.

Ormond, Alexander Thomas. *Concepts of Philosophy.* New York, Macmillan Company, 1906.

Ortega y Gasset. *The Dehumanization of Art and Other Writings on Art and Culture.* New York, Doubleday & Company, 1956.

Osgood, Robert E. *Ideals and Self-Interest in America's Foreign Relations.* Chicago, University of Chicago Press, 1953.

Perkins, Dexter. *The American Approach to Foreign Policy.* Cambridge, Harvard University Press, 1962.

Perry, Ralph Barton. *Puritanism and Democracy.* New York, Vanguard Press, 1944.

Peters, Paul. *Massive Retaliation: The Policy and Its Critics.* Chicago, Henry Regnery Company, 1959.

Pusey, Merlo J. *Eisenhower the President.* New York, Macmillan Company, 1956.

Ridgway, General Matthew B. *The Korean War.* New York, Doubleday & Company, 1967.

Riley, Isaac Woodbridge. *American Philosophy: The Early Schools.* New York, Dodd, Mead & Company, 1907.

Rovere, Richard H. *Affairs of State: The Eisenhower Years.* New York, Farrar, Straus & Giroux, 1956.

Rovere, Richard H. *Senator Joe McCarthy.* New York, Harcourt Brace Jovanovich, 1959.

Sapin, Burton M. *The Making of United States Foreign Policy.* New York, Frederick A. Praeger, 1966.

Schelling, Thomas C. *Arms and Influence.* New Haven, Yale University Press, 1966.

Schelling, Thomas C. *The Strategy of Conflict.* Cambridge, Harvard University Press, 1963.

Schlesinger, Arthur M., Jr. *The Bitter Heritage: Vietnam and American Democracy 1941–1966.* London, André Deutsch, 1967.

Seabury, Paul. *Power, Freedom and Diplomacy: The Foreign Policy of the United States.* New York, Random House, 1963.

Spanier, John W. *American Foreign Policy Since World War II.* Rev. ed. New York, Frederick A. Praeger, 1962.

Stevenson, Adlai. *Major Campaign Speeches of Adlai E. Stevenson, 1952.* New York, Random House, 1953.

Taft, Robert A. *A Foreign Policy for Americans*. New York, Doubleday & Company, 1951.

Tardieu, André. *The Truth about the Treaty*. Indianapolis, Bobbs-Merrill Company, 1921.

Thomas, Hugh. *The Suez Affair*. London, Weidenfeld & Nicolson, 1967.

Thompson, Kenneth W. *American Diplomacy and Emergent Patterns*. New York, New York University Press, 1962.

Thompson, Kenneth W. *Political Realism and the Crisis of World Politics: An American Approach to Foreign Policy*. Princeton, Princeton University Press, 1960.

Toynbee, Arnold J. *Civilization on Trial*. New York, Oxford University Press, 1948.

Twining, General Nathan F. *Neither Liberty Nor Safety: A Hard Look at U.S. Political and Military Strategy*. New York, Holt, Rinehart & Winston, 1966.

Waltz, Kenneth Neal. *Man, the State and War*. New York, Columbia University Press, 1959.

Warburg, James P. *Faith, Purpose and Power: A Plea for a Positive Policy*. New York, Farrar, Straus & Giroux, 1950.

Warburg, James P. *Our War and Our Peace*. New York, Farrar, Straus & Giroux, 1941.

Warburg, James P. *The United States in a Changing World* New York, G. P. Putnam's Sons, 1954.

White, William S. *The Taft Story*. New York, Harper & Row, 1954.

Woodhouse, C. M. *British Foreign Policy Since the Second World War*. New York, Frederick A. Praeger, 1962.

Wriston, Henry M. *Diplomacy in a Democracy*. New York, Harper & Row, 1956.

Young, Kenneth T. *Negotiating with the Chinese Communist: The United States Experience, 1953–1967*. New York, McGraw-Hill, 1968.

Books on Dulles

Beal, John Robinson. *John Foster Dulles*. New York, Harper & Row, 1959.

Berding, Andrew H. *Dulles on Diplomacy*. Princeton, D. Van Nostrand Company, 1965.

Comfort, Mildred Houghton. *John Foster Dulles: Peacemaker*. Minneapolis, T. S. Denison & Company, 1960.

Drummond, Roscoe and Gaston Coblentz. *Duel at the Brink: John Foster Dulles' Command of American Power*. London, Weidenfeld & Nicolson, 1960.

Dulles, Eleanor Lansing. *John Foster Dulles: The Last Year*. New York, Harcourt Brace Jovanovich, 1963.

Dulles, Allen W. "The Cost of Peace," *Foreign Affairs*, XII (July 1934), 567–78.

Dulles, Eleanor Lansing. "Time and Decisions," *Foreign Military Commitments: The Forensic Quarterly*, XLIII (August 1969), 277–85.

George, Alexander L. "The 'Operational Code': A Neglected Approach to the Study of Political Leaders and Decision-Making," RAND Corporation, RM-5427-PR (September 1967).

Halle, Louis J. "The World of George Kennan," *The New Republic*, CXLV (August 7, 1961), 21–23.

Halle, Louis J. Review of *John Foster Dulles: A Reappraisal*, by Richard Goold-Adams, *The New Republic*, CXLVII (December 8, 1962), 17–18+.

Halperin, Morton H., and Tang Tsou. "United States Policy toward the Offshore Islands," *Public Policy*, XV (1966), 119–38.

Hughes, Emmet J. "The Chance for Peace in 1955," *Life*, XXXVIII (May 30, 1955), 19–23.

Kennan, George F. "America and the Russian Future," *Foreign Affairs*, XXIX (April 1951), 351–70.

Kennan, George F. "Disengagement Revisited," *Foreign Affairs*, XXXVII (January 1959), 187–210.

Kennan, George F. "Let Peace Not Die of Neglect," *New York Times Magazine* (February 25, 1951), 10+.

Kennan, George F. "Overdue Changes in Our Foreign Policy," *Harper's*, CCXIII (August 1956), 27–33.

Kennan, George F. "Peaceful Coexistence," *Foreign Affairs*, XXXVII (January 1960), 171–90.

Kennan, George F. "The Future of Our Professional Diplomacy," *Foreign Affairs*, XXXIII (July 1955), 566–86.

Kennan, George F. "The Illusion of Security," *The Atlantic Monthly*, CXCIV (August 1954), 31–34.

Kennan, George F. "The Sources of Soviet Conduct," *Foreign Affairs*, XXV (July 1947), 566–82.

Kennedy, John F. "A Democrat Looks at Foreign Policy," *Foreign Affairs*, XXXVI (October 1957), 44–59.

Kissinger, Henry A. "Limitations of Diplomacy," *The New Republic*, CXXXII (May 9, 1955), 7–8.

Kissinger, Henry A. "Military Policy and Defense of the 'Grey Areas,'" *Foreign Affairs*, XXXIII (April 1955), 416–28.

Kissinger, Henry A. "Missiles and the Western Alliance," *Foreign Affairs*, XXXVI (April 1958), 383–400.

Kissinger, Henry A. "Reflections on American Diplomacy," *Foreign Affairs*, XXXV (October 1956), 37–56.

Morgenthau, Hans J. "Critical Look at the New Neutralism," *New York Times Magazine* (August 27, 1961), 25, 76–77.

Morgenthau, Hans J. "Immaturity of Our Asian Policy," *The New Republic,* CXXXIV (March 12, 1956), 20–22; (March 19, 1956), 14–16; (March 26, 1956), 13–15; (April 16, 1956), 14–16.

Morgenthau, Hans J. "Impact of the Loyalty-Security Measures on the State Department," *Bulletin of the Atomic Scientists,* II (April 1955), 134–40.

Morgenthau, Hans J. "Instant Retaliation: Will It Deter Aggression?," *The New Republic,* CXXX (March 29, 1954), 11–14+.

Morgenthau, Hans J. "The Decline and Fall of American Foreign Policy," *The New Republic,* CXXXV (December 10, 1956), 11–16; (December 17, 1956), 14–18; CXXXVI (January 7, 1957), 15–17.

Morgenthau, Hans J. "To Intervene or Not to Intervene," *Foreign Affairs,* XLV (April 1967), 425–36.

Morgenthau, Hans J. "Yardstick of National Interest," *Annals of the American Academy of Political and Social Science,* CCXCVI (November 1954), 77–84.

Moskin, Robert. "Our Foreign Policy is Paralyzed," *Look,* XXVII (November 19, 1963), 25–27.

Murphy, Robert. "Interrelationship of Military Power and Foreign Policy," *DSB,* XXXI (August 30, 1954), 291–94.

Murphy, Robert. "United States and the Uncommitted World," *DSB,* XXXI (July 5, 1954), 3–6.

New York Times. 1945–1959.

Platig, E. Raymond. "The 'New Look' Raises Old Problems," *The Review of Politics,* XVII (January 1955), 111–35.

Remak, J. Review of *John Foster Dulles: A Reappraisal,* by Richard Goold-Adams, *Saturday Review,* XLV (November 17, 1962), 27.

Reston, James. "Prospects for Stability in Our Foreign Policy," *Foreign Affairs,* XXVII (October 1948), 34–43.

Shulman, Marshall D. " 'Europe' versus 'Detente'?," *Foreign Affairs,* XLV (April 1967), 389–402.

Thompson, Kenneth W. "The Limits of Principle in International Politics: Necessity and the New Balance of Power," *The Journal of Politics,* XX (August 1958), 437–67.

Time. 1952–1959.

The Times (London). 1952–1959.

Wohlstetter, Albert. "The Delicate Balance of Terror," *Foreign Affairs,* XXXVII (January 1959), 211–34.

Wright, Quincy. "Realism and Idealism in International Politics," *World Politics,* V (October 1952), 118–26.

Wriston, Henry M. "Young Men and the Foreign Service," *Foreign Affairs,* XXXIII (October 1954), 28–42.

Yoshida, Shigeru. "Japan and the Crisis in Asia," *Foreign Affairs,* XXIX (January 1951), 171–81.

Articles on Dulles

Bennett, J. C., et. al. "Concerning Mr. Dulles," *The Christian Century,* LIX (October 25, 1944), 1231.

Berle, A. A. "Secretary in Search of a Foreign Policy," *The Reporter,* IX (July 7, 1953), 8–11.

"Candidacy for the Senate," *Nation,* CLXIX (September 17, 1949), 261.

Challener, Richard D., and J. Fenton, eds. "Which Way America? Dulles Always Knew," *American Heritage,* XXII (June 1971), 12–13 +.

Chamberlain, John. "John Foster Dulles: A Wilsonian at Versailles, This Famous Lawyer May Be Dewey's Secretary of State," *Life,* XVII (August 21, 1944), 84–86 +.

"Containment and Liberation," *Commonweal,* LVII (February 6, 1953), 442.

Davis, Forrest. "The G. O. P.'s Mr. Hull," *Saturday Evening Post,* CCXVII (September 9, 1944), 24–25 +; (September 16, 1944), 20 +.

"Dulles as Demagogue," *Nation,* CLXIX (October 15, 1949), 361.

"Dulles in the Gutter," *The New Republic,* CXXI (October 24, 1949), 6.

Egan, L. "Practical Men Around Thomas E. Dewey," *New York Times Magazine* (September 12, 1948), 10–11 +.

Harsch, Joseph C. "John Foster Dulles: A Very Complicated Man," *Harper's,* CCXIII (September 1956), 27–34.

Hatch, A. "Men Around Dewey," *Harper's,* CXCVII (October 1948), 38–46.

"Hitler's Backers, U.S. Bankers, and Mr. Dewey's Mr. Dulles," *In Fact,* X (October 30, 1944), 1–2.

Ickes, Harold L. "Dulles the Indispensable," *The New Republic,* CXXII (May 1, 1950), 16.

Ickes, Harold L. "Enough of Dulles," *The New Republic,* CXXII (January 16, 1950), 30.

Ickes, Harold L. "Looking Forward Backwards," *The New Republic,* CXXI (November 21, 1949), 16.

"In Justice to Mr. Dulles," *The New Republic,* CXIII (November 20, 1944), 647.

Jenner, William E. "America's Case Against Secretary Dulles," *American Mercury,* LXXXII (April 1956), 63–75.

"John Foster Dulles," *The Christian Century,* LXI (October 25, 1944), 1224–25.

Kohn, Hans. Review of *War or Peace,* by John Foster Dulles, *The Survey,* LXXXVI (June 1950), 333–34.

Kuhn, Arthur K. Review of *War, Peace and Change,* by John Foster Dulles, *The American Journal of International Law,* XXXIII (July 1939), 631.

Lerner, Max. "The World of John Foster Dulles," *The New Republic*, CXXII (May 15, 1950), 18–19.

Miller, William Lee. "The Moral Force Behind Dulles' Diplomacy," *The Reporter*, XV (August 9, 1956), 17–20.

"Mr. Dulles Approves Yalta Formula," *The Christian Century*, LXII (March 21, 1945), 357.

"Mr. Dulles' Record as Tough Negotiator with Business Outlook," *U.S. News and World Report*, XXV (August 20, 1948), 36–37.

"Mr. Hull and Mr. Dulles," *Time*, XLIV (September 4, 1944), 22.

Morgenthau, Hans J. "John Foster Dulles," in Norman A. Graebner, ed., *An Uncertain Tradition: American Secretaries of State in the Twentieth Century*.

Niebuhr, Reinhold. "The Moral World of Foster Dulles," *The New Republic*, CXXXIX (December 1, 1958), 8.

"Objection: Indefensible Tactic Against a Lawyer," *Commonweal*, XL (October 13, 1944), 604.

"On Mr. Dulles and What To Do About Him," *Soviet Russia Today*, XV (July 1946), 6–7.

Osborne, John. "Statesman on the Stump," *Life*, XVII (October 31, 1949), 72–74.

"Pepper Links Dulles to Nazis," *In Fact*, XIV (March 24, 1947), 1–3.

"Pro-Nazi Ties of Marshall's Adviser," *In Fact*, XVI (December 8, 1947), 3–4.

"Reluctant Internationalists," *Commonweal*, LVII (January 16, 1953), 367.

Reston, James B. "Dulles and History," *Foreign Policy Association Bulletin*, XXXVIII (July 1, 1959), 156+.

Reston, James B. "John Foster Dulles and His Foreign Policy," *Life*, XXV (October 4, 1948), 130–32+.

"Schroeder Scandal," *In Fact*, XVII (March 22, 1948), 3.

Shepley, James. "How Dulles Averted War," *Life*, XL (January 16, 1956), 70–72+.

"The Suppressed Dulles Story," *In Fact*, XX (October 24, 1949), 3–4.

"U.S. Money Behind German Revival," *In Fact*, XV (August 18, 1947), 1–3.

Vayo, J. Alvarez del. "Vishinsky versus Dulles," *Nation*, CLXXI (October 21, 1950), 357–58.

"Vishinsky Wasn't First," *New Masses*, LXV (October 14, 1947), 3–5.

"Will Democrats Center Fire on Dulles?," *The Christian Century*, LXI (September 27, 1944), 1091.

Articles and Speeches by Dulles

[Arranged in chronological order. The list does not include the numerous speeches, press conferences, and remarks of Dulles in the *Department of State*

Bulletin (DSB) or Press Releases by the Department of State, but does include those cited or quoted.]

Dulles, John Foster. "The Indemnity Terms: Justification of Allied Demands: A Reply to Mr. Keynes," Letter to *The Times* (February 16, 1920), 10.

———. "Reparation Problem," *The New Republic,* XXVI (March 30, 1921), 133–35.

———. "The Reparation Problem," *Foreign Policy Association Bulletin,* II (June 1921), 1–4.

———. "Allied Indebtedness to the United States," *Annals of the American Academy of Political and Social Science,* XCVI (July 1921), 173–77.

———. "The Allied Debts," *Foreign Affairs,* I (September 1922), 117–32.

———. "The Dawes Report and the Peace of Europe," *The Independent,* CXII (April 26, 1924), 218+.

———. "Our Foreign Loan Policy," *Foreign Affairs,* V (October 1926), 33–48.

———. "Conceptions and Misconceptions Regarding Intervention," *Annals of the American Academy of Political and Social Science,* CXLIV (July 1929), 102–104.

———. "Should Economic Sanctions be Applied in International Disputes?," *Annals of the American Academy of Political and Social Science,* CLXII (July 1932), 103–108.

———. "Hungary: Report of Mr. Dulles to the Committee on Hungarian Long-Term Debt," *Institute of International Finance Bulletin,* No. 61 (March 1, 1933), 15–19.

———. "The Securities Act and Foreign Lending," *Foreign Affairs,* XII (October 1933), 33–45.

———. "The Road to Peace," *The Atlantic Monthly,* CLVI (October 1935), 492–99.

———. "The Problem of Peace in a Dynamic World," *Religion in Life,* VI (Spring 1937), 191–207.

———. "As Seen by a Layman," *Religion in Life,* VII (Winter 1938), 36–44.

———. "Administrative Law: A Practical Attitude for Lawyers," *American Bar Association Journal,* XXV (April 1939), 275+.

———. "The Church's Contribution toward a Warless World," *Religion in Life,* IX (Winter 1940), 31–40.

———. "The Church's Role in Developing the Basis for a Just and Durable Peace," in *When Hostilities Cease: Addresses and Findings of the Exploratory Conference on the Bases of a Just and Enduring Peace.* Chicago, Methodist Church Commission on World Peace, 1941.

———. "Peaceful Change," *International Conciliation,* No. 369 (April 1941), 493–98.

Dulles, John Foster. "The Aftermath of the World War," *International Conciliation*, No. 369 (April 1941), 265–71.

———. "The Effect in Practice of the Report on Administrative Procedure," *Columbia Law Review*, XLI (April 1941), 617–27.

———. "Toward World Order," in *A Basis for the Peace to Come: The Merrick-McDowell Lectures for 1942*. New York, Abingdon-Cokesbury Press, 1942, 31–57.

———. "Peace Without Platitudes," *Fortune*, XXV (January 1942), 42–43+.

———. "A Righteous Faith," *Life*, XIII (December 28, 1942), 49–51.

———. "Six Pillars of Peace," *Vital Speeches of the Day*, IX (April 15, 1943), 405–407.

———. "Ideals are not Enough," *International Conciliation*, No. 409 (March 1945), 131–41.

———. "Statement of Political Propositions which Underlie a Just and Durable Peace," *International Conciliation*, No. 409 (March 1945), 170–77.

———. "Beyond Our Expectations," *Time*, XLVI (July 2, 1945), 21.

———. "Peace is Precarious: Can We Keep It?," *New York Times Magazine* (August 19, 1945), 12+.

———. "The General Assembly," *Foreign Affairs*, XXIV (October 1945), 1–11.

———. "Our Vital Peace Decision," *Vital Speeches of the Day*, XII (October 15, 1945), 7–8.

———. "The Churches and World Order," *Life*, XX (March 18, 1946), 34.

———. "Drifting into a New Dark Ages?," *U.S. News and World Report*, XX (March 29, 1946), 27.

———. "A First Balance Sheet of the United Nations," *International Conciliation*, No. 420 (April 1946), 177–82.

———. "Thoughts on Soviet Foreign Policy and What to do About It," *Life*, XX (June 3, 1946), 112–18+; (June 10, 1946), 118–20+.

———. "State Control versus Self-Control," *Vital Speeches of the Day*, XII (July 15, 1946), 593–95.

———. "Europe Must Federate or Perish," *Vital Speeches of the Day*, XIII (February 1, 1947), 234–36.

———. "Report on Moscow Meeting of Council of Foreign Ministers," *International Conciliation*, No. 432 (June 1947), 449–59.

———. "What Shall We do with the U.N.?," *The Christian Century*, LXIV (September 3, 1947), 1041–42.

———. "Free State versus the Police State," *Vital Speeches of the Day*, XIII (September 15, 1947), 719–20.

———. "The Christian Citizen in a Changing World," in *The Church and the International Disorder: Reports of the World Council of Churches.* London, SCM Press, 1948, 73–114.

———. "Not War, Not Peace," *Vital Speeches of the Day,* XIV (February 15, 1948), 270–73.

———. "Can We Guarantee a Free Europe?," *Collier's,* CXXI (June 12, 1948), 20+.

———. "The Meaning of Freedom," *Vital Speeches of the Day,* XIV (July 15, 1948), 581–83.

———. "Peace with Russia," *The Christian Century,* LXV (August 25, 1948), 849–51.

›———. "Moral Force in World Affairs," *Readers' Digest,* LIII (August 1948), 105–108.

———. "Moral Leadership," *Vital Speeches of the Day,* XIV (September 15, 1948), 706–708.

———. "What the U.N. Is and Might Be," *New York Times Magazine* (October 24, 1948), 10+.

———. "Discussion of Greek Problem," statement before Committee I of the U.N. (October 26, 1948), *DSB* XIX (November 14, 1948), 607–13.

———. "The Future of the United Nations," *International Conciliation,* No. 445 (November 1948), 579–90.

———. "U.S. and Russia Could Agree," *U.S. News and World Report,* XXVI (January 21, 1949), 32–36.

———. "What I've Learned About the Russians," *Collier's,* CXXIII (March 12, 1949), 25+.

———. "Reputation and Performance in World Affairs," *Vital Speeches of the Day,* XV (May 15, 1949), 465–68.

———. "Improving Relations with Russia," *U.S. News and World Report,* XXVII (July 8, 1949), 30–33.

———. "North Atlantic Pact," *Vital Speeches of the Day,* XV (August 1, 1949), 617–24.

———. "The Blessings of Liberty," *Vital Speeches of the Day,* XVI (February 1, 1950), 231–36.

———. "How to Take the Offensive for Peace," *Life,* XXVIII (April 24, 1950), 120–22+.

———. "New Aspects of American Foreign Policy," address before American Society of International Law (April 27, 1950), *DSB,* XXII (May 8, 1950), 717–20.

———. "A Policy for Peace Insurance," address at International House (May 16, 1950), *DSB,* XXII (May 29, 1950), 862+.

———. "The Korean Experiment in Representative Government," address before the National Assembly of the Republic of Korea (June 19, 1950), *DSB,* XXIII (July 3, 1950), 12–13.

Dulles, John Foster. "The Interdependence of Independence," address at Sesquicentennial Fourth of July Celebration, *DSB*, XXIII (July 17, 1950), 91–92.

———. "To Save Humanity from the Deep Abyss," *New York Times Magazine* (July 30, 1950), 5, 34–35.

———. "Korean Attack Opens New Chapter in History," address before Commonwealth Club (July 31, 1950), *DSB*, XXIII (August 7, 1950), 207–10.

———. "Uniting for Peace," statement before Committee I (October 9, 1950), *DSB*, XXIII (October 23, 1950), 651–55.

———. "U.S. Unopposed to U.S.S.R. on Peace Observation Commission," statement before Committee I (October 19, 1950), *DSB*, XXIII (November 6, 1950), 752–53.

———. "Door to Peace," *Vital Speeches of the Day*, XVII (November 1, 1950), 39–42.

———. "Where Are We? A Five-Year Record of America's Response to the Challenge of Communism," address before the American Association for the United Nations (December 29, 1950), *DSB*, XXIV (January 15, 1951), 85–89.

———. "Peace May be Won," address before American-Japan Society (February 2, 1951), *DSB*, XXIV (February 12, 1951), 252–55.

———. "Essentials of Peace with Japan," address at Whittier College (March 31, 1951), *DSB*, XXIV (April 9, 1951), 576–80.

———. "Peace without Fear," address before United Nations Association of Japan (April 23, 1951), *DSB* (May 7, 1951), 726–31.

———. "What will Happen now in Japan," *U.S. News and World Report*, XXX (April 27, 1951), 30–34.

———. "The Challenge of Today," address at University of Arizona (May 30, 1951), *DSB* (June 11, 1951), XXIV, 935–37.

———. "Japan's Future," *Newsweek*, XXXVIII (September 10, 1951), 31–32 +.

———. "How the Peace was Made," *Life*, XXXI (September 17, 1951), 32–33.

———. "Can We Stop Russian Imperialism?," excerpts from address before Advertising Council at Detroit (November 27, 1951), *DSB*, XXV (December 10, 1951), 938–41.

———. "Security in the Pacific," *Foreign Affairs*, XXX (January 1952), 175–87.

———. Statement before Senate Foreign Relations Committee (January 21, 1952), *DSB*, XXVI (February 4, 1952), 186–90.

———. Transcript of "Meet the Press," NBC Television (February 10, 1952).

———. "Importance of Initiative in International Affairs," *Vital Speeches of the Day*, XVIII (March 15, 1952), 333–35.

———. "A Policy of Boldness," *Life*, XXXII (May 19, 1952), 146–60.

————. "Danger in Our Defensive Mood," *Newsweek*, XXXIX (May 26, 1952), 39.

————. "Far Eastern Problems," *Vital Speeches of the Day*, XVIII (June 1, 1952), 493–95.

————. "Foreign Policy in the Presidential Campaign," *Foreign Policy Association Bulletin*, XXXII (September 15, 1952), 4 +.

————. "Freedom and Its Purpose," *The Christian Century*, LXIX (December 24, 1952), 1496–99.

————. Hearing before the Senate Foreign Relations Committee, 83rd Cong., 1st Sess., on the Nomination of John Foster Dulles, Secretary of State-Designate, January 15, 1953 (Washington, Government Printing Office, 1953).

————. "Purpose of Resolution on Captive Peoples," statement before House Foreign Affairs Committee (February 26, 1953), *DSB*, XXVIII (March 9, 1953), 372–73.

————. Memorandum on John Carter Vincent (March 4, 1953), *DSB*, XXVIII (March 23, 1953), 454–55.

————. "The Making of Treaties and Executive Agreements," statement before Senate Committee on the Judiciary concerning S.J. Res. 1 and S.J. Res. 43 (April 6, 1953), *DSB*, XXVIII (April 20, 1953), 591–95.

————. "Morals and Power," address at National War College (June 16, 1953), *DSB*, XXVIII (June 29, 1953), 895–97.

————. "U.S. Constitution and U.N. Charter," address before American Bar Association (August 26, 1953), *DSB*, XXIX (September 7, 1953), 307–10.

————. "The Power of Moral Forces," address at First Presbyterian Church, Watertown (October 11, 1953), *DSB*, XXIX (October 19, 1953), 510–13.

————. "The Moral Initiative," address before Congress of Industrial Organizations (November 18, 1953). *DSB*, XXIX (November 30, 1953), 741–44.

————. "We Have the Initiative," *Nation's Business*, XLII (January 1954), 24–27.

————. "The Evolution of Foreign Policy," address before the Council on Foreign Relations (January 12, 1954), *DSB*, XXX (January 25, 1954), 107–10.

————. "Report on Berlin," broadcast on Four Power Foreign Ministers Conference (February 24, 1954), *DSB*, XXX (March 8, 1954), 343–47.

————. "Intervention: The Story of International Communism in the Americas," address before the Tenth Inter-American Conference (March 8, 1954), Department of State Press Release No. 121 and *DSB*, XXX (March 22, 1954), 419–26.

————. "Policy for Security and Peace," *Foreign Affairs*, XXXII (April 1954), 353–64.

Dulles, John Foster. "The Mutual Security Program for 1955," statement before House Foreign Affairs Committee (April 5, 1954), Department of State Press Release No. 178 and *DSB*, XXX (April 19, 1954), 579–83.

———. "Toward a Free Korea," address before Third Plenary Session of the Geneva Conference (April 28, 1954), Department of State Press Release No. 219 and *DSB*, XXX (May 10, 1954), 704–707.

———. "The Mutual Security Program for 1955," statement before Senate Foreign Relations Committee (June 4, 1954), Department of State Press Release No. 297 and *DSB*, XXX (June 14, 1954), 921–25.

———. Statement by the Secretary on the European Defense Community (August 31, 1954), Department of State Press Release No. 486.

———. Determination in Case of John Paton Davies, Jr. (November 5, 1954), *DSB*, XXXI (November 15, 1954), 752–54.

———. "Red Tactics will Vary—So will Ours," *Nation's Business*, XLIII (January 1955), 24–26.

———. "Our Foreign Policies in Asia" (February 16, 1955), *DSB*, XXXII (February 28, 1955), 327–31.

———. "Report to the President" (May 17, 1955), Department of State Publication.

———. Address on U.S. Foreign Policy, (June 24, 1955), *DSB*, XXXIII (July 4, 1955), 6–10.

———. "Entering the Second Decade" (September 22, 1955), *DSB*, XXXIII (October 3, 1955), 523–29.

———. Address before American Legion (October 10, 1955), *DSB*, XXXIII (October 24, 1955), 639–43.

———. "Report on the Foreign Ministers Conference" (November 18, 1955), *DSB*, XXXIII (November 28, 1955), 867–72.

———. "Russia Faces New Frustration," *Nation's Business*, XLIV (January 1956), 26–27.

———. "Freedom's New Task" (February 26, 1956), *DSB*, XXXIV (March 5, 1956), 363–67.

———. News Conference (May 22, 1956), Department of State Press Release No. 272 and *DSB*, XXXIV (June 4, 1956), 920–26.

———. "Cost of Peace" (June 9, 1956), *DSB*, XXXIV (June 18, 1956), 999–1004.

———. News Conference (July 11, 1956), Department of State Press Release No. 380 and *DSB*, XXXV (July 23, 1956), 145–50.

———. Statement before Emergency Session of the General Assembly (November 1, 1956), *DSB*, XXXV (November 12, 1956), 751–55.

———. "Mutual Security: A New Approach," statement before Senate Special Committee to Study the Foreign Aid Program (April 8, 1957), Department of State Press Release No. 194 and *DSB*, XXXVI (April 29, 1957), 675–79.

———. "Dynamic Peace" (April 22, 1957), *DSB*, XXXVI (May 6, 1957), 715–19.

———. Statement before the Senate Appropriations Subcommittee (April 30, 1957), Department of State Press Release No. 255 and *DSB*, XXXVI (May 20, 1957), 795–99.

———. Statement before the Senate Foreign Relations Committee on Mutual Security (May 22, 1957), Department of State Press Release No. 310 and *DSB*, XXXVI (June 10, 1957), 926–31.

———. Statement before the House Foreign Affairs Committee on Mutual Security (June 10, 1957), Department of State Press Release No. 351 and *DSB*, XXXVII (July 1, 1957), 3–8.

———. "Disarmament and Peace" (July 22, 1957), *DSB*, XXXVII (August 12, 1957), 267–72.

———. "Challenge and Response in United States Policy," *Foreign Affairs*, XXXVI (October 1957), 25–43.

———. News Conference (October 16, 1957), *DSB*, XXXVII (November 4, 1957), 708–14.

———. "Atlantic Alliance," radio interview (December 3, 1957), *DSB*, XXXVII (December 23, 1957), 987–90.

———. "Challenge to Liberty," *Vital Speeches of the Day*, XXIV (February 1, 1958), 231–36.

———. "Our Cause Will Prevail," *Life*, XLIII (December 23, 1957), 12–13.

———. "Sharing Nuclear Knowledge with Our NATO Allies" (April 27, 1958), *DSB*, XXXVIII (May 5, 1958), 740–42.

———. "Our Changing World" (May 11, 1958), *DSB*, XXXVIII (May 26, 1958), 847–50.

———. "The Challenge of Change," statement before the Senate Foreign Relations Committee (June 6, 1958), *DSB*, XXXVIII (June 23, 1958), 1035–42.

———. "The Foundations of Peace," *Vital Speeches of the Day*, XXIV (September 15, 1958), 706–709.

———. "John Foster Dulles Talks to Britain," transcript of television interview with William Clark (October 16, 1958), Associate Television Limited Publication.

———. "Dulles Talks to the British," *U.S. News and World Report*, XLV (October 31, 1958), 78–81.

———. "Principles and Policies in a Changing World" (November 18, 1958), *DSB*, XXXIX (December 8, 1958), 897–904.

———. "Policy for the Far East" (December 4, 1958), *DSB*, XXXIX (December 22, 1958), 989–94.

———. Statement before the Senate Foreign Relations Committee (January 14, 1959), Department of State Press Release No. 31.

277-84; and Suez expedition, 289, 291-94

Egypt, 82, 255, 259; and Czech arms deal and US aid, 255, 265, 266; and Baghdad Pact, 267, 277; and Communist China, 268; and Aswan Dam and Suez crisis, 264-91

Eisenhower, Dwight D., 9, 64, 175, 188, 191, 273, 306, 319, 323; and Dulles relationship, 6-7, 163-65, 185, 222, 283; and Republican party, 7, 167-68, 182-83, 184, 187; and Communist China, 82, 295-96; and NATO and US troops, 87, 220-21, 239; runs for president, 161-62, 163-70; and Taft relationship, 169-70, 191; and McCarthy, 170, 186-87, 191; and issues on taking office, 182-83; and Congress, 183-84; and Cabinet, 185-86; and internal security issue, 194, 197-98; and Bohlen appointment, 200-201; and Bricker Amendment, 204-205, 207; and military policy, 222, 227, 230, 232-34, 306, 311; and Indochina, 243, 245-47, 250, 251, and Aswan Dam, 269-70; and Suez crisis, 279-82, 284, 286-89; and Suez expedition, 290-93; and Taiwan Straits crises, 299-301; and Sputnik, 311

"Ethical solution," concept of, 72-78, 119-20

European Defense Community (EDC), 215-19, 231, 244

European unification, and Dulles, 56, 85-87, 166, 212-15, 344n79; and Truman Administration, 212, 215

European Recovery Program, 86

Fascism, 47, 76

Federal Council of Churches, see Commission on a Just and Durable Peace

Ferguson, Homer, 201

Finland, 262

Foreign aid, 67-68, 158, 256, 258, 272; see also Congress

Foreign policy, nature of as basis for

study, 6-7, 9; and continuum in, 55, 306-307

Formosa, 59, 60, 96-97, 99, 100, 102, 146, 316-17; see also China, Republic of; Taiwan Straits crisis

Forrestal Diaries, 81

Fosdick, Harry Emerson, 14, 15, 16

Foster, John Watson, 12, 17-19, 21-22

Four Power Foreign Ministers Conference (Berlin, 1954), 104, 233, 242, 248-49

Four Power Treaties (1922), 309

France, 36, 41, 45, 47, 73, 82, 87, 147, 213, 220, 302, 303, 305; and World War I reparations, 27-28, 30; and allied debts, 38; and "liberation" issue, 178; and EDC, 213, 215-19; and Indochina, 242-43, 244-45, 249; and Baghdad Pact, 266; and Suez crisis, 277-78, 283-86; and Suez expedition, 290-93; and US estimates of 1955 summit positions, 319-21

Franks, Sir Oliver, 63, 64, 315, 316

Fulbright, William J., 103, 214

Geneva Conference on Indochina and Korea (1954), 7, 103-104, 148, 210-11, 241-250

Geneva Conference (1955), see Summit

Genocide Convention, 162, 183, 208-209

George, David Lloyd, 30

George, Walter F., 207

German Peace Contract, 182, 217

Germany, 24, 41, 74, 108, 133, 149; and World War I reparations, 21, 27-31, 37, 38, 44; and Ruhr occupation, 36-37; and World War II, 42-43, 45, 46, 47, 73

Germany, Democratic Republic of (East), 177, 302

Germany, Federal Republic of (West), 166, 215, 217, 231; as EDC issue, 213, 215-18; and Berlin crisis (1958), 302; and reunification of, 302, 319, 321-22

"Gray areas," deterrence problem of, 240-42

Gross, Ernest, 160